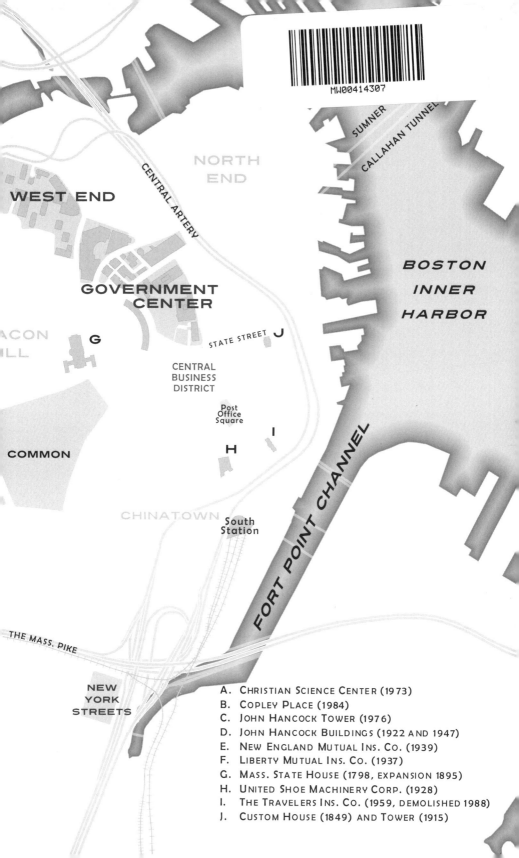

WEST END

NORTH
END

CENTRAL ARTERY

SUMNER

CALLAHAN TUNNEL

GOVERNMENT
CENTER

BOSTON
INNER
HARBOR

BEACON
HILL

G

STATE STREET

J

CENTRAL
BUSINESS
DISTRICT

Post
Office
Square

I

COMMON

H

CHINATOWN

South
Station

FORT POINT CHANNEL

THE MASS. PIKE

NEW
YORK
STREETS

A. CHRISTIAN SCIENCE CENTER (1973)
B. COPLEY PLACE (1984)
C. JOHN HANCOCK TOWER (1976)
D. JOHN HANCOCK BUILDINGS (1922 AND 1947)
E. NEW ENGLAND MUTUAL INS. CO. (1939)
F. LIBERTY MUTUAL INS. CO. (1937)
G. MASS. STATE HOUSE (1798, EXPANSION 1895)
H. UNITED SHOE MACHINERY CORP. (1928)
I. THE TRAVELERS INS. CO. (1959, DEMOLISHED 1988)
J. CUSTOM HOUSE (1849) AND TOWER (1915)

Insuring the City

Insuring the City
The Prudential Center and the Postwar Urban Landscape

Elihu Rubin

Yale University Press
New Haven and London

For my parents Zick and Carol Rubin

Published with the assistance of the Frederick W. Hilles Publication Fund
of Yale University.

yalebooks.com

Designed by Jena Sher
Set in Galaxie Polaris type by Amy Storm
Printed in China by Regent Publishing Services Ltd.

Library of Congress Cataloging-in-Publication Data
Rubin, Elihu, 1977–
Insuring the city : the Prudential Center and the postwar urban landscape /
Elihu Rubin.
    p.   cm.
Includes bibliographical references and index.
ISBN 978-0-300-17018-4 (alk. paper)
1. Office buildings—Massachusetts—Boston. 2. City planning—
Massachusetts—Boston—History—20th century. 3. Prudential Center
(Boston, Mass.) 4. Boston (Mass.)—Buildings, structures, etc. I. Title. II. Title:
Prudential Center and the postwar urban landscape.
  NA9053.O3R83 2012
  725'.230974461—dc23   2011040560

A catalogue record for this book is available from the British Library.
This paper meets the requirements of ANSI/NISO Z39.48-1992
(Permanence of Paper).

Jacket illustrations: *front*, A postcard view of the Prudential Center and
the Mass Pike in 1965 (Photo by Roger Maconi, used with permission);
back, The Prudential Center in 1968, with the War Memorial Auditorium
and Sheraton Hotel in the foreground (figure 37; Courtesy of the City of
Boston Archives).
Title page: The future site of the Prudential Center, ca. 1920 (figure 38)

10 9 8 7 6 5 4 3 2 1

Contents

Acknowledgments

This book was written in Berkeley, San Francisco, Brooklyn, and New Haven, and I have debts to all four cities for sparking my urban imagination even as I trained my thoughts on Boston in the 1950s and '60s.

The source of this book is a dissertation I wrote at the University of California, Berkeley, where I was lucky to find a rich intellectual environment spread across three academic departments: Architecture, City and Regional Planning, and Geography. I want to thank all the teachers and fellow students who made my experience there so rewarding. Foremost are my three dissertation committee members. I came to Berkeley to study the landscapes of American cities with Paul Groth, and he served as my adviser from day one. More than anyone, Paul has shaped the way I see the built environment and I thank him for his generous stewardship of this project. Like Paul, Richard Walker stimulated my passion for fieldwork, and he nurtured this project with an intuitive grasp for the big picture and always with good humor. Doing urban theory with Greig Crysler was an integral part of my Berkeley experience, and I have benefited greatly from his incisive comments and encouragement.

In the Department of Architecture at Berkeley, Nezar AlSayyad, Galen Cranz, and Kathleen James-Chakraborty inspired my work and the interdisciplinary view I take toward my field and future career. In the Department of City and Regional Planning, I had the opportunity to work closely with both Betty Deakin and Martin Wachs, and this book bears their imprint in its attention to the history, theory, and practice of transportation planning. I was aided by a research grant from the University of California Transportation Center. I also want to honor the memory of Alan Pred of the Department of Geography, whose courses helped me see the city — and myself — as a process of becoming.

At Yale, where I was introduced to architecture as an undergraduate by Vincent Scully and where I have been teaching since 2006, I am indebted to Dean Robert A. M. Stern of the School of Architecture for his encouragement and support. I am grateful for the wisdom and insights of Alan Plattus, my undergraduate thesis adviser and present colleague, who helped me see in the Prudential Center a modern incarnation of the medieval corporate enclave. And I thank Douglas Rae for his confidence and good counsel.

I knew I had found the right profession when I experienced the visceral pleasures of paging through 1950s corporate archives, feeling between my fingers the thin carbon copies of internally circulated company memoranda. I am grateful to Gabrielle Shanin and Dorothy Wolfe at Prudential Financial, Inc., for making their company archives available to me and for creating such a pleasant setting to conduct research. Dorothy began her career at Prudential in 1947 and worked there as a designer and supervisor of actuarial publications until she retired in the 1980s. In 1995, Dorothy was recalled to service as Prudential's archivist and historian at the company's head-quarters in Newark, and she remained in that position until her death in 2010. I regret that Dorothy will not see this book, to which she contributed so much. At the Perini Corporation in Framingham, Massachusetts — now Tutor-Perini — Paul Kavanaugh heroically dug through boxes of old materials with me to unearth photographs and old magazines. I thank Robert Band and Donna Tannar at Tutor-Perini for their coopera-tion with this project, as well as Ethan Anthony of Cram and Ferguson. Bob Bliss and Renford Taylor of the Massachusetts Turnpike Authority allowed me to rummage through the boxes of archival materials in the Pike's Weston warehouse. At the Jackson Homestead in Newton, I thank Susan Abele for so adeptly managing the city's his-torical documents. I thank Mary Daniels and Inés Zalduendo at Harvard's Loeb Library for helping me locate documents and images from the Walter Bogner papers. At Travelers Insurance in Hartford, Mary Beth Davidson made available key items from the company's archives. Librarians at the Boston Public Library, the City of Boston Municipal Archives, the Bostonian Society, the Avery Architectural Library at Columbia, New York Public Library, and the Sterling Memorial Library at Yale were also very helpful.

Special thanks to James Luckman for sharing with me the papers of his father, Charles Luckman, located in the basement of the Luckman Plaza on Sunset Boulevard in Los Angeles. I am grateful to Clay Stalls at Loyola-Marymount's Leavey Center for the Study of Los Angeles, which agreed to accept the Charles Luckman Papers and where they are now available to future researchers.

Amy DeDonato drew site plans for the Prudential Center at several moments in its evolution (they appear in figure 48) and I thank her and James Andrachuk for their dedication to the task. Terah Maher took beautiful photographs of the Prudential Center, several of which appear in this book, and helped prepare images for publication. Maki Takenouchi worked carefully to digitally rehabilitate the postcard used as the cover image, and I thank Carole Maconi for allowing me to use the striking photograph taken by her husband, Roger. Stacey Maples and the staff of the Yale University Map Collection came through in the clutch to produce the endpaper maps. Thanks to Kara Mason, who helped prepare the manuscript for submission to Yale University Press.

Several other researchers who have studied the Prudential Center and the Mass Pike have provided me with valuable guideposts. Cynthia Horan, who has also been my colleague at Yale, was generous with her research materials, encouragement, and advice. In 2005, I toured the Prudential Center with Benjamin Waterhouse and Paul Groth, and Ben's excellent paper on the Prudential Center served as an important reference. Jean Riesman's essay on William F. Callahan — the "Maharajah of the Macadam" — was an invaluable resource. I want to acknowledge, too, the work of historian Thomas Hanchett, who resourcefully analyzed the context of Prudential's real estate investments of the 1950s. Conversations with David Luberoff, Fred Salvucci, Yanni Tsipis, and Gary Hack were immensely helpful. I owe a debt to Richard Longstreth, who gave generously of his time to respond to the manuscript and discuss it with me. I am grateful to Alice Truax, who made excellent suggestions on the introduction and conclusion. It has been a pleasure to work with Michelle Komie at Yale University Press and I thank her for championing this project. Many thanks to Katherine Boller and Sarah Henry at Yale Press, and to Phillip King for his immensely helpful and careful editing. Many people have contributed to this book; its errors are mine alone.

So many friends and companions in the Bay Area, New Haven, Boston, and New York have helped me see this project through. I want to thank my aunts and uncles — Shale Stiller, Ellen Heller, Jeffrey Fischman, Charlotte Fischman, Susan Gesner, and Bill Danziger — for their loving support. My brother, Noam, has been a constant ally. I am inspired by the memory of my uncle Leonard Rubin and my grandfather Dr. Benjamin Moses. I would like to acknowledge the contributions of my dog, Leyla, for her stalwart insistence that I get up early to start each day of writing. What is true for urban development is also true for book writing: confidence is critical. I thank my parents, Carol and Zick Rubin, for their love and unfailing assurances. In many ways, this book would have been impossible without them, and I dedicate this book to them.

Introduction
Insuring the City

Boston's Prudential Center from the north bank of the Charles River in Cambridge, ca. 1970. To the right of the fifty-two-story tower is the Sheraton Boston Hotel, and to the left are the Pru's three apartment buildings and second office tower, 101 Huntington. (Courtesy of Prudential Financial, Inc.)

You begin to glimpse it from your car when the sinuous ribbon of the Massachusetts Turnpike crests some fifteen miles outside of Boston: the dull, gray tower that heralds the Prudential Center. Never the critics' darling, the "Pru," built in 1965, is yet the awfully great symbol of Boston: a square-plan tower with an illuminated antenna spire, the letters of the corporation that built it affixed at the top like a typographical cornice line. From a distance, it resembles a modern campanile — like the medieval bell towers of Italian towns, a civic icon in the skyline (fig. 1).

A moment later, the image on the horizon splits and the view from the road reveals a taller, shimmering slab: the John Hancock Tower, completed in 1976 and designed to outshine the drab Prudential (fig. 2). The Hancock — slyly insubstantial, an iridescent mirage — is considered by many critics to be the more elegant and appealing of the two insurance towers, although it is perhaps best known for the initial tendency of its mirrored glass panels to dislodge and crash to the ground. After many decades, there they stand: dueling emblems of the life insurance companies that built them and physical affirmations of the intangible product they represent: financial security. They are also somewhat quaint talismans of an anonymous, even bewildering, global financial culture in an age when the local commitments of large corporations are nebulous and hard to perceive.

It was not always this way. Insurance companies have long viewed themselves as playing a special role among American businesses. Ordinary businesses were perceived as heedlessly pursuing profit for its own sake. But insurance companies carried a greater responsibility: they managed the public's welfare and self-consciously cultivated the civic posture of a social institution. In the milieu of postwar urban redevelopment, the Prudential Center in Boston is material evidence of one company's efforts

left **Figure 1** The Boston Extension of the Massachusetts Turnpike and the interchange with Route 128, ca. 1965. The Prudential tower is the tallest building on the horizon. (Courtesy of the Tutor-Perini Corporation)

right **Figure 2** The dueling insurance towers of John Hancock (at left) and Prudential, 2011. To the right of the Prudential Building is 111 Huntington Avenue, a thirty-six-story skyscraper built in 2002 as part of the ongoing additions and renovations of the Prudential Center complex. (Photo by Terah Maher) to assert such a posture and to insure the future of a struggling city. The story of those efforts also illuminates an equally significant midcentury phenomenon: Boston's transition from a nineteenth-century city, organized tightly around rail-based transport and a concentrated business district, to a regional one, organized around highways and easy parking.

In 1945, the Prudential Insurance Company surveyed its digs — an agglomeration of buildings that had become an urban campus on Broad Street in downtown Newark — and decided to "break the whole thing up." For the next two decades the company embarked on an ambitious corporate restructuring, establishing semi-autonomous "regional home offices" in seven cities across North America. Casting about for a location for its Northeastern Home Office, Prudential came across a nearly thirty-acre railroad yard in the Back Bay district of Boston. The site was perfect: here Prudential could not only erect an impressive monument to itself but also make a big impact in a city that needed help.

Like other American cities in the 1950s, Boston was preoccupied with urban obsolescence and created a political and legal structure to facilitate redevelopment. The principal crisis was "decentralization" — of industry, jobs, and population (especially the white middle classes) — which threatened to leave the city an empty core, the hole in a metropolitan doughnut, left to languish in its slums (substandard neighborhoods) and blight (depreciated and ill-maintained properties). There was a pervasive sense that the city needed to overhaul its constituent parts — the streets, housing, and business facilities — in order to compete with the suburbs and rebuild its declining tax base.[1]

When Prudential announced in 1957 that it would construct a group of buildings, including its own Northeastern Home Office, on the sprawling site of the rail yard in Back Bay (fig. 3), the city applauded the corporation's bold move: it appeared that the insurance company had not only solved an immediate problem — the redevelopment of an intractable parcel that was widely seen as an impediment to the growth of the city — but also set the stage for a broader revitalization of the urban and regional economy. With the City of Boston struggling to right its economic fortunes, Prudential's pledge to invest $100 million in a "Rockefeller Center–like group of buildings" was a welcome vote of confidence.[2]

As it happened, however, Prudential's intended site on the outskirts of the central business district was also pivotal to the Massachusetts Turnpike Authority's plans to construct an urban extension of its toll highway. Where Prudential imagined a gleaming new city, the Mass Pike's chief William F. Callahan pictured a high-speed urban throughway barreling into the heart of Boston where it would link up with the Central Artery,

Figure 3 Before Prudential stepped in, the developer Roger Stevens distributed this photograph of the Boston and Albany Railroad yards, belonging to the New York Central, in 1953 to promote his efforts to redevelop the parcel "along the lines of New York's famed 'Rockefeller Center,'" as noted on the back of the picture. The dominant structure in the Boston skyline is the old John Hancock Building completed in 1947. (Courtesy of the Boston Public Library, Print Department)

the recently built elevated highway that cut a swath through the downtown. Callahan and his engineers targeted the rail corridor leading to the site as the path of least resistance for constructing a modern road, which they saw as crucial to securing the city's future. What began as a rivalry developed into a physical, political, and financial partnership to transform the relics of nineteenth-century railroad infrastructure into a unified megastructure for the motor age.

The first of Prudential's buildings opened in 1965 and included the signature tower — fifty-two stories tall and clad in an aluminum-framed curtain wall — flanked by four low-lying commercial pavilions, a concrete-slab hotel, a municipal auditorium, built by the city, and a sequence of open plazas. Three apartment towers, two department stores, and a second office tower were added by 1970. Prudential also granted an easement through the site for the Pike's "Boston Extension," from which one looping exit ramp delivered cars to a three-level parking garage that formed the base of the Prudential Center. Working together, the Mass Pike and the Pru created a massive highway interchange in the city and transformed a neglected piece of railroad infrastructure into a physically joined, self-contained landscape organized around the car (fig. 4).

The literature of postwar urban redevelopment has focused on the consolidation of political power, the changing economic function and social composition of metropolitan areas, the local impact of federal policies, and the guiding hand of strong public bureaucrats. Often neglected in this story, however, is the influence of corporate decision-making in reshaping the physical landscapes of major American cities. Moreover, the buildings and landscapes themselves — the highways, garages, office towers, plazas, and commercial spaces that are common elements of these cities — are underexplored in the political and economic analyses. At the same time, these urban redevelopment ensembles and corporate buildings are typically viewed as too undistinguished to attract much attention from architectural historians. Only a few redevelopment projects or corporate buildings have been introduced into the canon of postwar design, and the Prudential Center in Boston is not one of these. My intention is not to revive the Pru's reputation as "good architecture," but rather to engage the Prudential Center as a culturally significant landscape that exemplifies the production of urban space in postwar America.[3]

This is a case study of the role of corporate aspirations, values, and pretensions in shaping the American city. Like all case studies, the story of the Pru is unique, and we will follow its particular strands: the ambitions of an insurance company (Prudential), the history and politics of an American city (Boston), the road that united them (the Mass Pike), and the architect who moved from selling soap to promoting urban development (Charles Luckman). So this book involves forays into business history, politics, and urban planning. It remains grounded, however, in the making and meaning of the structures themselves. In the remainder of this introductory chapter, I aim to place the story in the context of four central themes: first, the dynamic interplay between public policy and private companies in the redevelopment of cities; second, how the railroads, which had formerly dominated urban land use to a large extent, gave way to new forces, notably insurance company investment, in shaping the landscape of the

Figure 4 Aerial photograph of downtown Boston, ca. 1968, looking east, showing the Prudential Center at lower right and the Boston Extension of the Mass Pike extending from it toward the upper right. The Charles River is at the left; the green strip of Commonwealth Avenue runs parallel to it in the center, leading to the Public Garden and Boston Common, beyond which is the financial district and the Central Artery. (Courtesy of Prudential Financial, Inc.)

city; third, the civic aspirations of insurance companies like Prudential and their impact on the buildings and landscapes they created; and, fourth, the challenge of urban and architectural design in the motor age, when cities sought to reinvent themselves by accommodating the automobile without forfeiting their distinctive identities.

CORPORATE STRATEGY, URBAN POLICY

The Prudential Center of Boston was one of seven regional home offices (RHOs) planned by Prudential in the 1940s and '50s to decentralize its Newark-based management. Large insurance companies had long constructed branch offices — often impressive, high-profile structures — as they grew and expanded their markets. Prudential's RHOs represented a more integral effort to reinvigorate the company's bureaucratic struc- ture, effectively splitting the large company into semi-autonomous regional units. What began as an internal policy of administrative decentralization, however, evolved into a prominent building program and urban planning phenomenon. In the spirit of its famous "Rock of Gibraltar" slogan, Prudential built massive promontories that dominated their urban landscapes. At the same time, Prudential's physical presence — for example, in Los Angeles, Houston, and Chicago, as well as Boston — had important spatial and economic ramifications: stimulating the market for commercial real estate; pro- moting the economic prospects of each city; and reshaping the geographical contours of the business district. Prudential's RHOs were also expressions of the insurance company's self-image as a benevolent force in American cities and social life. Considered together, they illustrate the formative role of corporate strategy in urban development.

My interest in corporate policy is a counterpoint to the story of urban renewal that has focused on the formation of locally constituted "pro-growth coalitions." In political terms, these coalitions paired progressive Democratic mayors with reform-minded Republican business leaders. Businessmen coalesced around "Citizen Committees" of one variety or another, sometimes organized with the encouragement of local aca- demic institutions. Simultaneously, municipal governments formed Redevelopment Authorities in compliance with the Federal Housing Acts of 1949 and 1954. Under Title I of the 1949 act, these authorities applied for and administered federal grants, brandishing the powers of eminent domain to seize property and working under the ideological cover of the public interest to rid the city of slums and blight. Federal funds subsidized the costs of land acquisition, clearance, and assembly for large parcels that were designed to entice private development, which would in turn yield a new tax base. For Boston and many other cities, urban renewal was viewed as the only way to break the cycle of disinvestment and the social decline it implied. In this scenario, Chester Hartmann wrote in his study of renewal in San Francisco, "the private investment community thus comes to be seen as performing functions in the public interest."[4]

What began as a federal program intended to ameliorate housing conditions for the urban poor became the catalyst for an extensive rebuilding of downtown landscapes around urban highways, parking lots, civic centers, shopping centers, and middle-class apartment housing. In some cases, vital and socially coherent neighborhoods were misunderstood as a "slum," "blighted," "decadent," or "sub-standard" area and replaced with highways or high-rises intended for very different users than those being displaced. In Boston, the West End and the New York Streets neighborhood (a section of the South End) were early casualties of the heavy-handed clearance style of renewal.[5]

Prudential did not require the Boston Redevelopment Authority to assemble its parcel, which was bought in its entirety from the railroad — which was one reason that the insurance company did not attract the outrage that some of Boston's early renewal projects did. Prudential fully understood, however, the value of its investment to the city, and it exploited it accordingly. The insurance company was unwilling to go forward with its ambitious proposal without a guarantee that it would be spared Boston's notoriously high property tax, which was widely viewed as an impediment to growth. At first, the mayor, John Hynes, proffered an informal agreement that established a predictable tax schedule. But Prudential would be satisfied only by a legally binding pact, insulated from the challenges of local rivals. The next solution would have sheltered Prudential under the tax-free umbrella of the Massachusetts Turnpike Authority. This plan was rejected by the Massachusetts Supreme Judicial Court, which could not imagine the "public purpose" of a private real estate development. With political interest still keen in response to this rejection, the Massachusetts legislature amended the state redevelopment law (Chapter 121A) to certify Prudential as a limited-dividend urban redevelopment corporation empowered to develop land in the public interest and entitled to special tax treatment. The Supreme Judicial Court approved the new law, finally adopting a "modern view of public purpose."[6] The "modern view" recognized that "blight" could be defined as any parcel that would not otherwise be redeveloped by the "ordinary operations of private enterprise."

Like the politicians who led the federal government, Prudential's decision-makers were planners and policy-makers of national scope. Like the federal government, which supplied many billions of dollars to American cities to adopt urban renewal plans, Prudential implemented policies on a national basis that shaped the practices of local actors. In Boston, Prudential's insistence on tax clemency hastened the amend-ment of urban redevelopment law. A rider to the new law abolished the City Planning Board and enshrined the Boston Redevelopment Authority as the chief arbiter of land use in the city, setting the stage for the city's broader program of urban renewal.

The Pru's decision to reshape Boston by building its tower over the abandoned rail yard in the Back Bay reinforced the view that the Prudential was a special type of urban actor: a company with resources and patience to implement a national policy that was informed by its distinct civic identity. Prudential shared this attitude and sense of scale with the federal government. Working in tandem — and sometimes in tension — the Pike and the Pru took on many of the functions of the state by defining the public interest and together planning the future of Boston.

FROM "OCTOPUS" TO "MIGHTY PUMP"

In *The Octopus,* his novel published in 1901, Frank Norris characterized the Pacific and Southwestern Railroad (a fictitious stand-in for California's Southern Pacific Railroad) as a creature with its tentacles intertwined in every feature of the nineteenth-century economy, social life, and built environment.[7] The federal government helped to spur the spread of railroads across the United States by offering immense land grants to the trailblazing railroad companies, and many of them explicitly formed land companies to manage their diverse holdings. The Pacific Railroad Act of 1862 not only delivered the rights-of-way to the railroads free of charge, but also offered them ten square miles of land for every mile of track built. The government perceived a public interest in subsidizing the private development of railroad lines as a way to unify the nation, inhabit its spaces, and spur its economic growth.

A twentieth-century analog of the railroad was the insurance industry, which in its own way inserted itself into the physical, economic, and social fabrics of American life. In 1964, a writer in *Fortune* described Prudential as a "mighty pump" of economic growth, a mechanism that accumulated a great reservoir of capital from the premiums of its policyholders and in turn pumped the cash into investments across the economic landscape. *Fortune* reported that two of the three largest private companies in the world were insurance companies: Prudential and Metropolitan Life.[8] From the start, Prudential was a business enterprise with a conspicuous public presence, with agents pounding the pavement of America's growing industrial cities and the company as a whole immersing itself in the larger processes of urbanization.

Many parallels can be drawn between the railroads of the nineteenth century and the insurance companies of the twentieth. Railroads were pioneers in the field of corporate administration, and so were insurance companies. As large railroad companies bundled together smaller systems and administered far-flung networks, they developed complicated bureaucratic structures to operate their facilities and manage their services.[9] Similarly, Prudential was organized as a multidivisional corporation, with many executive vice presidents reporting to the top man. Prudential's regional home office program was the physical result of an innovative policy of corporate decentralization. Like railroad companies, insurance companies were landowners and real estate developers on a vast scale.

In the fast-growing industrial cities of the East, railroads became important land-owners beginning in the early nineteenth century. In many large cities, the railroads were part and parcel to the process of urbanization, not only as providers of transportation but also as shapers of urban form. This was the case in Boston, where the railroads approaching the city from the west and the south guided the character of the city's physical growth. The Boston and Worcester Railroad (later it became the Boston and Albany) charged across the Back Bay marshlands on a graded viaduct; the Boston and Providence Railroad crossed the Back Bay from the southwest. The two intersecting tracks, Walter Muir Whitehill said, "formed a great St. Andrew's cross of railway lines through the Back Bay [that] . . . eventually led to the filling of the entire area."[10] This was the future site of the Prudential Center.

As rail power declined in the twentieth century, the real estate properties that these companies held became their chief assets: as rail lines were abandoned, opportunities for development presented themselves and these assets were sold off. Railroad companies looked to capitalize on their urban land holdings — the corridors, tracks, terminals, passenger and freight depots, support structures, and yards used to store and manipulate rail cars. These were often large tracts of land established in the nineteenth century near the commercial core of the city. Transportation expert Wilfred Owen observed in 1959 that the relocation or retirement of these facilities was "providing substantial real estate capable of conversion to more appropriate uses and has at the same time removed one of the principal causes of downtown decay."[11]

Urban redevelopment in the 1950s and '60s was frequently centered around railroad sites. Railroads had helped to construct the industrial metropolis and were signs of its vigor, but after World War II many planners saw urban rail infrastructure as outmoded, a source of property devaluation, and an impediment to growth. Prudential's investments in Boston and Chicago, where the Mid-American Home Office was built on railroad air rights, marked the passing of the Octopus — the nineteenth-century railroad trust — and the ascent of the "mighty pump" — the insurance industry. Like other insurance companies acting in American cities, Prudential used its immense resources to produce white-collar office landscapes over the embers of dying rail facilities.[12]

Prudential was aware that its activities in Boston were part of a broader effort to revive city centers and fight urban decay, and linked its plans for the Prudential Center to the Penn Center project in Philadelphia and the redevelopment of the Golden Triangle in Pittsburgh — a neighborhood on the city's peninsular tip at the confluence of the Allegheny and Monongahela Rivers.[13] In 1946, the Pittsburgh Urban Redevelopment Authority pioneered the effort to employ eminent domain to condemn and clear a large, unified parcel from an ensemble of smaller, blighted properties in the Golden Triangle to prepare for a modern building project there.

The Pennsylvania Railroad owned a large percentage of the property in the Golden Triangle. In 1967, the journalist Jeanne Lowe, a noted chronicler of urban renewal, described the triangle as a "grimy, flood-battered industrial blight of warehouses, overhead rail freight trestles and tracks which in the late nineteenth century came to disfigure the site of Pittsburgh's birthplace." The city had sunk into "dirt and decay," Lowe wrote, but a coalition of business elites, guided by Richard King Mellon and gathered under the banner of the Allegheny Conference on Community Development, extracted commitments from local corporations that they would stay and rebuild the downtown as an important headquarters city rather than abandon it.[14]

In his critical assessment of urban renewal, Martin Anderson pointed out that insurance companies were among the essential sources of finance capital for the large-scale development opportunities made possible by Title I land clearance.[15] This was the case in Pittsburgh, where representatives of the Allegheny Conference proactively sought the investment of insurance companies, and the Equitable Life Assurance Society emerged as the key investor in the Golden Triangle redevelopment project. Equitable saw a need for modern office space; its plan called for tall structures set in a sequence of lawns and landscaped walkways, described as "non-income-producing amenities which Equitable, as the developer, would have to maintain and support." The insurance company's real estate consultants and architects from the firm of Eggers and Higgins planned cruciform-plan office towers that were designed to maximize access to light and air (fig. 5). The ensemble — dubbed the Gateway Center to recall Pittsburgh's historical role as an entrance to the West for pioneers — also featured a garage system connected to the new expressways that hugged the riverfront along the former rail corridor. Equitable paid the full value of the site, $12 million,

Figure 5 The Gateway Center and Plaza in Pittsburgh, financed by the Equitable Life Assurance Society, ca. 1953 (Collection of Library and Archives Division, Senator John Heinz History Center, Pittsburgh)

to the City of Pittsburgh, plus a $1 million "toll charge" to the Urban Redevelopment Authority "for the privilege of using the public power of eminent domain."[16] The process of transforming central Pittsburgh from a sooty, noisy, dirty place where many uses of the industrial city mixed together into a cleaner, white-collar landscape was called the "Pittsburgh Renaissance," and held up as a model of business-led renewal.

Like the Back Bay rail yard where Prudential planned its mixed-use office complex, the Golden Triangle was located at the periphery of the established office district, which was also being rebuilt with new office towers for U.S. Steel and Mellon Bank. And as we shall see in Boston, there were downtown property owners in Pittsburgh who worried that the new Gateway Center would make their own buildings seem out of date, if not obsolete. Bypassing these parochial squabbles, Richard Mellon asked the officers of Pittsburgh corporations to move into the new center as an act of "civic responsibility."[17] Pittsburgh Plate Glass would occupy an entire building of Gateway Center. The executives of many of the city's leading corporations were eager to move into larger, more efficient quarters that would allow them to centralize administrative operations. Jones and Laughlin Steel, for example, which had been operating out of three different buildings in the central business district, could now consolidate in a single structure.

There were concerns that the design of the Gateway Center left much to be desired and raised the challenge of urban and architectural design at the scale of the automobile. An editorial in *Architectural Forum* came down hard on the plan of the ensemble. "The arrangement of the towers in their park is purely mechanical; the landscaping between them makes no fresh statement about our grand new world." As for the architecture itself, "the steel-clad structures are . . . lacking in proportion, texture and dignity."[18]

Despite the design's formal stiffness and aesthetic banality, *Architectural Forum* insufficiently acknowledged the "fresh statement" that the Gateway Center made by breaking with the established mode of city-building — the accumulation of piecemeal developments that were built out to the edges of the lot — and boldly reshaping urban space to accommodate the car. The center featured underground and peripheral surface parking that separated automobile from pedestrian traffic and an internal street system that was integrated with the city's new highways. Moreover, the physical presence of the three towers in a park confirmed the commitment of a national insurance company, coupled with local boosters and operating under the legal cover of the public interest, to dramatically reconstruct the city's built environment and assert its position as a vital business location.

Like Prudential, the Equitable wanted its project to be seen in the context of Rockefeller Center, a view promoted in the architectural press. In its assessment of the

Gateway Center project, *Architectural Forum* pointed out that "the 23 acres in Pittsburgh offered an opportunity to carry the Rockefeller Center concept much further."[19] Part of that concept implied that the Equitable could make a profitable investment and, in the same action, contribute a public service by graciously providing open spaces and sponsoring the modernization of the urban core. The Equitable would look like an urban savior in both financial as well as spatial terms. With the Gateway Center as a key model, Prudential eyed the Back Bay rail yard as a broad tableau — ostensibly "pre-assembled" by virtue of its prior use — to assert its own civic largesse.

Another key precedent for the Prudential Center in Boston transpired in Philadelphia, where the Pennsylvania Railroad had long been indivisible from the city's industrial prosperity and urban growth. In 1881, the railroad located its Broad Street station right next to the monumental new City Hall and brought with it sixteen tracks, erected on an above-grade viaduct, from the Schuylkill River. Jeanne Lowe called it a "block-wide 'Chinese Wall' which, as time went on, cast a blighting pall over development in the western half of the city's center."[20] In 1952, the railroad announced plans to demolish the station and redevelop the land. City planners in Philadelphia, led by Edmund Bacon, had long dreamed of a modern, mixed-used commercial core in the place of the railroad, and battled to exert influence over the redevelopment process to ensure a unified plan that would accommodate car and truck traffic, open space, and transit connections. A balance had to be struck between the planners' vision and what real estate developers would finance; or, as Mayor David Lawrence put it, "to combine the acquisitive instinct and the public good."[21] When the Equitable passed on the investment opportunity, it was Prudential that furnished a $7.5 million loan in 1954 to the New York–based developers, the Uris Brothers, enabling them to erect the first structures of Penn Center, which came to include several office buildings, an underground shopping concourse, open plaza space, and a train and bus transfer node.[22]

In Boston, the transition from the railroad (the octopus) to the insurance company (the mighty pump) could not have been more literal. The train yard of the Boston and Albany Railroad was a dark and uninviting trench that stretched across nearly thirty acres, a bastion of coal-driven pollution, and a vestige of the city's outworn past. In its place, Prudential Insurance Company executives envisioned a gleaming new city designed for automobiles and office workers, presided over by a signature office tower that housed the regional operations of a powerful national corporation and symbolized its commitment to the future viability of that city.

THE CIVIC AMBITIONS OF A PECULIAR BUSINESS

Insurance companies are important players in architectural history because of their attentiveness to the cultural dividends of shaping in urban spaces, including visibility and prestige. As a case in point, a key piece of Prudential's regional home office policy called for making visible urban landmarks, clearly labeled with the company's name. Prudential wanted to be seen as a prominent urban actor that had its finger on the pulse of growing Sunbelt economies, on one hand, and that refused to allow the great cities of the northern industrial belt to languish, on the other. As one Prudential executive who was important in the implementation of its decentralization policy put it, "The Prudential believes strongly in the future of the downtown city."[23] The public relations value of the regional home offices — as a sign of the large company's local commitments and as a literal signboard advertisement — were all part of what he called the "Extra Dividends" of his company's decentralization plan that fell outside of its strictly organizational function. Each a robust investment in urban real estate, the RHOs ratified Prudential's stature as a national institution and affirmed that life insurance was beneficial to the community — the product itself as well as the impacts of its investments. In this way, Prudential's RHO program reflects the insurance industry's self-conscious relationship to architecture and its symbolic function in the postwar era.

Prudential's urban policy, and its expression in the Prudential Center in Boston, called out to a long relationship between insurance companies and important urban architecture. Indeed, the civic pretensions of insurance companies came with architectural implications. More conventional companies were satisfied by mere *commercial* architecture, buildings that were principally utilitarian and attractive enough. But insurance companies aspired to the majesty and scale of *institutional* architecture and thus sought to join the ranks of ecclesiastical, academic, cultural, and government buildings. Distinguished architecture, defined by elaborate surface treatment, gracious interior spaces, rich materials, or sheer height, was a form of conspicuous consumption for insurance companies like Prudential.[24]

The Conspicuous Consumption of Architecture

In the heyday of the industrial city, American insurance companies were frequent patrons of noteworthy architecture. They were not the only business enterprises with the aspirations of a civic institution, a group that included newspapers and leading national firms like Singer (manufacturer of sewing machines), L. C. Smith (typewriters), or Woolworth (five and dime stores). American businesses commissioned leading architects to design prominent buildings that would be viewed — by the press, by other business leaders, by ordinary people — as credits to their host cities and advertisements for the companies that built them (fig. 6). These buildings were more than just functional containers of economic activities; they were jewels in a crown of collective urban achievement.[25]

Figure 6 Postcards of the Singer Tower (1908), the Woolworth Building (1913), both in New York, and the L. C. Smith Building (1914) in Seattle

Insurance companies soon took the lead in this endeavor. More than sewing machines or typewriters, life insurance companies needed to project material security to back the peculiar product they sold. Life insurance policies established a monetary equivalent for human life, and there were moments in the early history of the enterprise when it was viewed as a dirty business. As sociologist Viviana Zelizer has written, "Putting death on the market offended a system of values that upheld the sanctity of human life and its incommensurability."[26] Though its beneficiaries were widows and children, critics were put off by the application of business practices and life expectancy tables to what had been the domain of family, church, or locally organized mutual benefit societies. Insurance companies promoted their public obligations and cultivated an ideology of benevolent power. The quasi-public role had positive business value. Historian Morton Keller has written, "It was as useful to emphasize the social duty to sell insurance as it was to stress the social obligation of buying it."[27] The theme of the corporation's social responsibility was especially salient in the case of "industrial insurance" — pioneered in the United States by Prudential in 1875 — which entailed the collection of small weekly premiums from working-class households in growing urban areas.

Insurance companies, and acceptance of their products, expanded apace with the growing industrial metropolis. Along with extensive advertising campaigns and the adoption of corporate mottoes and emblems, one way that insurance companies reassured potential clients of the moral probity and economic security of their products was by commissioning urban landmarks. There were additional financial spurs for insurance companies to invest in office buildings. The companies needed to house large clerical staffs, with executive suites and white-collar production lines that prepared insurance policies. At the same time, until the 1940s, insurance companies were prohibited by law from investing directly in property outside of their own office structures. To get around this barrier, insurance companies invested heavily in their home and branch offices, structures that housed local operations while also providing speculative office space for other firms. Each headquarters or branch office building thus presented the opportunity for an otherwise unavailable real estate investment, coupled with a conspicuous branding statement.

The insurance company tradition of visually impressive architecture began in the 1870s, when young insurance companies sought to establish themselves as serious institutions. New York's Equitable Life Assurance Society, founded in 1859, set the tone when it held a competition to solicit designs for a headquarters building in 1867. The winners of the competition were architects with experience designing monuments for both public and private clients, Arthur Gilman and Edward Kendall, who teamed with George Post. Located on lower Broadway in New York's financial district, the building was rendered in the Second Empire style of architecture, modeled on Napoleon III's additions to the Louvre in Paris. The building's double-height windows, classicist detailing, granite facade, and mansard roof became symbols of cosmopolitan prosperity. Above the entrance portico was placed a marble sculpture called "Protection," which featured the company's emblem, the "Guardian Angel of Life," protecting a widow and an orphan.[28] Many other insurance companies followed Equitable's lead and built similarly styled buildings. In 1890, Prudential hired George Post to design a head-quarters structure in Newark. The fashion for mansard roofs had passed by then, and Post rendered a stone fortress with turrets, a structure that projected permanence and strength (fig. 7).

Figure 7 Postcards of the Prudential Building in Newark (1892), designed by George Post, and Metropolitan Life on Madison Square Park in New York (1909), designed by the firm of Napoleon Le Brun and Sons

As insurance companies continued their search for civic iconography, they often fused symbols from church and state. In 1909, Metropolitan Life hired the architects Napoleon Le Brun and Sons to design a replica of St. Mark's Campanile, the bell tower associated with the cathedral in Venice, featuring its loggia and pyramidal spire. It was a popular image. George Post had proposed variations on the tower to suit the expansion plans of both Equitable and Prudential, but both were rejected (fig. 8). Met Life was delighted with the imagery. Vice President Haley Fiske called the tower "an advertisement that didn't stand the company a cent because the tenants footed the bill."[29] Architects added four large clock faces to each side of the square shaft and capped the pyramidal crown with a searchlight. Met Life used the tower extensively in its advertisements, billed as "the light that never fails." Like Prudential's Rock of Gibraltar, the Metropolitan's tower represented sureness and constancy.

Midtown Manners

Met Life's tower punctuated the company's move from downtown to Madison Square Park at Twenty-third Street. Around the time that Prudential built its bunker in Newark, Met Life was busy assembling land around Madison Square and staked out a midtown office district in what was then still a residential area. The move was a statement of fiscal confidence as well as a deliberate real estate strategy, and others followed. The Flatiron Building in 1902 defined the southwest corner. In 1928, the golden octagonal pyramid at the top of the New York Life Insurance Company, designed by Cass Gilbert, came to occupy the northwest corner of the square on the block formerly occupied by Madison Square Garden itself. The drift northward to Madison Square was a sign that downtown was getting crowded. This fact was crystallized in 1915 when the Equitable replaced its original structure, destroyed in a fire, with a massive structure that rose forty stories straight up from the sidewalk. The building was widely considered a bulky intrusion and was one factor that hastened the adoption of a comprehensive zoning ordinance in 1916.[30]

The move from downtown toward midtown was not confined to New York. In smaller cities like Hartford, Connecticut — an important insurance center since the mid-nineteenth century — insurance companies seeking to expand looked for large, mostly unbuilt sites outside the central business district. When Aetna Life Insurance Company planned its new headquarters in the 1920s, the company established a different sensibility for civic prestige, one that emphasized horizontal expansion rather than height. Architect James Gamble Rogers designed a neo-Colonial mansion, modeled after Charles Bulfinch's Old Connecticut State House building in Hartford (completed in 1796). Placed in lushly landscaped grounds, the red-brick building rose six stories with massive projecting wings that framed a central pavilion (fig. 9). The entry colonnade was topped with a Corinthian temple front and golden-domed cupola.[31] As we will see in Chapter 2, Aetna's midtown campus was part of a pattern that was followed in Boston, where insurers left Second Empire–style buildings downtown for larger sites in the Back Bay. Like other insurance companies making forays into what were still residential districts, Aetna's red-brick mansion combined prominence with neighborly decorum. However, the presence of the insurance company often paved the way for other business enterprises and identified important avenues for commercial development.

If the move to midtown — by Met Life and Aetna, for example — was a response to the growing city, it was also an investment in that growth. After World War II, however, this pattern changed. It is instructive to follow the trajectory of Hartford's Connecticut General Life Insurance Company, organized in 1865. In 1924, Connecticut General left the downtown structure it had inhabited since 1905 — it was designed in 1873 by H. H. Richardson — for a larger site on Elm Street, facing Bushnell Park in the vicinity of the statehouse. Even though the new structure, designed by James Gamble Rogers, was expanded in 1938, the company soon outgrew that space as well. But instead of expanding again on the urban site, in 1950 Connecticut General purchased a 280-acre parcel in Bloomfield, Connecticut, about five miles outside Hartford, where it built a

left **Figure 8** George Post's massive tower, a proposal for an addition to Prudential's urban campus in Newark, would have dwarfed his original headquarters building (Collection of the New-York Historical Society)

Figure 9 From midtown mansion to suburban campus: postcards of *(top)* the Aetna Life Insurance Company building (1929), designed by James Gamble Rogers, and *(bottom)* the Connecticut General Life Insurance Company building (1954), designed by Skidmore, Owings, and Merrill

low-rise, modernist campus in the suburbs. In making the move, the company decided that an efficient and attractive work environment — one that contained many employee amenities, including a bowling alley and tennis courts — outweighed the benefits of a downtown location.[32]

Like Aetna's midtown mansion, Connecticut General's suburban estate was an expression of power underwritten by the patronage of distinguished architecture. The main building, a low-slung structure designed by architects from the large office of Skidmore, Owings, and Merrill under the leadership of Gordon Bunshaft, was lauded in *Life* as "one of the finest office structures in the country."[33] It embraced the taut steel-and-glass curtain wall of modernist, International Style architecture. At the same time, Connecticut General's move pointed out a crisis in the status of the city in the motor age and reflected a broad disenchantment with urban environments at mid-century. How could the city fit into the emerging pattern of highways and preserve itself as a business and office center in the face of the benefits and convenience of a suburban location? Connecticut General's president, Frazar Wilde, used the occasion of the new building's dedication to tackle the question head-on by hosting a symposium, "The New Highways: Challenge to the Metropolitan Region." Connecticut General offered its own suburban estate as one answer to these problems.

But in Boston and its other regional home offices, Prudential did not take this course of leaving the city. While Connecticut General was happy to disappear into the rolling suburban hills, Prudential was unwilling to abandon the longer tradition of civic prominence in an urban setting. Prudential did, however, seek to distinguish itself from the congested mass of buildings in the central business district. It hedged its position by finding midtown sites for its regional home offices, where it built self-contained "cities of insurance" and boasted many of the amenities that would be taken up by Connecticut General on its campus.

Connecticut General's abandonment of the central business district demonstrated a larger trend: the suburbanization of corporate headquarters. Prudential, however, acted on an institutionalized urban consciousness and explicitly sought the "extra dividends" derived from a midtown location. Partly by building in a new area, the company was able to have a higher profile: the big "Prudential" emblazoned across the skyline; the impact of leading a greater reshaping of the city; the chance for an insurance company (a company specializing in managing risk) to take a bold urban step and to be recognized for doing so.

City in a City

In the nineteenth and early twentieth centuries, large commercial buildings internalized many of the functions of the city, including street-front retail shops, internal arcades, connections to transit, and ornate lobbies that were semi-public extensions of the street. Frank Woolworth promoted his skyscraper on lower Broadway as a "city within a city," following a pattern of large office buildings that combined many functions in a single structure, including semi-public shopping arcades and circulatory spaces. In addition to sheer architectural splendor, the building possessed its own critical mass and presented itself as an integral piece of the machinery of the city and a civic improvement.[34] Even more ambitious were the large railroad terminal modernization projects, such as those at the Cleveland Union Terminal and Grand Central Terminal in New York, from the first quarter of the twentieth century, and Rockefeller Center, which was an explicit model for the Prudential Center and other large postwar urban complexes updated for the motor age.

The Cleveland Terminal and Grand Central projects pioneered the development of air rights over railroad facilities and the connection between self-interested business maneuvers and the broader reshaping of urban structure. Like the Prudential Center, each was a centrally planned ensemble, constructed over a span of time and with each building suited to its particular function. A brief look at these projects contextualizes Prudential's ambitions for a postwar "city in a city" that evoked the civic aspirations and architectural grouping of Rockefeller Center with the infrastructural coordination of the Cleveland Union Terminal and Grand Central projects.

The Grand Central project began when the New York Central Railroad, a syndicate of several lines assembled by Cornelius Vanderbilt, made the decision to erect an all-electric terminal on the site of its Grand Central Depot to compete with the West Side terminal planned by its rival, the Pennsylvania Railroad. The railroad's chief engineer, William J. Wilgus, devised a wide-ranging plan that included capping the vast rail yards that stretched north of the terminal and placing a lid over the tracks south of Ninety-sixth Street, which became Park Avenue. This daring plan capitalized on the railroad's holdings by allowing revenue-producing development over the air rights. Grand Central was the centerpiece of a veritable "terminal city" that included hotels, office buildings, and apartment towers on the roughly forty-eight acres of railroad-owned land that adhered to Manhattan's grid between Forty-second and Fiftieth Streets. In the new terminal itself, the great vaulted space of the main concourse was surrounded by an array of retail arcades and passages that connected the station to city streets and the emerging rapid transit system below. In the course of implementing the modernization of its own terminal facilities, the railroad enacted a masterful real estate scheme.[35]

In Cleveland, the Union Terminal complex grew out of the determination of two brothers and real estate developers, Oris P. and Mantis J. Van Sweringen, to unify the city's tangled knot of railroad facilities in a single terminal building and to construct office, hotel, and retail structures in the air rights above the tracks. The brothers' first priority was to build a rapid transit line connecting their suburban land development, Shaker Heights, to downtown Cleveland, and in 1909 they began to buy up land around Cleveland's Public Square to locate a terminus. The Van Sweringens' initially limited goal blossomed into a proposal for a Union Terminal that included nearly every major railroad as well as the city's electric streetcars, rapid transit, and interurban lines. The terminal housed an intricate network of lobbies and shopping arcades that connected nine different buildings across a seventeen-acre site. The twelve-story Higbee Department Store and one-thousand-room Hotel Cleveland framed the southeast corner of the Public Square. The Medical-Arts, Builders Exchange, and Midland Bank buildings rose at the back of the site, designed with U-shaped floor plans and light courts to break up the massing. Architects from the Chicago office of Probst, Anderson, Graham, and White — successors to Daniel Burnham's practice — used granite and limestone cladding to unify the collection of distinct buildings. The crowning achievement was a fifty-two-story office tower — the tallest outside Manhattan until the Prudential tower was built in 1965 — that fused the shaft and loggia of Venice's campanile with the tempietto, or circular chapel, used by McKim, Mead, and White to crown the 1913 Municipal Building in New York. Reinforced by the sheer height of the tower itself, the result was a resounding statement of civic iconography (fig. 10). The Cleveland Union Terminal group marked a breakthrough in large-scale urban planning. The project brought together many of the functions of the city in an integrated unit, making a seamless transition between transportation facilities below and the network of offices, stores, and restaurants in the complex above.[36]

The best known and most influential of the "city-within-a-city" projects of the early twentieth century was Rockefeller Center, which set the standard for a successful grouping of commercial buildings that persuasively claimed the mantle of civic space. Rockefeller Center was developed in the 1930s by a private consortium led by John D. Rockefeller, Jr., on seventeen acres in midtown Manhattan owned by Columbia University. When original plans for a new hall for the Metropolitan Opera dissipated, Rockefeller signed on as chief sponsor for the construction of a building complex that would ultimately house offices for Time-Life, the Associated Press, Eastern Airlines, and the U.S. Rubber Company, among others. An elegant sequence of relatively low pavilions facing Fifth Avenue and framing an outdoor retail promenade surrounded a central open space featuring a skating rink. Presiding over the ensemble was the slim, cliff-like, seventy-story tower named for its chief tenant, the Radio Corporation of American (RCA). The team of architects who worked on the project produced a largely symmetrical site plan that adhered to the street grid, though the massing and orientation of each building was tailored to its flagship tenant, a feature that broke the monotony of the plan. All buildings were clad in Indiana limestone accented with vertically fluted spandrels. The addition of a new, private street, Rockefeller Plaza, interrupted the city's grid and aided circulation across the site. Underground, an extensive network of tunnels and concourses, lined with shops, connected the complex. Provisions were also made for a parking garage (fig. 11).[37]

The buildings of Rockefeller Center set the standard for dignified corporate architecture before the steel-and-glass facades of International Style buildings became the architectural signature of American corporations. Moreover, the complex demonstrated that the private planning of a large commercial project could be widely accepted as a public asset. One facet of this was Rockefeller Center's extensive art program — including murals, freestanding statuary, and detailed relief sculpture — as well as the inclusion of galleries and other quasi-public display spaces. These amenities did not immediately reward investors in terms of rentable property, but they helped Rockefeller Center make a claim as a civic space. Prudential's model of patronage looked back to Rockefeller Center.[38]

Like these earlier developments, Prudential viewed its Boston center as a "city in a city," a vast conglomeration of office space, public plazas, and shopping arcades, a massive development that was designed as a coherent whole. Unlike Rockefeller

Figure 10 Postcard of the Cleveland Union Terminal group, built between 1917 and 1930

right **Figure 11** Photograph from a souvenir brochure of Rockefeller Center in midtown Manhattan

Center, however, the Prudential Center in Boston, and Prudential's other regional home offices — except for the Western Home Office in Los Angeles, which had some admirers — were not widely considered aesthetically distinguished pieces of architecture. In a review of the building program in 1955, writers for *Architectural Forum* remarked that none of the RHOs were "likely to win any really first-rank architectural awards." *Fortune* characterized the architecture as "modern Prudential style."[39] Nonetheless, Prudential used architecture to assert its civic values by the sheer force of urban redevelopment in an uncertain economic climate. Prudential had the wherewithal to take on expensive, long-term projects with serious political implications, and thus turned private urban development into a civic undertaking.

THE MOTOR AGE AND THE PROBLEM OF OBSOLESCENCE

Prudential wanted to play the role of urban patron in the motor age. S. Westcott Toole, a Prudential executive who helped formulate the regional home office strategy, pointed to the Prudential Center as an example of the company's commitment to solving "major urban problems of building in metropolitan areas." This was true in two ways: Prudential had awakened Boston's business leaders to a new era of investment in their own city, and Prudential helped modernize Boston's physical landscape. "For the first time in the building of a downtown real estate project," Toole said, "the needs of both pedestrians and motorists will be successfully met in a single architectural plan."[40]

Until 1920, accessibility to the business district was defined by mass transit. But after 1920, the "riding habit" declined and more Americans began driving cars and patronizing outlying business districts. City leaders faced a two-pronged crisis: the drift of business activity from the center to more accessible districts and intense traffic congestion in the core. The crisis of decline and abandonment was well represented in contemporary urban discourse.[41] Urban analyst Raymond Vernon observed that the rise of cars in the central business district had "taxed the obsolescent street system of the area almost beyond endurance." He identified "Boston's narrow crooked street system" as one example of obsolescence that contributed to congestion, a factor that pushed business functions to the fringes of the center city.[42] The challenges posed by cars in the city and the cost of modernization were central to traffic expert Wilfred Owen's analysis of the "metropolitan transportation problem."[43]

The Mass Pike's William F. Callahan assigned himself the mission to fix all that and modernize Boston's transportation landscape. His answer was better highway access, and he seized on the Boston and Albany corridor as the most efficient route from the western suburbs to the center city. Unwilling to cede control to the state's Department of Public Works (which he had once headed) and wait for federal funding to trickle in, Callahan advocated private financing of the Boston Extension through the fickle bond market — a market that was ultimately fortified by Prudential's commitment to purchase a large measure of the bonds.

The Pike and the Pru also embodied a new urban form intended to curb the decentralization of the city's office and commercial functions by mimicking the suburban logic of accessibility. Victor Gruen proposed this vision in its most ambitious form for downtown Fort Worth, which he wanted to convert into a pedestrian precinct ringed by highways and parking garages. Wilfred Owen called it a "total strategy for attacking obsolescence and restoring vitality" to the urban center. On a smaller scale, urban renewal was creating opportunities for private developers to assemble large sites, superblocks, and produce integrated building complexes. In 1964, the critic Mildred Schmertz pointed to the Prudential Center as one example of this proliferating urban form, the "downtown center," where architects were more likely to design complexes of buildings — "self-contained little cities" — than individual buildings. The new business centers were "welcome islands of safety for pedestrians . . . surrounded by elaborate traffic arteries."[44]

Insurance companies and governments were the major patrons of this new urban form. Alongside the Prudential Center, Schmertz focused her attention on Constitution Plaza in Hartford, where Travelers Insurance Company stepped in to rescue a flailing urban renewal project. The city's redevelopment agency had targeted the "Front-Market" area that lay between the central business district and the Connecticut River for slum clearance in the early 1950s, but the private developer — F. H. McGraw Company — was unable to secure financing. In 1960, Travelers organized a subsidiary corporation to finance, construct, and operate the office and hotel complex and persuaded key local businesses to stay in the city, including Connecticut Bank and Trust, Phoenix Mutual Life Insurance Company, and WTIC, the city's largest broadcaster, all of which were considering a move to the suburbs. Architect Charles DuBose planned the twelve-acre downtown center with eight office and commercial buildings, underground garages for eighteen hundred cars, and a sequence of landscaped walks and plazas. Buildings were designed by several of New York's leading commercial firms, including Kahn & Jacobs and Emery Roth & Sons, which teamed up with DuBose to design the eighteen-story tower that housed a major branch of Connecticut's oldest bank, Hartford National Bank and Trust Company. The Hotel Corporation of America — the initial hotelier at the Prudential Center — operated the new Hotel Sonesta, a twelve-story and 315-room facility (fig. 12). The complex was closely tied to state highway plans and the ramps from Interstate 91, careening beside the Connecticut River, neatly linked to many acres of parking garages that formed the building podium. *Architectural Record* recognized that Travelers was a well-endowed patron, "willing to pay for plazas."[45] Travelers had a significant stake in Hartford, where its massive thirty-four-story tower, built in 1919, anchored the business district and overlooked

Constitution Plaza. The insurance company's commitment to rescuing what might have become an urban renewal fiasco served as a powerful counterpoint to Connecticut General's departure from the central city and offered another answer to the challenge of the new highways for the metropolitan region, to fight back and "reverse the trend toward decentralization and the flight to outlying areas."[46]

In Boston, it would have been less expensive to leave the Mass Pike Extension as an open cut through the site, creating two distinct parcels. Both Prudential and its architects, Charles Luckman Associates, however, agreed that the "long range values" of the site could be preserved only if the entire parcel was developed as a single, integrated project. Prudential's view on this matter in Boston was consistent with its other RHO projects, including the very first, in Los Angeles, where Prudential chief Carrol Shanks insisted on buying a larger site than was strictly necessary and convinced the city to de-map one of its roads that ran through the parcel.

Prudential and its architects linked the public value of the Prudential Center to its site planning, which left plenty of open space for people to gather; its impact on traffic planning, with its ring roads that would mitigate congestion in the Back Bay; and the solipsistic assertion that the singular, unified quality of the plan, bridging the channel for the Mass Pike, itself protected the "long range values" of the project and thus the public interest in sound urban development.

PLAN OF THE BOOK

This book develops the themes outlined in this introduction through a detailed study of the context and the planning of Boston's Prudential Center. Chapter 1 tells the story of the Prudential Insurance Company and its ambitious plans to establish regional home offices in cities across America. The Prudential's RHOs were far more than divisions on an organizational chart. They were physical headquarters that had profound effects

Figure 12 Postcard of Constitution Plaza in Hartford, an urban renewal project financed principally by the Travelers Insurance Company

on the landscapes of the cities where they were built. Chapter 1 presents the corporate context in which the Prudential, the self-styled Rock of Gibraltar, established its massive promontories in American cities. The chapter explores Prudential's urban policy, examining the company's adoption of a decentralized corporate structure and its establishment of regional home offices in cities throughout America. The case of Chicago, in particular, presaged the study of Boston by illustrating the complex interplay of corporate policy and governmental urban policy in a city struggling to regain footing.

Chapter 2 situates our study in Boston and provides a selective history of the economy and landscape of the city, from the mid-nineteenth century to the 1950s, when the Prudential Center was planned. Boston, like other American cities, was preoccupied with urban obsolescence and renewal, and it erected a political and legal structure to try to facilitate such redevelopment. When the Prudential came to Boston, it had to navigate its way through these political structures and, in the process, became an "urban redevelopment company" in its own right. Chapter 3 focuses on the political history of the Prudential Center and the company's bid to redevelop the Back Bay rail yards with a gleaming commercial complex. It analyzes the interconnected political and legal events that gained for an insurance company the favored tax treatment that had been reserved for organizations whose primary purpose was to fight urban blight.

Chapter 4 demonstrates how the development of the Prudential Center became inextricably bound with the development of Boston's road system and, in particular, the extension of the Massachusetts Turnpike into downtown. The interplay of the Pike and the Pru was in the first instance geographical, because the Pru's intended location was pivotal to the Pike's plans to make the city more accessible to automotive traffic, and in the second instance legal and political: the Pru navigated a triangular relationship with the Pike and the Boston Redevelopment Authority to gain recognition — and favored tax status — as a legislatively sanctioned and quasi-public player in the rebuilding of Boston. The journey to quasi-public status was a complicated and sometimes perilous one, including side trips to the highest court in Massachusetts to pass on the legality of the enterprise. The Prudential indeed became an urban redevelopment corporation in reality as well as in legal fiction: the Pru, together with the Pike, became the mover of a major shift in the Boston landscape, expanding the "downtown" to a second midtown area.

When the deals between the Pru, the Pike, and the city were signed and sealed, an anxious Boston awaited the physical results: the new buildings and their surrounds. Chapter 5 examines the design choices made by the Prudential for the Boston regional office, beginning with the selection of a "businessman" architect, Charles Luckman, and looking closely at the bureaucratic aspects of the design process itself. The Pru has never been loved by architectural critics. Indeed, some aspects of the center, such as its retail spaces, were at least initially colossal failures. This chapter discusses why Prudential chose Luckman, the businessman-architect, and avoided working with modernist eggheads like Walter Gropius, who had already proposed a "Back Bay Center" for the same site. It also discusses incrementalism: we are accustomed to looking at large developments like the Prudential Center from that era and maligning them as monolithic constructions. But the Prudential Center was not dropped in place overnight. It was built over many years as Prudential responded to changing political and economic conditions. It has been a very restless landscape.[47]

Chapter 6 reflects on the lessons learned from the Prudential Center for the understanding of urban development, not only as a matter of politics and economics but also as an example of how private and public actors and concerns interact to shape the physical landscape of American cities. We will consider the legacy of the structure and spaces that the Pru gave to Boston, both in the 1960s and continuing to the present. The Prudential Center and other similar redevelopment projects from the 1950s and '60s have been attacked as a corporate land-grab in the name of the public interest. Were the "enlightened" self-interests of corporations like Prudential in fact less enlightened than they wanted to believe? Many large corporations and real estate developers in the 1950s have been accused of profiting from policies established to help the poor. Prudential was no exception. But the detractors of such projects do not acknowledge that they operate with 20/20 hindsight. Many of us today regret the foisting of large corporate estates on the urban landscape; we long for the architectural diversity and mix of uses in the city they replaced. But we do a disservice by ignoring the perspective of planners — municipal and corporate — who were fearful in the 1950s that American cities were dying.

Finally, I sometimes use "Prudential" or "Boston" as the subject of a sentence. It is not my intention to duck the question of institutional agency. "Prudential" and "Boston" are stand-ins for a group of individuals working together in an organization: they are the vice presidents, attorneys, and consulting engineers who represented the corporation; they are the politicians, city planners, and municipal staff who constituted the local government. My argument places "Prudential" in the same legal-institutional framework as "Boston." This latter entity was a place-based institution with explicit geographical borders. Prudential was (and still is) a national corporation managing many billions of dollars of assets. Nevertheless, Prudential was as influential as local governments in its effort to redevelop the postwar American city.

Chapter 1

Extra Dividends
Prudential's Urban Vision

Prudential's Mid-America Home Office, facing Grant Park in Chicago, ca. 1955 (Courtesy of Prudential

Between 1948 and 1965, the Prudential Insurance Company of America, at that time one of the largest corporations in the world, launched an expansive program of administrative decentralization. Wary of over-concentrating their operations in Newark, New Jersey, Prudential's corporate planners opened semi-autonomous regional home offices in seven cities across North America. What began as an effort to reinvigorate Prudential's bureaucratic makeup evolved into a prominent building program and urban-planning phenomenon. In each case — first in Los Angeles and followed by Toronto, Houston, Jacksonville, Minneapolis, Chicago, and Boston — Prudential's physical presence had important economic and spatial ramifications. The new RHOs stimulated the market for commercial real estate, promoted the economic prospects of each city, and reshaped the geographical contours of the business district.

Prudential's decentralization program embodied a deliberate urban policy, and corporate executives came up with a set of internal principles to develop the RHOs. As a rule, Prudential planners favored large, undeveloped sites outside the established central business district where they were free to construct expansive office campuses. At the same time, the insurance company committed to building in the city rather than decamping for the suburbs. The company's urban posture called for imposing, landmark buildings with towers that broadcast Prudential's name. The public relations value of the regional home offices — as a symbol of the large company's local commitments and as a literal signboard advertisement — were all part of what one Prudential executive called the "Extra Dividends" of his company's decentralization plan.

This chapter explores the sources and consequences of Prudential's urban strategy. Prudential executives believed that the RHOs, each a self-assured investment in urban real estate, amplified the company's local prestige, national presence, and posture as a public institution. This civic self-consciousness appealed to Cold War–era executives who believed that the insurance industry could embody the public interest both as a facilitator of urban renewal and, more broadly, as a guarantor of the nation's social welfare. This chapter discusses the Prudential approach as it applied in Los Angeles, Houston, and Chicago. The next two chapters will turn to the application of this approach in Boston.

THAT MIGHTY PUMP, PRUDENTIAL

In a 1964 profile of Prudential for *Fortune,* writer Robert Sheehan looked for a metaphor big enough to describe his subject: "[Prudential is] a kind of universal power plant, vast of maw and spout, breathing in and breathing out. Its function is the collection and redistribution of the people's savings. As the giant mechanism pumps away, there are few U.S. businesses — or few U.S. citizens, in fact — that escape the effect of either its updraft or its downdraft." The image is dynamic and immense. More than just a machine that pumped money, Prudential was a living, breathing thing whose respiratory action implied the dual nature of the insurance enterprise: "Prudential is, in reality, two distinct but complementary businesses. One is Prudential the life underwriter and salesman of financial security. The other is Prudential the investor." Breathing in, the corporation collected premiums from its 37 million policyholders — roughly one in five Americans in 1964 — amassing more than $2.5 billion a year. Breathing out, this heaving leviathan dispensed policy claims and made income-generating investments that suffused every aspect of the American economy and society. Prudential was the third-largest private corporation in the world, Sheehan reported, ranking behind only American Telephone and Telegraph and insurance company rival Metropolitan Life in total assets.[1]

The *Fortune* article included an illustrated chart of the polished new regional home offices, significant real estate assets and also the most visible signs of Prudential's fiscal confidence and national ambitions. But the RHO buildings were only one small piece of the company's larger investment portfolio. Prudential was the nation's largest private financier of home and farm ownership, executed by a national network of mortgage-loan offices, and financed a wide variety of commercial and residential developments. Prudential placed direct loans with U.S. industrial concerns and counted many of the most prestigious names in American business as borrowers, including IBM, Chrysler, and Union Carbide. Like many other insurance companies, Prudential was an active player on the bond market and had recently begun investing a small percentage of its assets in common stocks. Large departments in Prudential's home office in Newark were staffed with money managers and investment specialists, many with backgrounds in Wall Street and banking.

Prudential competed not only with other insurance companies in sales but also with banks and trust companies to invest the national pool of personal and pension-fund savings. Prudential was more than an ordinary business enterprise, however. Its ultimate mission was to provide for widows and orphans. As Sheehan wrote in *Fortune,* "[the] aggregate view of Prudential as an economic mechanism does not, of course, do complete justice to the company's character, motivation, and deep-down purpose. Life insurance was a belief before it was a business; it is a missionary effort, largely, that propels the 'pump.'"[2] That belief was that life insurance was a private solution to a public need: collective financial security. From its inception, Prudential cultivated a public image and internal self-consciousness as a company with broad social responsibilities that performed quasi-public functions.

Corporate Purification

The lore of Prudential's social accountability was rooted in the story of its founder, John F. Dryden, the "frayed young dreamer from Maine," who made it his personal mission to bring "industrial insurance" to the United States. Life insurance blossomed as an American enterprise in the 1840s and '50s, when the Equitable, New York Life, and Mutual Life of New York began to market "ordinary" policies to urban professional classes. The "Big Three" competed vigorously for dominance in the field in the decades after the Civil War, when a general aura of mortality coupled with the rapid growth of cities and their middle classes spurred the popularity of life insurance policies as a way to plan responsibly for the future. In contrast, John Dryden envisioned a "poor-man's insurance" that would provide some modicum of financial security for the families of working-class people. After dropping out from Yale, Dryden worked as an agent for Aetna, in Hartford, and other large insurance companies before coming to Newark to found the Widows and Orphans Friendly Society, which served as a collection agency for its members. The Friendly Society fit the model of a nineteenth-century mutual aid institution that filled the breach in an urban-industrial society where traditional forms of social welfare, including the extended family, had begun to dissolve. But it was not a profitable business enterprise and was being run essentially as a charity. Dryden sought to join the concept of the Friendly Society with an innovative British concept of "industrial insurance," pioneered by the Prudential Assurance Company of London. Dryden promised his early investors that his concept of insurance for the working classes was not a charity but "a sound business — a business of providing help for others in time of need."[3]

There were two key elements to such an enterprise: the collection of modest weekly premiums and the application of actuarial science to draw up life-expectancy tables that established premiums and managed the company's risk by spreading it across a large number of people. Newark's conservative financiers were initially reluctant to invest in the relatively untested concept. But Dryden's persistence eventually won over a small cadre of progressive backers. In 1875, Dryden altered the charter of the Newark Widows and Orphans Friendly Society and founded the Prudential Friendly Society. Two years later, with its business accelerating, the company's board changed the name again to the Prudential Insurance Company of America, selling policies to working Newarkers for as little as three cents a week. In its early days, Prudential agents went door-to-door each week, literally insinuating themselves into the fabric of the city, collecting the small sums that in aggregate formed the pool of capital to be reinvested by the company at a profit.[4]

Insurance companies like Prudential balanced their dual roles as public service corporations and financiers by establishing conservative investment policies. Dryden was an outspoken proponent of measured investing, declaring in 1884: "Our investments have been confined exclusively to Government bonds and first mortgages secured by improved real estate worth at least twice the amount loaned. . . . We make security the first consideration, the rates of interest secondary."[5] In his study of the life insurance enterprise between 1885 and 1910, the historian Morton Keller explained: "The traditional yardstick of satisfactory insurance investment — that the market value of the company's assets should equal the policy reserve — did not require highly productive fund placement."[6] Bonds in large, secure institutions such as government and railroads qualified as sound investments. And by investing heavily in mortgage loans, Prudential and its competitors also established a persistent link between insurance and housing. In those early years, the companies did not pursue industrial stocks or other securities they considered too vulnerable to economic fluctuations and thus inappropriate for an institution that held the public's money in trust and prized security. The investments of insurance companies were an important part of the overall urbanization and industrialization of American cities.[7]

Despite efforts to project a benign image, the large insurers were not beyond public reproach. In 1905, Charles Evans Hughes — later the governor of New York and the chief justice of the United States — led an investigation commissioned by Senator William W. Armstrong of New York into the business practices of large insurance companies. The results damaged the industry's reputation for benevolence. Hughes exposed a litany of infractions: corporate nepotism, inflated salaries, self-perpetuating directorships, costly marketing techniques, political meddling, dubious investment activities, and "executives who thought of themselves more as financiers than as insurance men." Some insurance companies responded by reorganizing their corporate charters. In 1915, Prudential became a "mutual" company, whereby ownership was transferred from stockholders to the policyholders themselves. Keller called this a "ceremony of corporate purification."[8] The Armstrong investigation publicized the fact that insurance companies were important conduits of capital flow throughout the national economy and sparked the proliferation of state regulations to guarantee the regional recirculation of locally collected savings. Prudential internalized this principle when it constructed regionally autonomous home offices in the 1950s.

Regulation and Real Estate

With government bonds and home mortgages viewed as safe investments with predictable yields, among John Dryden's earliest investments were eight mortgages on Newark property near the Prudential's first office, a basement space on Broad Street.[9] Prudential's interest in the mortgage loan business drove the company to establish a network of field offices to inspect properties. In the 1920s, Prudential made many individual loans for the construction of small homes. In the 1930s, Prudential sought to minimize foreclosures by initiating a "reconstruction policy" that extended forbearance to the many delinquent and defaulted loans on homes and farms. The policy was formulated as part of an expansive mortgage loan network, an infrastructure that bolstered the company's national stature and sales operations.

In 1922, a New York statute allowed insurers to invest directly in housing projects. In this case, government turned to insurance companies to provide a public good — shelter — where the private housing market had failed. As Harold Wayne Snider has suggested, "the purpose of this statute was to help alleviate a shortage of housing rather than to broaden investment outlets." The architectural historian Roberta Moudry has argued that insurance companies had an ideological interest in modern housing practices designed to enhance the health and hygiene of urban working classes. In 1929, New Jersey allowed insurance companies to invest 5 percent of their assets in housing as long as the project was linked to "slum clearance." In 1930, Prudential began the Chellis Austin housing project on three and a half acres in the Ironbound area of Newark, and built 407 units in six 6-story apartment buildings that occupied less than 50 percent of the site. In this case, Prudential did not require the state's power of eminent domain to acquire the site; the insurance company negotiated directly with landowners.[10]

Following New Jersey's lead, many state redevelopment laws were drafted in the 1940s with the explicit intention of encouraging insurance companies to invest in large-scale housing projects. These statutes offered tax concessions and made eminent domain available to insurers acting as housing redevelopers, with the caveat of limited profits. Under New York's Redevelopment Companies Act of 1942, for example, Metropolitan Life financed the construction of Stuyvesant Town and Peter Cooper Village on a broad swath of "slum" territory on Manhattan's Lower East Side after it had been assembled and cleared through the state and local government's power of eminent domain in the early 1940s.[11] The redevelopment statutes of the 1940s foreshadowed the formula by which Prudential sought tax concessions for its regional home office in Boston, the Prudential Center.

After World War II, insurance companies lobbied state legislatures to gain increased access to real estate markets. Beginning in 1948, many states amended their laws regulating life insurance investment practices. Henceforth, insurance companies could invest directly in real estate and act as owner-operators. Prudential immediately entered the housing arena, constructing garden apartment complexes across the United States. In the 1950s, Prudential was an early player in the market for federally guaranteed mortgage loans for suburban homes. Prudential mortgage specialists established lending policies that favored large-scale "community builders" working in green-field sites at the metropolitan fringe. Prudential financed commercial development as well, especially suburban shopping centers, including the upscale Short Hills Mall in New Jersey. Even as it looked for urban sites to construct its regional home offices, Prudential was actively reshaping the metropolitan and regional landscape at its expanding edges.[12]

Insurance and Government

Prudential had already opened the Western Home Office in Los Angeles when the company's president, Carrol M. Shanks, was called to testify before a subcommittee of the House Judiciary Committee in 1949.[13] In a manner less solemn and accusatory than Hughes's investigation in 1905, the congressmen struggled to grasp the sheer size and influence of insurance companies like Prudential. Shanks patiently described Prudential's boundlessness as a financial institution to the poorly informed politicians:

> We are not limited by any particular geographical area. We provide capital in the forms for expansion and modernization of business and industry. We enable families to buy and build homes and to own and operate farms. . . . The businesses which we have helped finance are a complete cross section of our economy. They include practically every type of business in every part of the country. They range from stockyards to the cosmetic industry, to abrasives, to television, from clocks to shipping, covering the whole field, including the great oil producing and refining companies and also the corner filling stations.[14]

The congressmen were shocked to learn that Prudential's single largest investment in any given year was United States government bonds. Prudential's capital helped underwrite the activities of government, but perhaps not inappropriately. Both the federal government and Prudential sought longevity and security. Moreover, the growth of insurance companies, Shanks insisted, would precisely echo the growth of the national economy as a whole — the two were inextricable. In his curt and forthcoming way, Shanks extolled the advantages of a national institution like Prudential: "As I pointed out, gentlemen, this is one of the important economic advantages of a large national company, the channeling of funds from the surplus areas to the areas of great and growing development where those funds are needed."[15]

Bigness and scope were assets, not detriments, to the national economy. Prudential could redistribute money from established areas with a large customer base (the industrialized East and Midwest) to developing areas where investment opportunities were plentiful. Shanks revealed that "Sunbelt" regions of the South, Southwest, and West received more in investment funds than were taken out in premiums — a revelation that prompted New York Republican Kenneth B. Keating to quip: "With all that money going down south from the Prudential Insurance Company, that eliminates the need of so much Federal money going to the South."[16] His colleagues laughed, but the comment was astute: insurance and government played overlapping roles.

Carrol Shanks maintained a clear idea about the fiscal role of his insurance company. Like *Fortune*'s image of a mighty pump, Shanks portrayed the financial character of Prudential in liquid terms, pooling and flowing without geographical restraint. "The life insurance company is a sales and service organization which accumulates reserves and hence has funds to invest," he announced to a group of realtors in Chicago. "It performs a gigantic pooling and redistribution service. These funds are directed into all parts of the American economy, wherever located geographically or in whatever segment or portion of our economy. They flow wherever there is a call for capital."[17]

Shanks believed that this flow of capital should proceed unfettered by too many regulations. He believed in the American system of what he called "free enterprise democracy," and believed that over-regulation would undermine the natural operation of this free-market system. Moreover, Shanks judged that businessmen were the best qualified people to foster economic stability and, by promoting stability, to bolster the American way of life. "If the business man is not to lead, who is?" Shanks's rhetorical question implied that neither politicians nor public bureaucrats were fit for this job. Shanks cultivated the reputation of business as a benevolent force in American public life, insisting that business decisions reflected the public interest more than did political maneuvering. Business, not government, contained the progressive power to resolve national problems. The weakness of the Russian system, Shanks insisted, was the draining of independent business leaders in favor of a stifling, planned economy. Democracy, for Shanks, was best preserved by corporate self-government, not the lordly oversight of cumbersome regulatory bureaucracies.[18]

United States congressmen in 1949 were willing to accept the important role of a large private company in the national economy and were interested in apprehending the principles that guided Prudential's ambitious postwar decentralization program. A very large corporation was in effect splitting off into several smaller ones — though each regional iteration of Prudential would itself be larger than almost any other competing insurance company. Shanks explained that each RHO was given enough autonomy to establish its own sales, service, and investment operations. Marketing would be locally responsive. Claims would be processed more efficiently. Executives would network with local business elites and regional bosses would gain leadership experience that benefited the company as a whole. And, finally, the buildings that housed these regional operations were local investments in urban real estate as well as important markers of Prudential's national standing.

BREAK THE WHOLE THING UP

"The service Prudential gave to the people of the United States was constant and inconspicuous," according to a convivial corporate biography of the firm published in

1950.[19] "Inconspicuous" was an inaccurate term, however, to describe Prudential's service to American people: the authors of this description confused omnipresence for inconspicuousness. Prudential's activities were so pervasively diffused through American social and economic life that they seemed to disappear into the atmosphere like so many particles of air.

In fact, Prudential had a very conspicuous presence in American visual culture, from advertisements in every imaginable medium to the architecture of its home and branch offices. In 1896, a young advertising man at the J. Walter Thompson agency hit upon the Rock of Gibraltar as Prudential's defining icon, and joined it with this phrase: "The Prudential Has the Strength of Gibraltar." The image, designed to symbolize the permanence, unbreakable strength, and even transcendence of the firm, was quickly adopted and disseminated (fig. 13).[20] The Rock of Gibraltar is a monolithic limestone promontory at the tip of the Iberian Peninsula. But an advertisement in *Life* magazine in 1898 featured a "Bright Boy (who reads the papers)" claiming that the Rock of Gibraltar could be found in Newark, New Jersey: "It is owned by the Prudential Insurance Company."[21]

Home Office, Branch Office

By 1910, the icon was branded across the nation. In large cities and small towns, Prudential established an extensive network of branch offices, opened for business among other Main Street proprietors. As historians of the company have noted, "The Prudential sign with its Rock of Gibraltar was a familiar sight on any Main Street, as well known to the farmers and ranchers of the Middle West and West as it was to the factory workers of New Jersey and New England."[22] In these early decades, each branch office functioned as a franchise of Prudential and reported directly to the home office in Newark, where policies were processed, claims paid, and investment decisions made.

As Prudential's national scope and exposure expanded, so did the home office complex in Newark. John Dryden first housed the Prudential Friendly Society in 1875 in the basement of the National State Bank on Broad Street in Newark. In 1878 he

Figure 13 Prudential's icon, the Rock of Gibraltar (Courtesy of Prudential Financial, Inc.)

rented a storefront and two floors in the Centennial Building on Market Street. In 1883, the company moved again, to the Jube Building on Market Street. By that time, Prudential had established its own actuarial department to calculate the risks associated with insuring particular policyholders. Each policy was recorded on a piece of paper that had to be filed, and Prudential created a printing department to supply its own forms. By the 1890s, the company had outgrown its rented office space. Dryden decided to build a home office to house the fast-growing firm and commissioned the prestigious New York architect George Post to design an eleven-story skyscraper, the Prudential Building, on Broad Street in the heart of Newark's flourishing business district (see fig. 7).

Post's design was a massive, heavy, and opulent building. Any structure of its size would have reflected the company's expansion and fiscal self-confidence. But the Prudential Building also used architectural iconography to project a fortress-like quality that evoked the attributes of strength and security. Post used turrets, canonical towers, and elaborate dormers with pointed roofs to suggest a fortified French Chateau. He borrowed from the style that H. H. Richardson had popularized, incorporating heavy, rounded archways of rough-hewn stone and deeply recessed windows. Two large stone lions sat atop the squat, rounded entrance archway, and various gargoyles were scattered across the facade. The building was a palpable contribution to Newark's urban culture and the importance of its central business district.

Despite its nostalgic external appearance, the iron-framed Prudential Building was a modern marvel with the most up-to-date amenities, including hydraulic piston-driven elevators, steam heat, running hot and cold water, gas and electric lighting, and telephones in every office. Executives had individual offices, but most of the space was given to open floors where the company's large clerical staff processed insurance policies. The Prudential was a huge urban production plant, with its own printing and mailing department, designed to function as a massive filing cabinet: "Millions of records had to be filed, indexed, and obtainable at a moment's notice."[23]

The Prudential Building was completed in 1892, but the staff soon outgrew it. Prudential acquired adjacent parcels and in 1901 four more buildings were in construction: the twelve-story Main Building addition, the twelve-story North Building, the eleven-story West Building, and the ten-story Northwest Building. In 1910, an addition to the North Building was erected. The Prudential buildings housed the colossal bureaucracy of a major financial institution. And though Prudential relied on the Rock of Gibraltar to symbolize the company, the stalwart architecture of the home office complex was also designed to advertise the company's dependability. The buildings were interconnected like a tight-knit urban campus, albeit one without very much open or green space. Prudential chronicler William H. A. Carr reported that "by the end of 1948 there were 11,526 employees, nearly 65 per cent of them women, working in a rabbit warren of seven buildings in the heart of Newark, the most important of the structures being linked by a tunnel which was completed in 1947" (fig. 14).[24]

Dividends of Decentralization

When he testified before Congress in 1949, Carrol M. Shanks had praised bigness. Scale and scope allowed Prudential to make sound investment choices without settling for quick profits or shortsighted convenience. But bigness had weaknesses that threatened to sabotage the company's future success. The most serious weakness was an elaborate, top-down bureaucracy that stifled innovation and obscured emerging leadership talent. Executives were overspecialized and acted too cautiously. Smaller companies were more nimble, more responsive to new ideas. Moreover, Prudential relied almost exclusively on the labor market in Newark for new employees. Robert Green, a vice president in Prudential's methods department, had a solution: "Break the whole thing up" (fig. 15).[25]

Figure 14 Prudential's interconnected campus of buildings in Newark is highlighted in this image from 1945 (Courtesy of Prudential Financial, Inc.)

Green proposed an ambitious program of corporate decentralization by establishing what he called branch home offices across the United States and Canada. In a memorandum to Carrol Shanks in 1945, he outlined the program's three principal objectives: "(1) To make the Company a truly national institution. (2) To give the Company stronger local significance in various sections. (3) To develop executive personnel." The branch home offices would be as independent as possible, each led by a senior vice president who would act like a president of a smaller company, "capable of passing judgment on sales problems, investment problems and general administration. He should have the good public relations sense and devote his interests and energy to promoting the Prudential throughout his area in all branches of the business." To achieve Green's goals, the regional executives "must be allowed plenty of leeway." The executive home office would remain in Newark to manage the company's overall accounts, perform most of the actuarial work, and coordinate between the regional homes.[26]

Green did not explicitly view the regional homes as real estate opportunities (he did not rule out renting space), but he understood the significance of their physical presences as a public image: "The point of location, nature of the office — whether rented or Prudential owned, type of building, etc. — will have some effect on local significance and public relations in the area," he wrote to Shanks. Green first suggested locating the branch home offices in cities where the Federal Reserve had established branches, each a key financial center, but quickly dismissed the idea: "We wish to be known as a service institution and not a financial institution, and, therefore, some variation might be desirable." Green shrewdly recognized that Prudential's civic orientation transcended mere finance. Shadowing the Federal Reserve would not send the right message.[27]

The concept of decentralization came from Prudential's methods department — what might today be called "corporate operations." But Shanks chose a man with experience in the public relations and advertising department as well as the real estate depart-

Figure 15 A chart illustrating the initial plan for Prudential's corporate decentralization, which called for seven regional home offices in the United States and Canada (Courtesy of Prudential Financial, Inc.)

ment to manage the regional home office building program: Samuel Westcott Toole. Robert Green was vaguely certain that decentralization would enhance Prudential's national standing and local significance. But Toole had a clear-eyed view of the "extra dividends" of decentralization, and he spoke about them frequently in his public appearances, as he said in one speech: "I refer to the advertising and public relations value derived from our attractive buildings." As an executive involved in the selection of building sites for the RHOs, Toole explained that Prudential chose "dramatic and strategic" locations in order to yield these "extra dividends."[28]

Wes Toole was fascinated by public image and name recognition. In 1947, he commissioned a nationwide survey to "obtain a scientific assessment of the public's attitude toward the Prudential." The survey included this question: "When you think of the leading life insurance companies in the country, which ones come to mind?" Forty-eight percent of respondents named Prudential. Fifty-six percent named Metropolitan Life. A similar survey was conducted in 1954, and Prudential came out on top, with fifty-six percent of respondents naming it as a leading insurance company. Toole attributed the increase to the Prudential's decentralization program.[29]

Toole, the ad man, constructed a compelling theory that linked geography, architecture, and visual culture to his company's public image and commercial success. In a speech to Prudential mortgage loan agents in 1957, he pointed to the recently constructed regional home office buildings: "I think you will agree that our buildings are strategically located so that they can be seen by hundreds of thousands of people each year and they therefore become living day to day advertisements of the Prudential and what the Prudential stands for." Toole understood that for architecture to function as advertisement, it had to be visually prominent and avoid being lost in the throng of skyscrapers in the central business district. To achieve this, there was a need for a buffer zone surrounding the building, so that views of the building would not be obstructed. Prudential's Chicago tower, opened in 1955, was just north of Grant Park, a public amenity that excluded multistory buildings. As Toole explained, Grant Park became like the building's own front yard, preserving an unobstructed view of the structure from Michigan Avenue. The building would be an instant landmark, with the name PRUDENTIAL spelled out across its top, visible during the day and lighted at night: "What better perpetual ad could the Prudential have than this beautiful 41-story structure standing majestically alone, but within easy access to everything required of a downtown location" (see chapter frontispiece).[30]

An Urban Institution

It was important to Prudential's planners that the company remain an urban institution. This was a point of pride for Wes Toole: "It should also be noted that in no case have we gone outside the city limits for a site for one of our regional home offices. The Prudential believes strongly in the future of the downtown city." Prudential would not join the postwar exodus of corporate offices to the suburbs. Yet Prudential's urban identity and the architectural principles that governed home office construction created a spatial quandary in the company's building strategies: how to find large sites that were geographically prominent and were also located in the center city. In 1955, Wes Toole delivered an address to the Real Estate Board of Newark, titled "The Outlook for the Central City." He argued that transportation technology, and the automobile in particular, had reoriented the urban region and challenged the preeminence of the central city. Toole noted that middle-class homes, commerce, and industry were increasingly unbound from the assets of urban concentration. But he did not think that service industries like his could afford to make the same choice: "The service industries will continue, in my opinion, to favor the central city. Can you imagine the large accounting firms, the big advertising agencies, the prominent law firms moving out to the periphery? I can't."[31]

Toole conceded that there were good reasons for businesses to leave the center city: traffic congestion, parking problems, high land costs, and heavy tax burdens. But these did not outweigh the disadvantages of moving to a suburban location, where firms would have to build and operate their own buildings. Moreover, suburban office centers were too dependent on the automobile. In 1955, Toole was not willing to abandon

Figure 16 The Plaza Building in Newark, ca. 1961, Prudential's headquarters building that replaced George Post's stone fortress, designed by the New York firm of Voorhees, Walker, Smith and Smith (Courtesy of Prudential Financial, Inc.)

the concepts that had established the preeminence of the central business district: the concentration of mass transit, the proximity of business contacts, and the traditions of social prominence and civic engagement. In fact, that year Prudential reaffirmed its commitment to downtown Newark. Despite all the emphasis on the regional home offices, Prudential announced that it was going to invest $20 million in its Newark headquarters, the "Corporate Home Office." The company's stalwart edifice, dating to 1892, would be razed and replaced with a twenty-four-story white marble tower with an adjoining seven-story pavilion, underground parking, and a street-level plaza (fig. 16).[32]

In his public speeches, Wes Toole urged his audience to support contemporary urban renewal plans that sought to eliminate the "slums" that surrounded the central business district. He called for more urban highways to redress the problem of new roads that bypassed the center city, thus making them less connected to their own regions. He supported President Dwight D. Eisenhower's proposal to throw federal funding behind the expansion of highways. Toole acknowledged that local authorities would have to improve urban parking facilities to accommodate the influx of cars. The challenges facing urban renewal efforts did not detract from Toole's optimistic outlook for the center city. But the regional home offices that Prudential proposed to build in several American cities ironically challenged the very urban principles that Toole championed. Unlike most other firms, Prudential could afford to build and operate its own buildings. And Prudential prized sites that were accessible to cars. Prudential wanted both the advantages of large, outlying sites as well as an urban address.

Location, Location, Location

Prudential's RHO location choices had both local and national significance. Locally, Prudential's buildings set new standards for the modern office landscape. The Prudential's local choices also reoriented the business districts, in some cases spreading them out from their established cores. And nationally, Prudential's RHOs anointed emerging financial centers, particularly in the South, and bolstered the fortunes of flagging cities, like Boston. In their written accounts — speeches, memoranda, and published recollections — Prudential's executives pointed to several logics driving location. Westcott Toole emphasized public image and visibility. Charles Fleetwood, of the Southwestern Home Office in Houston, advocated "accessibility" as a leading value.

Prudential chose RHO sites before the Interstate Highway System remapped American cities in the 1960s. Prudential Center in Boston most embodied the limited-access, highway-based logic of the regional city.[33] I think of the RHOs in Los Angeles and Houston as "boulevard" projects that anchored new business districts outside the downtown core along broad, arterial streets. The Mid-America Home Office in Chicago was built above the air rights of an urban rail yard — a project that presaged the Boston Prudential Center — and stretched the boundaries of the central business district away from the tight confines of The Loop and toward Lake Michigan. In Jacksonville, Prudential assembled two properties on the east bank of the St. Johns River where it constructed a lavishly landscaped nineteen-acre office campus featuring a twenty-two-story tower faced with limestone.[34] In Minneapolis, the North Central Home Office (NCHO) was built as a low-slung campus within city limits but well outside the central business district along a relatively undeveloped state highway (fig. 17).

As a consistent principle, Prudential's planners sought to control large swaths of land to protect against encroaching developments, particularly those they perceived could threaten land values. As a rule, Prudential buildings were developed as landscaped campuses on many acres of land, with surface parking lots, indoor and outdoor recreational facilities, cafeterias, and auditoriums.[35] These were more than just large buildings; they were office complexes. They were built within city limits, a fact trumpeted by Wes Toole when he claimed that Prudential "believed in the center city," but they also hedged on the risk of a strictly downtown location. These were autonomous "cities of insurance," nearly districts unto themselves. Many of the buildings were very well adapted to their settings, notably Walter Wurdeman and Welton Becket's Prudential Square on Wilshire Boulevard in Los Angeles. It was the largest office building in the vicinity and also addressed the street with a department store pavilion and retail strip set in a broad, landscaped sidewalk and small square plaza. But it is possible to think of the RHOs as a group, a fact accentuated by a shared architectural ambiance, what Robert Sheehan had called "Modern Prudential Style."[36]

Modern Prudential Style

In an unsigned feature article in 1955, *Architectural Forum* described the architectural manifestations of Prudential's corporate decentralization. The magazine tallied 3.7 million square feet of office space and $75 million invested in Prudential's decentralization and expansion program. Los Angeles opened in 1948, Houston in 1952, and Jacksonville, Minneapolis, and Chicago in 1955, and the writer depicted the five RHOs as a building type that shared a set of characteristics. In terms of interior organization, Prudential's new architecture reflected the modern insurance "production line," with broad, loft-like, open-plan floors organized with long rows of electrically powered work stations. "The bulk of its work, processing thousands of insurance and investment transactions daily, is done on long white-collar production lines, with paper as the raw material and more paper as the end product." A single piece of paper was processed by specialized divisions before the policy was mailed back to the holder. These production line divisions — such as medical, underwriting, and issue — were spatially

Figure 17 *top* The South Central Home Office was built on a nineteen-acre parcel across the river from downtown Jacksonville. The twenty-two-story tower, with two lower wings, was designed by local architecture firm Kemp, Bunch and Jackson. *bottom* The North Central Home Office, Minneapolis, was built as a low-slung campus within city limits but well outside the central business district along a relatively undeveloped state highway. The architects were Magney, Tusler, and Setter. (Courtesy of Prudential Financial, Inc.)

linked across the open floor plan, designed for "continuous work flow in spaces as large as a small factory," and a system of conveyors brought paper from one floor to the next. As a rule, Prudential's floor slabs were thicker than conventional floors, reinforced with thick steel rods to bear the weight of heavy filing cabinets and business machines. Each point on the floor's surface was as strong as the next, and modern work stations could be "placed at will" across the homogeneous plane.[37]

The exterior architecture of the mid-1950s RHOs also had common attributes. Sheathed in limestone with granite or marble accents, featuring mosaics and sculpture, the architecture looked back to the monumentality of Rockefeller Center — the model of a successful, civic-minded private development — or perhaps even the Rock of Gibraltar itself. *Forum* remarked on the overall pattern: "Like its favorite Rock, the Pru's last four buildings in particular are massive in shape, solidly embedded in the ground. . . . A utility tower is emphasized as a rocklike slab, labeled with the Gibraltar emblem and the company's name in letters big enough to be seen the desired distance. . . . The desired impact: the Pru is *big* but *local*."

The bulk of each building was artfully arranged in wings and towers, breaking up the exterior mass. As a rule, Prudential invited several local architects to propose a scheme for a new building before choosing one, though the company's internal building department oversaw the architects' work closely. While the approach was consistent, *Forum* judged the aesthetic results less than stellar: "Despite their obvious success in many respects, no Prudential building since the first one in Los Angeles is likely to win any really first-rank architectural awards. . . . The problem of how a large corporation gets really distinguished architecture is still a difficult one."[38]

Prudential's buildings, "like its salesmen, sell solidity and permanence." Instead of seeking distinction in modern architectural fashion, a whimsical pursuit, Prudential focused on sound planning principles to ensure each building's long-range value and to assert the regional goals of each RHO. These principles included visibility, accessibility, and fiscal security over the long term. The result was a particular urban type: the midtown office campus, on a large site with plenty of parking and employee amenities, yet featuring a tower — emblazoned with the name PRUDENTIAL — large enough to be seen by passing motorists on a well-traveled road. Prudential's locations struck a spatial bargain between the proximity to downtown amenities and accessibility at a regional scale. Visitors to a Prudential RHO were as likely to arrive at a regional airport at the metropolitan fringe, or commute from the suburbs, as journey from a downtown office or railroad station. The planning and construction of the RHOs in Los Angeles, Houston, and Chicago provide case studies of the Prudential policy in practice and prefigure the planning of the Prudential Center in Boston.

MIDTOWN ON THE MIRACLE MILE: PRUDENTIAL IN LOS ANGELES

In the 1920s, Los Angeles retailers moved west from the central business district along Wilshire Boulevard to enhance their accessibility to increasingly mobile and far-flung shoppers. The stretch of Wilshire Boulevard between La Brea and Fairfax Avenues was known as the "Miracle Mile," a trendy retail district dotted with art deco–style buildings. The Miracle Mile was an archetype for the linear, automobile-oriented commercial district outside of downtown. Prudential amplified this spatial trend by locating its Western Home on the Miracle Mile in 1948, hastening the decentralization of office space in Los Angeles along the boulevard. By the 1960s, this portion of Wilshire had become a high-density "midtown" office district.[39]

Westward, Ho! "The Shift from Center of Concentration"

In 1946, Carrol Shanks formed a small committee to advise him on the decentralization process. The committee's first recommendation was to start with a home office on the Pacific Coast serving eleven western states and Hawaii.[40] San Francisco housed the regional Federal Reserve Bank, but Shanks preferred Los Angeles, the anchor of Southern California's energetic economy. In a speech to the board of directors of the Los Angeles Chamber of Commerce in 1947, Shanks confided that "the selection of Los Angeles was not a difficult choice. The impressive growth of this section in all categories — and the vigorous promise of the future — seemed to make this a natural head office site for the West." Population and industrial development were both on the rise in the West. Shanks, a man with a head for numbers, had seen the "figures" and they were "breathtaking. One can't resist a thrill merely in reading them." Shanks couched Prudential's decision to open a Western Home Office (WHO) in Los Angeles in a grand historical narrative and spoke in prophetic terms: "We are at a great turning point in our national set-up. During the next few decades we are going to see a tremendous shift of the financial and economic control of industries to the West and to the Southwest." Shanks wanted Prudential not merely to follow this historical trend but to lead it. He wanted the Western Home Office to be a truly western institution, not a glorified branch office, but "autonomous to a high degree . . . it will control the destinies of Prudential — which is a great sales, service and investment institution — in the West."[41]

In 1948 Shanks addressed the Seattle Chamber of Commerce, titling his speech "The Shift from Center of Concentration." The title contained multiple meanings. In terms of the national economy, Shanks saw economic power shifting from the East to the West. He predicted that "the further expansion and growth of the [western region] . . . will bring about a substantial shift from the older, mature Eastern centers of concentration." Prudential would play an active role in this shift, "channeling large amounts of capital from the East to the West," a process that he believed would have a stabilizing effect on national capital flows. But Shanks's theme also contained a specifically urban-geographical meaning. He began by railing against the "artificial concentration of business" in the Northeast that was a result of business mergers and consolidations. These institutional arrangements had socio-spatial consequences: "Then there is the concentration of the people into the cities of that area. What a price they pay in wasteful, inefficient and unhappy life. Dirt, noise, congestion. Slums and deteriorating areas. In one Eastern City (probably in many) the taxes from the slum areas are only one sixth the cost of the city services for that area. Traffic jams and delays."[42] Shanks sought to spare western cities this undesirable urban condition, which mirrored at a national scale the Prudential's internal challenge: the bureaucratic bottleneck in Newark that the RHOs were designed to decongest. We can perceive this attitude in the site planning for the Western Home Office and other Prudential RHO projects.

Site Selection: The Miracle Mile

Shanks's decentralization committee (also a de-facto site selection committee) asked the director of Prudential's mortgage loan office in Los Angeles, Bill Scholl, to scout locations for the WHO. Scholl kept the process secretive. In his negotiations with property owners, Scholl feigned to represent an anonymous third party. Prudential had deep pockets, and sellers who knew the prospective buyer's identity would likely increase the price of land. Scholl identified an unbuilt ten-acre lot on Wilshire Boulevard between Curson and Masselin Streets, one block from an exposed swath of the La Brea tar pits. The subterranean tar pits extended beneath Prudential's proposed site, but an engineer assured Scholl and Prudential's committee that a light, low-rise building (fewer than ten stories) could be safely erected. This physical constraint also matched the city's ordinance for height limits on new construction. The engineer proposed that Prudential's new building float over the tar pits on a concrete slab, without foundations or pilings.[43]

The site-selection committee recommended buying half the site, more than enough space to erect a building that could house the projected staff and operations of the WHO. Shanks, however, insisted on purchasing the entire tract. This was the first indication that Prudential perceived RHO sites as real estate investments and not just physical plants to house internal operations. Shanks, who forecast immense economic growth in the West, must have perceived the long-term, speculative advantages of controlling a larger site. Shanks's executive decision also matched his urban ideology. Prudential needed room to stretch out and to insulate itself from "dirt, noise, and congestion." There was no indication that Shanks entertained specific opinions concerning architectural style or site-planning principles; he certainly could have imagined the need for a broad parking plaza. But perhaps the clearest motivation behind

Prudential's bid for an expansive urban site, larger than was strictly required, was the long-term security of land values. Shanks saw no reason to risk the encroachment of an unpleasant neighbor in the future. Such a neighbor could act without Prudential's approval, driven by an irresponsible, short-term profit motive, and without Prudential's public commitment to stability and enduring value.

The Building: Light Modern

George Post's Prudential Building in Newark was heavy. The Western Home Office in Los Angeles, designed by the large local firm of Wurdeman and Becket, was *light*. In the words of an official Prudential biography, "When the original home office was built, John Dryden had insisted on the heaviest material available. . . . The blue granite flagstones around the Newark home office were the largest ever quarried, weighing up to eighty tons. The Prudential western home office reflected the spirit of a later day. It was lighter in construction than almost any other building of its kind and size in the world."[44] The building had to be light because it rested on only seventeen feet of firm soil above the La Brea tar pits. It was erected without a basement on a concrete float instead of the more typically used steel pilings. Wurdeman and Becket used light-weight construction techniques to eliminate deadweight, including floors made of four-inch pumice concrete slabs and pre-stressed spandrels of the same material, which required fewer steel columns, beams, and girders than a more conventional building. The architects also used a lightweight fireproofing of pumice concrete and vermiculite plaster. Nonetheless, Prudential executives tethered their light building to the ground with a cornerstone shaped from a two-ton piece of the Rock of Gibraltar, a gift from the British government, which was laid on June 1, 1948.[45]

The Western Home Office was eventually dubbed "Prudential Square," which also referred to the small plaza facing Wilshire Boulevard. The 517,000-square-foot, $8 million building was executed in a spare, modern style (fig. 18). *Architectural Forum*, which featured the Prudential Building in May 1949 along with another new office building also designed by Wurdeman and Becket, for General Petroleum, heralded the building as "highly dramatic, thoughtfully conceived, carefully planned." The General Petroleum building, designed as an administrative headquarters, was located on a valuable site in downtown Los Angeles, which the architects filled to its allowable limits save for two internal courtyards. Wurdeman and Becket also designed an urban parking structure to complement the office building. But Prudential developed a less expensive eleven-acre site on Wilshire Boulevard that was assembled when the city agreed to close a bisecting street and allowed for a surface parking lot for one thousand cars at the rear of the site. *Forum* announced that "Prudential, free to spread out over two city blocks, is a special product of sprawling Los Angeles."[46]

The office floors of the Prudential Building featured tall ceilings and open plans designed for clerical activities. Casement windows ran from column to column to let in as much light as possible, complemented by an indirect fluorescent lighting system. *Architectural Forum*'s writers approved: "Seen from the outside, the long lines of lighting fixtures, parallel to windows, conform very effectively to the basic design of the long horizontal structure. Outside rows of light are kept going until midnight for advertising purposes." The building was entirely air-conditioned, but the architects were conscious of reducing the impact of the sun on the cooling system. They eliminated all windows on the west and east ends of the building and on all four sides of the central service core. The building's most distinguishing external features were the horizontal louvered sunshades — rendered in a shade of salmon — that projected from each floor. The sunshades dramatized the 325-foot sweep of the windows, which contrasted with the blank walls at the ends and in the central tower.[47]

Prudential's real estate team in Los Angeles planned Prudential Square with a nod toward the commercial quality of Wilshire Boulevard, with room for ground-floor stores that faced the street. Prudential occupied no space on the ground floor of the building except for a small information office in the lobby. The company provided a second-floor cafeteria for its employees that opened to a large patio on the roof of a low-slung commercial pavilion that contained stores, including a bank branch office and drugstore, facing the boulevard. Ohrbach's, the New York department store, agreed to rent space in the building, its first West Coast foray. Wurdeman and Becket designed a three-story wing for the department store with a mezzanine and sidewalk arcade. Behind the two- and three-story retail pavilions rose the wide, ten-story office block, interrupted by a central tower that housed the service core and also served as a dramatic billboard, with eight-foot-tall letters reading PRUDENTIAL, highly visible from Wilshire in both directions. The building's streetscape was broken up by a small plaza that lent the complex its name, Prudential Square, and projected the aura of a public amenity. This type of mixed-use development was unprecedented for an insurance company office structure; though it was a logical fit for Prudential's location on Wilshire Boulevard, which was in the heart of a premier shopping corridor. Conversely, the Miracle Mile's activities were mostly confined to shopping until the Prudential Building was erected.[48]

When he addressed the crowd at the opening ceremonies, Shanks stressed that the Western Home Office was "not a branch office. This is the home office for the 11 Western States and Hawaii, and the complete management of its affairs has been put into the hands of the western executives." This meant a "big dollar shift" from east to west, as control of $2.5 billion of insurance money would move from Newark to Los Angeles. Executives living in California would control upward of $20 million in investment funds

Figure 18 "Prudential Square," the Western Home Office on Wilshire Boulevard in Los Angeles, designed by Wurdeman and Becket, 1948. *bottom* A view of the Western Home Office driving east on Wilshire Boulevard, ca. 1950. The architects used the mechanical core of the building as a billboard. (Courtesy of Prudential Financial, Inc.)

every month. One local power broker, Norman Chandler, the publisher of the *Los Angeles Times,* was convinced that "the coming of Prudential to Los Angeles will have very far-reaching effects and may well be the guidepost for other eastern financial institutions."[49] Prudential's move to Los Angeles in 1948 established the company as an important player in a national shift of resources from east to west.

ACCESS TO PARADISE: HOUSTON AND THE GREAT SOUTHWEST

After establishing the Western Home Office in Los Angeles, Carrol Shanks moved swiftly to advance his decentralization agenda. He requested and received approval from Prudential's board of directors to open additional Regional Home Offices. For the Canadian Home Office, opened in 1950, Prudential rented eight floors of the Bank of Nova Scotia Building in downtown Toronto. Next Prudential came to Houston, where it opened the Southwestern Home Office (SWHO) in 1952.

The Great Southwest

Shanks chose Charles Fleetwood, Prudential's vice president of the mortgage loan and real estate investment department, to head the Southwestern Home Office. Like the other RHOs, the building's cornerstone featured a "time capsule," and Fleetwood contributed a letter addressed "To whom it may concern in the year 2000" that described the establishment of the SWHO. He addressed the most obvious question — the choice of Houston to host this regional home office. Fleetwood reflected that the Southwest was postwar America's most dynamic economic growth region and Houston was poised to join Los Angeles as a key growth pole: "Houston had enjoyed remarkable growth during World War II and the post-war years and seemed on the threshold of even greater growth and economic development."[50] In his own letter for the time capsule, W. P. Hobby, president of the *Houston Post,* reiterated Carrol Shanks's belief that the balance of financial power in the United States was in a state of transition: "This Southwestern headquarters brings to Houston a significant development in the field of investment and finance. It is one more step in a process which may be described as a shifting of the financial center of gravity of this nation from the big industrial cities of the North and East to the South, Southwest and West Coast regions."[51] The development of the SWHO contributed to this trend and validated Houston's position as a leading financial center.

Following the pattern set by Bill Scholl in Los Angeles, Fleetwood emphasized the need for secrecy in the site-selection process: "The next step was to proceed quietly and locate and option a suitable building site in Houston before the cat was out of the bag." Prudential sought the advice of local real estate magnate Jesse Jones. Prudential had financed several of Jones's commercial real estate projects, and Fleetwood recalled that "Mr. Jones, then in his 75th year, was an old friend." Initially, Jones urged Prudential to locate in downtown Houston. In a somewhat self-serving gesture, he offered to sell Prudential one of his own parcels: an entire city block near the Houston Municipal building. But Fleetwood demurred, eschewing the opportunity to build on a large urban lot. Recollecting those early conversations with Jesse Jones and others, Fleetwood wrote about the choice to locate in a site that was within city limits but some four miles from downtown: "Mr. Jones felt that we should locate downtown in the center of the business district, if possible, and was surprised to learn that we had in mind buying a suburban site. We explained our reasons, namely that the nature of our business made it unnecessary for us to be downtown; that by going farther out we would be able to avoid traffic and parking problems, and provide better and more practical working conditions for employees for less money. Mr. Jones was not convinced, but recognized that our needs were different from that of the average business."[52]

The "average" business derived influence from a downtown location by virtue of proximity to other, more powerful institutions. This was a basic principle of the urban agglomeration economy and its physical expression in a dense central business district, where land values were high and buildings were commensurately tall and bulky. In this milieu, firms and their executives nurtured interpersonal relationships and formed business partnerships that sustained their enterprises. Leading industrial corporations — in Houston these were the large oil companies like Gulf and Shell — looked to their more average neighbors to perform specific tasks, such as banking, legal representation, accounting, and marketing. But Prudential represented a more expansive and autonomous corporate enterprise, one that internalized many of these secondary office functions. This is not to say that Prudential did not forge beneficial relationships with local businesses and professional firms. But Prudential was a heavyweight and created its own center of gravity. The firm was less sensitive to the typical advantages of a location in the central business district and freer to pursue its own agenda.

The Ideal Site

Houston's southwestern quadrant was bisected by Old Main Street, a broad boulevard that ran directly toward downtown. Fleetwood enlisted a local real estate broker, Ernest Hester of the firm Hester and Wise, to scout for sites in this general area. Hester quickly identified a 27.5-acre vacant site at the intersection of Old Main Street and Holcombe Boulevard, four miles from the central business district and near the Houston Medical Center and the Rice Institute. The site was also across the street from the recently constructed Shamrock Hotel, a $20 million development and a choice accommodation for business travelers. "This piece of land lying at the intersection of two main arterial streets," Fleetwood remarked in his time-capsule essay, "seemed to offer great possibilities as a site for an imposing building which would dominate the area and which would quickly become a well-known landmark."[53]

But Fleetwood was not entirely confident in his own instincts about the site, or even the best advice of his local experts, Jesse Jones and Ernest Hester. (After all, Jones originally favored a downtown site.) Fleetwood was cautiously inventing his own theory of the ideal regional location in an age of increasingly accessible jet travel and ubiquitous auto mobility. Fleetwood turned to a nationally recognized expert to see if his intuitions corresponded with broader urban trends. He hired Homer Hoyt, a well-known real estate consultant, to prepare a "Survey of Regional Office Location in Houston, Texas." Hoyt's report, submitted in 1950, commenced with an overall picture of the Houston economy. He validated the appraisals of both Fleetwood and Shanks that Houston was an important urban center, a city that manifested the shift in American industrial growth from North to South. The report recognized Houston as a *growing* city, in terms of population, physical area, and industrial production. Between 1940 and 1947, Houston led the United States in per capita total investment in all new industrial plants. Hoyt reported the number of employees and annual payrolls of these new industries. Each employee, after all, was also a potential policyholder. The Port of Houston, a fifty-mile fabricated channel to the sea, ranked second in the United States in tonnage in 1950. Hoyt asserted that Houston had "already attained the position of the leading metropolis of the Southwest. . . . Houston is the most logical place in which to locate a new regional office building for the nine state area."[54]

Hoyt then assessed the downtown location offered by Jesse Jones, along with several suburban sites. He reasoned that a central location was at the nexus of the city's mass-transit infrastructure, principally a bus system. And Hoyt repeated the typical rationale for the agglomeration of office functions in the center city: "A central location affords proximity to other offices within walking distance, making it convenient for direct contacts. It has restaurants nearby and stores and shops which have an appeal to workers in lunch hours or after work. It is close to libraries, theaters and other places of amusement."[55] Hoyt evoked Westcott Toole's desire for a strong public image, saying that a large downtown building could create an "attractive vista." And he figured that a well-planned, twelve-story structure on Jesse Jones's full-block site could handle Prudential's office space needs and still allow for sufficient parking.

But Hoyt ultimately recommended an "outlying" site. Echoing Fleetwood's assessment, he acknowledged that "convenience of access to other downtown offices is not of primary importance to the Prudential, as it will be a largely self sufficient workshop. . . . Moreover, an outlying location with ample parking space will be more convenient to business men coming by automobile than a congested central location."[56] Prudential's sheer size and internal organization permitted its departure from the central business district. Local business contacts, especially those who needed loans, would gladly drive or take the bus down Old Main Street for an audience with Prudential's power brokers. Prudential executives had themselves discovered the convenience of air travel, a business trend that was quickly diminishing the dominance of railroads for inter-urban transport. The urban and regional geography of the postwar American city was increasingly liberated from the organizing presence of the urban rail terminal and the downtown hotels and office buildings located nearby. Hoyt addressed this issue with a broad appreciation of national trends and, thus, articulated a theory of regional office location that broke with the established logic of centralization.

In his survey, Hoyt developed this "outlying location" theory in more detail. He explicitly considered the Old Main Street parcel, which he identified as the superior site for such a location. In broad terms, Hoyt established a hierarchy of Houston's quadrants, with the southwest at the top. The east and southeast were heavily industrialized and contained low-quality dwellings. The east and northeast were "Negro areas" and were dismissed on that fact alone. "As far as character of the neighborhood," Hoyt asserted, "the office building should be located in the southwest sector."[57] And he claimed that the corner of Old Main Street and Holcombe Boulevard offered the best approach to a building site.

The location was convenient for Prudential's employees. Citing a recent study by the Plan Commission of Houston, Hoyt explained that forty-seven percent of Houston's downtown office workers lived in the southwest sector and many of them already commuted to the city along Old Main Street. Houston's bus system made frequent stops at the intersection of Old Main Street and Belaire Boulevard, one block from the Holcombe site. Hoyt also anticipated the completion of a new semicircular expressway and several other road improvements that would serve commuters from the city's other quadrants. The area boasted a set of "conveniences" that enhanced the desirability of the proposed site. Foremost was the Shamrock Hotel, which provided "the most modern accommodations for business visitors to the Prudential offices." The Shamrock and its many restaurants also featured performances by top entertainers, making it a desirable cultural destination. The nearby Rice Institute was building a new football stadium, another attraction. Hoyt anticipated a large regional shopping center at the corner of Bellaire and Main, giving workers "attractive nearby places in which to shop." Hoyt painted a picture of an emerging midtown commercial and office district that featured large-scaled buildings planned for broad tracts and organized along wide boulevards.[58]

Hoyt identified another key advantage of the Holcombe Boulevard site: its architectural visibility. A twelve-story building erected on the nearly thirty-acre site would create an impressive vista along Old Main Street, unfettered by the proposed low-rise shopping center. Hoyt's analysis addressed Prudential's concerns regarding the long-term value of a potential site. The southwest quadrant as a whole was characterized by high land values. Recent and proposed developments for the area — all of which were high-quality, well-planned, and large-scale projects produced by sound, future-oriented institutions — would not threaten that trend. Like the site for the WHO in Los Angeles, the Houston site was insulated — protected from hard-to-predict encroachments from shortsighted, small-scale, or otherwise irresponsible developers.

Office Building De-luxe

Having decided to purchase the site, Prudential looked for an architect. On Jesse Jones's recommendation, the company hired Kenneth Franzheim's Houston-based firm for the project. Though he never received graduate training, Franzheim had practiced architecture since his graduation from MIT in 1913. He worked in Boston until World War I, and then he became a partner with C. Howard Crane in Detroit, specializing in the design of commercial buildings and airports. In 1928, at the request of Jesse Jones, Franzheim came to Houston, where he collaborated with Alfred C. Finn on the design of the Gulf Building at 712 Main Street. Oil companies were chief patrons of Houston's urban architecture, and the Gulf Building was one of several skyscrapers that adorned Houston's central business district in the then-fashionable art deco style. The Gulf Building, for a time the tallest in Houston, was characterized by stepped-back massing; recessed, ornamental spandrels; ornate metalwork; and an elaborately appointed lobby featuring classical motifs in relief and frescoes of "Modern Houston." Among Franzheim's many works in 1930s Houston was the Oil and Gas Building, finished in 1937. The petroleum industry was spared the worst effects of the Great Depression, and Houston's economy was buoyed by the discovery of large oil deposits in the 1930s. Nonetheless, the Oil and Gas Building was more squat and decoratively austere than the exuberant Gulf Building and other towers of the late 1920s. The symmetrical massing featured a truncated tower with crenellations in the deco mode. The exterior design was organized vertically by a stark row of slightly raised shafts and an unadorned, double-height door frame, both characteristic of the stripped classicism that marked much official architecture of that period and foreshadowed Franzheim's own design for the Southwestern Home Office in Houston.[59]

Franzheim broke the SWHO building's mass into an asymmetrical composition of three interconnected towers, suggesting a miniature skyline four miles from downtown Houston: a twenty-one-story center section, a sixteen-story west extension, and a ten-story east extension. It was the tallest building by far outside of the business district (fig. 19). The central section turned its thin edge to Holcombe Boulevard, with vertical lengths of aluminum, framed in limestone, extending past the cornice line in a fashion reminiscent of art deco styling. The architecture was boxlike and plain, accented by the mottled texture of its stone sheathing, and the overall massing was imposing. Prudential executives — including Westcott Toole, Carrol Shanks, and Charles Fleetwood — insisted, as they did in Los Angeles, in clearly labeling the building as their own. The result was a three-story-high sign bearing the company's name and its trademark, the Rock of Gibraltar, cut from Texas granite and built flush into the east and west sides of the central tower.

The Rock of Gibraltar was joined on the ground by symbolic gestures of local place-attachment. Four pillars of Texas granite were used to articulate the main entrance and served as the porte cochère for the entrance drive. Prudential commissioned artist Peter Hurd to create a southwestern-themed mural of ranch life for a forty-six-foot curved wall in the lobby, which borrowed its title from one of Prudential's tag lines: "The Future Belongs to Those Who Prepare for It."[60] But these flourishes were over-shadowed by the building's principal selling points: the Prudential Building was Houston's most modern, technologically up-to-date, and amenity-laden office environment. The SWHO was among the first office buildings in Houston to employ an integrated air conditioning system that heated, cooled, and dehumidified the building. The open office floors, organized with flexible partitions, were completely wired for fluorescent lighting, office machines, telephones, buzzer systems, the "Edison Televoice System" (an early type of intercom), and a public address system. The third floor housed an employee health service, and the entire fourth floor was devoted to Photostat copying equipment and mail distribution. Nine large elevators were installed in the

Figure 19 The Southwestern Home Office in Houston, designed by Kenneth Franzheim, was dedicated in 1952 (Courtesy of Prudential Financial, Inc.)

building to accommodate peak loads. Even the toilets were organized with removable partitions to respond to fluctuating male and female populations of the building.[61] In 1953, Prudential's SWHO was featured in the magazine of Pittsburgh Plate Glass Company (PPG), a publication distributed to patrons and distributors of the company's products. The magazine trumpeted the SWHO as the "office building deluxe." The building's exterior was glazed with PPG's Solex, a "heat-absorbing and glare-reducing polished plate glass." Prudential also used PPG's "Herculite" doors and door frames. These material innovations, like the air conditioning and lighting systems, were there to make working at Prudential more comfortable for employees.[62]

The brochure produced to accompany the opening of the SWHO, *At Home in the Great Southwest,* announced that "a Prudential Home Office is a virtually self-contained 'city of insurance.'" Franzheim had designed a sprawling campus across the 27.5-acre site that included a surface parking lot for 705 cars, 114 of which were covered carports, complete with electrical lighting standards. The parking lots were connected to the main building by designated sidewalks and covered passages. The site had been heavily wooded. Much of it was cleared, yet the design preserved selected patches of trees. An underground sprinkler system was installed to maintain the professional landscaping improvements that featured many native plants. The forecourt in front of the main entrance was planted with azaleas and featured a fountain and sculpture by Wheeler Williams titled "Wave of Life," which depicted a man, woman, and child set in a small pool. The theme of the sculpture was apt, illustrating the normative family structure upon which the Prudential's business model was based.[63]

A Paradise for Office Girls

An important aspect of the building's design was its provision of recreational facilities, which the company viewed as important investments in the overall efficiency and appeal of the workplace. The availability of opportunities for recreation fostered employee contentment, creating a "Paradise for Office Girls," as described in *Life* magazine in 1955, and was part of what Prudential called a "sound personnel program and a necessary aid to efficient operation of the intricate business of life insurance."[64] Prudential installed two tennis courts on the east side of the building, as well as a softball diamond. Most outstanding was a large swimming pool at the southern end of the building, measuring seventy-two by forty-two feet. The text created for tour guides to use as they led visitors through the SWHO explained the presence of a swimming pool on the grounds of an insurance company building: "Such benefits as this pool provides for our employees more than pay their way. It costs money to employ and train people. Anything which reduces employee turnover is money well spent and good business for the Prudential and its policyholders. For example, if our clerical employee turnover were cut just 2% the pool would pay for itself."[65] In this view, a swimming pool helped retain employees. This was certainly the case for Oveta Smith, the eighteen-year-old "office girl" profiled by *Life,* who turned down a $180-a-month job at a maritime insurance firm for a $140-a-month job at Prudential because of the fringe benefits, which included "such unprecedented luxuries as a free swimming pool, free books, free lunches, free tennis courts — in surroundings suggestive of spacious and graceful living."[66]

THINKING OUTSIDE THE LOOP IN CHICAGO

The story of Prudential's Mid-America Home Office (MAHO) in Chicago centers on the convoluted political process of building on a complex urban site. Prudential's Chicago development was a prelude to the Northeastern Home Office (NEHO) in Boston, the Prudential Center, and emboldened company leaders to tackle a similarly ambitious project in an established yet economically flagging industrial city of the "snowbelt." Like the Prudential Center in Boston, the MAHO story heralded the transition from the railroad to an insurance company as the leading player in urban real estate. In Chicago, the Illinois Central Railroad sought to capitalize on its urban land assets while Prudential looked to erect a monument to its growing importance in the American economy and society.

City Salvation

As in Los Angeles and Houston, Prudential executives were stealthy in their search for a site in Chicago. They worked through local brokers and eventually negotiated anonymously with the landowner (the Illinois Central Railroad) through a trusted third party. Any developer who considered purchasing a significant swath of urban rail yard territory had to have plentiful resources. But the discretion that Prudential's managers exercised — and the cloak-and-dagger efforts they made to hide their identity from sellers — demonstrated how disproportionately powerful the mammoth insurance company was in the national economy. Land sought by Prudential immediately increased in value. Prudential's decentralization planners did all they could to limit the inflation of land values by shielding their intent as long as possible.

Prudential expressed interest in building in Chicago as early as 1949. The Los Angeles WHO had opened, Houston's SWHO was in the works, and a decision on the location of the Mid-America Home Office was imminent. Prudential contacted Leo J. Sheridan, president of a leading Chicago real estate firm, and asked him to suggest locations across the region; but Chicago, the commercial, industrial, and financial heart of the Midwest, was the clear choice. Nonetheless, Sheridan recommended an unconventional site: the Illinois Central Railroad was selling "air rights" to its rail yards lying just east of the Loop, north of Grant Park, and west of Lake Michigan. These air rights would give a purchaser the right to build above the rail yards without disrupting the railroad's activities, which would continue unabated below. Prudential executives were impressed by the prominence of the site, which the company's president Carrol Shanks called "one of the most dramatic in the country."[67]

Building above the Illinois Central rail yard required not only Prudential's sheer wealth, but also the institutional patience to see it through. Less financially stable developers, or those with a less refined sense of long-range purpose, shied away from engaging in what was bound to be a long and arduous process of negotiating for the air rights and for the ground-level parcels that would contain the building's supports. There would also have to be protracted negotiations with the city about zoning restrictions. But Prudential's executives thought the Chicago project was within their mandate as a public service corporation. They could solve a difficult land use and development issue for the city and lay claim to a coveted urban site at the same time.

Prudential retained James Brennan, a Chicago real estate attorney, to oversee the complex negotiations for the rights to build on this site. Brennan later explained this daunting task to a group of Chicago real estate brokers: "The site for years and years had been the object of acquisition by many influential and wealthy individuals and corporations, who hoped to build a skyscraper or several skyscraper edifices on the site but none of them were ever able to bring negotiations to a successful conclusion."[68] Brennan's comment suggests that Prudential, which finally did succeed in developing the site, arrived in Chicago as an urban savior, willing and able to undertake complicated and expensive negotiations in order to achieve a positive result for both the company and the city at large.

As in many large cities, the economic depression of the 1930s had deep impacts in Chicago that lasted into the early 1950s. The building industries were almost completely paralyzed. If not for the massive Field Building of 1934, there would have been a net loss in office space for the city of Chicago between 1930 and 1940. Many of the office towers built during the 1920s in the Loop were deposed to receiverships of bankrupt companies. In some cases, once-profitable commercial buildings were razed when property owners sought to avoid taxes on non-paying real estate. A typical example — if glaring from the perspective of architectural preservation — was when the Marshall Field Wholesale Store, designed by H. H. Richardson, was destroyed in 1930 so that the land could be sold to the R. G. Lydy Company as a surface parking lot. The architectural historian Carl Condit credited the Prudential Building with breaking the stagnation of postwar building in Chicago.[69]

Sheridan and Brennan commenced negotiations with the Illinois Central in 1950, but they had to first convince the railroad company that it was dealing with a reputable, albeit anonymous, partner. A federal judge, William J. Campbell, played a key role in providing this assurance. Sheridan revealed to Campbell the identity of his client, Prudential, and Campbell in turn advised the president of the Illinois Central, Wayne A. Johnson, who was a personal friend, that he was dealing with a responsible and able buyer. Judge Campbell's assurances underwrote the lengthy negotiations without disclosing the identity of the buyer. At first, the Illinois Central's representatives were doubtful that they could come to terms on such a complex development process. "The railroad could hardly be blamed for thinking that this was another impossible and speculative dream," Brennan recalled. "They had tried it before without success."[70] But Prudential would be different. Reporting on the recently released plans for the Mid-America Home Office in 1952, *Architectural Forum* stated the case plainly: "Not until a company with the resources of Prudential decided to build was anyone willing or able to go through the expensive process of acquiring title the hard way. This meant 18 months of negotiations during which 550 separate lots for caissons, impinging girders, columns, column footings and windbracing structures were separately defined and purchased."[71] Prudential had finally cracked the code to developing railroad air rights, and future developers, which the Illinois Central hoped to attract to the many acres of air rights still available on the site, could follow the wording of Prudential's deed for similar projects in the future.[72]

A Lawyer's Dream

The Illinois Central rail yard was exceptional among downtown Chicago building locations. Buffered by Grant Park and Lake Michigan, the prominent site promised permanent unobstructed views. This physical insulation had negative consequences, too. The three-and-one-half-acre site had no adjoining streets. At ground level, beneath Prudential's proposed building, were located no fewer than twenty-one tracks for passenger and freight traffic of the Illinois Central and Michigan Central Railroads, including passenger platforms for the railroad's suburban lines, a freight house, and a fifteen-story electric advertising sign. (The freight house and the sign had to be removed.) A projected building would have to be located above the Randolph Street suburban passenger station. Early in the site negotiation process, the firm of Naess and Murphy was hired to consult on architecture and engineering and was eventually awarded the contract to design the building. The Illinois Central planned to continue rail service on the site, and the architects had to demonstrate that it was possible to build a large office tower over a functioning rail terminal.

The purchase price for the air space and hundreds of small ground parcels was $2,270,315. Brennan, the real estate lawyer, described the time-consuming and expensive negotiations among architects, engineers, attorneys, and corporate representatives that convened nearly every day for a year and a half. Brennan, for one, relished his role and was stimulated by the task. It was groundbreaking work, both literally and figuratively, and gave the real estate attorney a moment to shine: "From a lawyer's viewpoint this deal was the quintessence of real estate law practice. It was a lawyer's dream. He was in the picture relatively early in the negotiations and formed a part of them. The contracts were novel with few precedents upon which he could rely. There was no 'boilerplate' in the two contracts written, except perhaps the introductory and closing sentences; all the rest was pure, creative draftsmanship." The agreement required legal imagination because it pioneered the concept of a three-dimensional "air-rights" space, where the railroad retained ownership of the space between the columns and caissons below the air lot levels. The negotiations affected the building possibilities for the site and explained why Naess and Murphy had to be called to consult early in the process. The eventual design was constrained by the negotiations that determined the caisson lots that Prudential would own. As Brennan put it, "Ordinarily, you buy a piece of land and then you make up your mind what kind of building you are going to put on it. This was a situation where we had to make up our minds exactly what kind of building we wanted to build before we knew what land we were going to buy."[73]

Prudential's site did not encompass the entirety of the Illinois Central holdings, and was locked within land that was zoned for industrial uses. Brennan explained how Prudential's negotiation team was "faced with a very grave situation in trying to guarantee that the buildings adjoining us, when they were erected, would not be objectionable to us." Prudential solved the problem by proposing restrictions on the surrounding property, effectively changing the area's zoning from industrial to commercial uses. The City of Chicago was willing to oblige this request in order to satisfy Prudential's concerns. The new zoning rules provided that no use could be made of the property "which shall be of more objectionable character or produce greater or more offensive odors, fumes, smoke, gases, dust, noise or vibrations than are now conducted on or under the property."[74] The Illinois Central was already electrified, reducing the railroad's production of these undesirable effects. Prudential agreed to build broad viaducts along three sides of its building and negotiated with the city to build a fourth raised street, effectively creating a new ground plane. Prudential was loath to bear the full cost of viaducts that subsidized future development for others and worked out a plan with the city for the eventual reimbursement of one half the cost of these new roads. Prudential had succeeded in unilaterally rezoning an emerging urban office district and it sponsored the city's public realm improvements that made the new district accessible.

Civic Duty

For the city of Chicago, the investments in infrastructure were well worth the expense to enable a massive taxpaying property improvement and the thousands of jobs that Prudential would bring. Prudential's successful interactions with the city relied on the support of Mayor Martin H. Kennelly, who seized his role to facilitate Prudential's investment. An official history of the Prudential Building in Chicago highlighted this cooperative relationship: "The keen interest with which Mayor Kennelly followed the negotiations and the important assistance which he contributed at many stages of the discussions reflected the high civic importance he attached to the enterprise and his great anxiety to see that the City of Chicago was selected for the Mid-America home office of Prudential so that Chicago might reap the future large benefits which such a development assured." This statement encapsulated the symbiotic relationships between pro-growth mayors like Kennelly and powerful financial institutions like Prudential: encouraging private development was a civic duty. For Prudential, the cooperation of local government was a key condition of its investment. In a letter to Kennelly, Shanks noted that "one of the impelling reasons why Prudential came to Chicago, was that we had confidence in the integrity of the government which you head up — that when the citizens of Chicago have a man like Martin H. Kennelly as mayor, it sustains my faith in the government of our cities."[75]

Mayor Kennelly, playing the part of the showman and booster so typical of big-city mayors, also saw Prudential's MAHO as a bullish investment in the urban fortunes of his city. At the ground-breaking ceremony in 1952, Kennelly crowed that "this Mid-America building has been conceived of a superb confidence in Chicago's future."[76] And at the ceremony marking the topping-out of the building's steel structure in 1954, Kennelly equated Prudential's private venture with the civic pride of his city and its citizens. The occasion of Prudential's development of the Mid-America Home Office in Chicago had captivated "the public interest." The mayor went on: "That interest has made the Mid-America building more than just another triumph of the architectural genius of the world-famous Chicago firm of Naess and Murphy. It has made it more than just another new skyscraper — more than just another big Chicago commercial enterprise. . . . [I]n many ways — this Mid-America building has become a civic project — a rallying point for Chicago's newly awakened civic pride. Millions of Chicago citizens regard it as the brightest new gem in the crown of 'Chicago — the Magnificent City.' They accept it as the symbol of the city's rebirth."[77]

On Spec

The Prudential Building opened in 1955, rising forty-one stories and including its own 350-car parking garage — at that time one of the largest parking facilities incorporated into an office structure in the United States (fig. 20). There were also pedestrian connections between the lower levels of the building and a 2,400-car municipal garage constructed under Grant Park and managed by the Chicago Park District. The building cost more than $40 million and was Chicago's first new skyscraper to open since 1934. On the fortieth floor was the "Top of the Rock" restaurant, managed by Stouffer's, and the forty-first floor featured a public observation deck. A ground-floor auditorium was designed to accommodate one thousand seats.[78]

Figure 20 The Mid-America Home Office sitting astride the Illinois Central tracks in Chicago, ca. 1955. Following Prudential's lead, the area beyond the building would be developed over the following decades. (Courtesy of Prudential Financial, Inc.)

The MAHO in Chicago marked a departure for Prudential because a large portion of it was rented out to other companies and firms. Each of the other regional head-quarters had been planned so that the Pru could eventually occupy the whole building. In the twenty-one-story Houston tower and twenty-two-story Jacksonville tower, Prudential planned to start by occupying the lower floors of the buildings' broad wings and renting the remaining space, but anticipated moving upward into the smaller tower floors as the regional home office grew.[79] In the smaller Los Angeles and Minneapolis buildings, Prudential occupied nearly the entire structure from the start. But the Chicago building, which *Architectural Forum* announced in 1952 as the fifth largest office building in the country and the tallest in Chicago, was explicitly an office struc-ture available for rental. Prudential positioned its new tower as the most desirable, most modern, best-serviced office space in the city for prospective tenants. Prudential planned to charge fifty percent more than the going rate for good office space in Chicago and offered a host of amenities and higher "space standards" to justify the premium. The Prudential Building, in this sense, did not compete with existing office buildings. It created a "de luxe building," as one official description boasted, "that will lift itself out of competition, so higher rentals can be charged to make the building pay off." Prudential offered tenants "advantages not found elsewhere in Chicago."[80]

In terms of building mechanics, *Architectural Forum* explained, Prudential's Chicago building set "a new high for many US office building standards and is well worth careful study to see just what improvements such a big, well-informed investor is willing to buy." In a list of superlatives, the magazine explained just what Prudential had bought, including, among others: the biggest tower floors (twenty thousand square feet) outside of New York City; the highest intensity lighting of any major U.S. office building; the highest electrical design load; the biggest floor-to-floor height (thirteen feet); the fastest high-rise elevators; more elevators than any office building built since 1929 (twenty-six passenger cars to serve forty floors); the biggest built-in garage serving a single building; and the biggest air-conditioning tonnage and heaviest air-conditioning design load, as well as other novel cooling techniques including the use of the Chicago River as a cooling agent.[81]

The MAHO building in Chicago combined so many services and amenities in one location that *Forum* described it as a "one-building Rockefeller Center." The compari-son to the New York landmark, which embodied a successful civic-oriented, private devel-opment, was a favorable one. The analogy emphasized the infrastructural scale of the Prudential Building, with its connections to the transit system and accommodations for the automobile. As did Rockefeller Center, planners of the Prudential Building positioned the MAHO as an urban institution. The facility included a "travel bureau," which consolidated ticket offices for rail, air, and steamship travel and could deliver tickets to the building's tenants on short notice. There were meeting and conference rooms equipped with motion picture, slide projector, and kinescope facilities (the last for previewing television programs). However, Prudential was wary of intimidating its neighbors or ruffling feathers among Chicago's established property owners. For this reason, Prudential began its search for renters by looking for out-of-town companies that wanted to move to Chicago. After that, it looked to firms whose offices were scattered about the central business district and who wanted to consolidate and streamline their operations.[82]

In terms of exterior architecture, *Architectural Forum* conceded that "Prudential will be no design experiment, no Lever House, no Alcoa, no UN Secretariat." It may have lacked the flash of the early International Style buildings then appearing in the skyline of a few cities, but Prudential's Mid-America building was a solid design: a clean, spare mass organized with vertical limestone piers running uninterrupted the full height of the building, featuring spandrels faced with a fluted aluminum skin. Stylistically, *Forum* saw the building as "contemporary with Rockefeller Center."[83] Despite its favorable connotations, Rockefeller Center was already twenty years old, so the comparison also presented Prudential's architecture as a dignified throwback. But Prudential was not inclined to take big risks in architectural style and must have perceived its building's likeness to Rockefeller Center as a positive selling point.

Corporate Policy, Urban Policy

Despite the City of Chicago's involvement, Prudential's principal partner in urban development was another private enterprise, the Illinois Central Railroad. At a press conference on March 1, 1951, Leo Sheridan, the realtor who brokered the deal, diplomatically praised both Prudential's Carrol Shanks and Wayne A. Johnston of the Illinois Central: "The real importance of the development, the beginning of which we are celebrating today, lies in the fact that it becomes a reality due to the vision, the prudent business sagacity, the courage and determination of two men . . . one heading one of the world's greatest insurance organizations . . . an organization devoted to the advancement of human interests, human welfare, and human happiness, under the system of private enterprise, and the other guiding the affairs and determining the policies of one of the great railroad systems of the world."[84] Sheridan predicted that Prudential's investment would lead others to make their own investments in Chicago. His statements dramatized the underlying soundness of a free enterprise system, in which enlightened corporate self-interest corresponded with the public interest at large.

At the ground-breaking ceremony in August 1952, J. M. Trissal, assistant chief engineer of the Illinois Central, alluded to the increasing tension between the American system of free enterprise and a planned economy and collectivist enterprise embodied by the Soviet system: "This occasion is particularly significant because it strikes a strong note of optimism in an unsettled world. It is a tribute to free enterprise, as we enjoy it in America, and will be a monument symbolizing the achievement of free men."[85] Two private corporations — a railroad and an insurance company — had worked together, over long and hard negotiations, to bring about the redevelopment of a seemingly intractable piece of urban real estate. Trissal passed the baton of urban growth from his railroad to the insurance company. The railroad had been essential to the land-making process, and served as the progenitor of vast urban fortunes. In the postwar era, wealthy insurance companies would claim this mantle. Trissal conveyed to his audience the heroic proportions of this endeavor:

> For more than a century, the Illinois Central has had a stake in the growth and development of Chicago's lake front and all of Mid-America. It was on this very property that the Illinois Central built its Great Central Station nearly one hundred years ago. To do this, it was necessary to reclaim area which was formerly Lake Michigan. Through Great Central Station passed thousands of pioneers on their way to populate and cultivate the lands opened to development by the completion of the Illinois Central Railroad. . . . The Illinois Central is proud of its part in the development of Chicago and Mid-America. We are happy to play a role in this new chapter of Chicago's progress, marked by the erection of the new Prudential Building on this spot — a Gibraltar on the Lake front.[86]

Needless to say, Mayor Martin H. Kennelly would not be shut out of the festivities: "I am glad . . . to accept my share of responsibility for the birth and up-bringing of this lusty lake-front 'baby.'" The Prudential Building, Kennelly trumpeted, would spur "the modern era of Chicago's rejuvenation. . . . It cannot fail to encourage other investors in Chicago's unlimited potential, because there is nothing so contagious as confidence." Kennelly pledged that the City of Chicago would not "do anything that would let Prudential down." Kennelly promised to "service" the Prudential Building in terms of transportation and parking. He devoted his short address to outlining future enhancements to metropolitan Chicago's transportation infrastructure, including improved mass transportation, parking facilities in the Loop, and several new "superhighway developments." Kennelly had mastered the physiological metaphors of urbanism and employed them dramatically: "No — Chicago is in no danger of dying from hardening of the arteries, nor from any disease of the circulatory system. The evidence is all about us that Chicago today is more virile — stronger in both sinew and spirit — than it has ever been."[87]

Prudential, Kennelly continued, had provided the city with a "psychological 'shot in the arm' that Chicago badly needed." He aligned the Prudential's significant undertaking with his own campaign for civic improvements. The mayor highlighted some of Chicago's city-initiated urban renewal projects that complemented Prudential's development, including new urban highways and municipal garage structures that were the infrastructural components of a modernized urban environment. Chicago's success, particularly with respect to the city's "fifty million dollar off-street parking program," was the "talk of the country" and had engendered a bit of jealousy from representatives of other cities foundering with postwar modernization. Kennelly even quoted from an editorial in the *Boston Daily Record:* "Pardon us, Chicago, if we seem a bit envious of your ability to get things done, for we are envious. . . . Chicago's reward for action, instead of words, is its first new skyscraper since 1934 — the forty-million dollar Mid-America building."[88]

More than a decade later, Boston would have its own Prudential skyscraper to boast about, one that required the acquiescence of local government to an even greater extent than in Chicago. The scale and complexity of Prudential's undertaking in Boston was greater than its previous regional home offices, and Prudential insisted on local tax concessions to hedge its risk. The Prudential Center was completed twenty years after the decentralization plan was conceived and might seem to embody a different generation of city building. Nonetheless, Boston's Prudential Center adhered to the key principles of the corporate policy that governed the establishment of regional homes, and Prudential's projects in Los Angeles, Houston, and Chicago presaged the Prudential Center in several important respects. Like Prudential Square in Los Angeles, Boston's Prudential Center built up a key midtown district. Like the Prudential Building in Houston, the Boston Pru would represent an extension of the city's economic life from the central business area to an outlying locale that was well connected to downtown. And, like the Prudential Building in Chicago, the construction of the Prudential Center in Boston involved a dramatic handing of the baton of urban development from the railroad to the insurance industry. Prudential learned from all of these efforts, so that by the time it announced its plans for a Northeastern Home Office in Boston, the company had refined and developed its ambitious mission: a mission that was nothing short of transforming the physical and economic contours of the cities that it inhabited and, by so doing, insuring their survival and growth.

Chapter 2

"I Hate Boston"
Setting the Stage

Aerial photograph of Boston, 1928, looking east. The Back Bay Fens is the open space at the lower left corner; the Boston and Albany rail yard is the unbuilt triangle just to the left of the center of the photo. The tall structure on the waterfront at the eastern edge of downtown is the Custom House Tower, then the city's tallest. (Courtesy of the Print Department, Boston Public Library)

I hate Boston. I don't know why. . . . The general spirit is so far, far, far back that it gets on my nerves. Lincoln Steffens

In 1948, the essayist David McCord published *About Boston*, a book that sought to capture the "sight, sound, color, flavor, inflection, and atmospherics" of his home-town. McCord focused on the dowdy charms of an old city, where rumpled patricians ambled from tidy townhouses on Beacon Hill across the ancient Common toward the cultural institutions of the Back Bay. He painted a richly described and affectionate portrait, not a critical piece, noting that he was "not here concerned with city government or dirty streets or book-banning or the pips of cheapness that any radar can detect within the city limits."[1] As a backdrop to the study of the rebuilding of Boston in the mid-twentieth century, this chapter focuses on precisely those aspects of the city that McCord chose to ignore: an ossified and corrupt political culture; the city's decaying physical plant and congested system of streets; Boston's reputation for conservatism (or, perhaps, puritanism) in the arts, including architecture; and, with respect to the "pips of cheapness," the similarly conservative culture of capital investment in Yankee Boston. This chapter provides a historical overview of Boston's economy, politics, and built environment, from the start of the nineteenth century to the middle of the twentieth. Some of the key events were part and parcel of the life and times of the entire industrial Northeast, while others — like the forty-plus-year reign of Mayor James Michael Curley — were unique to Boston. The upshot of this short history is to describe a postwar Boston that presented problems, challenges, and opportunities that were met by a new approach to insuring the city, an approach embodied by the story of Prudential.

GREATER BOSTON: THE RISE OF AN INDUSTRIAL REGION

McCord's elegant and wistful portrait ironically articulated the worst fears of urban boosters and other observers: Boston was a city of antiquated charms and long-cherished traditions, yet it was culturally outmoded and increasingly marginalized in the national economy. McCord's Boston was a pleasant village, moving at its own deliberate pace, a city of distinct neighborhoods where the irregular, curving streets of the colonial settlement still formed the basic patterns of city life. In 1868, Oliver Wendell Holmes called the Massachusetts State House, the golden-domed landmark designed by Charles Bulfinch in 1798 that crowned Beacon Hill, the "hub of the solar system." But if the world revolved around the Hub, as it came to be called, the city itself remained firmly in place. In the first half of the nineteenth century, Boston rivaled New York as an economic and cultural force. But its glory days as a preeminent metropolis were already on the wane, even if the city's elites refused to acknowledge that fact. In 1825, the Erie Canal connected the Hudson River to the Great Lakes, Chicago, and the West beyond, and New York City quickly became America's most important commercial entrepôt and financial center.[2]

The Industrial Region

Boston capitalists were once known for daring and innovation. The earliest fortunes were made in the China trade of the eighteenth century, when high-masted clipper ships tacked across Boston Harbor. Money amassed in commerce was used in the first half of the nineteenth century to spark an industrial revolution along the major rivers, like the Merrimack, of the city's hinterland regions. The woolen and cotton mills of Lowell and Lawrence produced textiles and garments that came to form the new base of Boston's export economy. Paper mills and soap factories were also established in these productive cities. Directly west of the city, Waltham was known as the "City of Five-Score Industries," where the famous Waltham Watch Company was established in 1854. The Boston region was a national leader in shoe production, in places like Haverhill and Lynn, to the north of Boston; and Brockton, to the south, which became the largest shoe manufacturing city in the country during the Civil War as a result of U.S. government contracts to produce boots for the Union Army. Among the key factors in the early industrial economy, especially in the textile industry, were Yankee farm girls. But after 1845, factories became dominated by immigrant labor, chiefly from Ireland, and the Irish dominated Boston's well-organized unions.[3]

Boston's economic vigor was already on the wane at the dawn of the twentieth century. Brockton's peak year of shoe production was in 1899, followed by a long, slow decline over the first half of the twentieth century. The New England economy prospered during World War I, spurred by the wartime demand for textiles, garments, and shoes. But the textile industry in particular was in steep decline at the start of the 1920s. Mill owners relocated their plants to the American South, where they profited from low labor costs, tax advantages, and lower rates of unionization. The Boston region, and New England as a whole, was suffering from high rates of unemployment well before the onset of the Great Depression, which only accelerated a downward trend. At the end of the 1930s, the large General Electric plants in Lynn were the state's largest employer, and G.E. prospered during World War II by producing piston-driven aircraft engines. War production temporarily restored full employment to the region's remaining mills, but this proved to be an ephemeral blip on the larger chart of economic decline.

Imperial Boston

Boston was a trading center — endowed with a deepwater port that was closely linked to the city's prosperity — and as late as 1930 Boston housed the nation's largest wool market in red-brick warehouses along the Fort Point Channel. The largest factories in the region were located in isolated company towns, but the city itself boasted a host of warehouses and steam-driven plants that crowded along an industrial belt encircling the central business district. Industrial Boston was organized around a cluster of rail facilities, the Fort Point Channel, the Charles River, and the harbor. In 1900, the Gillette Razor Company, founded by the visionary inventor King C. Gillette, was producing shaving devices in a South Boston factory. Roxbury (annexed by Boston in 1868) and East Boston (annexed in 1836) housed many small industrial concerns, including foundries, breweries, and factories producing a diverse set of commodities, from rope and cigars to suspenders and shoes. East Boston and Charlestown (annexed in 1874) cultivated maritime-based industries, including shipbuilding and repair. Boston was a city of wharves, and Boston Harbor played host to the fishing and whaling industries.[4]

Boston was the region's center for financial and commercial activities. Capital invested at the industrial periphery or in other ventures, such as western railroads and real estate, collected in the banking houses and financial trusts that lined State Street, a relatively wide and straight road that sloped toward Quincy Market and the wharves. State Street emerged in the nineteenth century as the spine of the business district, the home of financial institutions such as the Massachusetts Hospital Life Insurance Company at 50 State Street. Insurance was only a peripheral aspect of the company's larger purpose when it was chartered in 1818 as an investment trust for the city's elite. The John Hancock Mutual Life Insurance Company established its enterprise in 1862 at 41 State Street and began to grow swiftly after it introduced "industrial insurance" in 1877, selling the small policies pioneered by Prudential in Newark to the working classes of the growing city.[5]

Metropolitan Growth

In the nineteenth century, Boston's aristocratic politicians and leading citizens expanded the land mass and physical boundaries of the small, peninsular city to accommodate urban growth. The North End and West End became tenement districts for the immigrant working classes, but Beacon Hill, in the shadow of the State House on the north side of the Boston Common, remained an elite bastion of expensive townhouses. On the south side of the Common, a dense business and retail district sloped toward the many wharves that lined the harbor. The South End was filled in the 1850s and developers built gracious townhouses along rectangular squares, but the area never caught on as a fashionable district. The marshy flats of the Back Bay, first traversed by railroad viaducts in the 1830s, were filled between 1860 and 1880 and platted as a formal gridiron. The new district quickly became a high-class residential enclave and home to the city's leading cultural institutions. In the 1880s and '90s, Boston land developers established a set of streetcar suburbs to house the middling classes. And in the 1890s, Boston was the first American city to construct a subway designed to reduce the congestion of the business district.[6]

Beacon Hill elites had long maintained isolated suburban retreats. But the earliest "commuters" to Boston lived in spacious antebellum subdivisions in Newton and Cambridge, located near passenger stations built by railroad companies.[7] The exodus of professional classes from Boston's central neighborhoods increased in the late nineteenth century along the electrically powered streetcar lines.[8] Some of these newly middle-class Bostonians would themselves soon decamp for greener pastures of more suburban places, such as Newton to the west and Medford to the north, which rapidly evolved in the 1920s from independent, colonial-era towns to bedroom communities. The 1920s suburban settlements, though planned for automobile access, fundamentally depended on mass transit.[9] There was a clear physical connection between peripheral residential communities and the center city, still the location of the region's main employers. Automotive connections to the city were provided by a system of parkways, constructed during the 1920s and 1930s by the Metropolitan District Commission (MDC), and other state highways built by the Department of Public Works.[10] These highways were almost exclusively radial roads extending outward from the center city, with the exception of the initiation of a circumferential road, Route 128, also in the 1930s. The state's Master Highway Plan for Metropolitan Boston of 1948 sought to amplify these radial connections with limited-access expressways, and to complement them with a set of "loop" highways that allowed for suburb-to-suburb transportation that would open more land to suburban development, both residential and industrial.

Route 128 eventually became the key physical armature for the Boston region's postwar industrial resurgence based in high-technology firms, though the seedlings for such a boom were long in the making. In the early twentieth century, there were signs of a new industrial economy emerging from an alliance between the region's educational institutions, federal funding, and industry. Since its founding in 1861, the Massachusetts Institute of Technology — first located in Boston's Back Bay but eventually developing an expansive campus across the river in Cambridge — nurtured close relationships with the region's industrial concerns. In 1886, MIT graduate Arthur D. Little established the first "industrial consulting" firm in Boston, and his company advocated the establishment of industrial research laboratories that became an important part of Boston's regional economy. In 1922, MIT engineering professor Vannevar Bush founded the American Appliance Company, which produced refrigerators in Kendall Square, Cambridge. The small company eventually became Raytheon and maintained a strong collaborative relationship with MIT. Bush was crucial to the establishment of President Franklin D. Roosevelt's National Defense Research Committee (NDRC) on the eve of World War II, initiating a new model for federal spending on military technology and channeling millions of dollars of research contracts directly to Boston-area universities, especially MIT. The war years were an important time of growth for the high-technology sector, and Raytheon moved from producing radio tubes to radars and military armaments. By the early 1960s, Raytheon had spun off nearly 150 different companies. Most of them had relocated from the "Research Row" area of Cambridge, where they occupied existing warehouse and loft spaces, to new industrial parks located along Route 128. But while the region showed signs of an economic boom, the center city struggled. The new technologies were being developed and produced in Raytheon's Framingham complex, not in Boston. The proximity of these new industrial concerns, however, was a crucial aspect of Prudential's interest in Boston for its Northeastern Home Office. The city anchored a growing regional economy that promised an array of attractive investment and sales opportunities for the insurance company.[11]

"OUR FAIR CITY":
THE POLITICAL GEOGRAPHY OF URBAN DECLINE

In 1948, when David McCord composed *About Boston,* the center city was in economic decline. Boston was no longer either the bustling mercantile port of the 1850s or the robust industrial center of the 1890s. In the years immediately after World War II, many urban critics were frustrated by what they perceived as a debased system of local government — in Boston and many other cities — and sought to elevate the status of urban political discourse. In 1947, Robert S. Allen, a journalist and decorated military veteran, edited a collection of essays on the political leadership of American cities. Inspired by the fresh memory of America's victory in World War II, Allen introduced his book in strong terms: "We are a mighty nation, we Americans. Industrially and financially we are without equal. In the air, on land and on the seas we are all powerful. We alone possess the cataclysmic atomic bomb. But, ironically, while our victorious Armies are imposing democracy on millions in Europe and the Far East, local government here at home is a reeking shambles of corruption, incompetence, waste, and misrule." Allen spelled out "the melancholy story of the failure of good municipal management to take root in our cities." He called for "sensible city management," the kind of dispassionate management that had organized American victories in the two great wars of the first half of the twentieth century. Municipal governance had to catch up to the norms of efficient bureaucracy. Yet cities continued to rehearse "the same old story of boodling bosses and businessmen, of horrendous slums, of dirt and filth, disease and vice, of gross and shameless waste, of mismanagement and misrule, of crass disregard of public health and human dignity."[12]

Robert Allen meant his title, *Our Fair City*, as "ribald mockery." In fact, cities were in trouble. Though many middle-class people still worked in central cities, they now lived in suburban residential communities that resisted annexation to the big city. In Greater Boston, they were happy to let the city "stew in its own juice." Robert Allen saw *blight* in the physical environments of the city itself, but he was also startled by the "strangling blight of parasitic suburbs and satellite communities."[13] The middle classes were sabotaging their own livelihoods by ignoring the fate of the center city. The *Boston Globe* writer Louis M. Lyons filed a report on Boston for Allen's book in which he dolefully called the city a "study in inertia." Lyons described Boston's geographic, demographic, and political dilemma, where the city's "phenomenally narrow geographic limits . . . have shorn it of its middle class, leaving an aloof Brahmin minority politically smothered by an inert mass who are largely without a taxpayer's stake in their own dwellings."[14]

By the end of the nineteenth century, Boston's population had become largely composed of immigrants. In 1906, the emergent Irish Catholic majority expressed its political will by electing John F. Fitzgerald (known as "Honey Fitz") to the mayoralty, unseating Yankee patrician James J. Storrow and inaugurating a period of tension between Boston's aristocratic capital-holding classes and the working-class majority. In 1912, Honey Fitz was succeeded by James Michael Curley, who dominated Boston politics for the next forty years. Lyons described Curley as "big, bluff, theatrical, crude in his methods, but with a voice to melt brass." The Yankees were finally out of power and Curley was not one to let them forget it. As white middle-class households continued to leave for the suburbs (save for the Brahmin enclave of Beacon Hill and some parts of the Back Bay), Boston became what Louis Lyons called a "home of the poor." In 1940, a Housing Authority survey reported that a fifth of all Boston dwelling units were "substandard," without running water, private toilets, or centralized heating. "These are the harsh conditions of the voting population," Lyons reported. But despite their poor living conditions, the voting population did not easily tire of their "boodling boss," who was also their champion.[15]

"Curleyism" and the Politics of Land Use

When Robert Allen and David McCord wrote in the late 1940s, Boston was in the throes of political chicanery manifest in Mayor Curley's reign. Curley was first elected in 1912 and again in 1922, 1930, and 1946. He was twice sent to Washington as a U.S. congressman (1911–14 and 1943–47), and served once as governor of Massachusetts (1935–37). But James Curley was always essentially running for mayor. The son of Irish immigrants who settled in the streetcar suburb of Dorchester in 1864, Curley's political career embodied the ascendancy of Irish political power in the Democratic

Party and the efflorescence of machine politics. Curley's loyal constituents adored him. To them, he was a pugnacious populist who stood up for the common man. Early in his career, Curley was sentenced to jail for taking a civil service exam for a constituent. But Curley turned his misdemeanor into political capital when his reputation spread as a good-hearted politician willing to help out a friend. As one historian put it, "The idea of assisting the needy quickly became an essential part of the Curley appeal and legend. To thousands of Bostonians James Michael was a latter-day Robin Hood who stole from the rich and powerful to help the poor and needy."[16]

Boston's business elite distrusted Curley. They viewed him as an extortionist and a crook, too entrenched in the idiosyncratic world of patronage and political favors to successfully manage a city. Indeed, Curley delighted in his hostile relationship with Boston's business community, despite the fact that he relied on the business people to finance his administration through tax rolls and loans. In his autobiography, Curley fondly recalled an episode in which the president of the First National Bank of Boston refused to lend him money to meet the city payroll: "I decided a bit of political banditry was in order," Curley swaggered. He claimed to have told the banker: "There's a water main with the floodgates right under your building. . . . You'd better get that money up by 3 PM or those gates will be opened, pouring thousands of gallons of water right into your vaults."[17]

Political scientist Paul Peterson has written that "urban politics is above all the politics of land use."[18] Curley understood this perfectly. The city's main source of revenue was the property tax, which was based on the assessed value of real estate. The practice of assessing property was among the most corrupt in the city and a persistent source of antagonism between Curley and downtown property owners who felt that tax assessments were not only too high but also vexingly unpredictable and even arbitrary. Curley's political and fiscal strategy was to redistribute income from the core to the inner-city districts. Taxes on downtown real estate generated revenue for Curley's public projects in Boston's neighborhoods, the heavily immigrant (Catholic) and working-class districts that revolved around Boston's peninsular center. In the 1920s, Curley championed the expansion of the public realm in Metropolitan Boston, building parks, schools, branch libraries, and health clinics. He created a Municipal Employment Bureau to employ former soldiers. He oversaw the construction of public beaches, parks, playgrounds, and recreational facilities; he built roads, bridges, and tunnels to get to them. All of these projects entailed awarding contracts. This process was at the heart of "Curleyism," the political patronage championed by the mayor: firms that won contracts were expected to kick back to the Boss and donate to his campaigns. Meanwhile, Curley built up a loyal constituency by providing his people with jobs and services.[19]

The neighborhoods flourished at the expense of the center city. Curley instructed his assessors to squeeze as much tax revenue as possible from downtown properties, which were taxed at higher rates than residential real estate in the neighborhoods. Many of Boston's commercial buildings were owned by prominent family trusts, which could afford to pay taxes on downtown buildings even if they were not earning money from rent. Curley's biographer, Jack Beatty, noted, "Raising assessments on owners under no commercial imperative was a temptation that Curley rarely resisted."[20] Property owners could petition for tax abatements, but this was a tedious, case-by-case process that was mediated by a group of politically connected lawyers who negotiated settlements with the city. This Byzantine process became known as the "abatement racket." Property owners in Boston feared over-assessment and were thus deterred from improving their properties. Older buildings languished and few new ones were constructed. Some property owners even lopped off the tops of their buildings in an effort to lower assessments, an act that Jack Beatty characterized as "economic cannibalism."[21] Curley was unrepentant. He bragged about manipulating downtown property assessments and he was not above wielding the city's taxing powers to exact political reprisals. Curley recalled punishing the *Herald-Traveler* newspaper for opposing the construction of the Sumner Tunnel to Logan Airport in East Boston in the late 1920s. He wrote in his autobiography how he avenged this betrayal, "when [he] raised the assessments of the *Herald-Traveler* paper, along with other business in Boston which had not been paying their share of the tax burden."[22] This politicization of tax policy created an uneasy environment for new investments in downtown real estate, from the construction of new buildings to even modest improvements for existing buildings.

Not all the blame for the stagnation of urban development in the 1930s can be laid at Curley's feet. The entire nation was suffering from a vast economic depression that stifled new investments in nearly every sector of the economy. But Curley, despite his Robin Hood persona, was not notably successful in helping Boston recover from the Great Depression. Curley advocated relief programs and job creation for Boston's poorer citizens and championed liberal government expenditures. But his ambitious building projects were often stymied by a hostile state legislature dominated by Republicans. And though Curley was one of the first big-city mayors to support Franklin Roosevelt for president, FDR did not embrace the affiliation with this notoriously corrupt politician and kept his distance.

Thus, in the milieu of the Great Depression and Roosevelt's New Deal, Boston did not reap the benefits of federal largesse to the same extent as other leading cities. Federal grant-makers did not perceive Curley or his administration as responsible fiscal stewards, and Boston was largely passed over. In her study of New Deal landscapes, Phoebe Cutler wrote: "Only in Boston, where the WPA wallowed in politics and chicanery, did the New Deal riches fail to raise a surf."[23] What relief money that did surface was used to conduct surveys and create land-use maps and real estate inventories. But the tangible benefits of the New Deal were few in Boston.[24] On a national scale, the New Deal marked the federal government's first overt foray into the housing market.[25] Federal money for housing was funneled through local authorities. The Boston Housing Authority (BHA) was formed in 1935. New Deal–era housing policies, including the 1937 Housing Act, popularized the rhetoric of "blight" and the practices of "slum clearance" that set the stage for postwar urban renewal policies that had an even broader impact on the built environments and social makeup of American cities. Between 1937 and 1942, the BHA sponsored public housing projects in several outlying neighborhoods — purchasing land from willing property owners when possible, and using eminent domain when necessary.[26]

The Fall of the "Rascal King"

When Curley was elected once again to the mayoralty in 1945, Boston's dismayed business elite (then represented principally through the Chamber of Commerce and the Greater Boston Real Estate Board) initiated a concerted effort toward political reform. These interest groups wanted comprehensive tax reform. As political scientist Cynthia Horan puts it, they were hoping "not only to get rid of Curley but to abolish the entire system of ward politics that had produced him," and they advocated replacing the ward-based City Council with at-large representation.[27] The shift from cronyism (or, in this case, "Curleyism") to *managerialism* began in June 1947, when Curley was sentenced to the federal penitentiary in Danbury, Connecticut, for tax fraud.[28] With the blessings of downtown business leaders, the unprepossessing city clerk, John B. Hynes, was appointed temporary mayor. After several months, President Harry Truman commuted Curley's jail sentence, returning him to the mayor's office in November 1947. Boston historian Thomas O'Connor describes what happened after Curley resumed work: "In the course of the next frantic few hours, he interviewed sixty persons, found jobs for every one of them, and made a series of decisions involving millions of dollars for contracts relating to such things as parking meters, voting machines, and rubbish contracts. When his work was done and he emerged from his office, he boasted expansively to newspaper reporters: 'I have accomplished more in one day than has been done in the five months of my absence.'"[29]

Curley's ostentatious remark wounded John Hynes, who decided to challenge him for mayor in 1949, running under the banner of a "New Boston." Though he did not possess the mayor's charm or charisma, Hynes appealed to a diverse coalition united against Curley and was carried by a broad backlash against a city government that seemed mired in corruption. Hynes reached out to Yankee business leaders. He attracted the support of young World War II veterans. And he recruited the political talents of young stars from Boston's academic establishment. Hynes was able to exploit the personalized and quixotic nature of Curley's relatively disorganized machine. For Republicans, reform-minded Democrats, and, indeed, anybody who was anti-Curley, Hynes was the clear choice. He represented clean, businesslike government and an inclusive way forward, especially for young, educated elites, many of whom had assumed that they would have to leave Boston to succeed in business. Hynes was elected in November 1949. He split votes with Curley in the lower-class wards but prevailed in Republican bastions like Beacon Hill, the Back Bay, and other middle-class districts. Incredibly, Curley twice again challenged Hynes for the mayor's office in the 1950s, but lost both times. Hynes served for ten years before ceding the reins to John Collins, who also pushed for a "New Boston" and expanded the city's urban renewal program.[30]

Curley was a machine politician who perceived it as his duty to serve voting constituents and not merely bolster the business community. He stalwartly refused to acknowledge any coincidence between the public interest and private enterprise. To the contrary, he saw public interest and private gain as opposed to each other. There was something appealingly democratic about Curley's unyielding dogmatism on this issue: the idea that urban planning and public investment (in the built environment or otherwise) should be directed by popular wishes and not designed for private business interests. Postwar urban renewal regimes, beginning in Boston with John Hynes, represented a revolution in urban political thinking: progressive mayors perceived an inherent convergence between the public interest and business development. Growth was good for just about everybody, even if those sitting atop the capitalist hierarchy — those who owned factories, made investments, and amassed fortunes — would reap the largest share of the benefits. The political-economic ideology was simple enough: a rising tide lifted all boats. Urban renewal explicitly evoked the public interest by employing the constitutional powers of eminent domain to condemn privately held property (usually a contiguous set of small parcels) and assemble it for "higher and better uses." Private business interests in the 1950s actively organized and represented themselves as the "public interest" and, as a result, were able to receive government subsidies for their development projects. The development of the Prudential Center in Boston was a notable example of this process of private appropriation of the public interest.

Urban Decline and the Rise of Planning
By the 1950s a high-tech economic trend was manifest in the gleaming industrial parks that dotted the Route 128 landscape. As the journalist Elizabeth Hardwick wrote in 1959, Boston had "unlimited promise" for the "engineer, the physicist, the industrial designer, for all the highly trained specialists of the industrial age." But the center city

did not reflect these regional stirrings of economic activity. "In Boston the night comes down with an incredibly heavy, small-town finality," Hardwick wrote. In her eyes, the city had become physically derelict: "Downtown Boston at night is a dreary jungle of honky-tonks for sailors, dreary department-store windows, Loew's movie houses, hillbilly bands, strippers, parking lots, undistinguished new buildings."[31]

Many Bostonians shared this sense of the city's economic stagnation and physical deterioration. Some observers wanted to rebuild the antiquated city and start again. In his panoramic history of Boston's leading capitalists, Russell B. Adams, Jr., recounted a strangely morbid story that epitomized this attitude: "Speaking at a Faneuil Hall meeting in the closing month of 1944, architect William Roger Greeley had gone unchallenged when he lamented that Boston had not shared with London the 'advantage' of widespread destruction by aerial bombardment, leaving behind the rubble of an old city as a foundation for the new. In the absence of such wholesale but healthy razing, Greeley went on with graphically clinical metaphor, Bostonians needed to 'destroy our own diseased tissue and by heroic will-power rebuild our community as a worthy competitor of the newer type of city.'"[32] That Greeley could look longingly toward the devastation of London as an advantageous urban condition expressed more than just bad taste. His statement also indicated how closely the physical city was associated with economic and social well-being. Greeley articulated a generalized desire to produce new landscapes that would both reflect and generate a new, progressive era. He betrayed no nostalgia for the existing built environment, which he saw as physically decrepit and morally ambiguous. The architect acted on these impulses and in 1944 he chaired the "Boston Contest," which solicited broad-reaching proposals for the political and physical reorganization of the city and region. The winning team, led by Harvard political scientist Carl Friedrich, leaned on the anatomical metaphors of urban decay and disease. The city, Friedrich wrote in his team's statement, had "become ill, decaying at the core, because its vitality has not been a common concern of all those having a stake in it."[33] Friedrich's winning proposal — the "Harvard Plan," as it was known — called for a powerful metropolitan government to supersede the existing system of urban politics. Not surprisingly, distinguished members of Boston's business elite supported the Boston Contest, attended its meetings, and sponsored its proceedings.[34]

As it turned out, the Boston Contest was a planning exercise that produced few concrete results. Yet the winning Harvard Plan marked a key moment in the business community's desire to find common ground in an effort to right the economic fortunes of the city. The Harvard Plan also reflected the dominant feeling in academic planning and architectural circles that the core of the nineteenth-century industrial city had to be improved with drastic measures. José Luis Sert, the modernist architect who joined the faculty of the Harvard Graduate School of Design in 1953, articulated this attitude in the 1942 publication *Can Our Cities Survive?* Following the urban principles promoted by the International Congress of Modern Architecture (CIAM), Sert's text represented the challenges of postwar urbanism as a series of crises, analogous to physical diseases, that could be analyzed, diagnosed, treated, and eventually cured if the experts were only given the necessary authority. The essence of Sert's solution was blunt: the chaotic, clogged, and filthy nineteenth-century city — where housing, commerce, and industry dangerously mingled — had to be gutted and rebuilt along the strict principles of functional zoning. To save the center city, as William Greeley also believed, it first had to be destroyed.[35]

Academic tracts and blue-ribbon committees aside, there were statistics that suggested that Boston at the end of World War II faced a daunting set of economic and social challenges. The city's population had fallen by more than ten thousand between 1930 and 1940. The number of manufacturing establishments had also decreased, along with the number of wage earners and total wages paid by manufacturing activity. "By almost any index one chooses to use," one political scientist writes, "the central city showed evidence of being in serious trouble." Outside the central city, the Boston region was losing its manufacturing base, as textile manufacturers in particular fled to the temperate climates and open-shop labor practices of the Sunbelt. New England, as a whole, did not benefit from the wartime economic surge as much as other areas, like California. Boston had not recovered from the Depression years, when banks failed, businesses closed, and industrial production diminished. Boston's port facilities fell into disuse and disrepair. Real estate assets languished, as single-family townhouses were converted to tenements and boardinghouses. In his history of urban renewal in Boston, Thomas O'Connor described Boston in the 1930s and '40s as a "hopeless backwater," where there was a pervasive, palpable sense of the city's economic and physical deterioration. These problems were exacerbated by federal policies in the 1950s, which made it easier to build and purchase suburban homes in new subdivisions that relied on automobile transportation. Federal policies made it difficult to obtain mortgages on urban property and created an institutionalized bias against racially diverse neighborhoods. When Boston and other cities began to implement federally sponsored urban renewal in the 1950s, they sought to mimic the social norms and landscape forms of suburbanization in a desperate attempt to compete economically with their own suburban hinterland.[36]

The Politics and Rhetoric of Urban Renewal

When he wrote in 1947, Robert Allen had little faith in the ability of business leaders to put aside their individual self-interest in favor of collective reform. Allen felt that "the public" had abdicated its responsibility to oversee municipal government. Not much had changed, in other words, since the famed muckraking journalist Lincoln Steffens wrote *The Shame of the Cities* in 1904. Steffens had indicted the businessman as a "bad citizen, . . . a self-righteous fraud" and a chief source of corruption.[37] Allen and Steffens might have been pleased to observe that in the ten years following the publication *Our Fair City*, business interests in many American cities had begun to form citizen organizations that promoted ambitious programs of physical redevelopment, economic revitalization, and political reform. In Pittsburgh, led by the industrialist and banker Richard King Mellon, the Allegheny Conference unified business leaders who worked together with Democratic mayor David Lawrence to launch the "Pittsburgh Renaissance," which sponsored the rebuilding of the city's mixed-use, industrial core as a gleaming office center. Pittsburgh was heralded as an early example of "business-led renewal."[38] At nearly the same time, in New Haven, Connecticut, Mayor Richard C. Lee and his Redevelopment Agency chief, Edward Logue, pioneered the tricky process of unearthing federal grant money to launch urban renewal projects. New Haven became known as the "Model City," where a new form of urban governance, the redevelopment authority, was given broad powers to shape the physical, economic, and social futures of the city.[39] Similar pro-growth coalitions between politicians and business interests were formed in cities across the country, often taking advantage of federal programs aimed at relieving urban blight.

In Boston, John Hynes, and John Collins after him, were deeply vested in cultivating a friendly "business climate."[40] Yet Boston's Brahmin business community did not immediately trust Hynes. Ephron Caitlin, Jr., the Yankee president of the First National Bank of Boston, expressed this uncertainty: "Nobody had ever seen an honest Irishman around here."[41] But Hynes was cut from a different cloth than his predecessor, James Curley. Unlike the self-aggrandizing Curley, Hynes was soft-spoken, mild-mannered, forthcoming, and serious. Where Curley cultivated ethnic antagonism, Hynes sought common ground. Hynes actively solicited the participation of the business community in government affairs, forming special committees composed of leaders of local banks and insurance companies.

Under Hynes, Boston's pro-growth coalition took shape. An essential catalyst was the organization of the Citizen Seminars at Boston College, directed by the dean of BC's School of Business, the Reverend W. Seavey Joyce, a clergyman who also held a Ph.D. in economics. Joyce established the forum to bring business and political elites together to speak frankly about the future of the city and to build trust between public and private leadership. Beginning in 1951, the Citizen Seminars emboldened local business leaders to see themselves as a kind of "steering committee" for the fortunes of the city at large. Inspired by the Allegheny Conference in Pittsburgh, Boston leaders saw the benefit of a unified business-led coalition that transcended internal differences.

Over the course of these meetings, businessmen and politicians came to share a common vision for a "New Boston," one that called for both the modernization of the city's administrative bureaucracy and the renovation of the city's built environment. With political will, Boston could revitalize its slums and fight against the corrosive elements of blight. The city could rebuild its downtown office and commercial districts, create attractive housing for the middle classes, renew the region's transportation and port infrastructures, and even furnish new spaces for conventions and tourism. Indeed, Boston could begin to compete with the suburbs, which had become more attractive to residential, commercial, and industrial developers. If business and political leaders could achieve all this, "Boston would then be able to put an end to the flight from the central city, attract homeowners and customers back from the suburban shopping malls, promote a vigorous commercial activity, and attract substantial investments by outside corporations that would have real confidence in the city's future."[42]

The federal Housing Act of 1949 provided the institutional and financial framework to mobilize local consensus for urban change. The law represented a bargain between advocates of slum clearance and public housing, on the one hand, and those who supported private-sector redevelopment of the center city on the other. Title I of the Housing Act stipulated a federal write-down of the cost of acquiring, clearing, and assembling large parcels of land that had been designated as slums or blighted areas — terms that had been defined in the 1937 Housing Act. "Slums" referred to "any areas where dwellings predominate which, by reason of dilapidation, overcrowding, faulty arrangement and design, lack of ventilation, light or sanitation facilities, or any combination of these factors, are detrimental to safety, health or morals." The concept of "blight" was closely related to the slum, but did not refer exclusively to housing. Blight could result from the mixing of land uses, such as the encroachment of industrial or commercial uses in a residential area. As historian Mark Gelfand has written, blight could include any city neighborhood that was "no longer profitable to maintain or improve."[43]

For approved urban redevelopment projects that adhered to a "workable plan," the federal government would pay for two-thirds of the cost of land clearance, with the city absorbing the other third. Local redevelopment authorities negotiated with individual landowners to acquire the properties, forcing purchase under eminent domain when necessary. The law stipulated that private enterprise should rebuild on the cleared parcels and that new projects should be "predominantly residential" in character. However, this designation was sufficiently imprecise to render it essentially mute. In 1954, the amended Housing Act further distanced urban renewal (the term replaced "redevelopment") from its roots in public housing. Cleared slums or blighted areas near the central business district were deemed too valuable to allocate to housing for the poor. They created opportunities, however, to renew the center city for business purposes, middle-class housing, and "civic centers" to accommodate government offices and public plazas.

Urban renewal policy in the 1950s and '60s, in Boston and elsewhere, was aimed at purging the city of both the *urban village* and the *urban jungle* — the slum and the vice district, respectively. These low-rent neighborhoods were also low tax paying areas. Boston had two sacrificial urban villages: the New York Streets neighborhood in the South End, which was cleared for industrial uses, including the eventual construction of a plant for the *Herald-Traveler* newspaper; and the largely Italian West End, which was destroyed to make way for a large middle-class housing estate and the expansion of Massachusetts General Hospital. Boston's urban jungle was Scollay Square, a rowdy burlesque district clattering with sailors, transients, working-class revelers, and a variety of small-scale enterprises (dance halls, tattoo parlors) and light craft industries (cigar rolling, for example). Scollay Square was razed and replaced with a sprawling government center complex, with offices for local, state, and federal departments.[44]

In the early 1950s, the Boston Housing Authority was the local planning agency charged with administering federal renewal funds. The New York Streets project was the BHA's first attempt at assembling smaller parcels of privately owned land for large-scale commercial, and not residential, development. The project was conceived in 1952 under the misperception that industrial plants would locate on an urban site if the state subsidized development by clearing the land. The New York Streets had been created in the 1840s and '50s by the South Cove Corporation, a subsidiary of the Boston and Worcester Railroad (later the Boston and Albany), which filled the marshy cove along the Fort Point Channel and laid out streets named after cities in upstate New York served by the railroad. The land development was part of the railroad's larger efforts to extend its lines into Boston and construct a South Station. By 1950, the New York Streets had become a diverse immigrant community living in close proximity to the industrialized Fort Point Channel and the B&A's rail facilities. Contemporary newspaper accounts manipulated public opinion by characterizing the New York Streets neighborhood as a "Skid Row" area — illustrating how propaganda was a key element of urban renewal, perhaps as instrumental as the application of eminent domain itself. In his political autobiography, the African-American activist and Massachusetts state representative Mel King, who was raised in the New York Streets neighborhood, wrote about how newspapers shaped the public impression of this place: "The Herald-Traveler series which described the Dover Street area as 'Skid Row' was an important factor in the 'renewal' of the New York Streets. Labeling those streets as slums depersonalized the issue, and blocked out any understanding of the impact urban renewal would have on the lives of the people, like my family and friends, living there, and provided a rationale for replacing 'undesirable' elements of Boston with less troublesome 'light industry.' . . . Those articles helped reinforce the attitudes that allowed the city to come in and raze my family's house."[45]

There was no effective local resistance to question the BHA's claim that it was in the public interest, in the interests of Bostonians at large, to undertake this renewal effort. The thirteen-acre tract was razed — not for modern housing but for a private industrial project. William Zeckendorf, the flamboyant New York real estate developer, flirted with a proposal for the parcel, as part of a larger redevelopment of the South Station area; but eventually a Boston firm, the Cerel-Druker Redevelopment Corporation, took control of the property and sought investors. With no small irony, it was the *Herald-Traveler*, precisely the newspaper that maligned the neighborhood as blighted, that eventually constructed a plant in the renewal zone.[46]

The New York Streets project did not then, and has not since, attracted much outside attention. But Boston's next attempt at urban renewal gained more notoriety. In his complete history of urban planning in Boston, Lawrence Kennedy wrote: "The West End clearance symbolized all that was wrong with city planning in the 1950s because it bulldozed the homes of poor people and replaced them with an enclave for the wealthy."[47] The case of the West End is better remembered than the case of the New York Streets not only because of the scale of the undertaking but also because of the compelling literature produced on the subject, particularly *The Urban Villagers* by the sociologist Herbert Gans, Marc Fried's essay "Grieving for a Lost Home" on the psychological impacts of displacement, and Chester Hartmann's study of the relocation of the West Enders. Together, these documents revealed the myopia of early postwar planners who could not perceive meaningful social or economic relationships in visually chaotic environments. Gans called the West End an "urban village." In the 1950s, villages like these across the country were targeted for renewal by private developers and public-sector city-builders. They were seen as run-down, antiquated, obsolete, and even dangerous places that had the added misfortune of being located near central business districts. In the 1950s, Gans explained, "neighborhoods" were declared "slums." The power of this declaration was immense. The determination of a "slum" was a sociological judgment based on an oversimplified set of visual cues, governed by ideology, and often fabricated by redevelopment authority photographers who sought to document unseemly living conditions.[48]

As a poor neighborhood near the central business district, the West End was an obvious target for urban renewal. Its proximity to downtown office jobs made the area potentially attractive to middle-class, white-collar employees who liked to live near their places of employment. Gans neatly summarized the rationale behind urban renewal in the West End: "Boston is a poor city, and the departure of middle-class residents and industry for the suburbs has left it with an over-supply of tax-exempt institutions and low income areas that yield little for the municipal coffers. Through the federal redevelopment program, the city fathers hoped to replace some of the low-yield areas with high-rent buildings that would bring in additional municipal income. Moreover, they believed that a shiny new redevelopment project would cleanse its aged, tenement-dominated skyline, and increase the morale of private and public investors. This in turn would supposedly lead to a spiral of further private rebuilding in the city."[49]

Renewal planners believed that the West End should be torn down not only for the sake of the city but also to improve the lives of the people living there. The planners adopted what we now recognize as a narrow, paternalistic attitude toward acceptable norms of urban habitation. But the project was not designed to re-house the people who were displaced in more appropriate, modern housing. The city and its chosen private developer wanted to lure the middle classes back to Boston and turn a low-rent area into a sparkling new asset. The majority of West Enders did not believe they were living in a place that was substandard, and they did not want to leave. Though many residents were tenants, beholden to absentee landlords, the West End was a neighborhood that offered tremendous social sustenance. In the planning phases for urban renewal, Gans wrote, West Enders did not apprehend the real possibility that their neighborhood would be destroyed and they displaced: "They had watched the demolition of parts of the North End for the Central Artery — the city's expressway system — and while they disapproved, they realized that a highway was of public benefit and could not be opposed. But the idea that the city could clear the West End, and then turn the land over to a private builder for luxury apartments seemed unbelievable." As the project proceeded, however, disbelief turned to disillusionment. When residents learned that the development contract had been awarded to the second highest bidder and that he planned to build apartments that would rent for at least six times the going rate, they concluded that city government had struck a crooked deal. The action could not be justified by the public interest, people who lived in the West End reasoned, but made sense only in the context of a corrupt political system. "Many West Enders argued that only in Russia could the government deprive citizens of their property in such a dictatorial manner." The West End project did not foster a sanguine outlook for the possibilities of urban renewal in Boston, and Gans's book became a catalyst in the fight against the mass relocation of low-income householders. It was clear to contemporary observers — including political elites — that renewal could be violently disruptive and that the city had to improve its ability to communicate the nature and purpose of proposed urban changes to residents.[50]

John Hynes served as mayor throughout the 1950s and had begun, with mixed results, the process of physical modernization and administrative reform. But the rest of the job was left to John Collins, who became mayor in 1959 on an urban renewal agenda. Collins promptly lured Edward Logue from New Haven to serve as his redevelopment administrator, and together they launched an ambitious "$90-million plan for Boston," which proposed the rehabilitation of one quarter of all of Boston's acreage, an area that housed half of the city's population. Wary of the bitter taste lingering from the West End, Collins and Logue explicitly advocated a "rehabilitative" approach to renewal that emphasized the preservation of neighborhood character as opposed to wholesale clearance. Logue's citywide renewal program included a series of housing projects in the city's neighborhoods.[51] But the most notable and widely publicized project was meant to be a sign of the city's downtown revival and to spark the redevelopment of the commercial and business districts: the plan to construct a vast Government Center in Scollay Square. The most important political achievement toward realizing Government Center was convincing Franklin Floete of the U.S. General Services Administration (GSA) to locate a new federal office building in the disreputable Scollay Square district. With Floete on board, the Massachusetts legislature then agreed to locate a suite of state office buildings in the complex and the City of Boston decided to build a new, modern city hall in the same.[52]

As a guiding theory for urban renewal, Logue and Collins believed in the operative principle of *scale*. Urban renewal could not work on a piecemeal basis. Despite Logue's rhetoric of neighborhood sensitivity, this principle applied to a district like Scollay Square — the entire area had to be cleared — and it applied to the centralized coordination and administration of the program as a whole. Logue was also attuned to the concept of *momentum:* large projects had a catalytic effect on the public's attitude — or, at least, the attitude of leading private interests — toward renewal and boosted the city's self-perception. This outlook underscored the economic theory of urban renewal: strong and swift government action gave confidence to private developers and potential investors. Logue did not want to repeat the mistakes of the New York Streets or West End projects. He secured the commitments of federal, state, and local government to build at Government Center before initiating the process of acquiring land, relocating residents, and soliciting a physical plan. The prominent modernist architect I. M. Pei generated the initial site plan for Government Center, and a group of high-profile architects designed a bold set of public buildings and spaces. Groundbreaking ceremonies were held in September 1963, and buildings were ready for occupancy in 1968, just as Collins turned over the mayor's office to Kevin White (fig. 21).[53]

But the story behind the story of urban renewal in Boston was the Prudential Center. As we shall see in Chapters 3 and 4, the state legislation that enshrined Ed Logue's Boston Redevelopment Authority as the city's chief arbiter of urban land use was also the statute that formalized the Prudential Insurance Company's tax abatement.

THE
NEW
GOVERNMENT
CENTER
•
BOSTON
MASSACHUSETTS

Figure 21 Postcard of the "New Government Center," the centerpiece of Boston's urban renewal program, ca. 1965

The "Prudential Bill" of 1961 rewrote the state's urban renewal law to extend tax breaks to commercial enterprises. As a result, the insurance company's project would be officially administered by the Boston Redevelopment Authority. Prudential formally applied to the authority to proceed with its project under the rubric of urban renewal based on the "blighted" condition of the B&A rail yard and the prohibitively expensive obstacles to developing the site under the "ordinary operations of private enterprise," as specified in the state's revised urban renewal legislation. The topping out of the Prudential Center in 1964 was viewed by many, including Logue, as the chief harbinger of the "New Boston."[54]

BANNED IN BOSTON: CULTURE, CAPITAL, AND ARCHITECTURE

David McCord's brief mention of "book-banning" at the beginning of About Boston was a subtle indication of a conservative quality in the city's collective cultural leanings. He was referring to the phrase "Banned in Boston," which gained traction in the mid-1920s. In the midst of the high-flying jazz age, stodgy Boston elites were busy censoring literary works that they considered too risqué for public consumption. This cultural conservatism can be seen to extend to the city's architectural character and financial culture as well, which the Prudential planners would have to contend with.

The Watch and Ward Society, founded in 1878 as the New England Society for the Suppression of Vice — and which counted as members many of the city's Brahmin elite — monitored for obscenity the content of written material circulating in Boston.

There were many books that could not be sold in Boston, including Theodore Dreiser's 1925 novel *An American Tragedy* (probably because of its vivid evocations of alcoholism, prostitution, and abortion) and the 1926 novel *The Hard-Boiled Virgin,* by Frances Newman, which threatened middle-class attitudes toward women by portraying a sexually adventurous woman who chose career and independence over marriage and motherhood.[55] The noted essayist H. L. Mencken stood trial in Boston when the Watch and Ward Society tried to suppress an issue of his magazine, *The American Mercury.* Mencken had published a chapter from Herbert Asbury's book *Up from Methodism,* which told the story of a churchgoing prostitute, and the Watch and Ward demanded that the Harvard Square peddler who sold the magazine be arrested. In a theatrical protest, Mencken came to Boston, publicly sold a copy of the magazine to Watch and Ward member Reverend J. Frank Chase, and was placed under arrest. In 1925, Mencken published an angry diatribe against Boston's thin cultural tolerance titled "Keeping the Puritans Pure," bemoaning censorship as another form of upper-crust paternalism.[56] Once considered America's intellectual capital, Boston in the postwar period was better known for its priggishness. *Harper's* writer Elizabeth Hardwick wrote in 1959 that the character of the city itself was akin to the title character in John Marquand's 1936 novel about a proper Bostonian, *The Late George Apley.* Like Apley, Boston was "fussy, sentimental, farcically mannered, archaic." Boston represented to her a *lost ideal,* "wrinkled, spindly-legged, depleted of her spiritual and cutaneous oils, provincial, [and] self-esteeming."[57]

"Where's Boston?" Architecture and Urban Identity

Hardwick's loose description of Boston's cultural character can be extended to the realm of architecture. Geographer Mona Domosh has written about how "civic values" influenced the production and appearance of the built environments in nineteenth-century Boston and New York. Architecture was a functional container as well as a cultural product — an act of collective self-representation that could be read by a perceptive iconographer. New York and Boston, Domosh argued, offered two very different cultural responses to the socioeconomic upheavals of nineteenth-century industrialization. New York's eruptive skyline, constructed by an emerging industrialist class, expressed both wealth as well as a competitive jostling for prestige and status. Bostonians were slow to accept the New York skyscraper idiom or Chicago's practice of modern, steel-framed construction. Boston's rising bourgeoisie and established mercantile elite shared an interest in preserving the "Sacred Skyline," embodied by the highly ordered residential landscape of the Back Bay, punctuated only by church steeples, and the consistent cornice line of tall office buildings in the city's business district, which was shaped by strict height limits.[58]

There is a story, perhaps apocryphal, about W. Seavey Joyce — the dean of Boston College's Business School who convened the Citizen Seminars — that can be connected to the city's staid architectural character. Thomas O'Connor, the historian, reports that in 1956, Joyce returned to Boston by plane from an out-of-town trip — the first time he had flown into the city. The approach to Boston afforded Joyce a rare aerial perspective of his hometown: "As the plane neared Boston and banked lazily to begin its approach to Logan Airport, the priest overcame his aversion to heights long enough to look out the window at the scene below, which he now saw from a distance and a perspective he had never before experienced. As he gazed down on the low-lying protuberance of land beneath him, which was completely undistinguished, had no distinctive skyline, and not a single identifiable structure except the old Custom House tower, he exclaimed in a startled voice: 'Where's Boston?'"[59]

Joyce was looking for a landmark, a visual cue that distinguished Boston as a great city. But that visual cue was nowhere to be seen. At that time, the tallest building in New England was Hartford's 527-foot Travelers Insurance building, completed in 1919 and designed by New York architect Donn Barber as a massive office block with a broad tower, culminating in a pyramidal spire and a cupola containing a lantern. In Boston, the tallest building was the sixteen-story Custom House Tower (1915), designed by Peabody and Stearns, which was exempted from height restrictions because it was federally owned property. The tower was built on top of the 1849 Custom House, a four-faced Greek-revival temple featuring a Doric portico. But in 1956, the fact that the city's tallest structure was a government building erected forty years earlier was not an encouraging prospect for Boston's urban fortunes. The next tallest building was in the Back Bay, where the John Hancock Mutual Life Insurance Company erected a twenty-six-story tower in 1947. What should have been a boon to the city, however, became a cautionary tale. When the building opened, the insurance company was shocked to learn that its property assessment had jumped from $6.5 million to $24 million. The John Hancock had to go to court to reduce its tax load. Concerns over the city's high property tax and idiosyncratic assessment practices would haunt urban development through the 1950s.[60] In this section, I trace a selective history of tall buildings in Boston, with a particular interest in the role insurance companies played in commissioning impressive structures and in expanding the business district.

Tall Buildings in Boston

Beginning in the 1870s, life insurance companies were leaders in commissioning the first generation of tall buildings that surpassed the accepted norm of four-story commercial blocks and loft structures. The urban historian Robert Fogelson notes that corporate leaders "saw tall office buildings not only as a sound investment but also as a source of prestige and a form of advertising."[61] When fire ravaged Boston's business district in 1872, insurance companies were among the first to begin the rebuilding process.[62] The New England Mutual Life Insurance Company hired Nathaniel Bradlee, a prominent Boston architect, to design a five-story structure on Post Office Square sheathed in the fashionable French Second Empire style that was inspired by Napoleon I's additions to the Louvre in Paris. This architectural fashion was adopted for the Boston City Hall building (1862–65), designed by Gridley J. Fox Bryant and Arthur Gilman, endowing the richly detailed style with civic connotations.[63] The New York–based Mutual Life Insurance Company quickly followed suit and commissioned a matching Second Empire edifice on the adjoining lot. Architects from the prestigious Boston firm Peabody and Stearns modeled the Mutual Life building on its New York counterpart and included a 234-foot clock tower. The tower, drawn from a medieval Italian campanile, was not itself a common attribute of Second Empire architecture. Yet it became an oft-repeated symbol of the civic pretensions of insurance companies and other institutions. A stone's throw away stood the Equitable Life Insurance building, housing the Boston offices of the venerable New York firm, in yet another Second Empire–style building designed by Arthur Gilman. Although these early tall buildings were sumptuous affairs of neoclassical pastiche, their underlying impulse was to project dignity and a fussy sort of propriety.

After the fire in 1872, insurance companies were attracted to the development possibilities around the new Boston Post Office and Sub-Treasury Building (1868–75), a federal project designed by Alfred B. Mullett, who was then the supervising architect of the Treasury. The post office, too, was designed in the trendy Second Empire style. Post Office Square, as the area was called, represented an expansion of business offices into the warehousing district near South Station and marked an exodus from the city's established financial district anchored by State Street.[64] State Street was not abandoned, however, and in the 1880s, Boston capitalists began to rebuild office buildings there. Peabody and Stearns designed the ten-story Fiske Building in 1887 for a respected dealer of bonds and securities; and in 1889, H. H. Richardson's successor firm, Shepley, Rutan, and Coolidge, designed the fourteen-story Ames Building, headquarters for a large shovel-producing company.[65]

The new State Street structures stood more than 160 feet tall. They were masonry buildings and their heights were limited by the thickness of supporting walls. Chicago's Monadnock Building, at sixteen stories one of the tallest masonry structures ever built, was viewed as a limit to this construction technology. But the Monadnock was an exception to the rule of iron-framed buildings in Chicago. Boston architects and building financiers, on the other hand, avoided the iron, and later steel, frame that had been used so effectively in Chicago. Even though Boston-based capitalists Peter and Shepard Brooks financed many of Chicago's most important steel-framed skyscrapers of the 1880s, the local real estate community did not completely trust this relatively unproven technology. For Bostonians, the steel frame (increasingly used in the 1890s) was an audacious Chicagoan innovation, considered "too visionary" and "experimental." A Chicago architect, C. H. Blackall, designed the first steel-frame building in Boston in 1893, and was free to do so only because he also owned the building. Nonetheless, the building inspector insisted that the structure be engineered at triple the strength believed to be required for stability.[66]

Not everyone approved of tall buildings in Boston, and many contemporary observers of the building scene protested their construction. There were objections that tall buildings stole light and air from neighboring structures and thus created health risks. Critics claimed that tall buildings exacerbated downtown traffic congestion. Real estate developers thought that while tall buildings might appear impressive, they were not profitable. Boston's market for office space was not as heated as those in New York or Chicago. Despite their stature, the Ames, Fiske, and Exchange Buildings (another prominent office structure, built in 1891) did not charge premium rental rates and did not pay well on their investments. The historians Michael Holleran and Robert Fogelson write that "many contemporary observers questioned how well tall buildings anywhere paid during these early years and wondered whether they were not created more as monuments and advertisements than as sound investments."[67] Some Bostonians considered the Ames Building in particular to be a source of civic pride. But as a group, Boston capitalists favored discretion in their architectural expressions. This discretion reflected conservative Boston attitudes about money and even the financial instrument of the trust fund. The journalist Louis Lyons claimed in 1947 that "the trust fund was invented here and has found in New England its most elaborate use, with a full half of the assets of the region in what banks call 'conservative capital,' that is, in savings banks and trust funds which by their nature cannot be risked."[68] These "trusts" operated in a fiduciary, not an entrepreneurial, spirit. Skyscrapers were expensive and risky speculations, and they broke a law of conventional wisdom among Boston investors that warned against "putting upon land improvements that are worth much more than the land itself."[69]

Height Limits

In addition to their link to such economic conservatism, Boston's height limits were based on a shared public concern with urban congestion and expressed a conscious public policy of business decentralization. Height limits, urban property interests supposed, would spread commercial development over a wider area. In 1891, the state legislature's Joint Committee on Cities passed an ordinance limiting new construction to 125 feet (about eleven stories) in all Massachusetts cities, including Boston.

(The restriction exempted ornamental extensions such as steeples or cupolas.) In 1892, the legislature enacted a more nuanced building code that further restricted tall buildings on narrow streets. There was a broad consensus among Boston landowners who agreed on these regulations. Large landowners supported height limits because they assumed that development pressure would raise the value of their idle land. Downtown property owners supported height limits because they believed that their existing buildings would not be overshadowed or rendered obsolete by towering new structures. For them, tall buildings implied new, modern spaces that could steal tenants and spur unprofitable competition. In 1904, the legislature elaborated the height ordinance, providing for a "B district" throughout most of the city, limited to 80 feet, and maintaining the 125-foot limit in the "A district," the downtown business district.[70] New buildings on State Street were built to the limit, and height restrictions became a comfortable status quo — a legally enforced agreement among downtown property owners that they would forgo individual aspirations for taller buildings with higher property values for collective security through predictable and stable land values. The proof was in the pudding: "During a period [1890–1930] when real estate prices in other American cities went through devastating cycles, Boston was free of bust as well as boom."[71]

The national norm of flat height restrictions came to an end in 1916 when New York City passed the first comprehensive zoning ordinance that was designed to mitigate the height and bulk of large buildings by mandating setbacks.[72] Setbacks did not explicitly limit height but formed a building envelope based on street width. The goal was to expose as much of the sky as possible from the street, thus preserving ample access to natural light and air.[73] New York's zoning code became a norm for real estate capitalists, delineating an accepted formula with potentially universal applications. Boston's business district, meanwhile, was quickly built out to the 125-foot limit, implying that taller buildings could profitably be built. But New York financiers, frequently insurance companies, were hesitant to lend money to Boston developers working within the flat height restriction, a strong indication that by the 1920s the height limit had become a restraint on growth. A frustrated editor at the *Boston Herald* wrote, "By 1923, the president of the Massachusetts Real Estate Exchange could list specific projects which were 'held up because the big insurance companies of New York will not loan money under the present building [height] restrictions.'"[74] As a result, Boston was not fully integrated into the national real estate market, and this situation damaged the city's development prospects. Boston real estate interests began to question the height restriction, not only because the demand for office space required taller buildings but also because the comfortable aesthetic of a uniform cornice line had been threatened by those who admired New York's daring new towers. The construction of impressive skyscrapers in New York between 1905 and 1920 began to influence Bostonians' vision of the ideal skyline, which they associated with the city's economic success. Skylines were urban icons, and Boston's uniformity of building heights did not project a vigorous or exciting image. And yet there were enough supporters of height restrictions — those who were happy to see New York, and not Boston, claim those garish, oversized skyscrapers — that change in Boston was slow.

In 1928, the Massachusetts State Legislature finally passed a setback skyscraper ordinance. A structure could exceed 125 feet, but above that height had to step back one foot for every two and a half feet it rose. Freed by the new ordinance, Boston's most powerful corporations launched ambitious building projects. In 1929, the United Shoe Machinery Corporation, which controlled a large proportion of the nation's shoe machinery production and distribution, built a large new headquarters building at 140 Federal Street in downtown Boston. The twenty-four-story structure conformed to the 1928 code, its mass dramatically stepped back from the street and capped with a sliced-top pyramid. Boston-based architects Parker, Thomas, and Rice shaped the building's blocky massing, made of tan-colored brick over a steel frame, into vertical piers that framed recessed windows and spandrels. "The Shoe" introduced Boston to the design aesthetic of art deco, featuring elaborate metalwork, especially in the lobby, and minimal surface ornamentation in relief. The federal government also contri-

Figure 22 Postcards of key buildings, clockwise from top left: the New York Mutual (1875) and New England Mutual Insurance Company (1873) buildings on Post Office Square (courtesy of the Bostonian Society/Old State House Museum); the Custom House Tower (1915); the U.S. Post Office (1931); the United Shoe Machinery Building (1929)

buted to Boston's art deco scene. In 1930–31, Ralph Adams Cram's firm designed the Boston Post Office and Federal Building (replacing the Second Empire–style building on that site), a twenty-two-story office building that faced Post Office Square. The building's bulk — it occupied the entire block — was broken into a C-shape that allowed natural light to penetrate the office wings as well as the street. The building embraced the upward thrust of thin piers, typical of the art deco style, and was faced with vertical shafts of stone (fig. 22).[75]

Insurance-Deco and the Back Bay District

For the most part, Boston's new skyscraper ordinance in 1928 came too late. The national building boom of the 1920s had mostly passed, and very few new office buildings were built in Boston during the 1930s or '40s. There were three significant exceptions, however. Their sources were powerful insurance companies, and they were located in the emerging insurance district in the Back Bay. Insurance companies were the rare institutions that could afford significant real estate investments during the 1930s, though the architecture of these buildings revealed a kind of artistic stagnation in uncertain economic times. The Boston-based Liberty Mutual Insurance Company erected a new building at 175 Berkeley Street in 1937. In his architectural guide to Boston, Donlyn Lyndon dismissed Chester Lindsay Churchill's austere design: "If you did not have death on your mind before, passing by Liberty Mutual may quickly induce morbid thoughts of life insurance."[76] In 1939, the New England Mutual Life Insurance Company left its quarters on Post Office Square for a new building on Boylston Street in the Back Bay. The symmetrical building, designed by Cram and Ferguson, blended the stripped classicism that was popular with government buildings in the 1930s with picturesque details like a temple front and cylindrical cupola atop a clock tower. Two low wings and the entrance portico faced Boylston Street; the ten-story office slab and tower were set back from the street. The building was panned by critics and inspired David McCord to wax poetical:

Ralph Adams Cram
One morning said damn,
And designed the Urn Burial
For a concern actuarial.[77]

More recently, Donlyn Lyndon added his own dry critique, writing that the New England Mutual Life building was "a Cram & Ferguson opus so lifeless that it defies even unsympathetic description."[78] Yet this building helped establish the Cram firm as a trusted designer of insurance company office buildings.

The Liberty Mutual and New England Mutual buildings reinforced a westward spatial trend in the location of the Boston insurance industry that had begun in 1922, when the John Hancock Mutual Life Insurance Company commissioned Parker, Thomas, and Rice to design an office building on Clarendon Street, which they executed in a conservative, neoclassical style. Insurance companies had expanded the central business district in the 1870s when they established office buildings around Post Office Square. The move to the Back Bay in the 1920s and '30s represented a further push into an area that had been a principally residential district. This development was part of a national trend: insurance companies were among the early firms to decamp from cramped downtown locations for broader outlying sites. A key example was the Aetna Insurance Company, which constructed a sprawling colonial revival building at the outskirts of downtown Hartford in 1931. In 1926, Cram and Ferguson designed an imposing building for the Provident Mutual Life Insurance Company on a large parcel in West Philadelphia that featured a Corinthian temple front, clock tower, and cupola. Cram and Ferguson's design for the New England Mutual Building is more subdued than the Provident Mutual, but the similarities between them show how little insurance company tastes changed during that period.[79]

In 1947 the John Hancock expanded again and erected a twenty-six-story tower designed by Cram and Ferguson (fig. 23). The building displayed the vertical piers, stepped-back "ziggurat" massing, and pyramidal top typical of art deco. The lobby featured relief sculpture and elaborate murals. But the cornice lacked the extruding crenellations that endow art deco with so much of its vertical lift. The building is more restrained, more sober, than the sometimes effusive deco style. In 1947, the John Hancock building, clad in heavy limestone, was looking backward, not forward. Donlyn Lyndon called its style "retardataire deco," implying that it was behind the times and instantly out-of-date.[80]

Figure 23 An aerial view of the Back Bay insurance district in 1949, with H. H. Richardson's Trinity Chapel and Copley Square at the lower left edge. The courtyard building in the foreground is John Hancock's 1922 office building, with the 1947 tower behind it; just beyond is the 1937 Liberty Mutual building. The 1939 New England Mutual building is at the left of the frame. (Cram and Ferguson Collection, courtesy of the Fine Arts Department, Boston Public Library, and Cram and Ferguson Architects)

The 1947 Hancock tower is very handsome and a landmark. But the earliest post-war architects working in Boston confronted an architectural culture that was hostile to experimentation. Insurance companies in particular sought out established architectural styles that expressed the solidity and sanctity of the enterprise, and Cram and Ferguson had become the de facto architects of Boston's insurance district. It should come as no surprise that Prudential sought out Cram and Ferguson to serve as associate architects for the Northeastern Home Office project in Boston. Pereira and Luckman (and later Charles Luckman Associates), the coordinating architects, offered experience in large-scale master planning projects. But in choosing Cram and Ferguson, Prudential hedged its bet on the Los Angeles–based Pereira and Luckman by hiring an established local firm to help produce the architecture of the proposed new complex.

DIRTY STREETS: TRANSPORTATION AND MODERNIZATION

The insurance district represented an expansion of the business district, but also the drift of office space away from the cramped financial core of State Street and Post Office Square toward the bigger parcels of the Back Bay that were more accessible by arterial streets. The Prudential Center marked the culmination of this trend in spatial terms — a vast parcel that was designed in conjunction with an urban highway penetrating Boston's city limits from the west. While the insurance district of 1949 was highly accessible by major roads such as Commonwealth Avenue, Boylston Street, and Huntington Avenue, the Prudential Center was ultimately planned in coordination with the Boston Extension of the Massachusetts Turnpike, a limited-access highway that followed the route of the Boston and Albany rail corridor through the western suburbs and into downtown Boston where it connected to the Central Artery. This section explores the challenges to transportation planning in Boston leading to its eventual resolution with the Pike and the Pru.

As noted earlier, in 1948 David McCord had admitted that Boston suffered from "dirty streets," and he chose to overlook this banal topic in his portrait of the city, *About Boston*. But McCord's fleeting reference was not without significance. On the surface, he was saying that Boston's streets needed a good scrubbing. He may have simply meant that the city's street-cleaning services were not well organized or deployed. But to read more deeply, McCord betrayed a subtle disdain for the street — not as urban form, but as a place. The street was dirty: physically, yes, but socially, too. It was crowded, unclean, and even impure. As a source of urban form, McCord was drawn to the picturesque, irregular streets that were the legacy of Boston's colonial street pattern: "There is something about the curving of any path, urban or otherwise, that is more inviting to the pedestrian or traveler than the way that is straight."[81]

The Crooked and Narrow Streets of Boston

There have been many historical and quasi-historical renderings of Boston's idiosyncratic pattern of streets and their development over time. The most engrossing is Walter Muir Whitehill's magisterial narrative of the city's physical history, *Boston: A Topographical History*, first published in 1956 and now in its third edition. In 1920, Annie Haven Thwing published a doting portrait, *The Crooked and Narrow Streets of Boston*.[82] The 1930 Thoroughfare Plan for Boston, prepared by the city planning consultant Robert Whitten, included a lengthy article, "History of Boston's Street System," by Elisabeth Herlihy, the secretary of Boston's City Planning Board and a frequent writer on topics relating to Boston's planning and physical history. Herlihy wrote:

> To the pioneer upon the western prairie it is comparatively easy to lay out a prospective city in squares and streets of unvarying size and shape; to the colonist of 1630 upon the rugged promontory of New England, it was a different matter. Without the means of surmounting the natural obstacles in the way, he proceeded to adapt himself for them. Thus the narrow winding streets, the crooked ways and alleys, the short cuts, the curious twists and turns, the paths and lanes worn by the feet of the early settlers, and established for their convenience three centuries ago, remain today practically unchanged and even cherished by posterity for their early associations.[83]

At first, the Shawmut Peninsula — the site of first European settlement — was only tenuously connected to the mainland by a narrow neck, navigated by what would come to be called Washington Street, which served as the organizing spine of the colonial village. This situation changed little until the 1830s, when two railroad viaducts traversed the Back Bay and the "neck" was thickened and filled to support these transport connections to the west. The triangular intersection of the Boston and Worcester and the Boston and Providence lines created the urban form that became a large rail yard and eventually the site of the Prudential Center. Filled land, on the neck or elsewhere to enlarge the peninsula, was usually platted in a more orthogonal and less meandering fashion. In 1807, the seven commissioners of the Mill Pond Corporation, including John Quincy Adams, employed Charles Bulfinch to produce a plan for new land created by filling the pond at the city's northern edge. Bulfinch designed a perfect equilateral triangle divided by equally spaced linear streets.[84] In the 1850s, Boston's commercial and political elite conceived plans to fill the Back Bay, and the process of filling, street platting, and construction continued unabated for the next forty years.[85] The Back Bay was designed as a grid, with long east-west blocks and short north-south blocks anchored by the broad, tree-lined boulevard of Commonwealth Avenue, the district's central spine and chief public space.[86]

Though both were laid out in clear, geometric patterns, neither the Bulfinch Triangle nor the Back Bay was designed with the principal intention of moving traffic, a goal that became the governing obsession of urban planners in the twentieth century. The Back Bay was conceived as a real estate opportunity, a chance to expand the city's land mass to build a middle-class community. But at the turn of the twentieth century, Boston's urban planners, politicians, businessmen, and journalists were preoccupied with a foul and meddlesome problem that seemed destined to strangle both the economic well-being and moral rectitude of the city: congestion. The discourse about urban congestion and the images used to represent it have been in circulation nearly as long as the modern city itself. In photographs, engravings, and cartoons dating to the last quarter of the nineteenth century, images showed a mix of transportation apparatuses stuck in gridlock. Horse-drawn carts, electric streetcars, pedestrians, and eventually automobiles and motor trucks competed for space on the street. The concept and rhetoric of congestion, and the biological allusions it implied, accentuated a central tension in how we think about streets: are they strictly for circulation, or are streets *places*?

The Congestion Evil

Urban planning historian Asha Weinstein has traced the perceptions of congestion in Boston in the 1890s and 1920s and compares the solutions proposed in each of the two time periods — a subway and a "loop highway," respectively. Urban congestion was widely feared as a form of "strangulation" that threatened not only the economic vitality of the city but also the moral character of the community, compromised by cramped living conditions and the dangerous intermingling of bodies in the street. To be sure, congestion was a sign of economic vigor and the primacy of the central business district. But heavy traffic was also an impediment to the efficient circulation of goods and threatened the desirability and accessibility of downtown as a commercial district.[87]

One solution to congestion was to create multi-level streets. Two methods of achieving this were elevated rail lines and underground subways, both of which eliminated at-grade crossings for streetcars and opened up the street surface for other forms of transit. A subway was more expensive, but both were politically controversial because they implied the uneven enhancement or diminution of abutting property values. Private companies in New York and Chicago obtained charters to build elevated transit lines as early as the 1870s. But a proposal for an elevated transit viaduct in downtown Boston was rejected in the 1890s in favor of a subway, which was considered more reliable and less physically intrusive than an elevated line. Downtown business interests in Boston united to back the subway proposal. The Massachusetts legislature authorized the Boston Transit Commission to build a 1.5-mile subway beneath Tremont Street, in the heart of the retail district, which was leased and operated by the West End Street Railway Company.[88]

The intent of the subway was to free street space for the passage of other wheeled vehicles and pedestrians. But transit planning did not address the larger question of road planning at a metropolitan scale, a challenge picked up by the landscape architect Arthur Shurtleff in 1911. Shurtleff proposed an ambitious set of road improvements for the metropolitan region with the goal of rationalizing a discontinuous system of streets that had developed, as he saw it, merely by "natural" evolution. The existing pattern could be improved by minor design interventions in some instances, but it also required a set of new roads. Shurtleff recommended a system of radial and circumferential thoroughfares that would complete the ad hoc street network. The result would be an efficient, comprehensive system designed to facilitate the flow of "traffic" — a term that Shurtleff used broadly to embrace the movement of people, goods, and, in a more abstract sense, commerce itself. Like his forebears Frederick Law Olmsted, Charles Eliot, and Sylvester Baxter, Shurtleff perceived the transportation network as a constituent element of a metropolitan *circulatory* system that also included sewerage, water supply, and parks.[89]

Shurtleff's plans were mostly unrealized. But his image for Boston's new streets was influenced by a prevailing design paradigm: the boulevard, a modern street type that provided ample space for various transportation modes, sometimes organized around a landscaped mall. Boulevards were broad, multi-lane roads designed as urban amenities that also moved traffic. When Boston leaders later proposed a "loop highway" in downtown Boston, they adopted the boulevard form. This ambitious proposal was designed to circumnavigate the central business district and curve its way around the edges of the city's peninsular core. By the 1920s, the dramatic proliferation of motor vehicles, which competed vigorously (and dangerously) for street space, had added another element to the already meddlesome downtown congestion problem. The "loop highway" plan was initiated in 1923 by the City Planning Board and supported by Mayor Curley. This new street, also called the "intermediate thoroughfare," was designed to be one hundred feet wide, and was expected to cost nearly $33 million. The public expense of the road would be recouped, its advocates imagined, by increased tax assessments accruing to improved properties along the edges of the road and in the business district more broadly.[90] Thus, the loop highway was a plan to secure the fiscal integrity of downtown. *American City* magazine reported that the new thoroughfare was a "city-wide rather than a local improvement, and that the entire business district will derive a direct, substantial and assessable benefit therefrom."[91] Nonetheless, construction required land acquisition, either by willing sellers or through condemnation, and would be expensive. As it turned out, it was too expensive. Planning for the loop highway never got beyond the drawing boards and the state legislature eventually vetoed the project. Beyond sheer cost, the road was stifled by the lack of unified business support for the plan, and drew resistance from self-interested property owners who denounced public appropriations of private property.

Though it ultimately failed, the loop highway proposal introduced to Boston a key innovation in transportation planning: the development of "scientific" techniques to document and quantify traffic flow and assign a monetary cost to traffic congestion. In December 1926, Elisabeth Herlihy reported in an article for *American City* the results of traffic counts in Boston taken in 1924 and then again in 1926. The study, produced by the City Planning Board with the backing of the Boston Chamber of Commerce, reported a twenty-one percent increase over the two years in vehicular traffic entering Boston's central district. That number disguised the fact that automobile traffic had jumped by twenty-nine percent and motor trucks by twenty-one percent, while horse-drawn vehicles had declined by twenty-one percent. In lieu of entirely new streets, municipal government initiated a set of incremental measures to address the impact of cars and trucks on city streets, including street widenings, regulatory tactics to limit on-street parking and double parking, and other technological fixes designed to move traffic more efficiently.[92]

More ambitious than efforts to manage the flow of traffic at a single grade were proposals for elevated streets, repeating the basic idea behind elevated or submerged transit lines but applying it to automobile traffic. This was the driving concept for Robert Whitten's "Central Artery" in Boston, the centerpiece of his 1930 regional thoroughfare plan, prepared at the behest of Boston's City Planning Board. Whitten's plan was based on extensive traffic count statistics and left readers little room to question the idea that the city was choking with congestion. Whitten devoted the first half of his report to the exhaustive documentation and representation of the city's traffic congestion in a dizzying array of charts, graphs, and maps. The second half was a detailed proposal for a system of improved or new roads for metropolitan Boston. Whitten stated: "The Plan is based primarily on a recognition of the need for a modernization of the present highway system by the development of a limited mileage of express roads and parkways of generous width and permitting a continuous flow of traffic."[93] The concept of *continuous flow* was the ideological core of Whitten's proposal. *American City* picked up on this distinguishing feature and reported in 1930 that the Boston Thoroughfare Plan called for "the provision of continuous-flow traffic facilities."[94] When possible, this ideal flow could be attained through traffic circles, or roundabouts. But in dense urban areas it was necessary to build broad streets with an "express" underpass that allowed through traffic to avoid intersections with cross traffic. In the central business district, Whitten proposed an elevated "Central Artery" that was lifted off the ground on steel girders. Other key proposals included a tunnel connecting the center city to East Boston, via the Central Artery, and two highways approaching from the west and southwest that also linked with the Central Artery: the Blue Hills Radial and the B&A Highway, the latter of which would accommodate automotive traffic from the Back Bay and South End along the railroad's right-of-way.

Postwar Highway Plans

Whitten's plan gathered dust through the 1930s and into the war years. The concept of a Central Artery and many of Whitten's other recommendations were revived in 1947 when Governor Robert Bradford, a Republican, commissioned a study that led to the Master Highway Plan for Metropolitan Boston, published in 1948 and authored by the private consulting firm of Charles A. Maguire and Associates with the aid of DeLeuw, Cather and Company, a Chicago-based planning firm. The intent of this document mirrored the 1930 Thoroughfare Plan: to furnish the traffic statistics necessary to substantiate an expensive and ambitious highway-building program. The research methods of traffic engineering — traffic counting and origin-and-destination studies used to illustrate demand for new roads — had not technically advanced in the eighteen years between Whitten's report and the Master Highway Plan in 1948. But the rhetoric had been amplified, the techniques of visual representation were more compelling, and the physical proposals themselves were bolder. The individual data points from a series of origin-and-destination studies were accumulated into traffic demand statistics that were projected upon a map of the Boston region and labeled "desire lines" to sleekly dramatize the demand for modern, express highways that had built up during wartime. The Master Highway Plan explained this novel turn of phrase: "A desire line can be defined as a straight line between the point of origin and the point of destination of a trip or group of similar trips, without regard to routes traveled, in other words the line of travel if a direct highway existed."[95] The desire lines invariably led from the suburban periphery toward the center city. The 1948 plan proposed to satisfy those desires by translating them as directly as possible into a set of radiating freeways and also projected a set of circumferential highways that facilitated inter-suburban transport and allowed cars and trucks to bypass the City of Boston if necessary (fig. 24).

The Master Highway Plan coincided with a political mandate and fiscal policy to construct new roads. In 1949, the newly elected governor, Democrat Paul Dever, and state legislators, enjoying a Democratic majority, passed a $100 million bond bill for state highways, financed by an increase in the state gas tax. The money was turned over to William F. Callahan, who was reappointed as the commissioner of the Massachusetts Department of Public Works (DPW) after a ten-year hiatus. Callahan gave the highest priority to two links in the Master Highway Plan of 1948: the Central Artery designed to ease congestion through downtown Boston, and Route 128, the circumferential highway that he had initiated in his first term as DPW commissioner, between 1934 and 1939. These two projects for metropolitan Boston consumed nearly all of the $100 million bond dedicated to roads.[96]

In the 1930s, Callahan had launched a project to modernize and expand Route 128, which was the state's designation for a haphazard and disconnected series of local roads that weaved its way through Boston's suburbs in a vaguely circumferential pattern. Callahan wanted to build a divided parkway with limited-access interchanges that bypassed the small villages and towns that marked the awkward hinges of the old state road. Contemporary reports divided the new road into two parts — the "Northern Circumferential Highway" and the "Southern Circumferential Highway." In 1936, construction began on a small stretch of the road in the northern suburbs, but little progress was made, and nearly all highway construction came to a halt with the onset of World War II. When Callahan returned to the Route 128 project in 1949, he oversaw the swift construction of a twenty-two-mile section that completed the northern leg of

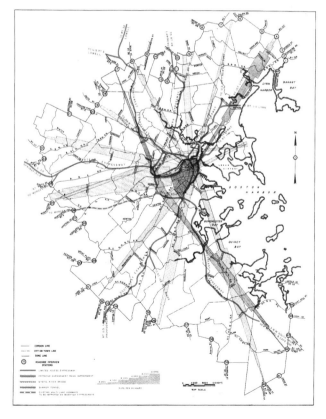

Figure 24 The 1948 Master Highway Plan for Metropolitan Boston charted proposed highways over the "desire lines" that insisted on them

the highway. But critics called the new highway a "road to nowhere." Did the region really need a modern roadway that connected small suburban hamlets while Boston was choking with congestion? Undeterred, Callahan went forward and divided the work into nine separate contracts to hasten its completion. Construction began in 1950, and the Northern Circumferential Highway was opened eighteen months later. Callahan left the Department of Public Works in 1952 to focus on his new venture, the Massachusetts Turnpike Authority, charged with constructing a limited-access highway from the state's western border to the outskirts of Boston. Callahan was succeeded at the DPW by John Volpe, who continued with the southern section of Route 128.[97]

The Central Artery was planned as the linchpin of the Master Highway Plan of 1948, a link in the "Inner Belt" that gave access to the central business district. Unlike Route 128, which entailed cheap land acquisition and minimal destruction of existing buildings, the urban highway was a major physical intervention. In his vision of the Central Artery in 1930, Robert Whitten produced a rendering of a delicate, steel-framed, elevated road neatly inserted amid the broad commercial structures of the business district.[98] Yet the Central Artery, launched in 1952 and completed in 1959, was designed at a much broader scale and required the procurement of expensive urban land parcels.[99] From the perspective of state highway planners, the Central Artery marked the culmination of more than sixty years of considering solutions to the congestion problem in downtown Boston. But when the wrecking ball came to town, there were vociferous protests. Meat wholesalers near North Station demanded that demolition halt until they could locate new quarters. Representatives of the garment, shoe, and leather trades, located in multipurpose loft buildings near South Station, pushed for an alternate route that would skirt the district. They were joined by community leaders in nearby Chinatown in an effort, ultimately in vain, to save their businesses and homes. The highway displaced hundreds of families in Chinatown and forced the partial demolition (it clipped the back end) of the recently completed Chinatown Merchants Association building on Kneeland Street.[100]

With the Central Artery under construction, highway planners debated the future of the region's highway infrastructure. Spurred by the Interstate Highway Act of 1956 — and its promise of abundant federal funding for road projects — state politicians, led by John Volpe, aimed to complete the image of the Master Highway Plan of 1948.[101] Volpe, who had returned to Boston after a stint as Eisenhower's inaugural federal highway administrator and positioned himself for a successful gubernatorial run in 1960, pushed hard for the completion of the Inner Belt highway built to the specifications of the 1948 plan. He faced a powerful adversary in William F. Callahan, at the helm of the Massachusetts Turnpike Authority. As we will see in Chapter 4, Callahan's plan for an urban extension of the Massachusetts Turnpike threatened to supersede the 1948 plan and replace the Inner Belt with a direct connection to the Central Artery from the west.[102]

A FINE OLD PAINTING OF CHARACTER

To those who scoffed at Boston's antiquated urban culture and languishing built environment, David McCord had a ready defense: "You would not stand in front of a fine old painting of character and say that it might be good if it had a new frame and a cleaning and a coat of varnish."[103] Yet the political and business leadership of Boston made precisely that assessment when looking at the "old painting of character" that was downtown Boston in 1948. Over the course of the following decade, a pro-growth coalition, led by Mayor John Hynes and backed by the local business and academic communities, initiated the first, if sometimes faltering, steps toward the spatial and economic restructuring of the city. There were signs in the mid-1950s that private capital was prepared to respond to Boston's urban renewal efforts and that the city's "antique barrier" would topple.[104]

In 1956, the large health insurance company Blue Cross and Blue Shield announced that it would build a twelve-story tower on Federal Street, just south of Post Office Square and across the street from the United Shoe Machinery building. The structure was designed by the noted modernist architect Paul Rudolph, and attracted attention from the architectural press for its bold use of precast concrete panels. In the Back Bay, construction was under way for a new office tower, financed by the New England Mutual Insurance Company, that would be leased by IBM for its regional headquarters. The six-story building was designed along modernistic lines by the New York firm of Harrison and Abramovitz, featuring a curtain wall with staggered glass panels.[105]

Also among the first to build in Boston was the Travelers Insurance Company of Hartford, which acquired a site adjacent to the Central Artery, then nearing completion. In 1957, Travelers announced its intention to erect a sixteen-story office tower that would house its Boston operations and provide top-quality office space for other firms. The announcement of the company's plan to build was received as a validation of the city's rebuilding efforts and demonstrated how the new highways had an impact on the location of new business structures. It was good news for the real estate outlook in Boston, reasoned *Globe* columnist Frederick McCarthy, when "smart business organizations such as insurance companies" decide to build office structures in the city.[106]

The Travelers Building was the first office structure built in the central business district since the "Shoe" went up in 1929; yet insurance company executives were convinced of the benefits of a central location. Travelers employed a large number of young women who, its male executives decided, enjoyed downtown shopping, entertainment, and access to transit connections at South Station. (A similar rationale was cited by Blue Cross and Blue Shield.) Early to sign on with the Travelers Building was the venerable industrial firm of Godfrey L. Cabot, Inc., which planned to manage its far-flung empire of mineral and fuel extraction and carbon-black production plants from four floors near the top of the building. J. Doyle DeWitt, the president of the Travelers, thanked his new tenants: "Our own faith in the future of this city is secured by your decision to join with us."[107] The building filled up quickly. Thomas M. Horan, vice president of the real estate firm Meredith and Grew, who helped orchestrate the deal, explained the building's popularity: "There is a serious shortage of modern, air-conditioned office space in downtown Boston."[108]

The design commission for the Travelers Building went to the New York architects Kahn and Jacobs, the firm responsible for many of the glass-curtain-wall buildings going up on Park Avenue and elsewhere in Manhattan, and its designers brought this modern sensibility to Boston. The building's edges were wrapped in alternating, unbroken bands of horizontal windows and spandrels of glazed blue brick. Vertical aluminum strips organized the main facade, which was punctuated by a windowless service core, clad in white brick. Large letters delineating THE TRAVELERS were affixed

Figure 25 Travelers Insurance Company Building, Boston, ca. 1960, Kahn and Jacobs, architects (Courtesy of Robert Allan Jacobs Collection, Drawings and Archives, Avery Architectural and Fine Arts Library, Columbia University)

at the top, facing inbound traffic on the Central Artery (fig. 25). The position of the utility core on the west side of the structure allowed for large, open office floors. The rectangular building sat in the middle of its rhomboid site, which accommodated a plaza and a small reflecting pool. The rear of the building had a parking area as well as a shipping and receiving ramp.[109]

The Travelers Building, along with the Blue Cross and Blue Shield and IBM buildings, represented important first steps toward the modernization of the city's office landscape. The two insurance buildings, in particular, demonstrated the impact on business location of the Central Artery and new parking structures — including a 950-car garage built in 1954 on Post Office Square (it had already been functioning as a surface parking lot) and a large, multistory municipal garage built nearby at Fort Hill Square in 1957. The new highway promised enhanced accessibility without having to forfeit the benefits of a central location. If the incentive of improved infrastructure wasn't enough, it was reported that Travelers had received assurances from the city regarding its property value assessments.

When the building opened in 1959, Travelers executives stressed its downtown location. "We are proud to have been among the first to put ourselves squarely on the side of downtown Boston's future," DeWitt beamed. The Travelers was not deterred by the negative reports emanating from the central city: "We heard reports of a downtown blight; of traffic problems; of the typical rush to the suburbs. But we were also made a witness to the hopes and plans of a dynamic City administration; vigorously supported by progressive Boston businessmen. We could not believe that one of America's principal centers of commerce was dying or even seriously ill." The promise of Boston's urban renewal program — that sustained public-sector commitment to rebuilding would attract private investment — seemed to be bearing fruit. DeWitt recalled his company's decision to move forward with the project in 1957, "inspired by the evidences of faith we saw all around us."[110] One evidence of that faith came from the city's efforts to launch its renewal program; another came from the city's ambitious highway-building program; and, surely another evidence of faith in the city came from Prudential, which had announced in January 1957 its intention to dramatically transform the sprawling Boston and Albany rail yard into a gleaming new district.[111] The proposed Prudential Center introduced a new scale and sensibility to urban development in Boston and would reframe that "fine old painting of character." Like the Travelers, Prudential was motivated to decrease the uncertainty of its tax burden. As we shall see, these efforts would be greatly tested.

Chapter 3
"We Believe in Boston" The Politics of the Prudential Center

PRELIMINARY STUDY 24

A detail of a photograph from Prudential's announcement on January 31, 1957, that it would construct the Prudential Center on the site of the Boston and Albany rail yard in Boston. On the right is Prudential president Carrol Shanks and on the left is Boston mayor John Hynes. (Courtesy of Prudential Financial, Inc.)

Prudential announced its intention to build a Northeastern Home Office in Boston at a luncheon hosted by the Greater Boston Chamber of Commerce at the Sheraton Plaza Hotel on January 31, 1957. For assembled politicians, business leaders, and newspaper reporters, Prudential's president, Carrol M. Shanks, delivered a rousing address that heralded a bright future for the city and its regional economy. Shanks then displayed a large image of the ground plan for the site: a twenty-eight-acre parcel in the Back Bay acquired from the Boston and Albany Railroad. But it was not until he unveiled a set of colored renderings of the Prudential Center that his audience perceived the enormity of his company's proposal (fig. 26). As one reporter put it, "The audience appeared stunned momentarily as it gazed in wonder at the two screens and listened to Shanks describe a project that will mean the revitalization of New England's economy."[1]

SIGHT AND SCOPE

When he arrived in Boston, Carrol Shanks appeared as a prophet of confidence, conveying that intangible yet critical factor in urban economics. His speech to the Chamber of Commerce, entitled "We Believe in New England," was received by local businessmen as a validation of the region's emerging high-technology and commercial economy and Boston's role as its financial hub. Shanks's tone blended prophetic economic analysis with the missionary zeal of an urban booster. The press widely reported the address as an important vote of confidence from a visionary corporate chieftain of national stature. Shanks emphasized that the proposed Prudential Center would benefit both his company and the city of Boston:

> I am told this represents one of the largest single areas within a metropolitan center ever to be developed at one time under a single plan. It is important to The Prudential.

Figure 26 Carrol Shanks (holding microphone) with Mayor Hynes (in dark suit), during a press conference to announce Prudential's intentions to develop the Northeastern Home Office in the Back Bay, broadcast on WBZ-TV. *right* A view of the rendering that was placed behind Hynes and Shanks, produced by Cram and Ferguson with Pereira and Luckman serving as coordinating architects. (Courtesy of Prudential Financial, Inc.)

But more than that, we believe it can serve as a stimulus for added vigorous growth and progress in the heart of one of America's very great cities. We have ambitious plans for this development, which will require substantial investment. The very existence of these plans reflects a firm conviction on our part that Boston faces a dynamic future. Our investigations into Boston and New England indicate that there is developing here a new economic empire, built upon modern technology. We believe in Boston. We believe in the entire New England Area.[2]

Yet Prudential's choice of Boston was not based on sheer faith. "This is the result of many months of research," Shanks told his audience. New England, the pioneering hearth of American industry, had fallen upon hard times as regional manufacturing dispersed to locations with cheaper labor. But in Shanks's broad view, these changes were ultimately for the best. What appeared locally to be a crisis was only part of a temporary, if painful, process of rebalancing the nation's free market economy: "The exodus of industries which provided New England with sometimes alarming sounding statistics is no reason to assume that New England will not progress: it simply means that businesses that belong somewhere else will go where it is most economical for them to operate, and those that belong in New England will stay here, or will come here and grow — as they have been doing in the past few years. In the end, when the transition period is finished, you will have a sounder economy than ever before." The cotton and textile mills had decamped for the South, but they were being replaced by high-technology industries that offered higher wages to fewer workers. The region's new companies — in electronics, military armaments, new consumer products, and industrial research — operated "on a high and complex plane." Let the old manufactories go, Shanks advised, and welcome the new world of radars, electronic components, and intellectual property: "These are the industries upon which the future economy of the nation will be founded."[3]

The economy of Boston's industrial region was improving, but Shanks believed that urban leaders had neglected the city itself. Like its broader economy, Boston's physical plant faced the challenge of obsolescence. A city's built environment performed economic functions and had to stay up to date to be productive and compete with other cities. Now cities also had to compete with their own suburbs, Shanks lamented. This meant that Boston had to be rebuilt with modern facilities that met suburban standards for accessibility, convenience, and amenities. Shanks predicted that Prudential's commitment to build a new office, commercial, and residential complex in the Back Bay would convince local businesses to stay in the city and even persuade other firms to relocate to Boston. This is what had happened in Chicago, where Prudential's Mid-America Home Office building encouraged local businesses to stay in the city instead of "moving into new areas, which a few years ago was an alarming possibility." Shanks noted that business leaders of Pittsburgh, under the guidance of the Allegheny

Conference, initiated a "sizable overhauling," channeling investment capital that might have gone elsewhere into the city's downtown office district. But Boston's investor class had too frequently passed over its own city, finding more distant beneficiaries of its capital. Shanks expected local capitalists to follow Prudential's lead and seek opportunities closer to home: "More and more of the money in this area can be put to work in Boston, in Massachusetts, and in New England. The returns here will be as good as anywhere else; in my estimation the investments will be at least as secure; and the money you invest in making local progress is money that, as it does everywhere, will pay you extra dividends in pride and contentment and security." Prudential championed this concept of "extra dividends," but Shanks made clear that psychological factors such as pride or contentment were secondary to Prudential's financial mission. He intoned: "Our project in Boston is being made strictly for business reasons and for profitable investment."[4]

City Within a City

The set of renderings of the future Prudential Center that Shanks displayed were credited to three firms: local architects Hoyle, Doran, and Berry; Metcalf and Eddy, a Boston engineering firm; and Pereira and Luckman, a national firm based in Los Angeles that would serve as coordinating architects. The images showed a vast campus of dramatic geometric shapes, centered by a fifty-story office tower and punctuated by two round, dome-roofed structures — the first to house a municipal auditorium that the city proposed to build, the second for a restaurant. It was a sparkling acropolis presented without an urban context and was hailed as a "city in a city." The main tower housed Prudential's Northeastern Home Office, but allotted nearly three quarters of the floors to outside tenants. Flanking the tower were rectangular low-rise commercial pavilions that framed a sequence of public spaces. The master plan also called for a slab-shaped hotel, attached to the city's auditorium, and five residential towers. One apartment tower matched the massing of the hotel. Four smaller apartment towers rose as a suite of identical fingerlike extrusions that mimicked the central tower's square plan, each neatly wrapped in steel and glass envelopes. The complex rested on an underground parking garage for a projected five thousand cars. Shanks summarized the concept: "This project is planned not only to provide peak efficiency for ourselves, but to provide high-class office space for rental to some of Boston's other businesses, and equally high-class apartments within Boston where people can live."[5]

In addition to building over the Boston and Albany rail yard, Prudential had options to augment the parcel with two smaller properties — the Mechanics Hall, at the site's southeastern edge, and several square blocks to the southwest that belonged to the Christian Science Church. The total site occupied more than thirty-one acres in the Back Bay. A press release echoed what Shanks had mentioned in his speech: "It is believed to be the largest single metropolitan site ever purchased for re-development." The "focal point" would be the central tower. The building contained over 750,000 square feet of office space and at fifty stories would be the tallest structure in New England. But the office tower was only the centerpiece of this massive project that encompassed more than twice the space of Rockefeller Center. Prudential officials proclaimed that the project would avoid the "cloistered atmosphere of a downtown development." A large portion of the plinth that capped the garage substructure would be left open for "plazas and malls, reflecting pools, fountains and sculpture, enclosed glass-walled walkways and other esthetic features." The overriding impression would be the "freedom of space."[6]

Mayor John Hynes was euphoric, if a bit startled by the image of such a massive new development. In a press release, Hynes enthused that the Prudential Center was "the biggest thing that has ever happened in Boston in a physical sense. There has never been anything here faintly resembling it." The governor, Democrat Foster Furcolo, was also swept up in the moment, declaring: "There perhaps has not been a single more significant event in the history of Massachusetts."[7] The hyperbolic politicians were likely inspired by the spectacular renderings of the proposed project, which promised a new scale, aesthetic, and planning sensibility for Boston's urban landscape. The Boston Globe's A. S. Plotkin, who covered architecture and real estate, reported: "Boston got an electrifying view yesterday of what its $100 million Back Bay 'city-within-a-city' will look like about five years hence." Prudential's project would "transform the dingy Boston & Albany railroad yards area into a spacious, picture-book vista of clean-lined structures. The emphasis will be on glassed-in, air-conditioned comfort."[8] To proper Bostonians accustomed to the more opaque and stolid built environment of masonry structures, Prudential's vision of a gleaming city of steel and glass was stunning: "The sight and scope of Prudential's plans for the now near-blighted area were breath-taking as they were unveiled on giant screens in the Sheraton ballroom. Rising high from about the center of the plot was a 50-story skyscraper which easily will dominate Boston's sky line."[9] The sheer size and look of the project made it seem like an overblown proposal, but Hynes insisted that it would be achieved: "I cannot over-emphasize that this is not something that may happen, this is something that will happen." Some cynics murmured that Prudential's plans were unrealistic. Hynes corrected this misimpression: "This is not a dream, this is an actuality. Prudential officials are not promoters, they are hard-headed businessmen who finance their own building program."[10]

Unobstructed Vision

To Hynes, Prudential's proposal marked a revolution in the city's self-image and he was determined to make that vision a reality: "Here it is before our eyes," the mayor said:

"It has been said, with some justification, that we have permitted our vision to become clouded — that we looked to the future as through a glass, darkly. Perhaps that is all too true. But from this time forward, from this very day forward, we shall have clear-eyed, unobstructed vision. The Prudential Company has wiped the mists from the glass."[11] In Hynes's view, Boston businessmen had been blind to the possibilities of their own city, but Prudential had opened their eyes. In an editorial, the *Boston Herald* reflected on the role of the outsider: "It has taken some non-Bostonians to sell Boston to the Bostonians." It seemed as though Prudential had come to Boston and found a very different city from the one inhabited by locals: "Those who attended the unveiling of the plans for the Prudential Center and heard President Shanks of the insurance company express his confidence in a great future for Boston and New England won-dered to themselves: Is this the Boston we have been living in?" Prudential conveyed a global vision of Boston, one that transcended the infighting and provincialism of the faltering city: "So, after all, this is Boston. We look at it and New England with newly opened eyes, and see a place for modern complex industries, a world research and educational center, a commercial link with Europe, Latin America and the vast resources of Canada to the north, and, as we take the contagion of Prudential, a society of dynamic and daring planners."[12]

If Prudential was a "contagion," it was the sanguine infection of fiscal confidence. The unveiling event was framed as a confirmation of Boston's economic and urban development prospects. The metaphor of vision was only one of many rhetorical devices used to extol the Prudential Center. At the press conference, an exuberant Hynes took simile to new heights to express his glee and promote the broader rebuilding of the city's economy and built environment: "Nothing like it has ever before happened to inspire us to take the bit in our teeth and to run at full speed ahead. Nothing that I know could better cause the mourners in our midst to sing a new song — a song of joy." Hynes turned to Shanks and regaled him: "Your confidence in our city, and in its future, enti-tles you to our undying gratitude."[13] Confidence itself had economic value, and Hynes was giddy over what he called the "tremendous psychological effect" of Prudential's rail yard project. "Confidence begets confidence, as it were," the mayor explained.[14]

The Prudential Center itself would generate a direct investment of over $100 million, and the complex would house twelve thousand new jobs. But "overshadowing these specific economic advantages" were the ripple effects across the larger invest-ment community: "The decision of the world's third largest company to construct a mammoth Prudential Center will have an impact nationally that will unlock the flood-gates of new private and federally-sponsored developments."[15] Hynes explicitly saw Prudential's investment in terms of inter-urban competition: "It will make Boston the envy of many of the larger cities. The Prudential decision to build in Boston marks the re-birth of the city. It is certain to inspire other such developments here. And it comes at an appropriate time, for the Boston community has come alive, so to speak, and realizes that the face of the city must change if Boston is to keep abreast of other cities and remain in competition with them. We know that other cities have been in competition with us. We are tremendously gratified that the Prudential has chosen Boston."[16]

How Hynes Steered the Pru to Boston

If Mayor Hynes was thankful to the Prudential, Carrol Shanks was equally gratified by the mayor's efforts to clear the hurdles in the path of Prudential's Boston proposal. There were two crucial obstacles: Prudential's desire to secure a tax concession and the Massachusetts Turnpike Authority's threat to claim the Boston and Albany rail yard for its own purposes, a Boston Extension of the turnpike. Hynes "worked tirelessly to help us untangle the complications," Shanks said at the January 31, 1957, press conference. "He has given us a new concept of what an asset to the city a great public servant can be."[17] In this shining moment, Shanks and Hynes could hardly have predicted the complications yet to come on the way to finally opening the Prudential Center in 1965. For Hynes, Shanks's announcement in 1957 that Boston would host Prudential's Northeastern Home Office was a vindication of a long effort to secure a developer for the Boston and Albany rail yard site and to stimulate investment in the city's real estate.

In 1970, the *Boston Globe* posthumously published an excerpt from a manuscript by John Hynes detailing his role in attracting Prudential to Boston. The editors explained that Hynes "had been urged to do this by friends who feared that his innate modesty would keep from the history books the details of the top event of his administration, and the birth, as it was, of the *New Boston,* and of a new spirit of urban renewal in the nation."[18] Hynes was mayor between 1951 and 1959, when renewal in Boston got off to a halting start with the New York Streets and West End projects. Yet his supporters sought to connect Hynes's political legacy to 1960s urban renewal and Boston's emergence as a major office center for both the public and private sectors. The Prudential Center opened in 1965 under the mayoralty of John Collins. Yet Hynes claimed authorship of the idea to turn the Boston and Albany's derelict urban rail yard into a major office development and he mediated the process of marketing the land to Prudential.

When he took office in 1951, John Hynes contemplated how he might restore confidence in the city's future. James Curley had left Boston on a weak financial footing. The city was dangerously close to fiscal insolvency, plagued by a shaky credit standing and an unappetizing menu of municipal bonds. Hynes resolved to pull off something big to silence the critics and soothe their "jittery apprehension," as he put it. He "went on the hunt for big game," seeking to attract a major investment from a national concern. In his mind, a major investment implied a significant real estate venture. Hynes hit upon the perfect place for it when he learned in May 1951 that the Boston and Albany Railroad Company, owned by the New York Central, had decided to sell its rail yard that fanned across twenty-eight acres in the Back Bay.

The parcel of land was widely viewed as an important opportunity for the development of the city. After the railroad's announcement, the Boston Planning Board hosted an open call for proposals. The Piasecki Helicopter Corporation suggested locating a heliport on the site. The most ambitious proposal came from the architecture firm of Cram and Ferguson. The plan called for the demolition of the Mechanics Building as well as the Lenox Hotel at the corner of Boylston and Essex Streets to expand the scope of the site. The focal point of the symmetrical plan — it resembled a City Beautiful–era civic center — was a large convention hall and open public plaza, surrounded by apartment buildings, office towers, and restaurants. The architects called for a concrete slab across the entire site that allowed the B&A tracks to continue unimpeded beneath it and provided a platform for a four-thousand-car parking garage. Even at this early stage, many observers saw in the railroad property a chance not only to pad the city's tax rolls with new commercial construction but also to modernize its infrastructure.[19]

These visions tantalized the Boston public. The city wanted its own Rockefeller Center in the Back Bay, the model evoked again and again in local newspapers, but who could afford to replace the railroad and advance an urban redevelopment at such a grand scale? At one point, the *Monitor* reported, Mayor Hynes even made overtures to John D. Rockefeller III to see if the scion would reproduce the family magic in Boston.[20] Some suggested that the city itself step forward and purchase the site, to avoid short-sighted, haphazard proposals by "money-hungry syndicates" and ensure sound long-term planning; but Hynes insisted that it could not afford to do so.[21] An opportunity arose in the spring of 1952, when Hynes met Mayor Haydon Burns of Jacksonville, Florida, who confided that Prudential had chosen his city to host the company's South Central Regional Home Office, "scouring away a pocket of rickety properties which had become an eye sore." Burns briefed Hynes on Pru's decentralization program and disclosed that the big insurance company was eyeing northeastern cities for another branch. This was the lightbulb moment for Hynes: "There popped into my mind a vision of a Prudential Building on the Boston and Albany land in Boston."[22]

Hynes was not the only one who saw great possibilities for the rail yard site. Not long after Hynes met with Burns, George Oakes, a leading Boston real estate man, bounded into the mayor's office on his own initiative with designs on the site. Oakes had persuaded the railroad to grant him an option to buy the land for $4.5 million and he wanted to broker a deal on the site. But first Oakes wanted the mayor's blessing in the form of a tax concession: a guarantee that the value of the property would not be assessed higher than the sales price, a necessary assurance for any potential financier. "This was a fly in the ointment," Hynes grimaced. The mayor asked Oakes if he had any connections to Prudential. Oakes knew the New York developer Roger Stevens, who had recently brokered the sale of the Empire State Building with Prudential money, and agreed to approach Stevens with the rail yard project. Stevens did have useful connections to Prudential — he was "known and respected by the Prudential officials," Hynes recalled — and the ambitious developer was enticed by the prospects of a large-scale urban redevelopment project. Stevens was nominated to pick up the option on the Boston and Albany land so as to make a direct overture to Prudential. Thus, the "courtship" between Boston and Prudential began: the former seeking to land an extraordinarily wealthy investor and the latter coveting a deep tax concession.[23]

Stevens and Oakes did not wait for Prudential's commitment to begin planning for the expansive rail yard site. The developer and the realtor recognized that the parcel offered a rare occasion to radically reconceive a large swath of urban land in the most modern, progressive terms. Stevens approached some of Boston's most distinguished urban planners, architects, and consultants to consider the program and spatial possibilities of a unified development on the site. Stevens contacted Walter Bogner, an architect and professor at Harvard, to help assemble a team to work on what was called the "Back Bay Center." The team, which called itself the Boston Center Architects (BCA), brought together luminaries from the local academic establishment, including Walter Gropius, then sixty-nine years old and a former dean of Harvard's Graduate School of Design; members of Gropius's firm, The Architects Collaborative (TAC); Pietro Belluschi, the Italian-born modernist who was dean of the architecture school at the Massachusetts Institute of Technology; and Hugh Stubbins and Carl Koch, eminent designers who had trained at Harvard with Gropius. Stevens commissioned a prolific New Haven–based traffic consultant, Wilbur Smith, to prepare a transportation plan, and hired Kenneth Welch to perform an economic analysis that gauged the market draw for what was projected to be a new midtown business district.[24]

It is possible that over the course of these preparations, Roger Stevens was acting as Prudential's clandestine real estate agent in the northeast. As we have seen, Prudential executives frequently worked through agents to mask their interest in urban real estate.[25] It is also possible that Stevens, with the aid of George Oakes, acted independently and was actively recruiting any number of possible investors. Certainly Stevens did not at first reveal the name of a client to his team of architects and planners, though Walter Bogner recognized that this group was likely designing an office tower for an insurance company — the type of institution with the financial wherewithal to consider such an ambitious project.[26] In 1954, the BCA plan for the Back Bay Center was published to great fanfare in the architectural press. Many of the basic concepts of this design — the "ring road," parking garage, unifying plinth across the site, and the program of a central office tower, hotel, residential towers, commercial blocks, and public spaces — would characterize the eventual design of the Prudential Center. The Boston Center Architects were not ultimately chosen to see the project through, but the developer Stevens clearly sought to elaborate and publicize an appealing vision for the Back Bay rail yard site that might entice potential investors.

In the fall of 1953, Stevens arranged a meeting in Newark between Mayor Hynes and Carrol Shanks. In fact, the meeting was more like a job interview, with "Boston," hat in hand, appealing to "The Boss," comfortably ensconced in his office. Prudential was slow to commit to a Northeastern Home Office project in Boston because of what Hynes himself called "the immovable tax hurdle." It was "all too clear that no development worth its salt would or could happen unless capital investors could be certain that they would not be victims of a tax monster with a voracious appetite."[27] The situation looked bleak in 1954. The railroad had stopped using the yards. Prudential was ambivalent and no other investor had stepped forward. In 1955, the New York Central's boss, Robert Young, pushed to close out Roger Stevens's option to buy the land. To the railroad executive, Stevens was sitting on a gold mine but unable to attract finance capital. Young's move forced the waffling Prudential to call his bluff. Unwilling to foreclose on a unique urban development opportunity, Prudential underwrote the option on behalf of Stevens. In 1956, Stevens assigned his rights to Prudential. At the start of the next year, on January 22, 1957, the insurance company formally purchased the 28.5-acre lot in the Back Bay for $5 million. When Prudential publicly announced its plans to build the Prudential Center on the Boston and Albany rail yards at an estimated cost of at least $100 million, the tax issue remained unresolved. At the January 31, 1957, press conference, Hynes made clear that Prudential had not been promised a real estate tax concession from the city. "Prudential pays its way everywhere it goes," the mayor said.[28] But he suggested that perhaps it was time for Boston to reconsider its tax policies, which were driving investment away to other cities.

TOWARD A TAX CONCESSION

Between 1953 and 1957, George Oakes — the realtor who shared credit for conceiving the Prudential Center — and John Hynes cultivated local support for the controversial Prudential project. Not everyone in Boston was thrilled by the possibility of a large new office and commercial district in the Back Bay. Downtown business leaders and property owners had several concerns. Prudential would insist on a significant tax abatement from the city, which seemed unfair to those property owners already burdened with high tax bills. Moreover, the Back Bay development threatened the spatial integrity, and thus land values, in the central business district; Prudential Center represented an instant "midtown" district that could favorably compete with downtown. Furthermore, Prudential Center's up-to-date office facilities were likely to lure tenants from existing buildings. More broadly, Prudential signified an unfamiliar and vastly powerful source of corporate wealth and influence that unsettled Boston's cloistered business community. Oakes and Hynes curried favor with local leaders, including heads of labor unions and members of the influential Catholic clergy, to soothe apprehensions and frame Prudential's investment as a boon to the city's collective economic fortune.[29]

On Prudential's side, Carrol Shanks delegated the task of considering Boston for the Northeastern Home Office to two of his executive vice presidents: Valentine Howell and Fred Smith. Howell managed the project from Newark; but Smith, who eventually relocated to Boston, was the more closely involved in Prudential's intricate negotiations in Boston. Smith's top priority was to resolve the taxation issue with the city. A secondary issue involved the Massachusetts Turnpike Authority, which wanted to be certain that Prudential's plans would not interfere with its own intention to construct the Pike's Boston Extension along the right-of-way of the Boston and Albany rail corridor. The fates of the Pru and the Pike were closely intertwined. In this chapter, we will see how Prudential's insistence on a tax concession shaped the course of urban redevelopment in Boston; in the next we focus on the pairing of the Prudential Center and the turnpike extension into Boston as an important part of the political process that allowed the Prudential project to succeed.

Informal Agreements

William F. Callahan, head of the Turnpike Authority, had eyed the Boston and Albany right-of-way as the most efficient route for an urban extension of the statewide turnpike since planning for the project began in 1952. In 1955, on Callahan's urging, the state legislature amended the turnpike's charter to authorize the extension, and the chief quickly moved to annex the Boston and Albany property. This move alarmed Prudential, which was actively considering a large project in the Back Bay. The company eventually negotiated an agreement that guaranteed the Pike an easement through the site for the Boston Extension and two railroad lines that were projected to remain in operation (as described in more detail in the next chapter). Prudential was satisfied with this accommodation, and Hynes had dodged a bullet.

The turnpike issue was only the first of Prudential's key concerns. It was Fred Smith's job to convince city administrators that the public benefits of the Prudential Center justified a major tax concession — specifically, freezing the tax assessment of the property for a period of years. In 1958, Prudential produced a pamphlet that introduced the Prudential Center in grand terms and outlined the case for a tax concession. It was "the most immense construction project ever attempted by Prudential. The most important single civic project in the history of Boston. And the largest enterprise of its kind in the country." Moreover, planning for the turnpike easement introduced costly engineering difficulties to an already expensive project. "The engineering's problems can be resolved: But even Prudential's resources are not large enough to contemplate taxation at Boston's present and probable levels." Prudential believed that the proposed development was important enough to Boston to justify "a very favorable — even unreasonable — concession." The insurance company was willing to accept an informal agreement with the city, trusting that future administrations would honor the plan. This was a risk: "The basis of this hazard, we realize, is pressure from other taxpayers who may choose to ignore the civic aspects of this project." For this reason, Prudential had not asked for an "unreasonable" concession, merely a fair one that would hold up in the future.[30]

The basis of this request was that the Prudential Center was a civic enterprise, a claim embedded in the urban design of the project itself. Prudential was paying for public space, including plazas and new roads. As Prudential put it, "At least one-third of the total cost is chargeable to civic improvement." Only twenty-five percent of the land would be used for revenue-producing buildings, with the remaining seventy-five percent developed as a landscaped park or used for transportation facilities and parking "to relieve local traffic." Prudential Center's site and scale were intertwined with broader infrastructural improvements to the city, including the road and rail easements, a ring road that circumnavigated the site, and the long-term integrity of the foundations themselves, which would be built on a nineteenth-century landfill with a high water table. The costs of these "civic requirements" were so high that "the true economic value of this development reflects only a small part of the actual cost." Both the City of Boston as well as Prudential would have to compromise: the former on tax receipts, the latter on profits.[31]

Equipped with this pamphlet, Fred Smith met with the key players — including John Hynes (his presence an indication of the high priority that the mayor placed on the project), members of the city's Board of Assessors, and representatives of the Massachusetts Turnpike Authority — on March 18, 1958. Smith stressed the "extra values" that Prudential's investment would bring to the city, including the enhancement of nearby property values. Smith also asserted that a project of the quality that Prudential intended to build — something "as attractive as possible" — would cost fifty percent more than a conventional or "utilitarian" facility on the same acreage. Prudential's designers and engineers had devised a method to mitigate local traffic impacts by encircling the site with a ring road, an added investment that was framed as a public improvement. Prudential was willing to engage in a very expensive undertaking on a site with innate difficulties — the easement and costly foundation work — and in one fell swoop transform an unpleasant and economically unproductive rail yard into a gleaming new multipurpose urban district. Prudential would construct a massive steel and concrete substructure to house a parking garage and allow transportation facilities to pass underneath. The technical imperative of a unified substructure and base emphasized the utility of maintaining the project under single ownership and management, as opposed to speculating on the site or selling off smaller parcels in an ad hoc fashion. Mayor Hynes judged the unified, planned quality of Prudential's proposal as an inherent advantage over piecemeal development.[32]

Fred Smith argued that a standard tax arrangement, one determined as a proportion of the assessed value of the property, was unfair to Prudential because it ignored the positive external impacts implied by a development of this size, expense, and distinction. Smith proposed an income-based approach to Prudential's property taxes and requested an assurance that the tax would not exceed twenty percent of gross revenues for a period of ten years after the completion of construction, to be followed by a mutual reassessment of the situation. Prudential estimated a total income of $15 million and agreed to pay $3 million a year in taxes. But Prudential needed time to get its feet on the ground and therefore requested a fixed, escalating land tax for the anticipated seven years of construction. Hynes and his assessors provided their informal consent to this proposal and the assembled participants signed a memorandum confirming this understanding. "It was fully understood at the meeting that this kind of agreement . . . would have no legal or binding validity," Hynes recalled. "Despite this awkward contingency, the Prudential was willing to accept the agreement in the belief that it would be officially honored by any future city administration."[33] In the early spring of 1959 the contractors drove the first of 144 steel and concrete caissons into the bedrock 145 feet beneath the rail yard site.

"Less Lofty Reasons": Local Resistance to a Tax Deal

Even as work on the foundation commenced, a dismayed subset of local businessmen cried foul and threatened to challenge Prudential's informal tax agreement in court. "There were those who believed that the concord was in contravention of constitutional principles and, for less lofty reasons, believed that the Prudential should be granted no tax incentives of whatever kind," Hynes later recalled.[34] There was good reason to suppose that the unofficial pact between Boston and Prudential would not hold up in court. In fact, Prudential's 1958 agreement was a reprise of an equivalent effort from three years earlier, when John Hynes sought legislative approval for a tax concession for the identical site. The direct recipient would have been Roger Stevens, who represented the Back Bay Center, but the benefits would have applied to any developer. State lawmakers drafted a bill that asserted the public's interest to develop a large project on the Boston and Albany rail yard. The proposed law was based on the premise that the prevailing tax structure made it unlikely that private capital would develop the site on its own and that the yard would degrade into "an area of economic blight and a potential breeding place for criminal and juvenile delinquency and will therefore adversely affect the value of adjacent properties." Without tax relief, lawmakers assumed, private enterprise could not afford to "undertake orderly and integrated development." The orderly, integrated, and thus *planned* nature of a proposed project was instrumental to establishing its public purpose, for "the public interest requires development in accordance with a broad plan, including transportation connections, a street system, parks, parking facilities, and a convention hall or civic auditorium." These provisions amounted to a set of "public purposes" that made special tax treatment both "desirable and necessary."[35] The legislative act authorized a "Back Bay Development Commission" to acquire the land through eminent domain. The commission was responsible for generating an overall plan and guaranteed that the private developer would execute the public uses indicated in the plan. As was common practice with constitutionally suspect new laws, the state senate submitted the bill to the Supreme Judicial Court of Massachusetts for review in 1955.[36]

To the immense satisfaction of local business interests who opposed this isolated tax dispensation, the court rejected the bill. Political scientist Cynthia Horan explains the court's rationale: "Unlike the legislature, the court did not view the project as generating significant benefits for the city, but rather concluded that the promotion of economic growth through a tax concession to a private company merely furthered private profits, not the public interest, and was thus not a suitable basis for a tax concession."[37] In its advisory opinion, the state's highest court held that a tax deal did not meet the constitutional requirement of "proportional and reasonable" assessments because the law charged the corporation "less than its share of the public expense."[38] Other taxpayers had to pay taxes each year on the full value of their property, notwithstanding income or profit. Why should a singular corporation be treated differently? The court rejected the legislature's articulation of the public interest.

The state's proposed Back Bay Development Commission was an early model of an urban redevelopment agency designed to implement a "public purpose" by facilitating the development of blighted land. In its 1955 ruling, however, the Supreme Judicial Court opposed public subsidies for private development: "Public money cannot be used for the primary purpose of acquiring either by eminent domain or by purchase private lands to be turned over or sold to private persons for private use." This was true even if the private developer planned to include a variety of public uses, such as open, landscaped plazas. Moreover, the court was unwilling to concede that the rail yard was blighted or had become a slum. "There is only an apprehension lest it become one," the court held. Declining property values did not, in themselves, define a blighted area. The possibility of an *indirect* public benefit by virtue of an increase in the value of adjacent taxable property also failed to qualify as a "public purpose." The court suggested that less direct means to facilitate development of the site, such as amending zoning and building regulations, might be acceptable, but a tax concession for a private developer was not.[39] Given this opinion, the tax question hung over the Prudential project like a low-hanging cloud: why should the company's tax agreement of 1958 be treated any differently by the courts?

If some opponents of a tax concession for Prudential genuinely believed that such an allowance for a wealthy private corporation did not represent sound public policy, those harboring "less lofty reasons" were more concerned with protecting their own financial interests against the threat of the Prudential Center. The Back Bay site was only one mile west of the central business district, but it was considered foreign turf to downtown property owners. Historian Thomas O'Connor explains this attitude: "Downtown businessmen and financiers feared that this new-fangled development was simply one more move that would only add to the frightening stampede already drawing too many paying customers out of the central city and into the suburbs."[40] When disgruntled downtown boosters threatened to challenge the eventual tax agreement in court in 1959, a wary Prudential halted construction until a more secure tax arrangement could be secured.

In 1953, when George Oakes and Roger Stevens approached Prudential with the notion of developing in the Back Bay, the Boston and Albany rail yard site appealed to the company's strategists like Westcott Toole and Valentine Howell. The parcel satisfied every principle that Prudential had established for an ideal RHO site. The rail yards were located in the city — affirming the company's commitment to urban real estate — but the site comprised a vast area that Prudential could control and plan as a unified district. "We immediately saw the potential advantages of the property," Toole told a gathering of the Massachusetts Savings Bank Association in 1957. A tall building on the site could be framed to command views and would function as an architectural landmark. The visual prominence of an attractive tower generated the "extra dividends" of advertising and public relations value that Toole championed. The site was accessible, too. It was well served by mass transportation facilities, including subways, streetcars, buses, and commuter rail. "Equal in importance to mass transportation is private transportation," Toole added. Prudential's location at the western fringe of the city was poised to intercept downtown-heading traffic along major arterial streets, like Huntington Avenue. Reversing his colleague Valentine Howell's earlier assessment, Toole said that a highway connection would be favorable, though not essential: "Should the proposed toll road and other highway facilities now under consideration by the Turnpike Authority go through, they will certainly add to the locational advantages of the site."[41]

Toole would have bristled at any suggestion that the Prudential Center portended a flight to the suburbs. In his view, Prudential's administrative decentralization was an expression of his company's faith in cities, including Boston. He sought to reassure local business leaders of this fact in his 1957 talk. First Toole explained Prudential's desire to choose "dramatic and strategic" locations for its RHOs. He also emphasized "that in no case have we gone outside the city limits for a site for one of our regional home offices. The Prudential believes strongly in the future of the downtown city."[42] Yet Toole may have made the downtown Boston bankers even more nervous when he extolled the virtues of Prudential's Back Bay location, accentuating the fact that the proposed Prudential Center marked an independent business district with distinct advantages over the downtown area. Toole's vision of the future center city was very different from the one shared by Boston's established business interests.

This pointed to the paradox of Prudential's "city-within-a-city" in Boston. On the one hand, the complex was its own, self-sufficient midtown business district. And yet Toole claimed that an urban location was an advantage for a company like Prudential: "Among the reasons for this are the good labor markets which the cities provide and the accessibility to banks, other financial institutions, legal firms, advertising agencies and business libraries. In addition, there is the availability of specialized business training for adults, good stores, good hotels and recreation facilities."[43] For Toole, Prudential's Back Bay site *was* a part of Boston's downtown business district. It was certainly *within* the city, as opposed to a suburban location. But to Bostonians, the Back Bay was a very different place from the central business district. Toole's broad perspective on Boston's urban geography conflicted with the local vision, which saw quite clearly the subtle, micro-geographical differences within city limits.

Merger: The Pike and the Pru

Fred Smith of Prudential recognized that some Bostonians were restive about the tax agreement he had reached with Mayor Hynes and that real estate interests were organizing to thwart the plan. "Some Boston groups wanted Prudential to restrict the height of its main office tower to only 26 stories, and to promise that no recruiting for office space in it would be sought among Boston commercial tenants in other buildings," the *Globe* reported. Meanwhile, Prudential executives wanted a secure tax deal with legislative backing. Lacking that, Smith asserted, they were prepared to "pack up and get out."[44] But in 1960 a new plan emerged that conjoined the Prudential Center with the Boston Extension of the Massachusetts Turnpike that promised to satisfy the Pru's concerns.

By the spring of 1960, William F. Callahan had shrewdly come to see the Prudential project as the vehicle through which he might promote his own highway plans to the City of Boston. And so Callahan recommended talks with Fred Smith over the future of the Prudential Center site. Eager to formally link his turnpike extension with the development of the Prudential Center, Callahan proposed that the Turnpike Authority claim the entire site through its power of eminent domain and lease the air rights to Prudential. The theory was that the Pike, a tax-exempt entity, would own the property, thus protecting Prudential from real estate taxes. This solution appealed to Prudential, which had not reached a binding tax agreement with the city on its own. An internal Turnpike Authority memorandum prepared for Callahan on April 9, 1960, discussed the negotiations between the Pike and Prudential. It alluded to several uncertain issues relating to the management of the Prudential Center, which would legally be owned by the Turnpike Authority. Who would control the garage and public plazas? Who would be responsible for policing the site? Furthermore, the most important issue was still in question: "Can the Authority indemnify the Prudential against the imposition of local real estate taxes?"[45] The Pike and the Pru were entering uncharted legislative waters, but they were willing to give them a try.

On April 29, 1960, the *Boston Globe* stretched an eight-column headline across the front page that hailed a "Merger of Toll Road–Prudential Center Planned in $300 Million Package Deal," accompanied by a photograph of the deal's brokers: William F. Callahan; Louis R. Menagh, Jr., executive vice president at Prudential who had assumed the helm of the Northeastern Home Office; the state attorney general, Edward J. McCormack; Prudential's Fred Smith; Governor Foster Furcolo; and Mayor John Collins. Under this arrangement, the Turnpike Authority would annex the B&A rail yard and construct the Boston extension along the rail bed from Route 128 to the Central Artery. At the rail yard, the Pike would build a vast three-level underground garage for twenty-five hundred cars, plus an interchange with access ramps from the highway to the garage just east of the site near Copley Square. The Pike would lease the air rights to Prudential, which would build the Prudential Center on a platform above the garage, though the Pike would technically hold title to the buildings. The Turnpike Authority's status as a public corporation made the entire project tax exempt, and the Pru was sheltered by the Pike's sponsorship. The Pike agreed to pay the city $3 million a year in lieu of taxes — the same arrangement, rejected by the state supreme court, that Prudential had made with the city in 1958. The garage was used as the legal basis for the project's constitutional standing, fulfilling the requirement of "public necessity" by reducing traffic congestion.[46]

Three hundred Boston businessmen gathered at the Sheraton Plaza Hotel to learn that a special law had been drafted to achieve this result, and the Supreme Judicial Court would again be asked to weigh in on its constitutionality. Should the court approve, construction on the merged project would begin immediately. The *Globe* further reported that Prudential had agreed to buy a significant portion of the bonds that would finance the extension. In a calculated, magnanimous gesture, Prudential also announced a $250,000 gift to the city toward the construction of the municipal auditorium. But there was an important proviso: "Unless the legislative and court roadblocks are successfully overcome, the conference was warned, Prudential will pull out." A labor union official and board member of the recently formed Boston Redevelopment Authority, Stephen McCloskey, voiced his concern that Prudential might renege and leave the city with a "30-acre parking space." Attorney General McCormack also noted that losing Prudential would mark a major "psychological blow" to the city. But Prudential's Fred Smith reassured the audience that the company was eager to proceed and hoped this resolution would stick.[47]

With the Turnpike Authority as the lead sponsor, the charge of establishing the merged project's public purpose now fell principally on the urban highway itself. By claiming jurisdiction over the site, Callahan also steered the project toward his allies, including the governor, a Democrat. On May 2, 1960, Foster Furcolo issued a letter to the state legislature in support of the turnpike's plan to annex the rail yard. The governor declared that the Boston Extension was in the public interest because it would "greatly relieve the pressing demands for increased traffic facilities and promote the health, safety and general welfare of the public."[48] Garage and truck terminal facilities were essential to the turnpike's utility and would be built in conjunction with a looping interchange — the "Prudential-Garage Interchange" — planned for an adjacent parcel east of the Prudential site. These facilities were necessary for "limiting traffic hazards and handicaps and relieving congestion on public streets."[49] But the garage would be expensive, and the Turnpike Authority had an obligation to develop income-producing properties in the parcel's air rights to generate an additional form of revenue, to supplement user fees (tolls), to guarantee its bond commitments. (Conversely, this novel revenue stream would also help market turnpike bonds.) Furcolo reported that Prudential had agreed to the turnpike's plan and he was introducing a bill — drafted by his attorney general, Edward McCormack — to the legislature that would permit the construction of both the garage and the Prudential Center. "The bill contains tax exemption and indemnity provisions which are necessary to assure the development of areas above the garage by private capital," he explained to lawmakers. Neither the Turnpike Authority nor its chief tenant (Prudential) would pay taxes on the project, nor should they be expected to do so, the governor insisted. Together, the Pike and the

Pru "will be in all respects for the benefit of the people of the commonwealth, for the increase of their commerce and prosperity, and for the improvement of their health and living conditions." In light of these public benefits, additional taxation was unwarranted. Governor Furcolo resolved to make the bill an "Emergency Act," effective immediately on his signature.[50]

It appeared that the Pike had guaranteed the Pru for Boston by generating a creative solution to the tax question. But the Supreme Judicial Court of Massachusetts quashed the deal. In an advisory opinion, the court stated that such an arrangement would be unconstitutional. While the Turnpike Authority might have special status as a tax-exempt public service corporation, the Prudential did not and could not acquire such status merely through the protective aura of the Pike. The court allowed that the turnpike extension along with the garage and truck terminal might well serve a public purpose. But the Prudential Center would surely exacerbate precisely those negative traffic conditions that these features were designed to ameliorate. The judges immediately understood that the proposed law before them was a direct response to "financial problems in respect of the so called 'Prudential center,' now under construction in the Back Bay section of Boston." The primary purpose of the new law remained a tax cut for a private enterprise, like the rejected 1955 bill for a tax concession on the rail yard site. The only difference was that in the new bill the Massachusetts Turnpike Authority was substituted for the Back Bay Development Commission.[51]

But even as they turned their thumbs down on the proposed law, the justices pointed to a way forward for the Prudential Center by alluding to a 1956 advisory opinion they had issued that recognized that the "problems of urban planning, development and renewal are increasingly in the area of public interests" and that "new forms for public participation in their solution may be within constitutional limits."[52] The court elaborated the concept of an urban redevelopment corporation, which, although technically a private enterprise, was an "instrument of the commonwealth" that performed public functions: "Urban redevelopment corporations, although in a sense private corporations, perform functions for the public benefit analogous to those performed by various other types of corporations commonly called public service corporations, property owned by them and used in such service may receive favored treatment in the matter of taxation."[53] The Supreme Judicial Court had thus suggested a way in which private interests, acting as quasi-public urban redevelopers, could propose projects that warranted tax concessions, so long as the proposed project was subject to some form of public oversight. To follow through on this suggestion, the state had to reexamine its urban redevelopment law, Chapter 121A, originally chartered in 1945.

Prudential as an Urban Redevelopment Corporation

Beginning in the 1940s, several states enacted urban redevelopment laws in order to subsidize the private rebuilding of blighted urban areas, the elimination of which was considered by the state to be a public purpose. These statutes made available to private developers the state's privilege of eminent domain to acquire, clear, and market large tracts of land. The developers were also given financial incentives to play a role in slum clearance. In Massachusetts, the state legislature enacted a slum clearance and redevelopment statute, Chapter 121A of the Massachusetts General Laws, in 1945. Chapter 121A granted tax exemptions to private redevelopers proposing "primarily residential" projects. Massachusetts was one of several states to enact a redevelopment law in advance of the federal Housing Act of 1949, which opened federal coffers to local states that initiated redevelopment programs. Chapter 121A entrusted the function of public oversight to the state housing board or the individual city's housing authority — in Boston's case, the Boston Housing Authority, which had been established in 1935. The law was amended in 1953 and again in 1954 to elaborate on the undesirable conditions — including "substandard," "decadent," and "blighted" open areas — that justified acquisition and clearance by the BHA.[54]

In the aftermath of the court-rejected "merger" of the Pike and the Pru, Attorney General McCormack took up the task of amending Chapter 121A with the specific intention of facilitating a tax break for Prudential. This required two feats of creative legal rhetoric: extending the definition of "blight" to include the Boston and Albany rail yard site, and expanding the spectrum of allowable redevelopment projects to include commercial and other uses outside of the "primarily residential" clause. The result was Chapter 652 of the Acts of 1960. In its first section, the new law broadly redefined the type of project allowable under redevelopment law: "'Project' [means] any undertaking consisting of the construction in a blighted open, decadent or sub-standard area of decent, safe and sanitary residential, commercial, industrial, institutional, recreational or governmental buildings and such appurtenant or incidental facilities as shall be in the public interest."[55] The new law consolidated the administration of urban redevelopment under the newly formed Boston Redevelopment Authority, which would be responsible for assessing the public's interest in a proposed project. The redevelopment authority subsumed the functions of the BHA, acknowledging the importance of a coordinated program of urban modernization. The law also provided that an "Urban Redevelopment Corporation" embarking on such a redevelopment project would be eligible for a forty-year tax exemption. Chapter 121A specified payments in lieu of taxes to the municipality, including an income-based excise tax that amounted to five percent of a project's gross income, and an additional annual one percent tax on the assessed value of the land and buildings. Because Chapter 121A redevelopers would be "limited dividend" corporations, they were allowed no more than a six percent return on investment, with any surplus returned to the city.[56] The effect of the new law was to eliminate almost all property taxes and substitute for them the income-based approach championed by Prudential.

In Chapter 121A, the state proclaimed the public's interest in alleviating a broadly defined group of social and physical circumstances, including "blighted open, decadent or sub-standard" areas. The key term was a "blighted open area," which was defined as "a predominantly open area which is detrimental to the safety, health, morals, welfare or sound growth of a community because it is unduly costly to develop it soundly through the ordinary operations of private enterprise."[57] Blight implied a constellation of negative social conditions, but its essential quality was that it was expensive to remedy. For example, arduous physical conditions such as the existence of ledge, rock, or unsuitable soil that might make redevelopment expensive contributed to blight. Another factor, which was spelled out in the 1960 amendment to Chapter 121A, was unusual expense "incident to building around or over rights of way through the area." This language, of course, was tailor-made for the situation of Prudential's Back Bay rail yard site. The 1960 act also specifically declared that no project could interfere with an extension of the Massachusetts Turnpike into the city of Boston, a clear reference to the Prudential Center situation. The act specified that "inappropriate or otherwise faulty platting or subdivision" and "diversity of ownership of plots" were also elements of blight that could make "unduly costly . . . the ordinary operations of private enterprise."[58] The act thus reflected a preference for large-scale land assemblage that superseded prior property divisions.

A "decadent" area, according to the act, was likewise a threat to the safety, health, morals, welfare, and sound growth of the urban community, but focused more on the physical decline of an urban locale. Decadent areas harbored buildings that were "out of repair, physically deteriorated, unfit for human habitation, or obsolete." Real estate in decadent areas could be seized for the nonpayment of taxes or mortgage foreclosure. Decadent areas were seen as deserving special attention not only because of inadequate air, or open space, but also because "diversity of ownership, irregular lot sizes or obsolete street patterns make it improbable that the area will be redeveloped by the ordinary operations of private enterprise." Echoing a concept from the description of a "blighted open area," the law favored physical redevelopment at a grand scale — not piecemeal improvements by individual property owners — and advanced a vision of large tracts developed under single owners with relatively sparse land coverage. The definition of a "sub-standard" area overtly addressed housing conditions and inveighed against "dilapidation, overcrowding, faulty arrangement or design, lack of ventilation, light, or sanitation facilities."[59] These ominous urban districts were not only economic liabilities but also breeding grounds for health problems and social malaise, and the state had every reason to facilitate private redevelopment that promised to redress these liabilities.[60]

The press immediately understood the direct purpose of the new redevelopment statute, and began calling it the "Prudential Bill." As one journalist wrote, the statute promised to enable the project to move forward unhindered: "The same building plans will be followed. The same tax payments will be made to the city. The same route will be followed by the Massachusetts Turnpike Authority for its toll road extension — tunneling underneath the Prudential Center and into the heart of the city."[61] Senate president John Powers pushed for the swift passage of the bill and Mayor John Collins organized a rally to support it, featuring a talk from Mayor Burns of Jacksonville on the positive impacts of the Prudential project in his city. But not all legislators favored the bill, fearing that it cut too broad a swath for future tax breaks to commercial developments. One legislator remarked, "It would mark a major step in the ever-widening interpretation of what constitutes the 'public interest' — broadening it to include commercial projects even though no slum clearance is directly involved."[62] Once again, the legislature submitted the statute to the Supreme Judicial Court for an advisory opinion. This time, the court approved the amended redevelopment law. An editorial in the *Christian Science Monitor* announced: "In an advisory opinion that was both meticulous and broad, the Massachusetts Supreme Judicial Court has told the Legislature that its second attempt to define the big civic project as a 'public purpose' eligible for special tax treatment is constitutional."[63]

The court decided that a project's public purpose was not compromised merely because most of the buildings that would be constructed there would not be dwellings. The court located the public interest principally in eliminating blight, not in the specific program for future development on the site: "There is no constitutional requirement that a blight, for example, if removed in the course of urban redevelopment, particularly if it is found to be one not about to be eliminated by private capital, must be replaced by residential buildings." The court was satisfied with the law's delegation of administrative oversight and public regulation to the Boston Redevelopment Authority, which would bear the ultimate responsibility for guaranteeing the public benefit of the project. In all, the court was sympathetic to Prudential's plans for the rail yard site: "If the Prudential center again is used as an example, there are many public advantages to be considered. These would include the elimination of grave doubts as to the future use of a great area, now largely vacant or occupied by a nearly obsolete, unsightly, railroad freight yard; covering over a railroad right of way; improvement to neighboring properties; the encouragement of prompt action unlikely to be undertaken by private enterprise in the foreseeable future; stimulation of other building and opening a new opportunity for urban growth at what might be a time which is appropriate but of short duration; and new facilities made available to public use."[64]

In its 1955 opinion, the court had not been convinced that the Back Bay rail yard constituted a blighted open area. But circumstances had changed. When it looked at the Prudential project as an example, the court noted that the Boston and Albany Railroad had been eliminating service and that an idle site at the rail yard lay in the path of the growth of the city.

LIGHTING THE FUSE:
PRUDENTIAL AND URBAN RENEWAL IN BOSTON

With the consent of the court, the Massachusetts Legislature was ready to act on the "Prudential Bill" in late August 1960. The new law promised to jump-start the Prudential Center as well as a host of other urban renewal projects administered by the Boston Redevelopment Authority. Michael Liuzzi of the *Christian Science Monitor* grouped the Prudential Center with the plans for a new Government Center downtown: "The Massachusetts Legislature is on the verge of enacting new laws which should nail down the two great centers around which Boston is rebuilding — the Prudential center in the Back Bay and the government center due to stretch down from Beacon Hill across Scollay Square."[65]

According to the *Monitor,* the new law had lit a fuse for the rebuilding of Boston, which would begin to take on a new character as a modern office center: "The Boston labor force is moving steadily toward a predominance of clerks and typists, engineers and secretaries, researchers and financial specialists, technicians of all kinds." This new employment structure also implied big physical changes to the city, which needed extensive modernization: "Grimy red-brick structures of five or six stories, built before 1900, are spread over 36 per cent of the 'central business district,' according to Boston City Hall figures. A change was due, and the change will probably be drastic. The fact is, Boston has been taking on a new character for several years now — which is only just beginning to show up in the new facades and a changing skyline."[66] The new character of the city would be heading upward, literally, in a series of new skyscrapers. The most significant new office structures being planned in the central business district were the ones that would house government activities.

A Tale of Two Centers

The Prudential Bill represented an upheaval in established development politics, giving the Boston Redevelopment Authority (BRA) a larger role than urban development agencies had ever had in the past. In recognition of this increased importance, the legislature passed an auxiliary measure that extended the terms of membership of the BRA for five years. At the same time, state lawmakers were considering a bill that authorized the construction of a state office building at the proposed Government Center in Scollay Square. The Prudential Center and Government Center, both under the auspices of the BRA, had been joined in public and political consciousness.[67] On September 2, 1960, the *Christian Science Monitor* reported that the "light is green for Hub centers," with the Prudential Center now worth $150 million and the Government Center weighing in at $100 million. Later that month John Collins announced the city's commitment to a $90 million redevelopment plan, with the Government Center at its core.[68]

Despite the buoying news of the new redevelopment law, all was not well at the Prudential Center site. On August 24, 1960, Prudential had turned off the dewatering pumps at the Back Bay construction site, flooding the recently completed concrete foundation poured over the steel pilings. The press dubbed it the "Prudential Lake," Boston's newest body of water (fig. 27).[69] Prudential officials insisted that they had flooded the site to prevent the erosion of the foundations. That may have been true, but the Prudential Lake was a sign that the court's advisory opinion and the imminent state legislation were only the first steps in a long process. Prudential was unwilling at

PRUDENTIAL CENTER
Boston, Mass.
Date 4/16/62 Photo No. 9

Figure 27 The Prudential Center site flooded, 1962, following the shutdown of the water pumps in 1960. Buildings on Huntington Avenue line the left side of the picture. (Courtesy of the Tutor-Perini Corporation)

that time to move briskly forward with construction until its proposed development was formally approved by the Boston Redevelopment Authority. Flooding the site may also have been a strategic move to create an atmosphere of urgency around the project.

Speaking for the Public

In early September 1960 the governor of Massachusetts signed the new piece of redevelopment legislation, and the acting chairman of the BRA urged Prudential to promptly submit its application to develop the Back Bay rail yards "in conformance with the provisions of Chapter 121A."[70] In January 1961, Prudential formally submitted its application, tailored to the language of the amended bill. Prudential made the case that its project area, the rail yard site, constituted a blighted open area, "unduly costly to develop . . . soundly through the ordinary operations of private enterprise," and described in detail the precarious physical conditions that impeded redevelopment of the Back Bay site. The application asserted the extreme expense of engineering any type of construction on the geologically unstable site. The entire Back Bay district, including the rail yard, was filled on a marshy swamp with a dangerously shallow water table. Prudential proposed to construct a coffer dam around the site to maintain the integrity of the wood pilings that supported most of the other buildings in the Back Bay and would sink steel and concrete foundation caissons 145 feet deep into the bedrock. (Some of this work had already been executed by Prudential.) An additional obstacle was the provision for a railroad and highway easement that diagonally split the site. Prudential proposed the construction of a large, substructural cage that housed the easement, capped with a plaza that covered most of the project area. The sum of these factors, the application argued, made a compelling case for Prudential's unified, integrated proposal and that the "coordinated architectural and engineering planning for the construction of all improvements therein be undertaken at one and the same time."[71]

In its function as the public sponsor of the Prudential project, the BRA held a public meeting to review Prudential's application on March 22, 1961. The meeting was essentially a public confirmation of the Prudential Center by a long list of boosters. The transcript of the meeting reveals a theatrical recitation of the merits of the Prudential Center, with little evidence of genuine public participation. Nine illustrious Bostonians appeared before the BRA, an ensemble of business and political luminaries, to advocate the project and urge its swift development. Prudential also produced thirteen "expert" witnesses on behalf of the project, including its architectural designers, engineers, and an array of city planners and consultants from around the country. Only six citizens of Boston spoke in opposition to Prudential Center, with varying degrees of influence and persuasiveness. Overseeing this highly stacked hearing was the appointed chairman of the BRA, Monsignor Francis J. Lally, a close aide to Boston's influential Cardinal Richard Cushing. The assignment of Lally to the unsalaried chairmanship of the redevelopment authority was a clear nod to the influence of the Catholic Church in Boston. Lally was, in essence, a political figure — but he endowed the authority and its public meetings with an aura of religious sanctity.[72]

Attorney General McCormack announced the support of state government behind the Prudential project and reminded the audience that the Supreme Judicial Court had already sanctioned this avenue of urban redevelopment. He explained that it was now the BRA's job to serve as the authority that ruled on the public benefits of the Prudential Center and to determine if the project area indeed constituted "a predominantly open area which is detrimental to the safety, health, morals, welfare or sound growth of a community because it is unduly costly to develop it soundly through the ordinary operations of private enterprise." Many of the statements were short and forceful. Governor John Volpe urged the board to endorse "the greatest proposed development in Boston's history. . . . This mammoth building and development project means a rebirth for Boston and the State." He called it a "shot in the arm for the Massachusetts economy." State senator John Powers, a frequent candidate for mayor of Boston, offered the backing of the entire legislature and urged the project's swift approval. Powers mused on the difficulties of urban development in Boston, which seemed to be more extreme than in other places: "Will somebody start building? . . . Let's get this thing on the road, please," he exhorted the BRA board. Powers was surprised by the relatively sparse turnout for the public meeting — not to oppose the project but to celebrate it. He thought that many thousands of people should have paraded to the hearing in a righteous outcry to advance the Prudential Center project: "Here is the most important thing that happened in my time, or, Monsignor, in your time," Powers asserted. "Let's start to build and put people to work and rehabilitate this city. I say that to your Board and everybody concerned. We are not going to be charged with irresponsibility or dragging our heels. This is a non partisan matter; this is the future of this city. We can't afford to lose it."[73]

Prudential's lawyer, Henry H. Meyer, introduced several officials from the company, starting with S. Westcott Toole. Toole explained that Boston was an obvious choice for Prudential's NEHO; the challenge was finding a site that allowed for a "large building such as the Prudential constructs." In the past, Prudential had to assemble smaller sites to form a large one, making the preassembled site of the rail yard parcel in the Back Bay particularly enticing: "It was large enough for us to do something really dramatic which would revitalize the entire city."[74] Prudential's in-house engineer, Alfred Linkletter, who was the executive general manager of the home office buildings and plant department, spoke about the physical challenges of developing the site, and outlined in detail the "complex subterranean soil conditions" on the site that had necessitated expensive testing and foundation work.

The architect Charles Stanton represented Charles Luckman Associates, the lead architects for the project. The architectural firm had "advised Prudential that only an overall and integrated development should be considered for highest and best utilization of land vs. any piecemeal approach to development," Stanton explained. To further its overall plan, Prudential had acquired the Mechanics Building — an adjacent parcel — "to guarantee long-range values" of the site. This integrated approach required covering the tunnel that would house the transportation easement with a "slab" or "lid" to level the building plane: "It created a base from which the superstructures could rise and on which pedestrians could circulate easily and safely." This tactic also allowed for the construction of a garage, "so necessary to any urban project today." Prudential had forfeited additional building space to design a ring road around the site to mitigate traffic congestion, which Stanton believed was "mandatory in the interest of sound long-range planning." In Stanton's narrative, the conditions of the parcel triggered architectural reactions, and the overall design emerged as the result of an in-depth analysis of the site. His testimony rationalized Prudential's proposal as a logical, master planning solution, not an idiosyncratic or ideological design.[75]

After presenting the physical details of their proposed project, Prudential officials paraded before the BRA an impressive group of real estate and city planning experts. These witnesses were Prudential's way of reminding the local audience of the extraordinary opportunity represented by this proposed investment in Boston. Though Prudential appeared before the BRA as a supplicant, perhaps some Bostonians did not realize that the city needed Prudential more than Prudential needed Boston. Henry Meyer first introduced Joseph Skinner, a Boston real estate appraiser who presented a detailed assessment of Prudential's project area. Skinner offered a broad historical overview of the Back Bay rail yard site, explaining how it had been formed between two intersecting railroad viaducts in the 1830s. In Skinner's view, this inauspicious founding had set a negative course for what became a blighted area. The area had become a "no man's land" between the Back Bay district and the South End, halting the westward expansion of the Back Bay at Copley Square. Skinner felt that only the integrated Prudential project could turn the area around.[76]

Charles Blessing, the director of planning for Detroit, who had studied architecture, planning, and civil engineering at MIT, also spoke out against redeveloping on a small scale and situated the Prudential Center in broader urban trends. Cities across the nation had "begun to recognize the fallacy of proceeding on a piecemeal, haphazard, narrow approach to their eventual renewal." Blessing directed urban renewal projects in Detroit and advocated a broad, comprehensive approach under the auspices of a singular redevelopment authority. Blessing was confident in the "soundness of the concept of a continuing partnership of public and private initiative in the rebuilding of a great city."[77] And Theodore Hazlett, the general counsel for the Urban Redevelopment Authority of Pittsburgh, likened Prudential's project to the Gateway Project in his city, financed by the Equitable Life Assurance Society. In both cases, a large insurance company had stepped in to redevelop derelict railroad facilities and correct their adverse affects on the expanding business district.

Henry Meyer also called on James Downs, the founder and chairman of the Chicago-based Board of Real Estate Research Corporation, to testify on Prudential's behalf. Downs's firm had produced a study of the rail yard site for Prudential: "When we were asked to examine the potentials of the Back Bay Yards in 1956, I must say for the City and community of Boston, in all truth, that I saw here a much more impressive opportunity than I did for the Prudential." Cities competed with one another to attract "vital job-giving facilities," Downs explained, and had to advance proactive policies to entice investors, including tax incentives: "It more than justifies the use of public powers which are here envisaged — not to serve a vested interest, but to bring economic dynamism and security to the people who make up this urban area." Between them, Prudential's guest witnesses articulated a national consensus behind the basic precepts of urban renewal — public subsidy of private development for the greater good — and chastened Bostonians to consider themselves lucky to have drawn Prudential's interest.[78]

Those citizens who raised objections to Prudential's application did not contest the project itself, but lamented its association with the Massachusetts Turnpike Authority's plans to construct a Boston Extension along the B&A railbed. These opponents were placed in an awkward position of having to resist the Prudential Center in order to stop the road. The first of these speakers was Daniel Rudsten, a former state senator from Boston and general chairman of the Massachusetts Citizens Committee, a group organized to resist the turnpike extension. Rudsten assured the hearing that he was "for the Prudential Center," but he and his committee could not stomach the highway that had been coordinated with it. "I, myself, and this group which I represent are vitally and vigorously opposed to the 8-lane toll road that is coming into the Prudential Development and under it, and that is designed to branch out into Copley Square with cloverleafs and ramps. We feel that is the most irresponsible kind of city planning in the world. No City Planner of any intelligence will condone it." Good transportation planning, Rudsten believed, would adhere to the Master Highway Plan of 1948, in which a Western Expressway would extend from Route 128 only as far as an Inner Belt. Rudsten saw this matter as a question of *urbanism* — the confluence of the city's social and physical qualities — and feared the reconstruction of Boston as a bland suburb: "The thing we must ask ourselves — and you, yourselves — is, what kind of a City are we building for Boston's future? Are we building a suburban shopping center with a lot of automobiles, or building a city of people who are working and playing together, of the homes and shops and business firms of industry, of theater and restaurants and playgrounds and esplanade concerts. Is not this the kind of a city we want, or are we just going to build a monstrous or monolith of buildings and surrounded with an 8-lane toll road that will be like a moat with the rest of Boston becoming a village, deteriorating around the back of it." The new toll road would bring so many cars into Boston that they would never be able to build enough parking spaces for them, until "no more cars would come to Boston because there would not be enough left of Boston to come to." For Rudsten, the turnpike extension was an affront to sensible city planning, and he bemoaned the fact that Callahan had managed to intertwine the two projects.[79]

But Rudsten recognized the awkward implications of his position: "It has gotten to a point where anyone who resists this type of planning has been put in a position of being against Prudential — we are not. We want the Prudential, but want it with sensible planning." He had solicited a letter from the newly elected president of Prudential on the question of the highway, and Louis Menagh had responded: "During the recent highway discussions we attempted to make it absolutely clear that the Prudential has taken no position whatever in what kind of a road goes through our area or whether there is any road at all. We are obligated to provide the easement to the Turnpike Authority. . . . Our position was merely that before proceeding with our Development we had to know what was going to happen." As was their policy, Prudential executives distanced themselves from the internal wrangling of Boston's particular political battles. For his part, Rudsten offered to take the issue directly to the citizens of Boston: "I call to your attention, I offered to have my Committee support and take an impartial poll of the people of Greater Boston — two million of them — to verify my charge that 99 per cent of them want the Prudential but do not want an 8-lane toll road into the center of town," a comment which drew applause from the audience. The redevelopment authority board patiently tolerated Rudsten's comments, but James G. Colbert of the board stressed the fact that the question of highway planning was "not within our province."[80]

Lawrence Ryan, an attorney for the Massachusetts Turnpike Authority, spoke after Rudsten, and hoped to disarm the former senator's comments. He explained that engineers from the turnpike and Prudential had worked for many months to integrate their plans. "I am amazed at the position taken by the previous speaker, because any change at this eleventh hour in those plans of the Prudential would, for example, nullify this hearing." But the BRA board was unwilling to engage in a debate over the turnpike extension. James Colbert cut Ryan short: "You know we have no control over where the highway goes, so why don't you confine yourself to this Application." Monsignor Lally, the chairman, chimed in: "Stick to the issues, please, Mr. Ryan."[81]

But the questions of the Pike and the Pru were not as distinct as the BRA might have imagined. Herbert Gleason, an attorney and member of the Ward Five Democratic Committee in Boston, read a statement from the committee that expressed its support for the Prudential Center. But he did not stop there: "The Committee also wishes to record its profound regret, however, that the Center has become tied in with the extension of the Massachusetts Turnpike beyond the proposed Inner Belt in Brighton. While favoring a freeway over a toll road from Weston to Brighton, the Committee takes particular issue with the extension of a huge private traffic facility into the heart of the already congested downtown area. Representing as we do so many people whose comfort and property will be demolished by the toll road, we must protest this sacrifice of the welfare of the city to private interests."[82] The private interests in this case were not Prudential's, but the Turnpike Authority's. Gleason believed that the railroad right-of-way should be preserved for transit facilities. Rudsten, Ryan, and Gleason each recognized what the BRA board was unwilling to admit: that the Prudential Center and the turnpike extension had become a singular piece of urban infrastructure, and approving the former almost certainly sanctioned the latter.

Other members of the audience at the public hearing intuitively grasped this as well. An unnamed man, late to the meeting, spoke up from the floor:

(FROM THE FLOOR:) Mr. Chairman, I am speaking against the land taking.

THE CHAIRMAN: Are you speaking in favor of the Application?

(FROM THE FLOOR:) I just got in here. I am for the Prudential but I am not for this indiscriminately taking land property, and my property is on the route of which the land-taking is supposed to be.

THE CHAIRMAN: On the Prudential site?

(FROM THE FLOOR:) No, but it's on the line, on Mountfort Street.

THE CHAIRMAN: That is not the issue. Before us is the Prudential Application. We are not able to hear anything on that question; we are here to discuss the Prudential site. We are not here for taking or redistricting, like Stuart Street and Copley Square. That will be heard at another time.

(FROM THE FLOOR:) Can we be heard? I am a property owner. Can we be heard?[83]

Robert Knowles, another Boston resident, likewise did not want to impede the Prudential Center but objected to the turnpike ramps projected for the eastern side of the structure. He felt that the looping ramps would destroy the Copley Square area. "Why couldn't these ramps that are going into the Prudential be eliminated?" he asked. Chairman Lally would not entertain this question: "The ramps of the toll road are not under our jurisdiction at all. That is the Mass. Turnpike Authority and they will have to make a decision on that."[84]

A somewhat eccentric view came from Mrs. Dwight Strong, who objected to the Prudential Center on philosophical terms: "I sit here now registering disapproval of the Prudential project in view of the fact that it is quite apparent to me that it is a monolithic example of materialism." But the most eloquent opponent, willing to attack the Prudential Center on its own terms, was Joseph Lee, a prominent Beacon Hill patrician and member of the Boston School Committee. Lee systematically rebutted the claim that Prudential's application to redevelop the rail yard could be justified under the definition of "blight" as defined in Chapter 121A. Lee insisted that the area under consideration was not, in fact, "detrimental to the safety, health, morals, welfare or sound growth of the community."[85] Lee rejected Prudential's claim on each of these points:

Is the area detrimental to safety? No. Well, is it detrimental to health — will it disease people? No. Is it detrimental to morals — a lot of criminals living out that way? No. Is it detrimental to the welfare of the community? No. The welfare of the Commonwealth is not the slightest bit injured by this open area. On the contrary this area has given a house-jammed, traffic-jammed city a little respite from congestion. Can you find the area detrimental to the sound growth of the community? No. The area has aided in the sound growth of the community; that is pretty well shown by a great metropolis which has grown up around that area, a metropolis of some three million in the last three hundred years, which doesn't seem to be very detrimental to sound growth.[86]

If the technical challenges of building on the Back Bay site made this area too expensive for private enterprise to develop, Lee argued, it followed that the same could be said for nearly every inch of Boston, much of which was also built on nineteenth-century landfill. Never before were special concessions necessary to cultivate private investment; why should the city start now? In this manner, Lee rejected the very premise of Chapter 121A.

The most biting criticism came from a citizen named William P. Foley, who attacked the nature of the hearing itself and called it out as a sham. "This is not a citizen participation public hearing," he argued; "this is a newspaper participation public hearing. This is not a vested interest citizen participation public hearing. This is a public hearing where financial interests have established a public hearing to conform with a law that was to benefit people in this type of government. . . . The Constitution states clearly that no one should be allowed to establish a kingdom. This is becoming a kingdom." But

Foley was stifled by the presence on the board of Monsignor Lally, for his allegiance to the church conflicted with his opposition to Prudential: "I am telling you in my way, in a public way, how this Prudential is affecting me. I do not like to discuss this matter and have to clash in a heated argument with a member of the Clergy. I prefer that a member of the Clergy were not sitting on that Board and that these people here have something to do with the church." But Foley could not contain himself: "The Prudential is receiving unfair and unnatural tax concession. I used the word 'unnatural,' again, because it establishes a kingdom." Foley may have damaged his credibility by his whimsical reference to a "kingdom," yet he rightly recognized what the BRA board was unwilling to discuss: that the Prudential Center project was linked with the turnpike extension and thus implied an auxiliary set of land takings that threatened local property owners. The board insisted that Foley and others confine their comments to the Prudential Center project, which few wanted to resist.[87]

A Final Legal Test

In November 1961, Prudential orchestrated a "friendly" court test of the project's viability under the new urban redevelopment law. This test case, *Dodge v. Prudential*, served as the company's final legal assurance before moving forward with the Prudential Center. The case tested the legitimacy of a contract between Prudential and one of the Prudential Center's principal tenants, the New England Merchants Bank of Boston, which planned to establish its main offices in the Prudential Center. Robert Dodge was a partner in the Boston law firm of Palmer, Dodge, Gardner and Bradford. Dodge was appointed by Prudential to serve as an agent to hold the leases made between Prudential and the bank. His court petition "seeks to ascertain whether or not the project has advanced to such a state as to warrant the agents turning these leases over to the Prudential Company." The lawsuit was a formality, though it did reassert the principles behind Chapter 121A; if the individual lease was legitimate, it would imply "a sufficiently dominant public purpose in the entire project to protect it from being declared illegal in a subsequent suit."[88] The court ruled affirmatively in December 1961, validating the lease between Prudential and the New England Merchants Bank, and, thus, the terms of the urban renewal contract between Prudential and the City of Boston. "This was the 'last green light' everyone had been waiting for," the *Christian Science Monitor* reported.[89] But it was a premature valedictory. In fact, the public meeting held in 1961, which so clearly demonstrated resistance to the Boston Extension of the turnpike if not to the development of the Prudential Center itself, foreshadowed additional travails as the Prudential waited for the Massachusetts Turnpike Authority to resolve its own struggles to carry out its plans for a highway connection to Boston.

Chapter 4

A Closed Loop
The Pike and the Pru

Workers from the Perini Corporation pour cement on the reinforced decking for the Boston Extension of the Mass Pike, ca. 1964. The just completed Prudential Tower is visible in the background.

At first, the Pike and the Pru were rivals. Each prized a piece of Boston's deteriorating rail infrastructure as the armature for modernization and development. The Boston and Albany Railroad provided a convenient right-of-way for the Pike's Boston Extension. The railroad's path cut across a thirty-acre switching and storage yard that Prudential wanted for its Northeastern Home Office development. It seemed like the two projects were mutually exclusive. But the two parties eventually came to see the utility of teaming up and plotted a joint venture that linked the highway and the Prudential Center. This way, the Prudential was guaranteed swift automotive access to its site and the Pike could bind its project to the Prudential Center, which in turn was tied to the city's hopes for an economic revival. What began as a rivalry evolved into a mutually contingent partnership in which the success of one insured the other.

As built, the Pike and the Pru formed a massive urban interchange: a looping exit ramp from the Boston Extension delivered cars to a three-level parking garage that formed the base of the Prudential Center. The unified spatial logic of the Pike and the Pru mirrored the railroad system it replaced: just as tracks led to a yard, so too must the urban highway lead to a central depository, the parking garage. But the coordination between the Pike and the Pru encompassed more than physical and even political aspects. In 1962, with the Pike struggling to raise money, Prudential pledged to purchase a quarter of the $180 million bond issue that financed the construction of the turnpike extension.

Chapter 3 reviewed the ways that Prudential influenced Boston's local redevelopment policies. The insurance company secured a tax break because the Prudential Center was viewed as a legitimate expression of the public interest. Like Prudential, the Turnpike Authority positioned its project as a manifestation of the public interest to bolster the future of Boston. This chapter discusses the history and politics of the Pike and its Boston Extension, the difficult choices and conflicts that it faced at the end of the 1950s, and how the balance between clashing interest groups was finally tipped by an outside influence: the Prudential Insurance Company and the forces of urban development that it brought with it.

PLANNING A NEW ROAD

In the spring of 1957, the main line of the Massachusetts Turnpike opened: 123 miles of limited-access superhighway that ran from the New York border to the outskirts of Boston. To celebrate the event, and to promote the continuation of the highway building project, the Perini Corporation — one of the Pike's main contractors — produced a cartoon on the back page of its quarterly *Perini News,* a magazine circulated internally and in the road building and civil engineering communities (fig. 28). In the cartoon, a "Turnpike Pilgrim" galloping down the Pike must rear his horse to a halt at the Route 128 beltway, where the highway's path abruptly ends. The Pilgrim's progress is impeded by the urban density that lies before him. The Pilgrim is not alone. On both highways, cars are marooned in gridlock, their drivers cursing and honking in desperation. One driver speculates: "Maybe they use helicopters from here — er sumpin." The Pilgrim himself is sweating with exasperation. His thought bubble displays a vision of the Massachusetts State House, that iconic "hub of the solar system," as dubbed by Oliver Wendell Holmes, which represented the ultimate central city destination. How could the Pilgrim reach the object of his desire? In fact, he didn't have to look far for inspiration — the answer was in plain view. The cartoonist has clearly rendered the passage cut by the Boston and Albany Railroad. The road to Boston was endowed with a ready-made right-of-way.

The text of the cartoon intoned: "Some folks know more than others where, when and how to build a road. How, when and where to now?" This question alluded to the well-known views of the chairman of the Massachusetts Turnpike, William F. Callahan. At the dedication ceremonies, Callahan declared that the turnpike "will not be completed until we take it into downtown Boston. It will be the salvation of Boston. My intention is to do everything within my power to bring this road into downtown Boston."[1]

As early as 1953 Callahan and his team of consulting engineers had identified the Boston and Albany right-of-way as the path of least resistance to the central city. Moreover, the junction of the Pike's main line and the metropolitan beltway, Route 128, had purposefully been designed to enable this future alignment. But Callahan's plan to

Figure 28 Illustration from the back page of the *Perini News*, Spring 1957 (Courtesy of the Tutor-Perini Corporation)

extend the Pike along the B&A route into Boston had become controversial. He and other turnpike advocates faced a series of obstacles: first, from the Prudential Insurance Company, which sought to claim a piece of the B&A infrastructure for its own purposes; second, from advocates of a freeway system that contested Callahan's stranglehold on road-building politics; and, third, from suburban politicians who resented the imposition of the turnpike through their towns. To understand how the Pike reached its crisis point in the late 1950s, we need to examine its political and organizational underpinnings — the public authority model that it adapted, the place of Callahan and the Turnpike Authority in Massachusetts political culture, and the relationship between road building and urban development.

The Public Authority Model

In 1952, just five years before the Mass Pike opened, the Massachusetts legislature chartered a new body, the Massachusetts Turnpike Authority, to construct a road from the state's western border with New York to a point "in the vicinity" of Boston. Toll roads had been common institutions in the early American republic. The Pennsylvania Turnpike, entered into service in 1940, revived the idea of using turnpikes to provide for statewide transportation needs modeled on the limited-access parkway, such as the Henry Hudson Parkway, which opened in 1934 along New York's west side. In the postwar era politicians and highway planners returned to the concept of an independent turnpike authority as an efficient institutional arrangement for building roads that the state could not otherwise afford. The idea for the Turnpike Authority came from William F. Callahan, who was already the chairman of the Department of Public Works and had many friends in the legislature. The Turnpike Authority, whose chairmanship Callahan promptly assumed, consolidated his control over the road-building enterprise in Massachusetts.[2]

The Turnpike Authority was modeled on "public benefit corporations" like the Port Authority of New York and the Triborough Bridge and Tunnel Authority, which sought to organize and modernize a region's transportation and port infrastructures. These authorities were given broad legal powers and proprietary funding sources, such as the right to float revenue bonds and collect tolls, to finance large-scale projects that were intended to support the economic growth of the city and the region as a whole. The public authority model was an institutional innovation that could be applied to the challenges of providing transportation, infrastructure, and housing. These projects required huge capital investments that the private sector could not, or would not, make on its own. The public authority model also crystallized the tension between rational planning, which looked at the region's infrastructure in theoretically objective terms, and the supposedly corrupt practices of the political establishment.

Turnpike authorities, organized by states, were one form of public benefit corporation intended to build the infrastructure for the modern metropolis.[3]

Although they were chartered by the state — and thus creations of a political system — public authorities of the Port Authority type were ideally insulated from political meddling. Transportation specialist and toll road advocate Charles Dearing explained in 1961 that public authorities were created to remedy the shortcomings of government. Special authorities were "created to compensate for the failure of the conventional and established forms of administrative organization, procedure, and finance, to satisfy 'effective' demand for the provision of public services such as roads, bridges, tunnels, and airports."[4] In the 1940s and early 1950s, many highway planners supported the public authority model of financing, planning, and constructing major road projects in the form of turnpikes. With a seemingly limitless demand for new roads but uneven sources of government funding, the turnpikes promised quick financing on the bond market. Although bodies like the Port Authority and the Triborough Bridge Authority were characterized as "public" or "quasi-public" corporations and drew political strength through legislative backing, they were in fact very closely linked to private financing by virtue of the bond market. Turnpike authorities marketed bonds, backed by the promise of future toll revenue, to private and institutional investors, suggesting that turnpikes were market-driven inventions that had to sell their future success based on traffic demand.

Not all turnpikes were created equal, however. A turnpike's success relied on the other pieces of transportation infrastructure that would feed the road and the popularity of the destinations it connected. The New Jersey Turnpike, completed in 1951, was an extremely successful operation because it connected key pieces of the regional transportation network. "Don't ever confuse the New Jersey Turnpike with any other toll road," warned Paul Troast, chairman of the New Jersey Turnpike Authority. "There is no other toll road that lies between the first and third largest cities in the country; there is no other toll road that could be projected that is fed by such facilities as the George Washington Bridge, the Holland Tunnel, the Lincoln Tunnel, the Pulaski Skyway, Newark Airport, our own Edison Bridge to the shore, Burlington–Bristol, Tacony–Palmyra, Camden–Philadelphia Bridges, and the Delaware Memorial Bridge."[5] These comments had important implications for planning the Massachusetts Turnpike. Like New Jersey's Troast, the Massachusetts Turnpike Authority's Callahan envisioned the Pike as knitting together a set of existing and proposed transportation assets. These included the Central Artery through downtown Boston, in construction by 1952; the Sumner Tunnel, which further connected the Central Artery to East Boston and Logan Airport; and Route 128 with its budding technology industries. Interstate connections between turnpikes were also crucial. At its western terminus, the Pike was designed to connect with the New York State Thruway — also financed with toll revenues — ultimately linking

Massachusetts by express highway all the way to Chicago and beyond. Each additional link enhanced the strength of the system as a whole, and turnpike planners believed that an urban extension of the Pike to Boston would exponentially amplify the utility of the system.

Unlike a toll bridge or tunnel, which was often an unavoidable funnel for traffic, a toll road did not monopolize the market for roads. Indeed, when the New Jersey Turnpike was being planned, Governor Alfred E. Driscoll promised that the turnpike would always be paralleled by other, toll-free roads and that these free facilities would be improved constantly. To advance in this competition, Troast formed a public information department and launched an aggressive press campaign that "dramatized our every act. . . . It was one of the most successful programs of public relations ever undertaken, as is witnessed by our first full month of operation."[6] He argued that demand for a turnpike could be produced through advertising and public awareness. The Massachusetts Turnpike Authority followed suit by establishing its own public relations department that issued a nearly constant flow of press releases and eventually produced several short television films about the Pike.

The Massachusetts Turnpike Authority: An Expanding Kingdom

The New Jersey governor's guarantee to his constituents that free roads would not be abandoned was also a pledge to his political allies. Leaders of state highway-building agencies viewed toll roads as competitors. Turnpikes bypassed the conventional circuits of highway financing and thus threatened the authority of state public works agencies. Toll road advocates like Charles Dearing defended turnpike-style financing, however, because it accelerated the capitalization of the road-building enterprise without the racket of political patronage or dependence on public highway funds. Bond-revenue financing could "get the roads built quickly where needed on the basis of traffic demand, and . . . the users are willing to pay in tolls for having these facilities available today rather than ten years hence."[7] Turnpike authorities appealed to Dearing because they were designed as temporary agencies that performed a specific job before they were retired and their assets subsumed into the state bureaucracy. The story of the Mass Pike and its chairman, William Callahan, however, calls into question the supposed advantages of a politically insulated and thus rational planning organization. In fact, the Turnpike Authority was a highly politicized road-building agency led by an idiosyncratic and powerful leader.

When the Massachusetts legislature chartered the Turnpike Authority in 1952, the intent was to create such a temporary, "self-limiting" authority. The enabling legislation, Chapter 354 of the Acts of 1952, charged the Turnpike Authority with providing for the "construction, maintenance, repair and operation of a self-liquidating express highway." The charter permitted the new public authority to issue bonds, charge tolls, and use eminent domain to acquire land, rights of way, and easements for the road.

The law's intent was to entrust the management of the highway to an independent agency, free of the constraints of state government, until the road was completed and its bonds retired. In an effort to insulate the Turnpike Authority from political pressures, Chapter 354 established eight-year terms for the authority's three board members, who were appointed by the governor and had to represent both political parties. But the charter had a "sunset clause": once the road was built and the bonds were retired, it specified, the authority would transfer ownership of its facilities to the state.[8]

In 1991, the Massachusetts office of the inspector general, led by Robert Cerasoli, issued a vitriolic report that claimed the Turnpike Authority had "lost sight" of the original intent to limit the agency's life span: "As this Report shows, the Authority does not wish to understand, and has no commitment to deal with, the original intent of its enabling legislation."[9] In fact, just the opposite occurred. William Callahan's vision for the Pike exceeded its original constraints, for he was not satisfied merely to build the road stipulated in the 1952 charter. The authority consistently sought to expand its portfolio of transportation assets, to issue new bonds and extend its indebtedness, and, in general, to preserve its institutional longevity.

A critical step toward increasing the scope of the Mass Pike was Callahan's effort to construct an extension of the highway from Route 128 to the heart of Boston. Callahan vigorously lobbied the state legislature for the legal right to build the extension. He was gratified in 1955, when the legislature enacted Chapter 47 of the Acts of 1955. This statute amended Chapter 354, which authorized the authority to build and operate a toll "from a point in the vicinity of the city of Boston," by adding, after the word "Boston," this clause: "or from point or points *within* said city."[10] This simple addendum was enough authority for Callahan to begin planning what was soon called the Boston Extension. But that was not all. In 1958, the legislature authorized the Turnpike Authority to acquire the Sumner Tunnel, which connected Boston to East Boston and Logan Airport, and to construct a second Boston Harbor tunnel, to be named the Callahan Tunnel (after William F. Callahan's son, Lieutenant William F. Callahan, Jr., who was killed in World War II). In 1963, the legislature passed Chapter 505, again amending Chapter 354 to allow the authority to lease air rights for development over the Boston Extension. All of these new legislative acts expanded the scope of Turnpike Authority operations and created an insular network controlled by that body. And while none of them preempted the "sunset clause" specified in the original charter, the turnpike's horizon line seemed to fade unceasingly into the future.

Chairman Callahan: "He Gets Things Done"

In his study of the Port Authority of New York, Jameson Doig stressed the importance of examining individual leadership in analyzing the workings of large, bureaucratic institutions. Bureaucracies cultivated a collective culture within an expansive hierarchy of decision makers, but the motivations of individual leaders could have a great impact on this culture. This observation is true in the case of William F. Callahan and the Massachusetts Turnpike Authority.[11]

When he became the Turnpike Authority's first chief executive in 1952, Callahan already had a wealth of experience developing infrastructure and building roads. A self-taught engineer, Callahan ran a dredging company in the 1920s and later owned a marine-engineering firm that specialized in the construction of dry-docks and port facilities. In 1934, Governor Joseph Buell Ely appointed Callahan as an associate commissioner of the Massachusetts Department of Public Works. In 1936, Ely's successor, James Michael Curley, promoted Callahan to be chief of the department. Callahan quickly recognized that DPW appointments were vulnerable to political trends. His tenure at the department was based on the ascendancy of the Irish-Democratic political machine. When the Republican Yankee blueblood Leverett Saltonstall won the governorship in 1939, Callahan was dismissed and replaced by a future rival, John Volpe.[12] During wartime, Callahan returned to the private sector to build dry-docks and other marine projects around the world. But he was restored to the chairmanship of the DPW in 1949 when Democrat Paul Dever became governor, and he held the position until 1953 when he resigned to focus his energy on the newly founded Turnpike Authority.

Callahan was a statewide political figure, supported by a broad network of Massachusetts lawmakers. *New York Times* reporter Anthony Lewis wrote in a profile of him in 1965: "The bond of affection between the Legislature and Mr. Callahan is one of the phenomena of Massachusetts politics. . . . Along with the motto 'He gets things done,' a popular saying is that 'He's never lost a vote in the Legislature.'" In 1951 a Republican legislator said Mr. Callahan was "more powerful than any elected official in the state." Callahan's cozy relationship with state representatives was not surprising. The road builder was in a position to award many millions of dollars in construction contracts and to make decisions about the routes of important new highways. What rural Massachusetts representative did not want his town connected by a glittering new highway? What politician did not have his own list of preferred contractors to support with no-bid contracts? The prospect of such hefty patronage was more than enough to cultivate the affections of state legislators. Lewis estimated that over his long career in the DPW and with the Turnpike Authority, Callahan had nearly $1 billion in public funds to dispense, which amounted to a "club of patronage."[13]

There were those who felt that Callahan's cult of personality transcended both the DPW and the Turnpike Authority. He ran a secretive institution outside of legislative purview. Anthony Lewis noted that "the legislation creating the Turnpike Authority does not allow any state official to look at the Turnpike's books, and the Legislature has ignored suggestions that it give the state auditor access to them. Nor does the Turnpike legislation require competitive bidding on authority contracts."[14] In 1960, Callahan was implicated in a bribery scandal. The prosecutor, Elliot Richardson, attacked his undue influence in the state's political culture.

> The most dangerous aspect of Callahan's operations is simply his attitude. . . . He's a master at manipulating the machinery of government — jobs, pressures, patronage, fund-raising for the Democratic party. It's as if he were saying, "Look, I didn't invent this system. My concern is building roads. To do that, I have to try to get through the clumsy constitutional machinery of the Commonwealth. I came up through a school that taught me how to win friends and influence people and I've played the game harder and better than anyone else." At some point, however, society pays too high a price for results. The ultimate effect of accumulated obligations is to get in the way of the state's legislators. Their obligations to Callahan are greater than to the public."[15]

There was a broader issue at stake that transcended individual scandals. To whom did Callahan answer? How much graft could be justified in the name of achievements for the public's use? Was Callahan merely playing the game of political patronage for the sake of the people? And could this be achieved despite his ability to corrupt the politicians who sustained his empire?

When Callahan was called to stand trial for corruption, the prosecutors accused him of running an idiosyncratic agency where great wealth was mediated by personal and political contacts. One example that came to light was the fact that Lou Perini, who owned the large construction company that built the Prudential Center and many sections of the Pike, was related to Callahan through his daughter's marriage. A reporter noted Callahan's simple response to these accusations: "He has never denied that, whenever the circumstances properly permit, he throws business to his friends. 'Would anyone expect me to give it to my enemies?' he asks."[16]

Callahan justified his actions and dismissed his critics. "Some people like to climb over your back politically. You've got to have critics. But usually they're people who haven't accomplished anything in their lives. I call them grocery-store philosophers, pen pushers." These were among his favorite pejorative terms, which Callahan used frequently for whoever stood in his way. The pen pushers and grocery-store philosophers were linked in his mind with do-nothing city planners who fussed over ideal schemes without achieving concrete results. Callahan insisted that his highway plans were devised by expert engineers who responded to hard data. He prided himself as a hard-charging builder who could get the job done. "There is a certain pride in building bridges, building roads," Callahan said. "One thing in life — I want to finish some of these jobs. Then I don't care."[17]

Some of his contemporaries paired Callahan with New York's "Master Builder," Robert Moses, who was also seen as dictatorial. Like Moses, Callahan obtained different state appointments that augmented his power base. In 1958 he was made chairman of the Massachusetts Parking Authority, which was then planning the $9 million garage under the Boston Common (itself a controversial project). Callahan also headed the three-member commission in charge of erecting the state office building at Government Center, the centerpiece of Boston's urban renewal initiatives. But more than any other part of his portfolio, the Turnpike Authority gave Callahan a political and financial base that allowed him to sidestep the ordinary democratic processes of taxation and budgeting.

Roads and Development

Callahan believed that the Pike was essential to Boston and New England's economy. This belief was based in large measure on his experience with another groundbreaking road project, Route 128. In his 1930s stewardship of the DPW, Callahan helped conceive the circumferential highway that was at first dubbed by critics the "Road to Oblivion" or "Callahan's folly."[18] Critics could not comprehend the utility of a road that ran in an arc — approximately twelve miles from Boston at any given point through the largely undeveloped countryside — without connecting any meaningful destinations. Construction on the road began in 1936 but stalled during World War II. The road gave an impression of a "make work" project during the Depression, a convenient way to distribute monies and give people jobs. But the road was also groundbreaking in terms of its style and engineering standards. Using an older two-lane state highway as its guide, Route 128 was designed as a multi-lane limited-access expressway with looping interchanges and a landscaped mall dividing traffic. Only eight miles had been constructed by 1947, when several bond issues and hefty state appropriations accelerated the project. Callahan made the road a priority when he rejoined the DPW in 1949, and the beltway opened in 1952.

One function of Route 128 was to serve as a grand bypass around Boston that would allow a driver to travel from Providence to Portland without facing downtown traffic. But in addition to providing such a bypass, the road would become the region's most important armature for land development in the 1950s. In 1955, *Business Week* lauded Route 128 as "a classic example of how a new road can change the traffic pattern of a metropolitan area — and completely remake the face of the landscape around it."[19] By making suburban tracts more accessible to cars and trucks, Route 128 unearthed the latent demand for industrial and commercial space on land abutting the "super-road" and facilitated the development of residential property in towns near the road. The well-established real estate company Cabot, Cabot, and Forbes developed many of the industrial tracts near Route 128's suburban interchanges. This included building low-slung, horizontal campuses for a growing electronics and aero-space sector, which had been incubated at the Massachusetts Institute of Technology and spawned in nineteenth-century red-brick lofts, warehouses, and garages in Cambridge. In 1956, *Architectural Forum,* reporting on Boston's development prospects, wrote that manufacturers were moving to these new industrial parks, "following the new highway system as industry followed rivers and railroads a century ago."[20]

In May 1954, the Turnpike Authority successfully marketed $239 million in revenue bonds to cover the costs of constructing the Pike. In November of that year, the *Christian Science Monitor* excitedly reported Callahan's expectation that "rich trea-sures of vast industrial expansion and increased tourist trade will be tapped when Massachusetts completes its 123-mile toll road from Greater Boston to the New York state line." Construction on the new "highspeed, limited-access highway" was set to begin, and the *Monitor* reporter looked back to "Callahan's folly" as a positive indicator: "If the experience of the new Route 128 is borne out by the toll road, hundreds of millions in new industrial development will spring up in the vicinity of the turnpike." Route 128 had opened up a crescent of Boston's outskirts as an attractive industrial location and vastly increased land values in the area. Before work on the turnpike had even begun, property near its fourteen planned interchanges had already increased in value. Callahan also predicted that the Pike, a crucial link in a broader network of state turnpikes and highways, would augment New England's truck-oriented trade. The Pike would bring "Massachusetts hours closer to the Midwest markets, as it will connect with a spur of the New York Thruway." Callahan also saw the Pike playing an important role in New England's tourist economy, evoking the notion of pleasure driving that was a key element of 1920s parkway planning. In particular, the Mass Pike would open up the scenic Berkshire Mountains to visitors from eastern Massachusetts.[21]

To carry out the Turnpike project, Callahan drafted many of his key aides from the state's Department of Public Works, including its former chief engineer, Philip H. Kitfield. Kitfield and Callahan collaborated to design the ultra-modern highway: "Into the road is built every possible safety device to make the road safe for 70-mile-an-hour speed. To combat driver fatigue, the road is being varied through gentle curves, through the separated opposing lanes of traffic sometimes being so widely separated that drivers traveling in opposite directions will not see one another. At other points, the opposing traffic lane will be separated only by a wide grass plot." Many of the Pike's key attributes — a designated right-of-way, the elimination of intersections, limited access at curving on- and off-ramps, and a protected view corridor — were pioneered more than thirty years earlier with the Bronx River Parkway, completed in 1923, and the Henry Hudson Parkway. These roads aimed to tame the automobile in a parklike setting. But the scale and engineering standards (such as turning radii) of those roads were antique compared with the Mass Pike, which was designed to carry freight traffic. Kitfield and his team built the highway to allow easy grades, a feature especially important to truck drivers. "Heavy trucks will be able to travel from one end of the toll road to the other without shifting gears even in the Berkshire Hills area."[22] To ensure the unimpeded flow of traffic, they located toll plazas off the main road at each of the fourteen interchanges, with the exception of the western and eastern termini. At the toll plazas, motorists entering the turnpike receive a ticket that they surrender upon exiting, paying to a uniformed attendant a cash toll based on the number of miles traveled. The highway opened on May 15, 1957, with a three-hour complimentary period in the afternoon, allowing a long queue of curious drivers, including many trucks, to experience the road before attendants began collecting tolls. The early results were positive, and toll attendants reported heavy use of the new road, including many drivers from nearby states.[23]

THE BOSTON EXTENSION

Callahan always intended to extend the turnpike to Boston, and he believed that the city's economic future depended on the Pike's ability to bring both goods and people in and out of the city. Route 128 and the mainline of the Pike had opened up suburban areas to industrial development and were important arteries for truck-based freight. Certainly these trucks needed to access Boston. However, Callahan also believed that the future of Boston as a commercial center would turn on the positioning of the Pike as a method of daily commuting into the heart of the city. For example, he pointed to Boston's languishing retail establishments: "I suggest a survey be made to see how many stores have had to reorganize or have wound up in financial trouble in the last five years."[24] These stores were struggling, Callahan believed, because they were no longer accessible to suburban consumers, who preferred large shopping centers with ample parking.

There were critics who charged that Callahan's efforts to construct the turnpike extension represented a significant expansion of his dominion. The turnpike, extension, Central Artery, and harbor tunnels would all be linked in a single system controlled by one man. But Callahan insisted that his interest in the Boston Extension was a magnanimous effort to revive the city's economy, not driven by personal political ambition. "It will not make any difference to me, personally, whether there is ever a road built into Boston and I am not interested in the politics." But the gruff road builder had little patience for those who did not share his conviction that a highway should be built to Boston or who doubted that the city's survival as an economic entity depended on highway access. In his typically flamboyant style, Callahan declared in a turnpike press release that "if a road wasn't built into Downtown Boston . . . they better look up Chief Chickatawbut's descendants [he is the Indian chief from whom Governor John

Winthrop purchased the land the city was built on] and arrange to give downtown Boston back to the Indians."[25]

The enabling legislation that chartered the Turnpike Authority stipulated a "self-liquidating" enterprise that paid for itself with toll revenue. To maximize toll revenue and thus to expedite self-liquidation, the extension sought to capture the most vigorous traffic movements in the state — those from Boston's western suburbs to the center city. If the Pike could capitalize on the desire to drive from the surrounding area into Boston, these "local users" — including daily commuters driving from the suburbs and exurbs to work in Boston — would greatly increase toll revenue. The Pike had to persuade potential bond buyers that there was demand, and hence fiscal viability, for the road. The Pike hired a group of transportation consultants and engineering firms to furnish the traffic demand statistics that could, in turn, rationalize the new road.

Engineering Demand

In 1953, the Chicago-based transportation consulting firm DeLeuw, Cather, and Company produced one of the first traffic projection reports for the Turnpike Authority. The report's succinct title, "Estimated Traffic and Revenues," revealed the essential logic of the turnpike: the more traffic it attracted, the more money it would earn, and the more likely that bondholders would be quickly rewarded. Other reports investigated the costs of acquiring rights-of-way and of the construction itself. DeLeuw produced a separate report that guided the development of authority-managed concession areas on the side of the road and another that recommended highway maintenance policies. But the principal goal of the "Estimated Traffic and Revenues" document was to estimate traffic demand, recommend the locations of traffic interchanges providing access to the turnpike, and devise an optimal toll schedule.[26]

The DeLeuw consultants had at their disposal a set of traffic statistics drawn from prior studies. They had access to the origin-and-destination studies used to produce the 1948 Master Highway Plan for Metropolitan Boston. Similar reports had been created for the state's other large cities, including Springfield and Worcester. For its 1953 report, DeLeuw conducted its own origin-and-destination surveys with a sample of approximately three hundred thousand motorists at thirty-one different stations along the major roads across the state. The traffic engineers used these interviews to determine the most common traffic movements. Following the practice established in the 1948 plan, DeLeuw charted "desire lines" to represent traffic patterns. Predictably, the most desire was charted between Boston and everywhere else, but especially Worcester, Fitchburg (a nineteenth-century industrial center along the Nashua River in north-central Massachusetts), and the suburban areas west of Boston. All of this data emphasized the premise of the Master Highway Plan of 1948: the most useful road in the state would satisfy the desire of drivers to reach Boston from the west.

The traffic engineers premised their traffic projections for the Pike as a whole on its anticipated urban extension. The farther into Boston the extension penetrated, the higher the traffic potential. In addition to connecting the state to its capital city, the Massachusetts Turnpike would also be "integrated with a comprehensive system serving many of the eastern states and promising to connect with Chicago and the Middle West within a few years."[27] Highway planners stressed the systematic nature of their proposals. Each new link in the chain amplified traffic demand across the system as a whole. But some links had a greater impact than others. In Massachusetts, the highest overall demand for road facilities was in the Boston region and, in particular, for roads that brought commuters to the downtown business district. The Central Artery had been designed to deliver these cars there. But the value of the Central Artery, planned as a leg of the Inner Belt highway as delineated in the 1948 Master Highway Plan, depended on its connection to a metropolitan system of highways. By promoting a turnpike link to the Central Artery, Callahan sought to supersede the 1948 plan and replace it with his own system. He wanted to position the Mass Pike as the region's essential commuter highway.

The Pike was designed to function like a frictionless, well-oiled machine, and its advocates accepted this ideal as fact. As a primary measurement of their work, the DeLeuw consultants wanted to establish the time savings generated by the proposed highway. This was a tricky task, because the road had not been built. The driving time on the nonexistent Pike had to be estimated and compared with the measurable amount of time then required to travel by existing roads. Thus the estimated time of making a trip was based on an idealized conception of turnpike travel. The road theoretically allowed for the uninterrupted flow of traffic at an average speed of fifty-five miles per hour (fifty for trucks), "excluding time for lunch and refueling stops."[28] Time savings could be translated into monetary savings, and the toll schedule was designed to allow drivers to make a "profit" by saving time: "The proposed rates are such that the tolls will be approximately one-half of the value of the savings in time and distance that will accrue to the users of the turnpike in various vehicle classification groups."[29] The route of the Pike shortened the distance between Route 128 and Albany by fourteen miles. But time savings would be even greater because of the higher speeds allowed — and enabled — by the new road. In terms of safety, the DeLeuw engineers pointed to the accident record of existing roads, and claimed that a controlled-access highway like the turnpike would improve on this record. "The life saving characteristics of toll roads are a matter of record," the report asserted without substantiation.[30]

The Pike had another edge over conventional roads, one that enhanced both the safety and the aesthetic experience of driving: the elimination of abutting commercial establishments as well as the signs and billboards that cluttered the roadside environment.[31] The Pike did not allow billboards, which were not only distracting and thus a safety hazard but also an offense to the natural beauty of the countryside traversed by the road. But motorists would get hungry and they needed to refuel. The Turnpike Authority planned to build and manage its own concession areas at designated spots along the way. The restriction of billboards and provision of concession areas were part of the legacy of the limited-access parkways of the 1920s and '30s and were standard features of all turnpikes beginning with the Pennsylvania Turnpike in 1940. The Pike would also maintain its own "Highway Safety Patrol" to regulate traffic, aid broken-down motorists, and dispense first aid when necessary.

In sum, the Turnpike Authority proposed to construct a massive, insulated landscape that it could wholly control in accord with its own perceptions of best practices. This was a very different model from that of existing state roads that cut across lands held by various private property owners who could do as they saw fit with their abutting land. The Pike made the case for a road designed in the public interest as defined by speed, safety, and convenience for the motorist.

"An Unimpeded Surface"

Starting in 1956, the Pike's efforts to construct the extension were tied closely with Prudential's contemporaneous plans to develop a large project on the Boston and Albany rail yard. At first, the two sets of plans were at odds with each other. In July 1956, Mass Pike officials were meeting with representatives of the New York Central, which owned the B&A, to discuss the acquisition of the railroad corridor. Early reports suggested that the Back Bay segment of the Boston Extension would be designed as an elevated highway on girders, like the Central Artery, to allow the B&A to continue rail service on two tracks. At the time, Prudential held an option to buy the twenty-eight-acre rail yard that the tracks passed through. Valentine Howell, speaking for Prudential, felt that the plans for a toll highway would jeopardize his company's designs: "I don't see how bringing a highway into the area on stilts is going to enhance the value of the property," Howell told the *Boston Herald*.[32]

The B&A roadway was not the only route being considered for the location of the Boston Extension, but it was clearly favored by Callahan and his engineers at the Turnpike Authority. A second proposal involved a route that followed the Charles River and required two river crossings before coming into Boston. This route was not as threatening to Prudential. Mayor Hynes did not take a public position on the route of the extension, though he was adamant that he wanted both the Pike and the Pru to go forward. "I hope we can have both. We need both. I don't want to have to sacrifice one for the other," the mayor said. Hynes suggested that even if the Pike did go through Prudential's rail yard site, there would still be enough usable land for Prudential to develop. But he also recognized that "the company will not want to erect a 20 million dollar office building on 'an island surrounded by highways.'"[33]

Prudential insisted that it was only interested in the B&A site and no other in Boston. Fred Smith, the company's local representative, was also reluctant to abandon Boston for another city. He claimed that Prudential was considering five other New England cities that were "statistically as good as Boston, but not emotionally as good." Prudential's concern was that a highway would ruin the B&A site and make an integrated development impossible there. Smith announced that both projects could work only if an "unimpeded surface" was left at the B&A yards. In that event, he said, Prudential would go ahead with its proposed development. The Pike and the Pru, along with the city and representatives from the New York Central, engaged in talks to reconcile the two projects.[34]

One compromise position was to terminate the Boston Extension at the proposed Inner Belt highway, which the Department of Public Works was then planning. "Prudential officials say this plan to end the toll highway before it gets to the B&A yards would leave them completely free to go ahead with their plans." However, this possibility raised a new set of concerns involving the coordination between the Pike and the DPW. "It would cause chaos if the turnpike were finished before the highways [were ready] to absorb the traffic [heading for] Boston." Prudential was principally concerned with a speedy resolution of this planning snafu. The company had begun the rebuilding of its home office in Newark and needed to quickly rehouse its Northeastern Home Office staff. Things came to a head in the summer of 1956, with the approach of the August 10 effective date of Prudential's $5 million purchase agreement of the B&A site from the New York Central. It appeared that if the Pike followed through on its plan for an elevated extension into the city, the Pru would abandon the purchase agreement. Desperate not to lose Prudential's interest in Boston, Mayor Hynes organized negotiations between the Pike, Prudential, and the City of Boston. Under the pressure of the impending deadline, there was a flurry of activity and an apparent resolution.[35]

On August 1, 1956, the *Christian Science Monitor* reported on the agreement that had been reached. The Boston Extension would come into the city via the Boston and Albany Railroad tracks through the Back Bay yards and on to South Station without jeopardizing Prudential's proposed development. The Pike agreed to abandon its plans for an interchange at the B&A rail yard site and instead secured an easement that cut through the site. (It was later decided that the interchange would be moved to a site directly east of the Prudential Center.) Prudential would erect a "shell" over the turnpike right-of-way through the site with supporting columns that would not interfere with the highway or railroad tracks. A parklike mall would rest on top of the shell at street level. The basic architectural concept of the Prudential Center had been reached: the idea of a large substructure that straddled the turnpike and was capped with the plinth. The substructural shell allowed Prudential the unimpeded surface it required for its development by creating a new, unified ground surface above the right-of-way.[36]

Fred Smith alluded to the complex mediations between the Pike and the Pru when he announced Prudential's purchase of the rail yards in 1957. He singled out the chief of the Turnpike Authority, William F. Callahan. "Mr. Callahan," Smith declared, "is the most stubborn and yet the most wonderful gentleman I've ever come in contact with. I love him." But Smith carefully hedged on his allegiance to the turnpike extension, which was itself a controversial project: "We have a contract with the Turnpike Authority for an easement when and if it is needed, and if and when the highway is constructed along the main line of the railroad."[37]

Opposition in the Suburbs

Prudential was not the only institution interested in Callahan's proposal to use the B&A rail corridor as the route for the turnpike extension. Residents of nearby Newton were also concerned that the turnpike's plans would adversely affect their city. In August 1956, not long after the Pike and the Pru reconciled their plans, the Newton Board of Aldermen established a Citizens' Toll Road Committee to consider the city's interests, "recognizing the far-reaching, permanent and detrimental implications for the City's future and the potential damage to homes, property and the general welfare of the community."[38] There were two pressing factors from Newton's perspective: the taking of land and homes by eminent domain from residents of four of Newton's "villages" that were along the path of the B&A (Auburndale, West Newton, Newtonville, and Newton Corner); and the fear that the road would displace the B&A's commuter rail service between Newton and Boston.[39]

The chief engineer for the turnpike, Philip Kitfield, reminded critics that decisions about discontinuing rail service were up to the railroad, not the Pike. When Newton residents complained that a highway would cut their city in two, Kitfield insisted that it already was — by the railroad.[40] Callahan did his best to separate the issues of the turnpike extension and the future of commuter rail service from the suburbs to Boston. In an undated turnpike memorandum, he tried to clarify the issue:

> There has been some misunderstanding as to the Turnpike's part in connection with the curtailment of service by the New York Central Railroad. Possible discontinuance

or curtailment of service by the railroad is a matter entirely up to them and any public agency which has jurisdiction over the matter. The Turnpike, if it comes into Boston over the railroad right of way, will interfere in no way with the railroad's operation as there are provisions in the Turnpike plans for sufficient space to retain two tracks along side the highway for its entire length from Route 128 into Boston.[41]

The B&A line, which was sunk below ground level through much of Newton, did in fact already represent a gash through the city's physical fabric; but a turnpike entailed a broader swath of linear land takings, as well as much additional land at the traffic interchanges.[42]

Mayor Howard Whitmore of Newton supported the alternative Charles River route that traced the border between Newton and Waltham. A Charles River route would use mostly unoccupied land publicly owned by the Metropolitan District Commission (MDC). The citizens' committee went so far as to suggest reengineering the Charles River itself: "Where space is insufficient, the river can be put into a conduit with the expressway on top." The committee had an additional concern (one that may have undermined concerns about the threat to rail service): its members did not feel that Newton citizens should have to pay tolls to drive into Boston. The Newton group voiced its strong feeling that, regardless of the route, a freeway would be preferable to a toll road.[43]

Freeway or Turnpike?

The chairman of the citizens' committee's subcommittee on public relations was Robert Kretschmar, who was also the executive secretary of the Massachusetts division of the American Automobile Association (AAA). In his capacity as the citizens' committee's publicist, Kretschmar urged that alternative road proposals be well publicized. And in his role with AAA, Kretschmar came out strongly against a toll road and in favor of freeways. He believed that a "Western Expressway" as defined in the Master Highway Plan of 1948 was superior to Callahan's turnpike.

By the end of 1956, a more generalized resistance, on both political and practical terms, to Callahan's proposed turnpike extension was developing around the national "freeway" movement. The Interstate Highway Act of 1956 had created a new method of financing expressways that made toll roads seem like an obsolete and untenable concept. This fact was reflected in the "slowdown in financing of new toll turnpikes" in 1957, as reported in the New York Times. In 1956, very few new turnpike projects floated bonds for financing. "Plans for building more than 1,500 miles of tollways in ten states were shelved last year, many for good." Investors no longer looked at turnpike bonds as good investments. "Toll-turnpike securities suffered severe price declines during the year," the Times reported. One reason was that all fixed-interest securities had declined in value due to a tight money market. But another reason was that many turnpikes were not performing well; they were not earning as much as their planners had expected.[44] The *Monitor* reported that "an end to the toll-road era is in sight" because of the trend toward federally aided interstate highway construction.[45]

AAA was a major supporter of the Federal-Aid Highway Act and believed that a system of toll-free expressways would encourage the greatest overall automobility, which was its mission to expand. AAA came out in favor of systematic highway planning as a progressive counterpoint to Callahan's style of piecemeal construction. Robert Kretschmar insisted, "Bay State motorists shouldn't be made to pay a toll to commute to Boston when they can have a free road." With the federal government offering to pay ninety percent of the cost of a freeway, motorists were "entitled to a free public road."[46] Motorists were already paying for road improvements with their gasoline taxes. AAA viewed a toll road as an odious form of double taxation that ran against the interests of the car-driving public.

In an editorial, the *Boston Herald* wrote: "The Massachusetts Turnpike Authority . . . has taken over the planning of major freeways. There is nothing in Boston history that quite compares with this calm assumption of public planning by Chairman Callahan of the Authority." The *Herald* argued that the Turnpike Authority had usurped the DPW's public planning power and hampered its ability to plan a free Western Expressway in conjunction with the Inner Belt. In a series of editorials, the *Herald* — which saw its base as Boston's working and lower-middle classes — complained that Callahan represented an investor class and not the people at large: "We are now to have a highway system to serve not the public but the turnpike investors."[47] If Callahan insisted that a highway to Boston was necessary to secure the city's economic viability, the *Herald* asked, would not a freeway serve the same purpose? Yet Callahan seemed bent on "hanging a toll road" like a noose around the neck of metropolitan Boston by monopolizing traffic to and from the west.[48] An editorial in the *Herald* in July 1956 announced that suburban commuters from the west of Boston would become "second-class citizens" should the turnpike extension go forward, forcing them to pay for access to the city when it should be free.[49]

The *Herald* objected both to Callahan's power mongering as well as to his urban planning. At issue were two different visions of the spatial role of the Central Artery in Boston. The toll road would link directly to the Central Artery as a single highway piercing central Boston. But the 1948 Master Highway Plan saw the Central Artery as part of a loop around and through the city completed by the Inner Belt. The *Herald* echoed the concern of some transportation planners who worried about the traffic impacts of a direct connection between the Pike and the Central Artery without the Inner Belt to distribute traffic evenly throughout the central city area: "The Master Highway Plan for Metropolitan Boston, with its Inner Belt Route tying in the radial express-ways, was an integrated and balanced whole. Then Chairman Callahan . . . scrambled the plan with his projected toll road into the South Station. The result will be the aban-donment of the Inner Belt circuit if Mr. Callahan has his way."[50] Some Boston city planners were more interested in the Inner Belt than the routing or financing of a western highway to Boston. "Boston municipal planners say that either a freeway or a tollway into the city would be acceptable," one reporter said, "but that they do not regard the toll highway as a substitute for the more essential Inner-Belt route around the city." The Boston Planning Board believed that the Inner Belt was "required" because it unified the suite of radial highways that connected the region to Boston and distributed that traffic evenly around the urban core.[51]

In February 1957 representatives from Newton and other opponents to the toll road attempted to stop Callahan's plan for a turnpike extension by presenting bills to the state legislature that would have rescinded the 1955 amendment to the Pike's enabling law that permitted the construction of an extension. But these bills failed to gain traction in the Callahan-friendly legislature. Callahan stressed the urgency of building a highway to Boston and insisted that a toll road could be constructed much more quickly than a freeway. The turnpike chief was unconvinced that federal high-way funds could be successfully marshaled to provide for all the roads required by the Boston region. "Remember, I know something about *Federal Aid* after 25 years," Callahan wrote in a memorandum in preparation for a state house hearing on the extension. "The Public has been fed the greatest propaganda on this Federal High-way money," he insisted. "I know how much money is available for the next 3 years. Government money for Interstate — approximately $104,000,000." Callahan tallied a list of state highway projects promised by the DPW and concluded that federal aid would fall short. If the Department of Public Works proposed to construct the western freeway to Boston, the agency would have to make some sacrifices — a fact that concerned lawmakers from western Massachusetts. "If the DPW will tell me what projects they will abandon; what year they will start and where the money is coming from, I will be guided accordingly," Callahan sneered. "I will gladly step aside and let the DPW build a freeway into downtown Boston, if they can prove they can. In the meantime, I intend to keep on with my study."[52]

Callahan wanted to move forward with a bond offering to finance the extension. His position was bolstered by the testimony of Robert Weeks, a partner in a Boston invest-ment firm, who believed that the bond market would be very favorable to a turnpike extension offering.[53] But the market for turnpike bonds would not cooperate with Callahan's plans for the extension. Two efforts to market the turnpike extension bonds in 1958 and 1959 failed. One reason was that the Pike was underperforming. In October,

Business Week magazine reported that the Pike had earned only fifty-four percent of its estimated revenue.[54] In December 1959 the Greater Boston Chamber of Commerce requested that the Massachusetts DPW move forward with plans for a Western Expressway, claiming in a letter to Commissioner Anthony DiNatale of the DPW that "the general condition of the revenue bond market precludes the early construction of a toll express highway."[55]

Getting There First

While the Pike was struggling to launch the extension project, Prudential was floundering with its efforts to secure a tax concession from Boston. As noted above, in April 1960 the two parties announced an alliance to merge the two projects in a "$300 million package deal," in which the Pike would annex the B&A rail yard and allow Prudential to build, tax free, over the air rights.[56] Prudential had already begun sinking foundations for the project that allowed for the turnpike easement, and this legal agreement reinforced those construction plans. The *Boston Globe* ran an image of the "Prudential Garage-Interchange" that accentuated the physical communion between the Pike and the Pru. As part of the agreement, Prudential agreed to buy "a substantial amount" of the turnpike extension bonds once the issue was floated. Callahan was optimistic about the prospects of a forthcoming bond issue. "Now we are in the black. . . . We are absolutely sure that we can sell the bonds."[57] However, the failure of the Pike and Pru merger, following its rejection by the Supreme Judicial Court in 1960, rejuvenated opposition to the turnpike, as freeway supporters redoubled their efforts to vex Callahan's plans.

In January 1961, Republican John Volpe was elected governor of Massachusetts. He made an inaugural vow to unseat Callahan's plan for a turnpike extension and to build a western freeway to the city instead: "You will never see a toll-way if a freeway is started. It's a question of just getting there first."[58] Volpe insisted that his desire for a freeway was not part of a political "test of strength," but the press could not resist the personality drama. The *Globe*'s transportation reporter, for example, in an article titled "Pros, Cons of Volpe-Callahan Hassle on Highways," cast the lead characters as rivals: "The hassle represents more than a personality clash between Volpe and his arch-foe, William F. Callahan. Mixed up with political cross currents is a basic clash in road-building philosophies. The biggest question is: How to pay for it?" Volpe's and Callahan's shared interest in road building diverged at the "philosophical" issue of financing. Callahan reiterated his concerns that federal money for highways would "dribble in too slowly" and maintained that "it would be long years before the job could be finished."[59] Callahan believed motorists were willing to pay a toll for a fast road to Boston if it could be built quickly, and he bristled at Volpe's efforts to scuttle his plans and challenge his authority. With customary braggadocio, he remarked: "I've only designed and built, including the Turnpike, approximately $800,000,000 worth of roads in this State but I suppose the pen pushers or grocery store philosophers, who never built anything in their lives, are better able to plan and say how and where roads should be built. People like these are the cause of the decline of Boston."[60]

But John Volpe was not a grocery-store philosopher. He was the democratically elected governor of the state and he believed that he had Boston's best interests in mind. He was a building contractor by trade; a former head of the Massachusetts Department of Public Works; and the first federal highway administrator, appointed in 1956 by Dwight Eisenhower to coordinate the emerging interstate highway system.[61] Volpe resented Callahan's effort to ram his highway down Boston's throat at the expense of the 1948 Master Highway Plan. Volpe thought that Callahan's idea of running the turnpike directly to the Central Artery would overtax the elevated urban highway and exacerbate downtown congestion. Callahan, on the other hand, cast Volpe as a dickering planner, whose preoccupation with an idealized road system might prevent the construction of anything at all. Callahan only wanted to build. "We have proven our competence as builders," read one turnpike press release. "We had a 123 mile toll road to build and we built it. . . . Now we have a highway to build . . . to and from Boston, and we are building it. Mr. Volpe's long range plans for Boston should be quietly buried. . . . Let the dreamers plan and plan and plan some more; but if you want something done, get a workman."[62]

PRUDENTIAL IN THE BALANCE

Looming behind the showdown between Volpe and Callahan was the Prudential, whose plans for the Back Bay development appeared to favor the turnpike extension. A. S. Plotkin wrote in the *Globe:* "The big insurance company has planned all along for the 'pike extension to cut through the foundation of the $150 million Back Bay project. . . . Prudential has spent a lot of money already for engineering design, based on leaving room for road and tracks. To change this design now would be costly and time-consuming."[63] But in public, Fred Smith hedged on his company's commitment to the turnpike. Smith was most concerned with a swift resolution of the highway question, which he regarded as an internal political battle. The critical issue was that Prudential required highway access to its site — the major avenues were no longer adequate guarantors of automobile access: "Prudential says it doesn't care whether it's a toll road or a free road. But it does want assurance soon that some kind of major access to Boston's expressways will be built."[64] Smith said that it was "very important to the city and to our project" for the Prudential Center to have a "superhighway" connection in order to deal with the Pru's anticipated traffic.[65] He wanted "somebody in authority" to solidify the plan; "since we have so much money riding on it, we would like to know what the solution is going to be." Smith's statement spurred state senate president John E. Powers, from South Boston, to insist that he would "personally lead the fight" against Volpe's freeway proposal should it delay the Prudential Center, which was "too important to the City of Boston to jeopardize."[66]

Volpe's Overture

Governor Volpe scrambled to integrate Prudential's demands into his freeway plans for a Western Expressway that stopped at the Inner Belt, about half a mile west of Prudential's Back Bay site. The governor claimed that his plan was compatible with the Prudential Center: "I would not have proposed the freeway plan if I thought it would disrupt Prudential's project."[67] Volpe pledged to build a special access road from the Inner Belt to the Prudential Center, possibly by improving Huntington Avenue for the short span, but he would not bring the freeway downtown. The governor was adamant that the freeway terminate at the Inner Belt, the loop highway that he considered the keystone of the region's highway plan and necessary to achieve "proper distribution of traffic" in metropolitan Boston.[68]

In answer to Callahan's charge that federal financing was not forthcoming, Volpe floated a plan to borrow $100 million to jump-start both the Western Expressway and the Inner Belt. Volpe hoped to secure the loans with short-term notes, because they required a simple majority in the legislature as opposed to the two-thirds approval necessary for a bond issue. But Democratic lawmakers in Callahan's camp were quick to denounce Volpe's scheme: "Massachusetts needs to borrow $100 million like it needs a hole in the head," said Secretary of State Joseph D. Ward. Ward accused the governor of seeking to reward his own cabal of favored contractors and supporters instead of Callahan's. The *Globe* assumed that in ideal financial terms, Volpe's freeway was superior to Callahan's turnpike. But Callahan's turnpike was "shovel ready" — how quickly could a freeway be planned and engineered? How long would it take the federal government to reimburse the state's loan to pay for the highway? And would the Prudential Center be further delayed in the process?[69]

Prudential was sitting on a stalled construction project. Because of uncertainties over the tax issue and the highway project, the company halted work in August 1960, after the foundations were poured, and abandoned the site. On August 25, the *Christian Science Monitor* wrote about the "Prudential Lake" rippling in the Back Bay after the insurance company ordered the water pumps turned off and the site flooded — in part to save money, but also to protect the foundations from erosion and eventual frost.[70] When Volpe met with Smith in January 1961 to pitch a "connector" road from the

Inner Belt to Prudential Center, the press treated it like a diplomatic summit with the future of Boston hanging in the balance. In principle, Prudential might have accepted Volpe's proposal of a purpose-built access road, as the company publicly insisted that it had no strict loyalty to one road or another. "What is highly desirable is a direct link from the Center to a major highway," said Smith.[71] But Volpe had neither the money nor a working plan to build the freeway. The Department of Public Works had not produced technical plans for such a road. Engineers at the DPW — perhaps unsure of their loyalty to Volpe or Callahan — were working under the assumption that the Turnpike Authority was going to build the highway. Volpe agreed to back off his fight with Callahan and allow the turnpike chief a chance to sell his bonds.

The Bond Market

The bond market had already proved "unfavorable" to the turnpike's issue in the 1950s.[72] The *Globe*'s A. S. Plotkin waxed poetic on this point: "The market for these bonds seems to be like a beautiful woman's favor: delicate and fleeting."[73] But the 1960s brought new hope for the turnpike bonds. Investors still looked at turnpike offerings with a "jaundiced eye," but revenues were rising with the increasing automobile traffic as the federal interstate highway program lagged with slow progress.[74] Many investors insisted on state credit backing for turnpike bonds, but Massachusetts refused to extend such credit. As one reporter put it, "Institutional investors are watching carefully to see how the Massachusetts Turnpike Authority's proposed $175,000,000 bond issue will fare in the market without state credit backing." Because insurance companies made up a large component of potential investors, "Wall Street bondmen expect the Prudential Insurance Company of America to act as 'sponsor' for the bonds of the roadway extension that will serve its $100,000,000 Back Bay Boston redevelopment project," the *Christian Science Monitor* reported. "The Prudential's 'sponsorship,' expected to take the form of buying a large block of the proposed Massachusetts Turnpike issue, will be a key factor in the bonds' salability in the absence of a pledge of state credit."[75] When the Turnpike Authority attempted to sell the bonds in April 1961, Prudential reiterated its pledge from 1960 and publicly committed to purchase $40 million of the $175 million offering. But Prudential's "sponsorship" was not enough to overcome the cloud that hung over the turnpike bonds, which flopped on the market. According to an article in the *Boston Herald*: "The Prudential Insurance Company of America said it still wanted to build its $100,000,000 development in the Back Bay, but expressed apprehension that the maze of uncertainties into which it had been plunged by the toll road abandonment might prove too costly and too time-consuming."[76]

In the spring of 1961, an impatient Prudential postponed its application for the Prudential Center to the Boston Redevelopment Authority. There were two issues. First,

Prudential had designed a tunnel through the project for the embattled turnpike, and second, it viewed a highway connection to the Prudential Center as crucial. A Prudential executive, probably Fred Smith, wrote to Monsignor Lally of the BRA: "Our statement that it is immaterial what kind of a road, or whether any road at all proceeds *through* the project, has been interpreted widely to mean that we have no substantial interest in an access road *to* the project. This is not the case. The project will not be practical . . . unless special access is provided to this area from a major artery."[77]

Prudential's announcement created a crisis atmosphere in the city. Turnpike supporters charged that a faction in Boston that opposed both the Pike and the Pru had sabotaged the bond sale. One turnpike supporter told the *Herald*, "The same people who ruined the toll road now are rolling up their sleeves to ruin Prudential." An unnamed Prudential source pointed to a nebulous "group" that sought to sink the Pike and the Pru in one fell swoop: "That group went underground for a time, but now is gloating it scored a great victory."[78] The "group" had sabotaged the Turnpike Authority's bond issue by circulating a document to one hundred financial firms across the country attacking the projected earning power of the Boston Extension. The report scared off many potential investors who passed on the bond issue.

The mysterious group was the Massachusetts Citizens Committee, which released "A Critical Review of the Boston Extension Project of the Massachusetts Turnpike Authority" to the press and potential turnpike investors with the hope of dissuading them about the value of such an investment. This report drew from an economic analysis of the extension produced by three transportation experts from Harvard and MIT — Martin Wohl, Charles Haar, and A. Sheffer Lang. The three professors claimed that the Pike was based on fatuous overestimations of traffic demand and underestimations of maintenance costs. The "Critical Review" concluded, "The Boston Extension project is a dubious economic venture and an undesirable method of meeting the expressway requirements of the Boston metropolitan area."[79]

The professors' report questioned the professional integrity of the consulting firms who furnished the Turnpike Authority with traffic statistics. The transportation engineers, DeLeuw, Cather & Company and Coverdale & Colpitts, produced traffic and revenue projections for the extension that seemed unreasonably high, far outstripping a list of the country's most heavily trafficked toll roads, including the segment of the New Jersey Turnpike connecting suburban New Jersey to New York City. Moreover, the Pike's consulting engineers did not have a good track record. They had vastly overestimated the popularity and income of the Calumet Skyway in Chicago, for example.

The three professors also attacked the Pike Extension from a planning perspective, because it contradicted the basic principles of the 1948 Master Highway Plan: "A turnpike extension largely ignores and downgrades the importance of the Inner Belt

Highway. Without the Inner Belt Highway, the entire metropolitan highway program will become unworkable." Echoing John Volpe's concerns, the "Critical Review" claimed that Callahan's piercing extension would "create chaos in the South Station area by dumping large volumes of traffic on the Central Artery and surface streets." The transportation academics represented a consensus position among city planners that a western "gateway" highway had to stop at the Inner Belt and proceed no further. In 1960, the Boston City Planning Board came out against the toll extension, claiming that it was against the objectives of the "General Plan for the Central Business District." The Turnpike Authority, the professors said, threatened to dismantle the long-term planning goals of the entire regional highway system in favor of accruing the most revenue for "the projects under its jurisdiction."[80]

Prudential was not among those investors who accepted the critics' assessment of the Boston Extension. The insurance company made its own investigation, rejected the negative report, and agreed to purchase $40 million of bonds. State Senator John Powers, vocal proponent of both the Pike and the Pru, saw Prudential's choice as a decisive commitment: "Imagine, the second largest investment firm, Prudential, which invests $15,000,000 a day, feels it is a good investment, and they certainly know what they are doing," he told the Boston Herald. Powers believed that a shadow force had colluded in an effort to sabotage the Prudential Center and, by extension, the city of Boston. "This has every indication of a plot against the city. This sort of thing, the unexpected rejection of a large bond issue like this, does not just happen."[81] The professors insisted that they were not part of a plot, but were merely performing a public service. Charles Haar evoked his public role as a disinterested intellectual: "We did this as part of our public function to supply technical information for the public benefit."[82]

Creative Financing

Callahan attempted to sweeten his extension bonds by requesting that the state legislature raise the maximum interest rate from 5 percent to 5 ¼ percent, but Governor Volpe refused to bring Callahan's message to the State House.[83] Undeterred, Callahan made his next attempt to market extension bonds in June 1961. But this effort was once again stymied when the Pike could not secure underwriters for the entirety of the $183 million issue.[84] A third attempt in November 1961 also failed to gain traction. The Pike's public relations director, Gordon McLean, glumly reported: "Nothing is happening. Everything is quiet now."[85]

But the Turnpike Authority's luck changed on January 22, 1962, when it was finally able to place $180 million of Boston Extension bonds with a syndicate of three New York investment banking houses. The underwriting firms — Allen and Company, Merrill Lynch, and Tripp and Company — bore the responsibility of marketing the bonds to their ultimate buyers. Conservative Boston financiers were startled by the Pike's strategy, which stretched the meaning of the word "sold." The three underwriting firms guaranteed the sale of the bonds, yet the ultimate buyers had not been identified.[86] The bond issue was organized into two parts: $100 million "Series A" bonds bearing 4¾ percent interest, and a second "Series B" issue of $80 million that started at four percent but would jump to five percent when the authority's original 1954 bonds were retired. *Boston Globe* business reporter Peter Greenough explained that this innovative structure created security for investors by promising the accelerated retirement of the original bonds. "Boston bond houses felt that this issue would reach a broader audience, one more receptive to taking calculated risks," Greenough said, and he predicted that the country's biggest insurance companies — Prudential, New York Life, and Equitable — would be at the top of the list to purchase these bonds.[87]

True to its word, Prudential announced that it would buy at least $40 million in bonds.[88] The state supreme court had recently confirmed Pru's status as a Chapter 121A redevelopment authority, and the insurance company was ready to build. Smith said the highway would "give us an immediate access road which we have wanted."[89] But Callahan was the star of the story. The *Times* said, "the sale of the bonds was seen as a political triumph for William F. Callahan."[90] Powers hailed the turnpike chief: "If ever there was a vindication of a public spirited man, this is it."[91] Callahan shared his victory with Boston: "The City of Boston is well on its way on a comeback that will again put it in the forefront of great metropolitan cities of the world," he told the *Boston Globe.*[92]

Figure 29 William F. Callahan inaugurates the Mass Pike Boston Extension construction project. On his left is Lou Perini, the contractor. On his right is Fred Smith, Prudential's main negotiator in Boston. (Courtesy of the Tutor-Perini Corporation)

Figure 30 Constructing the Mass Pike through Newton required extensive land takings, especially at interchange points, resulting in the loss of homes and property for Newton residents who lived near the railroad corridor (Courtesy of the Tutor-Perini Corporation)

Creative Destruction

On March 5, 1962, Callahan pressed a plunger to ignite the construction of the Boston Extension, as he triumphantly declared: "I only wish some of my critics and enemies were sitting on that ledge."[93] He stood on a dais with Fred Smith and Lou Perini, the lead contractor for both the Pike and the Pru (fig. 29). *Roads and Streets* magazine called the extension a "Contractor's Dream Project," worth $91 million. There were thirty-six months to build twelve miles of highway under a single contract that brought together three of the world's largest builders: the Perini Corporation, which managed the project, Morrison-Knudsen, and the Kaiser Company.[94]

The extension promised to reshape traffic patterns in the western suburbs and Boston. Though it followed the path of the depressed B&A roadbed through Newton, the Pike entailed a strip of destruction that altered many neighborhoods — in West Newton, for example, where a long-standing African American community was rent asunder by a wide-swinging turnpike ramp (fig. 30). In a press release soon after the bonds were sold, Callahan justified the trade-off: "We are fully aware of the hardships they will have to endure, no matter what the price may be; however, the public is paying an even greater price in death, injuries, inconveniences and inefficiencies because of sub-standard and dangerously overcrowded roads and streets that fail to properly serve the biggest segment of our metropolitan population."[95] Callahan's comments echoed the famous mantra of Robert Moses: "You can't make an omelet without breaking eggs."[96]

Callahan also suggested that he expected the Inner Belt highway, which he had never formally opposed, to go forward: "Engineering reservations will be made to provide from connections with the Inner Belt to integrate through, interstate traffic with Greater Boston traffic." But the Inner Belt was never built. One of the reasons was the Turnpike Authority's none-too-gentle handling of eminent domain proceedings, which were described as hostile and condescending. The experiences of the *other* publics, those who were displaced by the Pike, would haunt the future of highway building in Boston. Plans for the Inner Belt were thwarted in the mid-1960s by a diverse, cross-class coalition that led to Governor Francis Sargeant declaring a "moratorium" on highway construction in 1970.[97] Additional pieces of the 1948 Master Highway Plan, such as the Southwest Expressway, were also scrapped. In the final analysis, the Mass Pike's Boston Extension effectively scuttled more ambitious plans for a regional highway system. Instead, the Pike and the Pru built a single highway that pierced through the urban core along the path of least resistance. In 1962, the Pike and the Pru carried the day, insinuating a vision of the public interest — and the future of Boston — that reflected their own image.

Chapter 5

Designing the Center
The Business
of Architecture

Construction photograph from the Perini Corporation of the Prudential Center in 1964. The tower is finished and the Sheraton Hotel is nearly completed. (Courtesy of the Tutor-Perini Corporation)

In mid-September 1956, the architect Charles Luckman received a call — "out of the blue," as he later remembered — from Carrol Shanks, the president of the Prudential Insurance Company, explaining that his company had an option on a large parcel in Boston's Back Bay. "How would you like to do the master planning and a feasibility study for us?" Shanks asked. As Luckman recalled it, he met with Shanks in Newark the next morning and the two of them flew to Boston that afternoon to inspect the site.[1] Soon thereafter, Prudential hired Luckman's firm as the architect for the Prudential Center. The decision was not only an embrace of Luckman, a former corporate executive who had come to architecture as a second career, but also an implicit rejection of a group of Boston's most distinguished architects, including Walter Gropius and Pietro Belluschi, who had already prepared a plan for the same parcel of land — then known as the Back Bay Center — complete with motel, shopping mall, and a distinctive lozenge-shaped office building.

This chapter discusses the design and construction of the Prudential Center, with a central focus on the contrast between the high-style approach of the rejected Boston architects and the more pragmatic and corporate approach of Luckman, who got the job. In the realm of modern architecture, Prudential hedged its bets by choosing an architect better known for his business acumen than for his strong opinions about design.

THE BACK BAY CENTER

As noted in Chapter 3, Prudential was not the first to consider a large development project on the site of the Back Bay rail yard. When the New York real estate developer Roger Stevens bid to develop the site in 1953, he hired a group of distinguished Boston-based architects to consider site planning and architectural design for a speculative project called the Back Bay Center. The team included Walter Gropius, who had come to Harvard in 1937 after fleeing Germany, and members of the firm that Gropius started in Cambridge in 1945, The Architects Collaborative (TAC). Gropius and TAC were joined by other local luminaries, including Pietro Belluschi, then dean of the architecture school at MIT; Carl Koch and Hugh Stubbins, both of whom studied at Harvard with Gropius; and Walter Bogner, an Austrian-born and Harvard-based architect and planner who was the informal leader of the group that called itself the Boston Center Architects (BCA). Stevens also engaged two outside consultants to conduct special studies: Kenneth Welch evaluated the economic draw of the new commercial center and Wilbur Smith produced a transportation plan. The Back Bay Center was more than an architectural design. It was a statement of the economic and social functions of a new midtown district for Boston.

"A Cure for the Ailing Heart of Boston"

Stevens unveiled his proposal on September 11, 1953 (fig. 31). In a long report on the Back Bay Center, *Architectural Forum* distilled its urban strategy to a list of "six big ideas."

1. Attract the automobile back downtown from suburban shopping centers by providing superb traffic and parking facilities.
2. Once the traffic has arrived, store it in cellar parking. Above, float a 28-acre raft solely for pedestrians.
3. Add big-city excitement and power to the rural-shopping-center concept by building not just a castle of stores (840,000 sq. ft.) but also office buildings (1,400,000 sq. ft.), a convention hall (seating 7,500) and a 750-room hotel.
4. Arrange these buildings municipally around plazas and promenades. Instead of just letting the intervening spaces between buildings fall where they may, design the spaces first, then the buildings, and thus bring the Greek idea of the open central city core back to enrich urban life.
5. Subdivide the big plot for development horizontally, not vertically. Slice it into strata, not building lots.
6. Do it all with private money ($75,000,000 of it) aided not by federal support, but only by the cooperation of the city government.[2]

The proposal embodied a motor-age update on the large-scale commercial project coordinated with transport facilities, such as the Terminal Tower complex in Cleveland. Traditionally, a builder erected a discrete building on a lot or set of lots that were organized by existing surface streets. The Back Bay Center was a wholesale insertion of a new piece of urban infrastructure on a tabula rasa site with its own internal system of streets and a parking garage. The architects envisioned the center as a super-block complex that gave high priority to car circulation and created self-contained pedestrian enclaves.

Stevens believed that the Back Bay Center had the power to maintain Boston's position as New England's most important business location. He saw the project as a stopgap to the suburbanization of the city's economic functions: "The automobile runs on a two-way street," Stevens told *Architectural Forum*. "The motor that brings the city to the country can also bring the country to the city. By providing better facilities, our cities must bring back the patronage they have lost." Kenneth Welch, the economic consultant, predicted that the Back Bay Center would successfully compete with suburban shopping centers — including regional centers he himself had helped plan — and reassert Boston as the region's commercial focus.[3] Walter Bogner announced, "The

Back Bay Center is a cure for the ailing heart of Boston."[4] It would revive the city by pumping life again through its physical, economic, and social spaces. The project reflected Walter Gropius's conviction that the core of the nineteenth-century city had to be rebuilt for the people of the twentieth century by segregating modes of transport and providing pedestrian plazas that enriched civic life. Mayor John Hynes actively courted the privately financed project. Ultimately, however, Stevens failed to launch the Back Bay Center because he could not guarantee enough "cooperation" from city government by way of a guaranteed tax concession.

Design for Accessibility

A key goal of the proposed Back Bay Center was accessibility, both to people and — perhaps most of all — to their cars. As traffic expert Wilbur Smith declared, "Accessibility is requisite for marketability." The Back Bay Center's position at the western fringe of the city was strategically placed to "intercept" downtown traffic. The Back Bay Center — and the Prudential Center after it — would benefit from the proximity of nearby stations of the subway and streetcar lines that ran down Boylston Street and

Figure 31 The Back Bay Center, proposal by the developer Roger Stevens in 1954 (Courtesy of Harvard University Graduate School of Design, Frances Loeb Library)

Huntington Avenue. These facilities, however, were considered peripheral and not integral to the design. Smith designed a ring road surrounding the building site to channel traffic from city streets into the center and the large garage that would collect the parked cars. He engineered the ring road to handle peak traffic, unimpeded by direct crossings, traffic signals, or stoppages of any kind. It would be a constantly streaming rotary, a great collector and distributor of cars. The multi-level garage was to be split at its lowest level by an easement for the railroad (the turnpike extension had not yet been proposed) and was capped with a twenty-eight-acre "raft" of concrete that would host the center's structures. It would be the world's largest enclosed parking garage, with room for five thousand cars. "When they first showed me the site I didn't believe it could be done," Smith reported. "But now we know it can be done. You will be able to bring a car in there, park, and be upstairs in ten minutes."[5]

The design for traffic circulation distinguished the Back Bay Center from Rockefeller Center, the project it was inevitably compared to. Smith explained the key difference: "Circulation will not be by regular through-city streets, which make Rockefeller Center an extension of the horizontal traffic flow of the city around it. Instead, in Back Bay Center, people will enter at the base from a ring road and then move *up*."[6] Some criticized the plan for a center that would "sit behind its ring road somewhat like a castle city behind a moat." But, as the *Architectural Forum* editors acknowledged, "how else could the auto traffic be so deftly handled?"[7]

The centerpiece of the Back Bay Center was to be a six-sided, forty-story, lozenge-shaped office tower, whose broad facade looked toward the cars approaching Boston from the west. The tower would be surrounded by a department store, a "castle of stores" shopping area, office buildings, a 116-room motel, and a saucer-shaped convention hall that punctuated the western edge of the plan. For *Architectural Forum,* the structure that epitomized the project was the motel, where a visitor could check in from his car and park in front of his room. The motel was the endpoint of a traveler's "sociological trek." Increasing numbers of travelers were coming to cities by car rather than by train, and they needed lodging not only for themselves but also for their vehicles. The overall effect, *Forum* suggested, was "a melange of city efficiency with suburban dash."[8] The suburbs made shopping easy by providing automotive access and plentiful parking; the Back Bay Center would compete with the suburbs on those terms.

Giving Back to Pedestrians Their Right-of-Way

Walter Gropius made no apologies for the spatial conceit of the Back Bay Center. If the center was "an island in an ocean infested by automobile sharks," it was for the best. Gropius believed that social spaces for people should be removed from the street: "In the modern city a plaza for pedestrians may be more important than ever before. The pedestrian has been pushed against the wall in our cities. We have a beautiful net of highways for automobiles, but in the city we also have to give back to the pedestrian his right of way."[9] The enclosed shopping center — a multi-level promenade with a glass roof — allowed pedestrian shoppers to stroll comfortably. The buildings of the center framed a central plaza that was conceived as an outdoor room. The trick was getting the scale of the plaza right. It had to be just large enough to hold the peak rush-hour crowds, but not so large as to dwarf the individual person. In Gropius's view, the urban plaza represented a new core for community life. *Progressive Architecture* recognized the Back Bay Center with a "first design award" in 1954, noting with approval that "the pedestrian once again comes into his own," but not at the expense of his automobile.[10]

The Back Bay Center gave Gropius an opportunity to implement the urban ideas that he had been developing, along with other modernist architects affiliated with the International Congress of Modern Architecture (CIAM), since the 1920s. CIAM urban planning ideas were codified in the "Athens Charter" of 1933, principally written by the Swiss architect Le Corbusier, which advocated strict zoning of the four urban functions: dwelling, work, recreation, and transportation. The challenge was to foster community life within this new, segmented landscape. It was a challenge taken up in other CIAM documents, including *The Heart of the City: Towards the Humanization of Urban Life,* published in 1952 and edited by Jaqueline Tyrwhitt, CIAM president José Luis Sert, and Ernesto Rogers. In his lead essay, Sert wrote: "One of the first requisites of all of these centres of community life is the separation of pedestrians and automobiles."[11] The Back Bay Center exemplified what Sert and Gropius hoped for the city as a whole.

The Boston Center Architects may have had in mind Le Corbusier's influential 1945 proposal for the reconstruction of a civic core for Saint-Dié, a town in northeastern France destroyed in World War II, featuring a six-sided tower with a staggered "egg-crate" facade for government offices set in a monumental pedestrian plaza and facing a civic auditorium.[12] The Boston Center Architects adopted a similar facade treatment and presented it as an effort to connect the project to the city; it, too, had a six-sided office tower with small, staggered fenestration, as an homage to Boston's brick-style residential architecture.[13] It was the modernists' gesture at acknowledging regional culture in what was otherwise a steel and glass campus in the International Style.

The Pru Turns Thumbs Down to the Boston Center Architects

On October 11, 1955, the Boston Center Architects assembled at the offices of The Architects Collaborative in Cambridge to discuss the outlook for the project. Roger Stevens was bowing out. He had been unable to secure a tax concession from the city, without which he could not afford to launch the project. But an unnamed insurance company had emerged as a potential sponsor and solicited a scheme for a large office building. Fifteen days later, Bogner, Gropius, and Belluschi were in Newark to meet with Prudential executives, including Valentine Howell, who was planning the North-eastern Home Office, and Westcott Toole, who headed the regional home office pro-gram. Prudential's initial response to the Back Bay Center plan was skeptical. It appeared, as described in Bogner's handwritten notes, that the modernists' vision of urban revitalization was in conflict with the Pru's own conception of its Northeastern Home Office project.

Prudential viewed the Boston Center Architects' plan for a shopping center in the complex as too ambitious. "Prudential does not seem interested in stores, etc. as income producers," Bogner noted. The insurance company executives also balked at the plan's comprehensive scope and believed that "any large development must be carried out in stages, rather than on big blocks." Prudential was interested in the over-all visual impact of the project, reflecting Wes Toole's preoccupation with creating landmarks. "Prudential wants a show piece in its insurance building," Bogner wrote, "seen by greatest number of passing motorists. Therefore believes removal of Mechanics Building essential to create impressive view from Huntington Avenue." Bogner also noted that Howell advocated a "building with wings and a high tower as show piece," along the lines of Prudential's previously built RHO buildings.[14]

I have not found any documents explaining the Pru's final decision not to go with the Boston Center Architects and instead to hire Charles Luckman, who was at that time perhaps more notable as an administrator than a designer. But we can make some educated guesses based on the available information. Prudential was accustomed to working with proven commercial architects and established firms. The Boston Center Architects were perhaps too visionary for comfort. The Pru had a particular sort of cor-porate culture, and executives like Toole and Shanks could relate to Luckman. In addi-tion, Bogner noted, Prudential was afraid the Back Bay Center plans would cost too much. The insurance men seemed to fear that the Boston Center Architects, despite their distinguished reputations — or perhaps because of them — would promote their modernist ideas without due regard for cost. Luckman, in contrast, was known for cost control and administrative efficiency. Prudential was apparently less concerned with architectural distinction than with a special sort of symbolism — the towers that loomed over extended downtowns, with "Prudential" emblazoned on them. Should it be surprising that an insurance company concerned with promoting its image would gravitate to an architect who once achieved distinction by designing soap displays for grocery stores?

FROM SOAP SALESMAN TO ARCHITECT: CHARLES LUCKMAN

In his memoir, Luckman recalled being present at the earliest stages of planning the Prudential Center, and he positioned himself at the ear of Prudential's chief: "I persuaded Shanks that if Prudential announced a dramatic redevelopment project, as we proposed, it would have a ripple effect. Other builders and developers would buy up the adjacent seventy-five acres and the whole area would blossom." But it wouldn't be easy, Luckman emphasized. Prudential had purchased a difficult site from the perspective of land development. For one thing, the two major streets that bordered the site, Boylston and Huntington, sloped in opposite directions, requiring major earth moving to establish a building plane. Moreover, the entire Back Bay district was made of filled-in land that could not sustain the foundations for such a large project. "Until we did the soil borings we would have no idea how deep we would have to go to hit solid rock," Luckman later wrote, as if he had been unaware of the previous plan for the Back Bay Center and had to start from scratch.[15]

Autobiographies are acts of self-invention, and Charles Luckman's is no exception. Published in 1988 when he was nearly eighty years old, *Twice in a Lifetime: From Soaps to Skyscrapers* is full of jocular half-truths, loosely remembered quotations, and picaresque anecdotes of his dual careers: from his swift ascent to the helm of Lever Brothers, the soap company, to the principal of a large architecture firm that bore his name. Though he was trained as an architect, architecture was his second career, and what had come before always influenced his attitudes and actions in that profession. A brief look at Luckman's career in business will help us to understand his place in postwar architectural culture.

In 1946, *Time* magazine introduced Charles Luckman to readers as a blue-eyed "boy wonder" who quickly rose from a toothpaste salesman in Depression-era Chicago to president of the industrial soap production giant Lever Brothers at the age of thirty-seven. From the company's headquarters in Cambridge, Massachusetts, Luckman controlled a key node in a global "Empire of Soap" run by Lever Brothers' parent company, the Dutch-Anglo conglomerate Unilever.

In the press, Luckman was an all-American success story. An advertisement for *Fortune* magazine in 1947 described the young executive's vital statistics: "$300,000 a year at 37 — up from a $25-a-week soap salesman to the top boss of Lever Bros. Time: 15 years flat." The press hungrily picked up on Luckman's winsome, Horatio Alger–like story. He was the irrepressible Kansas City newsboy who dreamed of becoming an architect — and trained as one at the University of Illinois — but took a detour to the world of sales when jobs for architects were scarce in the 1930s. He won the hearts of small drugstore proprietors by designing signs and displays that helped move their soap inventories at a time when consumers were watching their wallets. He had an intuitive grasp of advertising and the power of media. To pitch Lever's Irium brand toothpaste, for example, Luckman hired the rising star Bob Hope to peddle *Irium to Mirium* on radio and, later, television.[16]

Luckman was far more than just a run-of-the-mill corporate chieftain and pitch-man. He was an ambitious man-of-affairs. A profile in *Fortune* in 1950 confirmed that by then Luckman had arrived as a public figure. He was presented as a progressive industrialist, a prolific speechmaker, and an articulate exponent of the American free enterprise system. Reflecting his wide recognition as a leader of industry, Luckman was asked to chair President Harry Truman's Citizens Food Committee, a Marshall Plan program that sought to persuade Americans to save grain to send to Europe. The French and Italian governments decorated Luckman for his role in this effort, recog-nizing him for combating the specter of Communism by helping to feed the hungry masses of war-torn Europe.[17]

Luckman was a master of the art of merchandising and public relations, and he applied these skills to corporate architecture when he recommended that Lever move from Cambridge to a new office building on Park Avenue in Manhattan. A new space was needed to consolidate Lever's expanding array of subsidiary companies. Beyond that, a striking new building would stand as an advertisement for the soap company. Luckman hired Skidmore, Owings, and Merrill to design the building. But he later took most of the credit for devising the architectural concept: "As a licensed architect who also happened to be the client, I could tell the architects what I wanted, and see that I got it. I spent many weekend hours walking up and down Park Avenue, trying to envision the kind of building I dreamed of seeing there. . . . Gradually, from somewhere in the depths of what I had learned in architectural school, a concept of a new kind of office building began to take shape in my mind." That concept drew on the most up-to-date building technologies — a steel structure glazed with a very thin curtain wall of large glass panels. Luckman also wanted the entire ground-plane to be "open to the pub-lic," an open-air extension of the sidewalk. At first, Unilever was alarmed by Luckman's proposal to construct a small structure that eschewed street-level retail stores, that "wasted" valuable land by not building to the limit, and that was not large enough to accommodate tenants other than Lever itself. But Luckman was able to persuade the Unilever directors of the long-term value of his approach — that "giving back to the street" would enhance Lever's standing.[18] And he was right. Lever House opened in 1952 and is widely considered one of the most important examples of postwar mod-ernist architecture, marking corporate America's adoption of International Style design principles.

Before Lever Brothers could occupy its new home on Park Avenue, Luckman fell suddenly from his corporation's grace. Observers speculated that his brash manage-ment style clashed with the principles of conservative stewardship championed by Unilever's European directors.[19] Near the end of 1950 he agreed to step down from the helm of Lever. This marked the close of the first chapter of Luckman's career. He was tempted by many offers to continue in business, but was lured by a different sort of offer from the architect William Pereira, a former classmate at the University of Illinois. The two men formed a partnership in Los Angeles, and Luckman happily returned to his first love — architecture — at the age of forty-one.

They made a good team, and each architect consciously adopted a distinct role: Pereira was the talent, Luckman the charismatic salesman. Pereira, playing the part of the artiste, wore a smock; Luckman brandished a pipe (fig. 32). "There was no possibility that I would ever become the 'smock' kind of architect," Luckman wrote. "I would stay with my no-jacket, rolled-up-shirt-sleeves, man-at-work attire."[20] The combination appealed to patrons, who saw Luckman as a fiscally responsible peer. He used his business experience as a selling point for the firm, and announced as much to potential clients. He used to tell them: "Pereira will be the architect. I'll be the businessman."[21]

The firm quickly attracted high-profile clients, aided by Luckman's high-powered Rolodex and his extensive contacts in both government and the corporate world. In 1953 the firm was asked by CBS chief William Paley to design a "Television City" in Hollywood, the first studio complex designed expressly for television production.[22] Pereira and Luckman's work for CBS led to the establishment of a branch office in New York. The firm became known for solving big architectural problems, and addressed a

Figure 32 A promotional photograph for Pereira and Luckman found among the Charles Luckman Papers, probably taken around 1953. Luckman, left, looks on as Pereira points to a detail on a blueprint. (Source: Charles Luckman Papers)

series of unprecedented programmatic challenges. Pereira and Luckman carried out the planning and design for the modernization of the Los Angeles International Airport and a series of large military projects for air and naval bases, including NASA's manned-spacecraft center in Houston.[23]

Architecture *IS* a Business

Despite the firm's success, Bill Pereira grew disillusioned with his partnership with Luckman. He was turned off by Luckman's drive to expand the firm. He thought architecture could not be managed in a bureaucratic fashion, but should be rendered with craft by the architect. For Pereira, the architect was a renaissance man; for Luckman, the architect was a team leader at the top of a corporate hierarchy. The two parted ways in 1958, and each formed his own firm. In a press release announcing the dissolution of the Pereira and Luckman firm, Pereira declared: "It is my conviction that I should limit the number of projects which my associates and I hope to undertake to those which we can contribute the most and which we can follow through personally from beginning to end."[24]

Luckman reported that only two designers and one project architect chose to go with Pereira. Luckman organized Charles Luckman Associates (CLA) by making each associate a "stockholder," entitled to a profit share. CLA assumed responsibility for many of Pereira and Luckman's larger commissions, including the Prudential Center. An early vote of confidence for the new firm came in when the president of the California Federated Bank Corporation asked Luckman to design a new office tower on Wilshire Boulevard, projected to be the tallest in Los Angeles at twenty-eight stories and located not far from Prudential's Western Home Office.[25] Many other banks and corporate clients followed suit, and CLA was soon designing large office complexes in cities across the country. Some critics thought the office buildings — which often paired a tower, placed on a podium, with a freestanding parking structure — were insensitive to local context and essentially interchangeable. Ada Louise Huxtable of the *New York Times* called the CLA design for the First National Bank of Oregon, which occupied a two-block site in downtown Portland that had been cleared with federal urban renewal funds, "a blind, insolent, formidable fortress raised against pedestrian humanity."[26] But suggestions like these did not seem to discourage clients. CLA was counted by *Fortune* in the top tier of American architecture firms in terms of total value of construction in place, in a group with Welton Becket (which occupied the top spot) and Harrison and Abramovitz.[27] In 1968 *Business Week* declared that Luckman sold architecture the way he sold soap: in bulk. Yet Luckman made clear that each project bore his personal imprimatur: "No project can be shown to a client before I've seen it and approved it," he said.[28] Luckman saw himself as an architect with an intuitive sense of space and style. He noted in his autobiography that he was personally registered as an architect in more than seventeen states.

But Luckman's principal architectural responsibility was as the front man, making business contacts and soliciting new projects. His blatant self-promotion, and the sheer volume of his firm's production, tended to dilute Luckman's cultural capital. In his book *The Favored Circle: The Social Foundations of Architectural Distinction,* the sociologist Garry Stevens writes that the architectural profession has a vested interest in asserting the autonomy of its field, to pretend that it somehow exists outside the practical world of real estate development, business practices, or fluctuations in the political economy.[29] Yet Luckman unflinchingly embraced these constraints on architecture; he even flaunted them.

In the early 1960s, CLA received a commission from the Pennsylvania Railroad to produce a new terminal as part of a larger urban development project for the railroad's property on the West Side in Manhattan. Preservationists bitterly protested the destruction of McKim, Mead, and White's terminal building, a landmark built in 1910, but the railroad went forward with its ambitious plans to capitalize on its West Side real estate holdings by building an office tower, theater, and sports arena on top of a new passenger terminal. A big part of the job was to coordinate the terminal's construction without interrupting the railroad's operations. When it was finished, Huxtable called the theater at the new Madison Square Garden "pleasantly unpretentious and handsome," noting its "simple, direct solutions with rational and appropriate details." The overall effect, she wrote, was "neither avant-garde nor high architectural art." Yet it was a grand space, designed "to serve popular pleasures for a great many people, on a vast scale, with efficiency and comfort." Madison Square Garden, Huxtable allowed, "deals, legitimately, in mass art. . . . Twenty-thousand hockey fans will undoubtedly love the new Garden, and 20,000 hockey fans need not be wrong."[30]

Indeed, Luckman's work was *mass,* not *class.* Some people thought he had no taste. In 1962, *Time* magazine ran another profile of Luckman, and noted: "The critics grumble that he is more a businessman than an architect. 'He is successful,' says one top Chicago architect coolly, 'because he produces anonymous architecture in a prescribed time and at the least cost and fuss to his clients.'" This type of censure never bothered Charles Luckman. Terrorizing clients was not a virtue for him, and he took pride in building on time and on budget. Beyond that, reasonable people could disagree on what constituted attractive architecture. According to *Time:* "Competitors cluck that Chuck Luckman could never sit at the same drawing board with a Mies van der Rohe or a Corbusier — or half a *hundred* top architects for that matter. Luckman airily dismisses such criticism. 'Unquestionably,' says he, 'other firms work as ably as we do, but they don't do it in the way we do.'"[31]

And what was that way? Was there a method behind Luckman's prolific architecture? *Time* called it "mass production," with designs coming off the "assembly lines." Luckman expressed his professional philosophy during a 1954 interview with a reporter from the *New Yorker* magazine for a "Talk of the Town" piece. Luckman said: "I am firm in my belief that architecture is a business, and not an art. . . . I handle the programming of a job. I organize it. What is the problem? What is the client trying to achieve? If we do a project that is mostly engineering, I staff it with engineers. If it is mostly architectural, I staff it with architects." Architecture, for Luckman, was the art of allocating human resources. He organized his firm as a multidivisional corporation, with planning, engineering, architecture, interiors, and research divisions. There was even a group dedicated to "design visualization," which exclusively considered the "look" of a building. Luckman initiated strict budget auditing with a cost-control department consisting of fourteen engineers whose sole function was "to see that nothing goes on the drawing board that will put the project over the budget." According to Luckman, his designers at first resisted this economizing, complaining that their creativity was being hemmed in. But they soon changed their tune: "They found that in order to design within a budget they had to be *really* creative."[32]

In 1962, Luckman was selected to design the United States Pavilion for the 1964 World's Fair in New York's Flushing Meadows–Corona Park, a commission that suggested the firm's prominence at that time. Luckman presented twenty-eight different schemes for the pavilion to Norman K. Winston, the United States commissioner responsible for the project. Winston eventually chose a low, boxlike structure, enclosed in translucent panels made with colored glass pieces and raised above the ground on concrete supports. Luckman's tactic of creating many choices for a client was typical of his style as an architect: he wanted to show all the possible options and empower the client to choose among them. This technique also revealed Luckman's aesthetic pliability. He had no design agenda, championed no style. He was more interested in satisfying the customer than he was in advancing a strict vision of good architecture. However, Luckman and the architects working at his firm were well aware of prevailing trends and techniques in contemporary architecture. The firm's design for the United States Pavilion fit with a broader pattern for federal architecture in the early 1960s of "modern, floating pavilions," including State Department architecture overseas, like Edward Durrell Stone's New Delhi Embassy.[33]

In 1968, Luckman was a featured speaker at the American Institute of Architects conference in New York, where he insisted that "Architecture *IS* a Business," and chided his colleagues for marginalizing the profession by focusing too much on design aesthetics. "If our profession is to survive in today's kaleidoscopic society, we must make our aesthetic contributions within the framework of business-like procedures and systems." Luckman thought that architects played too small a role in overall construction activity and that the built environment had suffered because of it. The architect had to reclaim his rightful position atop the building hierarchy; therefore, he had to become a *generalist,* "capable of coordinating the work of many specialists." In terms of output and range of projects, CLA was in a league with other leading firms that were also organized as multidivisional outfits of national scope with several regional offices, like Skidmore, Owings, and Merrill and Welton Becket and Associates. These were firms that internalized the planning, engineering, and architectural functions necessary to prepare large projects. Welton Becket made this embrace of multiple services his credo of "Total Design."[34]

Charles Luckman took his business model to its ultimate stage in 1968 when he sold his firm to a large conglomerate, the Ogden Corporation, and took charge of a new real estate subsidiary, the Ogden Development Corporation. Ogden was principally a scrap-metal and shipbuilding company, with interests in a variety of other areas including food businesses, restaurant chains, and transportation systems. The newly formed Ogden Development Corporation, with Luckman at its helm, planned an aggressive foray into real estate. One of Luckman's first projects with Ogden was Broadway Plaza in downtown Los Angeles. Hailed by the press as a "megastructure" when it opened in 1973, the project integrated office and hotel towers, parking facilities, and an enclosed shopping "Galleria" featuring a flagship Broadway-Hale department store.[35] Luckman saw Broadway Plaza as one example of how private developers can "solve the problem of deteriorating central cities on a scale and basis that is economically feasible."[36]

To Luckman, his role as a developer animated his conviction that the architect was the most qualified leader of the city-building process. He believed that by assuming the role of developer, the architect enhanced his impact on urban development and his position in society at large.[37] Yet the editors of *Progressive Architecture* expressed some concern: "So here we are," wrote Jan C. Rowan. "The road has been traveled all the way: The architect becomes a team, the team becomes a corporation, and the corporation becomes a subsidiary of another corporation. In the shuffle, what happened to the architect?"[38] The implication was that the architect was somehow compromised by incorporation. Luckman would have disagreed: the architect was compromised from the start. He was simply loath to admit it.[39]

Master Plans That Are "Do-able"

Though he emphasized the importance of business in architecture, Luckman was also an advocate of "design." He told a group of UCLA students that "we will be set back one hundred years unless we integrate the word 'design' into architecture." At its most superficial, "design" reflected the whims of an aesthete. Luckman railed against those dilettantes who were "boxed in by the narrow viewpoint of the what-does-it-look-like school to whom the 'image concept' is the beginning and end of all architectural wisdom." Good design had to be brought into the "total concept" of architecture, which also included engineering, construction, and economics. This meant dealing with complex political milieus and a myriad of specialists involved in the urban development process.[40]

Luckman, the pragmatist, dismissed utopian city planners who invented ideal scenarios for what the city "should be" instead of what it "could be." Luckman quoted with disdain an article from a "Manual on City Planning," in which the author exhorted readers, "'Are we to be forever satisfied with mere improvement? Shall we not instead completely rebuild our cities? Can we not ignore present obstacles and dream big dreams?'" Luckman dismissed such foppery: "Those plans could be fruitful only if the cities were to be obliterated by war. Is that to be the limit of our genius?" Luckman believed in master plans, but eschewed "revolutionary master plans." "I am opposed to 'dream-able' plans," he said. "I am in favor of 'do-able' plans." Luckman predicted tremendous building activity during the 1960s: "The United States this year will embark upon the greatest building boom the world has ever seen — as part of what will rightfully be called the Spectacular Sixties."[41] It was an opportunity that Luckman did not want to see squandered by the withdrawal of architects into the insular world of pure design.

In Luckman's view, planners who were preoccupied with utopian urban visions ignored the actual work of building the metropolitan physical environment. He believed that older cities, built with obsolescent infrastructural systems, required well-planned urban redevelopment projects targeted to specific neighborhoods. As an example of such a project, Luckman pointed to his firm's work in the Bunker Hill section of downtown Los Angeles, where CLA produced the master plan that guided the "transformation of a 136 acre semi-slum area in downtown Los Angeles into a modern center providing functional and aesthetic accommodations for living, working, shopping and recreation for more than 60,000 people."[42]

From "Humanization" to "Humanation"

Despite his rejection of planners who were "dreamers" rather than "doers," Luckman was not closed to modernist approaches to architecture and urban development. He was influenced by modernist ideas, but he gave them his own pragmatic spin. For example, Luckman took the idea of the "humanization" of American cities, as championed by Siegfried Giedion and other modernists, and transformed it into his own brand of "humanation."

Giedion, the architectural historian and critic who was for many years the secretary general of CIAM, shared an interest with Gropius, Sert, and other modernist architects in *humanizing* the core of the modern city. In an essay from 1951 called "The

Humanization of Urban Life," Giedion sounded his concern for humane spaces tailored to the pedestrian experience in the midst of the busy, chaotic city. He insisted that the pedestrian must be returned to a place of dignity in the urban core: "Today this right of the pedestrian — this human right — has been overridden by the automobile, and so the gathering places of the people — the places where people can meet together without hindrance — have been destroyed. Today one of our hardest tasks is the reestablishment of this human right, which is not merely imperiled but has been destroyed altogether." Giedion's answer was to "humanize" cities, and in an essay written in 1956 he pointed to the unbuilt Back Bay Center as an ideal illustration, where "a large area was consciously created for the sole use of the pedestrian, a protected zone within which he can wander free from danger." Giedion acknowledged that as a consequence, "the center no longer faces upon the street." But this was a small price to pay: "At last the pedestrian regains the right he had lost since antiquity, to move freely within a center of collective life."[43]

Luckman echoed Giedion's concerns for a humane urban environment. He stressed this theme in many of his invited lectures and public talks, putting his own spin on the notion of "humanization": "We as architects must and will devote more attention to the people who occupy our buildings. This is what I term 'the humanation of architecture.' We must fulfill their human needs and aspirations — we must enable them to live and work with happiness and dignity."[44] "Humanation" was Luckman's bastardized version of "humanization," yet his vision of urban space shared much with the leading modernist intellectuals.

Luckman talked about Lever House as a formative experience in shaping his spatial imagination. He pitched his idea for an open plaza at street level to the dubious directors of Unilever in 1950: "The final straw that broke the back of their belief in my sanity, was when I said I wanted the entire ground floor on Park Avenue left open so that people could walk in and feel a part of Lever; so that there might be a very human feeling at the ground level to contrast with the kind of slick and gleaming tower which I felt would properly reflect a soap company. To their everlasting credit, they gave me exactly what I asked for!"[45] At Lever House, Luckman viewed the street-level plaza as a contribution to the public realm of the city — a refreshing pause amid the dense brick and mortar of Park Avenue. Luckman believed that the Lever House principle could be applied to large urban projects to create more suitable environments for people. And once he took on the Prudential Center project, Luckman pointed to it as a model for the "humanation of cities." Despite its size and complexity, it was crucial that this "city within a city" not be overbuilt. It was designed for people by allowing them plenty of open space, which both Luckman and Prudential viewed as a civic gesture, a giving-back to the community: "We have done this by assigning 75 per cent of a 31-acre area to landscaping, reflecting pools, statuary, terraces, walkways, patios and sculpture gardens. Only the remaining 25 per cent is used to accommodate the buildings themselves." People needed this "freedom of space" because it was "the proper environment, the proper distribution of those things which are presumably free — the sun and the air." To deny the people these things would be to deny them the promises of America's founding fathers, and what Luckman took to be the foundational goals of city planning: life, liberty, and the pursuit of happiness. Landscapes that granted "freedom of space" and promoted "humanation" would help preserve those American values and even ward off "the malignancies upon which socialism and communism are born."[46] Luckman's assumptions about the good city represented a trickling-down of urban ideas from avant-garde intellectuals to commercial practitioners. He infused these ideas with his own brand of Cold War enthusiasm for the American free enterprise system that was rooted in his experiences as a business leader. It was a view shared by Prudential.

THE PRUDENTIAL PROJECT UNFOLDS

In his autobiographical recollections, Charles Luckman gave the impression that the Prudential Center emerged, fully formed, from a rational consideration of the client's program and the features of the site: "Our concept required that we make a firm decision at the very start on the shape and height of every building in the project, because we had to build the foundations for *all* the structures at the same time that the plaza level and garages were being built. If we did the foundations later, we would have to break through the plaza and garages each and every time we sought to lay a foundation for a new building. The Prudential directors understood the problem, and had the courage and foresight to approve our putting in the foundations for all future buildings."[47] But despite Luckman's later recollections, these sorts of "firm decisions" for the planning and design of the Prudential Center could not possibly have been made at the outset of the project. Prudential considered pulling out of the project on several occasions — and as late as 1961 — as its tax concession and the turnpike plans were debated, negotiated, and eventually resolved. Although the foundations for the entire 31.5-acre site were established at one time, Prudential did not make final decisions about what would sit atop those foundations in the same unified fashion. In fact, the company viewed the center as an ensemble of four precincts that were initiated at different times: (1) the central plaza, with commercial arcades and tower, (2) the hotel and convention center at the western edge, (3) the eastern precinct with two apartment houses and a Saks department store, and (4) a "far eastern" precinct with a third apartment tower and a structure for Lord and Taylor, another department store.

Planning the Site

After being hired by Prudential in 1956, Luckman's first task was to staff the project. He himself was based in Los Angeles, and the Prudential Center fell under the domain of Pereira and Luckman's New York office, led by Charles Stanton. The firm of Pereira and Luckman became the "coordinating architects," paired with a local firm, Hoyle, Doran, and Berry (HDB). HDB was the successor firm of Ralph Adams Cram, later called Cram and Ferguson, and was responsible for the New England Mutual and John Hancock buildings, each important pieces of the Back Bay "insurance district" that emerged in the 1930s.

When Carrol Shanks came to Boston in 1957 to announce his company's intention to construct the Prudential Center, he was armed with several large renderings of the project (see fig. 26). The ambitious images of a "skyscraper city" complemented Shanks's buoyant message about the economic prospects of New England and its capital city. The designers had rendered the Prudential Center as an ideal diagram, a massive, independent entity that floated in pure space, with no reference to its urban context. The Pru referred only to itself, anchored by its fifty-two-story tower that turned the same face in each direction like a beacon, gesturing at a distance if not to its immediate surrounds. The ring road that circumnavigated the site concretized the center's isolation from the city at large.

This initial plan revealed how the Pereira and Luckman and HDB team of architects divided the program into precincts and used symmetry to bring visual clarity to the plan (fig. 33). To the west was the convention center complex, with a slab hotel and

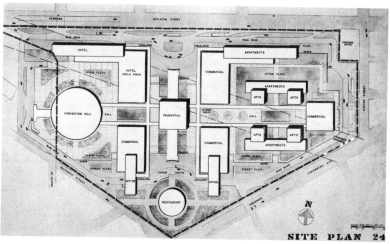

Figure 33 This plan, the first publicly released, was also used by Carrol Shanks to introduce the Prudential Center. Its title, "Site Plan 24," shows that Pereira and Luckman had already experimented with many versions of the plan, which here stresses a symmetrical resolution of the center's program. (Courtesy of Prudential Financial, Inc.)

saucer-shaped auditorium on axis with the tower. The center section included the tower and low-rise commercial buildings, with a circular restaurant at the southern corner. The architects placed the commercial blocks at the corners of the tower, producing four plazas that faced each side of the tower. One rendering illustrated the dramatic entrance concourses and reflecting pools that were projected for the north and south plazas. The eastern precinct of the site was for housing. Architects imagined four fingerlike apartment towers with small square floor plans. A landscaped mall

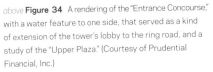

above **Figure 34** A rendering of the "Entrance Concourse," with a water feature to one side, that served as a kind of extension of the tower's lobby to the ring road, and a study of the "Upper Plaza." (Courtesy of Prudential Financial, Inc.)

right **Figure 35** Renderings of the Prudential Center were produced in quick succession in 1957 and 1958. In July, Fred Smith declared the image on the bottom to represent the "final working plans" for the Prudential Center. This scheme would remain essentially unaltered for at least three years. (Courtesy of Prudential Financial, Inc.)

running east from the tower culminated in a low, square-plan commercial block. On the northern edge of the site, bordering the busy commercial thoroughfare of Boylston Street, Pereira and Luckman planners placed a second slab containing more apartment units. In a rendering that HDB provided to the *Christian Science Monitor,* which noted "Glass and Steel Will Predominate," the Pru and its pedestrian plazas appeared as a vast, pastoral landscape insulated from the life of the city (fig. 34).[48]

Over time, Prudential released a series of variations on the scheme. The first of these came in May 1957.[49] The north and south entrance concourses remained, but the fingerlike apartment towers were now rectangular slabs, oriented to Boylston Street, each placed on its own pad of grass. An unreleased rendering, also from 1957, suggested that the architects did at least briefly consider designing a wider, slab-shaped tower. In July 1958, Prudential released "final working plans," and Fred Smith, its representative, announced, "This is it" (fig. 35).[50] The new plan coincided with Prudential's agreement with the city over tax concessions, the informal arrangement that was eventually debunked by the state supreme court. "The physical aspects of the center are now established," said Smith. In the July 1958 site plan, CLA planners abandoned the saucer-shaped restaurant and varied the site layout and floor plans of the apartment towers.[51] The commercial blocks were widened and simplified and would be broken up by covered arcades. The lobby extensions were removed and traded for broad forecourts with staircases that stepped down toward the ring road (fig. 36). The southern plaza was designed with a pool that could be used as an ice-skating rink. The tower itself appears thicker, less delicate, and without the vertical striping of the previous rendering — it is an undifferentiated rectangular prism except for a stepped-back observatory bearing Prudential's name. The site plan also shows that the ring road was simplified and scaled back, cutting off the far eastern portion of the site. HDB prepared four different proposals for the civic auditorium, and Mayor Hynes unveiled the city's choice in August 1958: a boxy design with a mesh-like screen that faced Boylston Street, to be named the City of Boston War Memorial Auditorium (fig. 37).[52] In December 1958, Prudential announced that the Boston-based Hotel Corporation of America would operate the hotel at Prudential Center and that Charles Luckman Associates would design the building.[53]

Laying the Foundation

In 1955, Walter Bogner reported that Prudential wanted to remove the Mechanics Hall at the southeastern corner of the site. As was his wont, Luckman later took credit for the idea. He claimed to have convinced Shanks to acquire a larger site by buying and razing the building, built in 1881, which he called "a sixty-year-old red sandstone monstrosity" (fig. 38). The Mechanics Hall housed Boston's largest convention hall, a

Figure 36 This rendering of the tower and north plaza accompanied the July 1958 rendering of the Prudential Center. Here, the tower appears as a glassy prism. The plaza level was accessible by two sets of escalators as well as the ceremonial staircase. (Courtesy of Prudential Financial, Inc.)

left **Figure 37** A photograph of the recently completed Prudential Center in 1968 focuses on the War Memorial Auditorium building, foreground, designed by Hoyle, Doran, and Berry (Courtesy of the City of Boston Archives)

right **Figure 38** The Mechanics Hall, ca. 1920, built in 1881 by the Massachusetts Charitable Mechanic Association. The hall contained the largest auditorium in the city until it was taken down in 1959 to expand the site of the Prudential Center. (Courtesy of Boston Public Library, Print Department; photo by Leon Abdalian)

function that would be assumed by the municipal auditorium that would be built in conjunction with the Prudential Center. Moreover, the sprawling building would have spoiled the "open plaza approach" to the Prudential Center that anchored Luckman's vision of the complex.[54] Prudential's demolition of the Mechanics Hall in January 1959 was the last physical obstacle to clearing the nearly thirty-two-acre site for the Prudential Center. This act of destruction was reported as the "first visible sign that the city's massive Prudential Center would actually be built as planned."[55] The *Monitor* announced that in the contest for a "New Boston," "modernity outflanks historic brick building."[56]

As construction commenced, Prudential gave priority to the center section of the project and hired the George A. Fuller Construction Company to execute excavation and foundation work for the tower and commercial plazas. Fuller installed a coffer dam that isolated this area from the rest of the site to protect against water seepage. Fuller hammered the tower supports — there would be 150 of them made of steel pipe caissons thirty inches in diameter — 140 feet below grade into bedrock before capping them with a ten-foot-thick raft of concrete that supported the tower's structural steel columns.[57] A three-foot slab of concrete would cover the rest of the site and serve as the floor for the garage and for the columns that would support the low commercial structures adjacent to the tower. April 3, 1959, marked the official groundbreaking for the Prudential Center. Mayor John Hynes shoveled dirt from the site into a lucite container to be preserved for posterity. He called it "the most historic dirt removal job in the history of the city of Boston."[58]

Prudential was prepared to proceed with construction on an ambitious timeline that would have led to completion of the project by 1962. But that schedule was delayed when the insurance company insisted on a formal guarantee of real estate tax concessions. The solution announced in April 1960 was to merge the construction of the Pru with the building of the Massachusetts Turnpike's Boston Extension, as we have seen.

The Pike and the Pru, having already agreed to an easement through the site, strengthened their collaborative efforts to integrate physical plans and turn the Prudential Center into one of the hoped-for turnpike extension's major interchange points. The ramps were to be placed at a site just east of the center, at the location of the B&A railroad's Huntington Avenue station that the Pike planned to acquire (fig. 39). It remained unclear in 1960 whether the turnpike extension would actually be built, however. Therefore, Prudential asked CLA to estimate the costs of preparing two alternative design scenarios: one that anticipated the extension, which required raising Huntington Avenue to permit the road to pass underneath it, and another that assumed the absence of the highway.[59]

When the Supreme Judicial Court upended the proposed bundling of the Pike and the Pru, an exasperated Prudential halted construction on the site. The project was shuttered on August 24, 1960, when the company ordered the "flooding" of the foundations to save the cost of pumping and to protect the completed work from the elements. The "Prudential Pond" stayed a watery or frozen space for nearly two years. As we saw, Attorney General McCormack hurried to prepare legislation to amend the state's urban redevelopment law, Chapter 121A, to guarantee to Prudential the tax break it demanded. With the new law in place, Prudential prepared an application for the Boston Redevelopment Authority, which had assumed administrative control of the project. The authority's public hearing in March 1961 thus became a pivotal point in

Figure 39 A diagram outlines the land takings required to construct the Prudential Center ramps to the east of the site and shows how the tower was sited just south of the turnpike easement. *right* A photograph taken from the Prudential tower shows the Boston Extension and the ramps east of the Prudential Center toward its connection with the Central Artery. (Courtesy of the Tutor-Perini Corporation)

the course of the project. The BRA had to determine whether or not the Prudential Center conformed to the new redevelopment law: was it in the public interest to grant a tax break to a private company that proposed a major real estate project for the rail yard?

Long-Range Values

Prudential's case for the public value of its proposal was closely tied to the expense of developing the entire rail yard site under a unified plan. Charles Stanton represented CLA at the BRA hearing and offered a detailed explanation of the architects' design strategy. When his firm first looked at the site, Stanton saw that the railroad easement presented a major challenge to "orderly site development." When further consideration had to be given to the Mass Pike, the planner's job was made even more difficult. It would have been easier and less expensive to leave an open cut through the site and develop two distinct parcels. But this approach would have damaged the "long range values" of the project that would be preserved only if the land was developed in a unified fashion. This required enclosing the highway easement to insulate for noise, vibration, and fumes and extending a "lid" that covered nearly the entire site. As Stanton explained, "This in effect created an elevated piece of real estate on a single level." He continued: "It is in truth, one building; it's completely contiguous, foundations, and substructure, slabs and construction generally. And then the separate buildings or superstructures, if you will, then rise from this 3-story base that covers the entire site."[60]

The ring road, too, was conceived with long-term planning goals in mind. To make room for it, Prudential voluntarily abandoned a large portion of buildable land at the perimeter of the site. Stanton reported that only thirty-two percent of the site would host "superstructures," with the rest of the space (including, presumably, the ring road itself) open to the public. Prudential's sacrifice asserted the company's "long range economic and civic values." Stanton's message was that the project's physical unity was itself a civic gesture.

Prudential's Wes Toole, who also appeared before the BRA, echoed Stanton's view that "whatever was built should be on a common plane as a single, integrated development." Toole explained to the BRA board that the B&A site was a perfect match for Prudential's regional home office development formula, which called for a large campus, including landscaping and parking space. The rail yard was ideal because it was a large, unified site that could be bought in a single purchase. "It was large enough for us to do something really dramatic which would revitalize the city," Toole explained.[61]

The BRA approved Prudential's application, but the company delayed construction until a "test case" of the new law had been tried, and announced a winter 1962 restart of the project.[62] When the Supreme Judicial Court decided this "friendly action" in Prudential's favor, the company was ready to turn on the water pumps at the site again, and to resume the flow of its corporate capital toward the construction of the Prudential Center.[63] It was a watershed moment for Boston, and some writers saw the new development as an episode in a great struggle between modernity and tradition: "Old Boston, fighting to free itself from the chains of tradition, is aiming at the complete upheaval, renovation, and replacement of its ancient structures."[64]

March 1962 marked the second beginning for the Prudential Center. The company hired the Perini Corporation as contractor for the center section. But Prudential had scaled back its ambitions for the project and postponed planning and design for the eastern apartment precinct. There was no evidence that the BRA objected to Prudential's diminished proposal. Nevertheless, it appeared that the premise of a singular foundation that would cover the entire site had been dropped — and, in retrospect, it appeared that Prudential and its architects had overstated the case in its public hearing.[65] The foundations poured by the George A. Fuller Company encompassed only the center section of the site. Prudential released images of a 9.5-acre parking area in the eastern sector landscaped with trees and shrubbery on either side of a cut that contained the Boston Extension of the Mass Pike (fig. 40). Attention was focused on the central and western part of the site, where ground was broken for the hotel in July 1962. Steelwork on the commercial pavilions and the tower commenced in September 1962 and proceeded apace until the topping-out ceremonies were held in January 1963. Perini began to install the aluminum-framed curtain wall in May 1963 (fig. 41).

"Warmer than the Tall Buildings on Park Avenue"

For the exterior of the tower, CLA aimed for a "lacy . . . textured effect." The wall was made of continuous vertical aluminum members and horizontal "fill-in" pieces, fabricated by Reynolds, the large aluminum company. The metal grill was filled with panels of structural glass in several shades of blue and green, creating a delicate, "lacy" quality. The five mechanical floors, given over to the building's electrical and ventilation systems, were faced with darker panels that horizontally segmented the tower's mass. "It will not give you the impression of a straight modern glass tower," Charles Stanton told A. S. Plotkin of the *Globe*. "It will be much 'warmer' than, say, the tall buildings going up on Park Avenue."[66]

Luckman paid special attention to the interior as well as the exterior of the tower. When he reviewed an image of the "Tower Skyroom," a restaurant at the top of the tower to be operated by Stouffers, Luckman concluded that the mood seemed "far too cold and barren. . . . I think that we should redo this interior so as to show real design and warmth." As opposed to minimalist restraint, Luckman wanted to inject some "design" into the architecture. Soon these images would go into publicity for the project, and he did not want to give the wrong impression.[67]

Luckman and Stanton's preoccupation with projecting a feeling of warmth signaled a dividing line between CLA's views toward contemporary architecture and other leading practitioners of a colder, more austere brand of modernism. These included the laconic master, Ludwig Mies van der Rohe, who teamed with Philip Johnson and the firm of Kahn and Jacobs to design the Seagram Building that opened on Park Avenue in 1958. Built as the headquarters for a whiskey company, the Seagram Building was admired by many for its visual clarity, elegant proportions, and craftsmanship. It was a deceptively sober building that coolly flaunted its sumptuous materials with what

This is the architect's rendering of Prudential Center in Boston, a unified business and civic development now in progress on a 31-acre site. The 52-story Prudential Tower will rise more than 750 feet to become the tallest office building in the world outside Manhattan. At the left is planned a 1,000-room hotel, and behind it, the City of Boston Municipal Auditorium. Other structures will house banking facilities, restaurants, specialty shops, and other retail stores. The Northeastern Home Office, serving the six New England states plus upstate New York, will occupy the first 18 floors of Prudential Tower. The remaining floors will be rented. The landscaped parking area at the right will be developed by Prudential later on, either as a residential area of apartment houses or as an additional business area.

Figure 40 A promotional image of the Northeastern Home Office from 1962 shows how the insurance company scaled back its plans to develop the eastern portion of the site. The last line of the caption reads: "The landscaped parking area at the right will be developed by Prudential later on, either as a residential area of apartment houses or as an additional business area." (Courtesy of Prudential Financial, Inc.)

Figure 41 A construction photograph from 1963 showing the base of the Prudential Center and installation of the aluminum curtain wall. The railroad tracks are in the foreground and the turnpike easement was encased with a steel and concrete cage. (Courtesy the Tutor-Perini Corporation)

one architectural historian has called "frigid hauteur."[68] CLA may also have sought to distinguish its design from the proliferation of glass-box office buildings on Park Avenue designed by Emery Roth and Sons, derided by critics for their cookie-cutter monotony.[69]

Spreading the Gospel of Humanation

With the steel frame rising to the sky, Luckman worked to promote the new district he was helping to create and to spread his gospel of *humanation*. Humanation, Luckman explained to a reporter, was an "architectural process to make the area attractive as a visiting place." Luckman gave special emphasis to the Prudential Center's eleven-acre pedestrian plaza that surrounded the central tower (fig. 42), noting with pride that the Pru would feature four times the open area of Rockefeller Center. The "Prudential Plaza" would be lined with shops and was anchored by the tower at its center. Stanton described it as a "proper setting for people" as well as the foreground to enhance the visual impact of the tower itself.[70] There would be two ways to access the north and south plazas. Each featured a monumental, branching staircase — coated in terrazzo — that stepped to a broad sidewalk adjacent to the ring road. CLA also designed escalators that ascended to the covered walkway that fronted the shops. For Prudential employees — presumably also people who deserved a "proper setting" — CLA designed an outdoor patio that extended from the second floor of the tower, its four corners resting on each of the four commercial pavilions.

If the plazas themselves were not enough to create a human-friendly setting for the 750-foot tower, CLA designed a slim channel of water that surrounded its base: a modern moat, transformed from its original purpose of defense to that of "aesthetic architecture." The ornamental pool was not a good fit for Boston's cold climate, but the architects were undeterred. They designed a heating system to keep the pool from

Figure 42 A rendering of the Skyroom restaurant at the top of the Prudential tower. *right* A rendering of the plaza and tower lobby illustrated the "modern moat" effect that CLA architects designed for the base of the tower. (Source: Charles Luckman Papers)

freezing over in the winter. Four cast-stone bridges spanned the moat from the plazas to the covered promenades on each side of the glass-walled lobby.[71] The moat set the tower back from the plazas, reflecting Luckman's conviction that the tower needed an uncluttered viewing platform to heighten its impact. And, to give the moat a feeling of warmth, Luckman advocated placing a sculpture in the moat's reflecting pools.[72]

In another sort of nod to "humanation," Prudential, with CLA's approval, commissioned Donald De Lue to produce a sculpture for the north plaza. Prudential wanted to stay away from "far-out" artwork and was drawn to figural or allegorical pieces.[73] De Lue produced *Quest Eternal,* a five-ton bronze statue of a nude man reaching to the sky (fig. 43). It was a monumental sculpture that celebrated the human form, like those of Atlas and Prometheus at Rockefeller Center. Although Stanton worried that it might be too risqué for the local audience (and that the architects would be blamed), it was installed after the center opened in 1965.[74] The architects were particularly pleased by Alfred M. Duca's quasi-abstract sculpture *Boston Tapestry,* a cast-iron screen that evoked the local scene, which was placed in the lobby of the Prudential tower.

Topping It Off and Moving Forward

The topping-out ceremonies for the Prudential tower were held on January 30, 1963. Prudential planned to identify the building with the company's name spelled out in seven-foot-high letters at the very top on the east and west sides of the structure. With the steel frame in place, Luckman and Stanton tried to discourage Toole from going ahead with plans for the signs, "particularly in light of the recent criticisms levelled at signs on the new Pan-Am Building in New York." CLA believed the signs were unnecessary to identify the tower, which even in skeletal form was "already a Boston landmark, just as the Empire State Building is in New York. The signs may only distract from its dignity and fine architectural appearance."[75] But Toole could not be persuaded to give up on one of the key principles of regional home office design.

In August 1963, Prudential confirmed that it would move ahead with two twenty-six-story apartment buildings, each costing around $20 million and to be designed by CLA (fig. 44).[76] The office tower was also starting to attract tenants. Prudential's Northeastern Home Office would occupy the first eighteen floors. The United Fruit Company made a splash in January 1963 when it announced that it had signed a fifteen-year lease to occupy more than 200,000 square feet — nine full floors — of the tower, where it would consolidate its headquarters. United Fruit's move established the new tower as a prestige building, and the company hired CLA to design its office interiors.[77] Seventy-six percent of the rental space was leased before the office tower opened. The seventy-one-foot antenna on top of the tower was operating by

left **Figure 43** Donald De Lue's *Quest Eternal,* a five-ton bronze sculpture, still punctuates Prudential's north plaza (Photo by Terah Maher, 2011)

above **Figure 44** Prudential released this image in 1963 to promote an enhanced vision of the Prudential Center featuring two twenty-six-story apartment towers in the eastern half of the site. The towers were sited at a right angle to each other, forming a landscaped plaza. (Courtesy of Prudential Financial, Inc.)

the fall of 1964, as the transmitter for several radio stations and Boston's first UHF television station.[78]

There were also positive signs that the Pru's retail plazas would draw tenants. Garber's Travel Service signed a lease for a space adjacent to the convention facilities at the hotel and auditorium. It was a strategic location, and president Bernard Garber expected to serve the high-flying executives who would soon be circulating through the new business complex.[79]

The Prudential Center was dedicated on April 19, 1965, when the central and western sections — with tower, commercial pavilions, hotel, and auditorium — were opened to the public. The first two apartment towers opened in the fall of 1967, and a third was added in 1968. The original plans for commercial structures also evolved in the late 1960s. Prudential was successful in attracting leading department stores to anchor the commercial presence of the center. Lord and Taylor opened in 1968, and Saks Fifth Avenue followed in 1971. In 1970, a second office building, initially named the South East Tower and later called 101 Huntington Avenue, opened, and a second hotel tower was authorized in 1972. CLA worked on all these projects.

The Bureaucratic Basis of Design

The enterprise of architecture includes not only creative leaps at the drafting table but also project organization, management, and bureaucracy. The managerial side of architecture is especially salient when the architect is Charles Luckman, who unabashedly viewed architecture as a business. His son, James Luckman, provided me with access to the previously unreported archives of Charles Luckman Associates' memos on the Prudential Center project.[80] The memoranda concern a variety of themes, including the levels of administrative hierarchy and the tensions that developed between constituencies. They also make clear that, grand plans notwithstanding, the project developed step by step, with many twists and turns along the way.

CLA's role in the project was complicated by the firm's multiple commitments to different tenants of the Prudential Center who needed their own architectural services. CLA was the primary designer not only of the Prudential tower but also of the hotel, apartment towers, and commercial pavilions. As the master planners for the project, CLA was also responsible for coordinating the efforts of the small army of contractors and subcontractors. Although Prudential was well aware of the firm's multiple roles, it still expected CLA to give priority to the insurance company's own needs. For Charles Luckman and his lieutenants, it was a juggling act, further complicated by the halting political process that occasionally cast the entire project into doubt.

The New England Merchants Bank

In October 1958, the New England Merchants Bank signed on as one of the first major tenants to commit to the Prudential Center. It was an important vote of confidence from one of Boston's venerable financial institutions, founded in 1831. The bank would construct a flagship banking hall and executive suites in one of the four commercial pavilions envisioned in the CLA master plan — the southwestern "A" block — and planned to rent the forty-ninth floor of the tower for cafeteria and private dining facilities.[81] The bank building was conceived as an independent structure that would require its own architectural services. Detailed consideration of the new bank structure was delayed until 1962, when Prudential resumed construction of the center. At that point, CLA secured the design commission from New England Merchants. In a gesture to his new clients, Luckman shifted the accounts of his Boston office from the State Street Bank and Trust to New England Merchants.[82]

New England Merchants president Richard Chapman had design ideas of his own. He was concerned about the "character" and "atmosphere" that the bank would project. Perhaps to counter the stereotype of coldhearted bankers — and echoing Luckman's concerns for the Prudential Center at large — Chapman wanted his bank to radiate warmth. And he was afraid that the center's contemporary design could, when applied to the bank, come off as flat and cold. Chapman communicated his ideas to Luckman, including the desire that the banking floor have "a primary 'focus,' which might for example be an extremely fine mural on the wall behind the tellers' area."[83]

Responding to his client's wishes, Luckman involved himself personally with the development of New England Merchants' interiors. In a memo to Stanton, he instructed: "Care should be taken that the scheme for the main banking floor does not become too busy as a result of the use of too many colors, materials, etc; 2) Sufficient color renderings of the final scheme should be prepared to fully present the concept in a manner easily interpreted by the client; 3) Great care must be taken in developing budgets, and the final design concept presentation to the client must include budgets developed as accurately as possible."[84] His memo exemplified three aspects of Luckman's overall participation in the project as the principal architect: attention to how small design details created overall tone, careful consideration of how plans were represented to clients, and watching the bottom line.

If the Boston bankers were not prepared to fully embrace contemporary design, Luckman did not challenge his clients' preferences. If Chapman wanted a "traditional Georgian room" with a faux fireplace in the directors' meeting suite, he would get one. It was Luckman's job to gratify his clients, not to push an aesthetic agenda, and he reassured Chapman that the banker's "requirements for a handsome and dignified interior design are, in my judgment, being met very satisfactorily."[85]

A Three-in-One Hotel

Prudential solicited proposals from hotel companies to lease and operate the center's hotel. Boston-based Hotel Corporation of American (HCA) emerged as the leading candidate. Prudential set a $17.5 million budget for the project, and hired CLA as the architects.[86] But Prudential left most of the decisions about hotel construction to HCA — it would be *their* building. HCA proposed a "3-in-1 Hotel" that combined a "modern conventional-type commercial hotel," an "intown motel" (reminiscent of the Back Bay Center's planned motel), and a "deluxe hotel" that offered luxury accommodations.[87] The hoteliers wanted to bring in a "concept designer" for the interiors — Harry End of Miami — and CLA accepted this plan on the condition that End's fee not be taken from CLA's own design budget for the hotel.[88]

Harry End specialized in organizing the spatial arrangements, materials, and thematic qualities of interior spaces, and he insisted on making small alterations to CLA designs. The hotel included many places to eat and drink, and End wanted to style them all. He insisted, for example, that the Rib Room needed its own bar. (This may have seemed like overkill, given that there were also plans for a Seafood Bar and Polynesian Room Bar.) He called for a draped fabric ceiling treatment for the Turkish Lounge. And, in an effort to open up the hotel's public spaces, End suggested eliminating the entrances that separated the restaurants from the lobby, so that passersby could peer in and circulate more easily. (HCA rejected this idea because of security concerns.)[89]

Charles Stanton saw End's involvement as an aggravation that would slow down the approval process as design moved from concept to working drawings. "The potential danger of End's entering the picture," Stanton wrote in a memo, "lies of course, in the possibility that he will want to make changes on work already approved, with, frankly, the possibility that he may need to justify his participation."[90]

Luckman himself expressed even greater concern about attribution for the design of the hotel project. HCA had failed to mention his name in an announcement published in *Hotel World Review and Hotel Management* in September 1960, and he feared that CLA would not receive due credit.[91] HCA allayed this concern. When Prudential announced the groundbreaking for the twenty-eight-story, thousand-room Hotel America in July 1962, the name of Charles Luckman Associates was attached to the project as "architect." But Luckman was sorely disappointed when the Sheraton Hotel Company, which assumed responsibility for the hotel when HCA backed out in 1964, produced a brochure that failed to mention CLA. The entry of the Sheraton, another Boston-based hotel chain, was a vindication for the company's co-founder and board chairman, Ernest Henderson. Henderson had served as president of the Greater Boston Chamber of Commerce in the 1950s and was part of a delegation that had helped woo Prudential to Boston in the first place. He hosted Carrol Shanks's announcement of the Prudential Center in 1957 at the Sheraton-Plaza Hotel. At that time, he coveted the lease on the center's projected hotel. A consummate urban booster, Henderson was energized by the prospect of using the large hotel, with a direct connection to the Municipal Auditorium as well as its own ballroom, banqueting hall, and meeting rooms, to promote Boston as a tourist and convention destination.[92] Although Sheraton initially lost out to HCA, when HCA withdrew from the project, Sheraton was quick to step in.

Sheraton was able to recycle most of the HCA plan, as executed by CLA, including the "three-in-one" concept, now branded as a "motor hotel," "cosmopolitan hotel," and "luxury tower suites." There would be five themed restaurants and a terrace swimming pool set in a "garden-resort atmosphere." The hotel and auditorium complex allowed Boston to compete with other cities for the lucrative business of hosting conventions. Even before the Prudential Center opened, major bookings through 1973 had been made.[93] One indication of the hotel and convention center's success came in 1972 when the Boston Redevelopment Authority authorized Prudential to augment the original hotel with a second twenty-eight-story structure containing an additional 428 hotel rooms, also managed by Sheraton.[94]

The Residential Side of Prudential

Prudential originally planned for as many as six apartment towers, but announced in August 1963 that it would go forward with two towers, each containing 271 apartments.[95] Prudential perceived great demand for in-town apartment living. Suburbanites were "rapping on Boston's door," eager to leave their detached single-family homes for more urbane digs. The developers of the West End renewal project — called Charles River Park, where the first group of apartment towers opened in 1963 — also believed this to be the case. Boston had seen very little new residential construction since before the Great Depression, and most rental units were located in fixed-up or remodeled old buildings. For suburban empty nesters who had grown accustomed to a high-amenity lifestyle, as well as for upwardly mobile young professionals, there was a demand for "higher-grade apartments."[96] And families moving into Boston from the suburbs on the crest of the apartment house boom were seeking homes closer to their workplaces and to the cultural opportunities of the city.[97]

Orville E. Beal, who became president of Prudential in 1962, announced that CLA would design the residential towers. CLA planned to face the apartments, which were framed in concrete, with "Boston's traditional red brick," a departure from the metal and glass that characterized the central plaza part of the project. The architects planned a "tree-studded park-like" plaza area that hovered some thirty feet above Boylston Street — a continuation of the roof that covered a three-story, seven-hundred-car garage for residents (fig. 45). A broad red-brick walkway connected the residential quarter to the main plaza. The *Globe* noted the intense interest in landscaping: "More than 300 matured trees will be growing in this residential park. More than 600 evergreens and flowering shrubs also will be planted. Tall trees will screen the commercial section of the project from the residential island."[98] Within the larger island of the center, CLA designed a suite of distinct sub-islands. The first tower was planned for young, single people, and included 101 studio units, 96 one-bedroom units, 47 two-bedroom units, 23 three-bedroom units, and four luxury penthouse suites. The second tower would have provided a higher proportion of larger units. In 1965, Prudential and CLA began planning a third, "Far East Apartment No. 5" (the first two were numbered 1 and 3). The original apartment towers, named the Fairfield and the Boylston, opened in 1968. The third, the Gloucester, opened in 1970 and included balconies, an additional luxury feature, on the same block at the eastern end of the complex as the Lord and Taylor building.

Filling In the Site

In the planning for Prudential's "city within a city," many other decisions had to be made involving stores, office towers, residential buildings, and the spaces and connections between them. Although CLA was billed as the coordinating architect for the entire center, the decisions in fact involved a diverse cast of actors that were sometimes in tension with one another — CLA, Prudential itself, tenants with their own minds, building contractors, and still other architectural firms.

In 1964, Prudential was in talks with Lord and Taylor about opening a department store in the "far east section" of the center.[99] Lord and Taylor, which was owned by the Associated Dry Goods Corporation, hired its own architects, Raymond Loewy and William Snaith, to design both the exterior shell and the interior merchandising layout. Snaith headed the architectural arm of the famed industrial designer Loewy's large enterprise. The firm had worked on dozens of Lord and Taylor branch stores and was among the nation's leaders in store design. Loewy and Snaith turned over their "production drawings" to CLA, which produced the final plans. The building for Lord and Taylor was scheduled to be ready for occupancy in mid-1968 (fig. 46).[100] The first floor of the Lord and Taylor building opened directly onto Boylston Street, and its second story had an outlet to the small, elevated plaza in front of the third apartment tower. These buildings in the far east section lay outside the ring road and were connected to apartment buildings 1 and 3 with an uncovered pedestrian bridge.

In July 1967, Prudential officials announced that the fifty-two-story Prudential tower was mostly filled, and that "recent studies indicate that the demand for prime office space in the city has not been fully met."[101] To respond to this need, the Pru unveiled its plan to build a second office tower, with 450,000 square feet of rentable

left **Figure 45** From a brochure for the Prudential Center apartments. The center of the landscaped plaza featured a cylindrical cutaway that looked down to the ramps of the garage that formed the podium for the towers. (Source: Boston Redevelopment Authority archives)

above **Figure 46** Lord and Taylor at the Prudential Center, opened in 1968, design concept by William Snaith of Raymond Loewy's firm. The brick-clad structure featured a recessed portico entrance that faced directly on Boylston Street. (Courtesy of Prudential Financial, Inc.)

office space and its own three-level, seven-hundred-car garage. At the same time, Prudential announced a two-story "specialty shop" to be operated by Saks Fifth Avenue (owned by Gimbel Brothers).[102] Charles Luckman Associates was retained as the architect for these new buildings. By this time, the first of the three residential towers was nearing completion, scheduled for occupancy in the fall of 1967.

Site planning for the second office tower and the third apartment building seems to have been developed in Prudential's own architecture divisions. The Pru's Alfred Linkletter mailed a plan as well as rough massing studies to Charles Stanton in 1966 that proposed a twenty-one-story "Southeast" tower that would gross 700,000 square feet, and he sought Stanton's reaction.[103] Stanton reported to Luckman that Prudential wanted a "very economical design" and had resisted CLA's suggestion of a tower with notched corners, which would have pushed the building taller to make up for the lost floor area at the corners. Prudential's rental agents in Boston saw no advantage there, and Linkletter preferred to fill out the corners and reduce the total height of the tower.[104] The involvement of Linkletter's office in determining site planning and building shape raised issues of who was ultimately responsible for the planning and design of Prudential Center.

As CLA's responsibilities for the design of the Prudential Center expanded, the strains between Luckman and his patron, the Prudential Insurance Company, also increased. In particular, Prudential felt that Luckman was not giving enough personal attention to the project. The insurance company expected more direct involvement from the heads of the architectural firms that it engaged. Prudential officials raised this concern in a memo to CLA written in 1962: "On all of our other projects such as Mid-America, Houston, Newark, etc., we have always had principals of the architectural firm involved conversant with all phases of the job, thus enabling them to better guide their field representatives."[105] CLA's organizational chart ran from Luckman himself to Charles Stanton, who ran the firm's New York office, to Serge Petroff, who was the project architect assigned directly to the Prudential Center. Petroff, in turn, managed a team of associate architects. But Prudential executives wanted to interact with the "top man."

Taken as a whole, CLA's internal memoranda — and the correspondence between the architects, Prudential, and the many contractors who contributed to the project — emphasize the elaborate bureaucratic organization of any major architectural project. It is clear that not only the architectural team but also Prudential executives played a strong role in determining the course of development at the Prudential Center. Architecture was not only "design," but also the management of the building process. What Prudential had told Walter Bogner and the Boston Center Architects in 1955 — that any large development had to be carried out in stages and could not be executed in one fell swoop — turned out to be true.

THE CRITICS ATTACK

Even before the Prudential Center opened, it had become a place that architectural critics loved to hate. Among the early critics were ideological allies of the Boston Center Architects, who believed that the Prudential Insurance Company made a grievous aesthetic and sociological error when it retained CLA rather than BCA to design the complex. In 1956, for example, Siegfried Giedion, the secretary general of CIAM, bemoaned the fact that the Back Bay Center plan would not be built and lambasted the politicians "who had no understanding of what Boston could have gained by such a community center for a great city — and of what it has now lost."[106] In strictly aesthetic terms, few would view the architecture of the Prudential Center — as individual buildings or as a larger ensemble — a great success. We'll never know for sure whether the company, the city, or the architectural world would be better off if Wes Toole, Valentine Howell, and their colleagues had chosen the Boston Center Architects rather than CLA to design the Pru. But when we undertake this exercise in the hypothetical, we will conclude that the answer is not as clear as the critics might have it.

The Prudential Center was still under construction, yet the critics sharpened their spears. They disdained the projected green- and blue-tinted tower as an artistic blight, and disliked the commercialism of the huge "Prudential" sign. "We welcome this new investment in Boston," commented architect Hugh Stubbins, a member of the Back Bay Center team, "but isn't it an intrusion on the public's senses to clad this huge structure in peacock blue, and remind us of its identity with the hammer blow of a sign at its top?"[107] Stubbins's remarks prompted Charles Luckman to reassure Wes Toole that the facade's colored panels would be rendered in shades of muted gray-greens, not "peacock blue." The Prudential tower skin was part of a contemporary trend toward a softer modernism that used colors and grills and screens to create texture instead of more austere glass walls; but the architecture critic Wolf Von Eckardt called it "just fussy."[108]

Perhaps more significantly, critics deplored the total concept of the Pru as a setback for urban development. To Ada Louise Huxtable, writing in 1964, the Prudential Center was a "slick developer's model dropped into a renewal slot in Anycity, U.S.A." She went so far as to call the Pru a "textbook example of urban character assassination" — "rigid," "routine," "overscaled," and even "megalomaniac." At a Harvard urban design conference, Von Eckardt declared that the Prudential Center was "totally out of human scale and has no relation to people and the surrounding buildings which, in turn, have no relation to this enormous tower."[109]

As the opening of the Prudential Center drew near in December 1964, the chorus of criticism became so loud that Mayor Collins felt the need to play architecture critic and at the same time urge a suspension of judgment. He called the Prudential Center "a citadel which has not forgotten the aesthetic values of a proud heritage. And while we're on the aesthetic . . . why don't we answer a few critics who disdain the design of this huge structure." By evoking a "citadel," Collins allowed that the Pru resembled a fortified enclave; but he waved off those who claimed that it fell short of contemporary modernist buildings then rising in Boston: "It is easy enough to refer irreverently to a major undertaking as a burden on the artistic sense of the public — but who could place the Prudential in a category inferior, say, to the dormitories at Harvard — the Earth Sciences Building at MIT — or even the new Boston City Hall, without proper reference to the surrounding locale? Why don't we wait and look at the complete relationships before we offer negative opinion."[110] Collins was referring to José Luis Sert's design for Peabody Terrace, Harvard's graduate student housing towers along the Charles River, and I. M. Pei's twenty-story concrete tower for MIT, which, along with the new City Hall and other buildings going up at Government Center, were being held up as icons of Boston's emergence as a host to distinguished modern architecture.

Luckman deflected the criticism of his design. "I'm very excited," he told the *Globe* soon after the center opened in 1965. "It's just as I envisioned it." He enjoyed the sight of people "sitting and resting" in the landscaped plazas and walkways that he had provided. "People were saying, 'Someone thought about us.' That's a pretty sad commentary on architects, that people have felt left out before." With its generous open spaces, the Prudential Center had been designed with "people in mind," Luckman insisted; armchair critiques from naysayers were hardly worth taking seriously.[111]

What If . . . ?

Although they did not express it in so many words, critics of the Pru's design seemed to bemoan the fact that the project had been entrusted to Luckman — viewed as more or less of an aesthetic philistine — rather than to the modernist greats assembled in the Boston Center Architects. As Robert Campbell, architecture critic for the *Boston Globe,* tartly observed, "Luckman sold soap better than he designed buildings." What if the Pru had made a different decision and enlisted Gropius, Belluschi, Bogner, and their fellow BCA architects to transform the work they had done on the Back Bay Center into the Prudential's Northeastern Home Office complex? Would the product have been received more enthusiastically by the architectural community? And would it have better stood the test of time?[112]

We can only imagine what a BCA-designed Prudential Center would have looked like by extrapolating from the designs for the unbuilt Back Bay Center. In terms of general spatial paradigm, the Prudential and its forebear, the Back Bay Center, had much in common. Both prescribed a ring road that would have isolated the center from surrounding streets. If the Boston Center Architects had been retained, instead of the imposing tower with PRUDENTIAL across the top, we might have had a pinkish pillbox of a building without any overtly commercial adornment. Instead of retail courts that spilled away from the tower toward the ring road, we might have had a more concentrated public space around the tower and an enclosed shopping mall.

Designers of the Back Bay Center left the middle of the site as a discrete open plaza, which was the core of what was intended to be a new civic center, albeit one presided over by a large office tower and a shopping mall. It was a pedestrian preserve in the midst of the fast-paced city that surrounded it; a place where citizens might gather and debate the issues of the day, as in an idealized image of the ancient Greek agora. Luckman may have intended to make just such a space with his retail plazas. But instead of hollowing out a core for the new city, the CLA plan placed the tower at the center of the design, which scattered the impact of the plazas. A writer for *Architectural Forum* speculated that the tower's central location was designed to preserve the highest land values at the center of the site.[113] We may speculate that CLA wanted to allow equal access to the Pru from both Huntington and Boylston Streets. From Prudential's perspective, placing the tower at the center of the site meant that motorists approaching on both avenues — and, ultimately, on the Mass Pike — would have equal visual access to the corporate monument. When the central tower was first proposed in 1957, it anchored a massive cross axis. As the project was broken into pieces, the center tower and plaza section were left as a fragment. CLA proceeded to arrange the buildings in a rigid, geometric order that failed to spark a relationship between buildings and plazas (fig. 47). But there is reason to question whether or not a pedigreed design by noted modernists would have been any more dynamic or appealing to people. The reason points to a larger challenge to the spatial logic of large-scale design in the motor age. The best urban open spaces are experienced as a pleasant

Figure 47 Construction photograph, north plaza, December 28, 1964 (Courtesy of Tutor-Perini Corporation)

relief from the intimacy of the streets that lead to them — there is a sense of discovery to these places that endows them with a feeling of spatial and psychic comfort. The Back Bay Center design may have rightly anticipated the convenience and popularity of interior shopping malls. Despite the architects' intention to design a new core for the modern city, however, we may wonder if the Back Bay Center might not have been equally criticized as an isolated behemoth disconnected from its surroundings.

Could the Back Bay Center plan have been brought off successfully? Perhaps. But there would have been many obstacles and challenges. First, we don't know what changes the Boston Center Architects would have had to make to stay within the Prudential's budgetary constraints and cautious, incremental planning. Would they have been able to adapt their design to the political and economic forces that affected the step-by-step approach to the Prudential Center? Second, it might have been difficult for the Prudential businessmen and the BCA visionaries to work together. In spite of the occasional strains between the Pru and CLA, there was still a certain rapport among businessmen that might have been more difficult to achieve with BCA. In terms of aesthetic distinction, the BCA-designed tower might have met the same critical fate as the Pan Am tower (later renamed the Met Life tower) built over the air rights of the New York Central Railroad behind Grand Central Terminal, which was designed by essentially the same group that worked on the Back Bay Center. The Pan Am building was maligned by critics as an ungainly intrusion in the midtown landscape and has been associated with the "shattering of the modernist dream."[114] More fundamentally, the Back Bay Center represented an urban vision not all that different from CLA's Prudential Center, and might have met the same resistance from critics. Like CLA, the BCA planners would have had to accommodate the highway easement that forced the elevation of the plaza level. Both embodied an insulated plan, divorced from the streets of the surrounding neighborhoods.

Writing just a week before the official opening of the Prudential Center in April 1965, the *Monitor*'s June Bibb described the scene at the end of the working day:

> Secretaries, executives, clerks, salesmen stream from the tower through tree-lined plazas. Passing fashionable shops, gliding down smooth escalators, and filling subways and the new Massachusetts Turnpike extension — they head for home. The working day is over for the tower's thousands.[115]

It seemed, at least at first, that the planners and architects of the Prudential Center had accomplished many of the same goals of the Boston Center Architects. The Pru embodied a vision of the postwar urban landscape as an efficient, frictionless enclave and a reprieve from the congestion and perceived discomfort of the city around it.

Chapter 6

The Legacy of the Prudential Center
Confidence, Criticism, and Change

SHERATON

The bowed fronts of townhouses and a landscaped median in the South End contrast with the towers of the Prudential Center (Courtesy of City of Boston Archives)

As he craned his head in 1964 to look up at the Pru's newly completed fifty-two-story tower, Mayor John Collins saw much more than an office building. He declared it a "bellwether of the renaissance of a city determined to regain its rightful place among the top municipalities of the world."[1] Boston had obtained the imprimatur of a great corporation that had demonstrated its faith in the city's future by constructing its Northeastern Home Office complex there. Indeed, the evidence suggests that despite the criticisms leveled against it from many quarters, the Pru helped to usher an era of business confidence in Boston. This new era was reflected by the reshaping of Boston's architecture — both in the old downtown and in the Back Bay — over the course of the following decades.

The Pru was not by anyone's lights an unqualified triumph. As time went on, many problems were revealed — both physical as well as financial — and some of them were eventually addressed by an extensive reexamination and refurbishment of the project; indeed, these revisions have continued into the twenty-first century. One indicator of the Pru's success over the long run, however, has been its demonstrated malleability. Designed as an enclave, with its ring road holding back the surrounding city and its podium resting on three levels of parking garages, recent alterations and additions have transformed the Prudential Center from an urban island into what is intended to be a piece of connective urban tissue. At the very least, the Pru is still there, still making its mark on the Boston landscape even if its tower now presides over a different supporting cast of buildings.

There is also a broader balance sheet that needs to be considered. The legacy of the Prudential Center includes the interplay of corporate, political, and architectural decisions that permitted it to be built in the first place. A major shaping force of postwar urban America has been the uneasy — and sometimes misguided — partnership between large corporations and government to protect against urban deterioration and to create the structures, byways, and ambience of the reimagined city.

INSURING THE PUBLIC REALM

To mark the dedication of the Prudential Center in 1965, Prudential put on a three-day pageant that was heavily covered by print, radio, and television media.[2] The center officially opened to the public on Sunday, April 18, with free access to the observation deck, guided tours of the Sheraton-Boston Hotel, a choral and symphony concert on the south plaza, and an Easter Parade. On April 19, the center was formally dedicated with a presentation of flags from all of the states represented in Prudential's northeastern region. After a benediction, the event was punctuated by a cannon salute triggered by an electronic signal sent from NASA's Mariner IV satellite, then orbiting Mars — a bit of theater that dramatized Prudential's role as a bridge between Boston's past and its space-age future. Following the pattern of the previous regional home offices, Prudential was presented with a fragment of the Rock of Gibraltar by the queen of England's consul general in Boston. It was installed in the lobby of the tower and inscribed with the year of dedication beneath an inscription chiseled into the greenish marble: "The Future Belongs to Those Who Prepare for It."[3]

To mark the occasion, Prudential organized a symposium called "The Free Society and Its Posture in World Affairs." It was held in the grand ballroom of the Pru's Sheraton-Boston Hotel and broadcast on WHDH television. Prudential engaged Walter Cronkite to moderate the forum and invited such luminaries as U.N. ambassador Adlai Stevenson and former prime minister Sir Anthony Eden to participate as panelists.[4] The purpose of the forum was to promote Prudential as a leading sponsor of public discourse and to establish the Prudential Center as Boston's chief site for such conversations. It demonstrated the company's commitment to playing a central role not only in Boston's landscape and financial life but also in its public realm and culture. Moreover, the symposium's Cold War subject matter alluded to Prudential's belief that a vigorous free enterprise system could meet the challenges of the day.

The dedication was scheduled for the weekend of Patriots' Day — a state holiday that commemorates the first battles of the Revolutionary War — and timed to coincide with the Boston Marathon, whose finish line was moved from Boylston Street to the north plaza of the Prudential Center.[5] The marathon is a Boston institution; it has been held every year since 1897 and is part of the enduring culture of the city. The Pru was making a concerted effort to insert itself into that culture, and the effort continued in the years following the dedication. Prudential became heavily involved with local philanthropies and continued to mobilize the Prudential Center itself as "an action place where things happen in Boston."[6] This effort included conscientious programming in the center's open plaza spaces, which hosted summer band concerts, square dancing, and even ice skating.

In keeping with its decentralization policy, the Prudential was determined to "earn for the company the reputation of a good corporate citizen in Boston and New England." By its own lights, it succeeded. Within a short span of years following the opening of the Northeastern Home Office, the company had transformed itself from an outsider into a local. In 1974, Thomas Allsopp, president of the northeastern office, reported that "Prudential now is regarded as a full-fledged member of the Boston business community and has a presence today in the state and the region which is far more important than it was a decade ago."[7] To be sure, these efforts were all part of Prudential's advertising and promotional activities; the company was seeking to increase the sales of insurance policies in the seven-state northeast district. Allsopp reported that this goal had been achieved.

INSTILLING CONFIDENCE

The Pru was the centerpiece of a cluster of projects that were meant to instill confidence in Boston as a modern city built on centuries-old foundations, and Prudential executives were fully aware of that intended impact. President Orville E. Beal, speaking at the Prudential Center dedication in 1965, was explicit about this. In Boston, he said, the insurance company not only looked to construct an efficient regional headquarters structure, but also "wanted to help meet some of this City's most pressing needs. One was the need for modern convention facilities. Another was the need for rebuilding investor confidence."[8] Some feared that the growth of the Back Bay area would draw companies and shoppers away from downtown and threaten its viability. Mayor Collins acknowledged this concern in 1964: "The fear has often been expressed in the past that the Pru would create another downtown on the other side of the City, thus cutting the City in half." The evidence, albeit circumstantial, was otherwise. Collins reported that a combination of "planning, private enterprise and redevelopment have co-operated to effect a city-wide renaissance rather than sectional competition."[9] Lending support to this claim, a Boston Redevelopment Authority survey in 1969 reported that, although many firms had relocated to the Prudential Center from the downtown business district, the downtown district maintained a near-zero vacancy rate. Indeed, the demand for downtown office space continued to grow and, by the mid-1960s, a commercial building boom was under way in downtown Boston.[10]

Among the first to reinvest in the old downtown was the State Street Bank, which became the flagship tenant of a \$20 million, thirty-story tower in the financial district.[11] Other Boston banks were soon to follow, and by the mid-1970s Boston had a cluster of new high-rises there. In addition to the new State Street Bank tower, completed in 1966, new buildings in the financial district were sponsored by the New England Merchants Bank, the Boston Company, the National Shawmut Bank, and Fiduciary Trust, among others. New England Merchants, which had signed on with the Pru as a flagship tenant in 1958, built its own forty-story tower at 28 State Street in 1970 on a parcel adjacent to the new Boston City Hall that had been cleared as part of the Government Center urban renewal project. Just across the street, Pietro Belluschi designed the forty-one-story Boston Company Building (1969). The Architects Collaborative, continuing its work after the death of Walter Gropius in 1969, designed downtown towers for both Fiduciary Trust (1971), on a location adjacent to the Central Artery, and Shawmut (1975) near Post Office Square. Hugh Stubbins designed the striking, washboard-shaped Boston Federal Reserve Bank (1977) near South Station.

Closer to home, one of Prudential's first neighbors to begin the rebuilding process was the Christian Science Church, which in 1965 announced a thirty-one-acre building project to expand its world headquarters, including a twenty-two-story tower for church administration, a six-hundred-car underground garage, and an expansion of the Church Park to seven acres, including a reflecting pool. Architect I. M. Pei, who had also been retained to do master planning for the Government Center project, was the designer.[12] The Pru was joined in the Back Bay by the sixty-story John Hancock tower, completed in 1976. The Hancock building, designed by I. M. Pei's partner, Harry Cobb, was a soaring, mirrored, trapezoidal-plan tower neatly placed on a relatively small block across from Trinity Church on Copley Square.

By the mid-1970s Boston had firmly reestablished its position as an important office center. Certainly Prudential executives themselves liked to claim that the Prudential Center "broke the log jam" on new commercial construction in Boston. Looking back in 1974, Thomas Allsopp surmised, "There seems to be a kind of corporate 'keeping up with the Joneses' that made many old buildings look inadequate to their owners after Prudential Center appeared on the Boston scene."[13] One BRA official speculated that the Prudential Center prompted John Hancock to build its taller tower "through good old-fashioned corporate competition."[14]

Few of the new commercial projects followed the urban redevelopment model established by the state redevelopment statute, Chapter 121A, that had permitted Prudential to develop land in the "public interest," however. Most firms, presumably, did not want the burden of establishing a public purpose, and the practice of ad hoc tax agreements between the mayor and developers persevered. Yet Prudential was often credited for igniting Boston's building activity. When surveying "tomorrow's Boston — a city of new scale and grandeur," one journalist concluded that "the turning point for the city came in the late 1950s when the Prudential Insurance Company of America decided to build a multimillion-dollar center on soon to be abandoned railroad yards in the Back Bay."[15]

It is difficult to isolate specific causes and effects in the context of an evolving national, regional, and urban economy. Yet there is reason to believe that the Pru's success in bringing off its challenging "urban renewal" project emboldened others to proceed with their ambitious projects, both in the Back Bay and in the old financial district. We may hypothesize that in the domain of urban development, as in financial transactions and other domains of life, confidence can be contagious: when public, quasi-public, and private actors see successful urban ventures, supported by public-private cooperation, they are more ready to take such risks and face such challenges themselves.[16]

THE WINDS OF TIME: RENOVATING THE PRU

Despite the fact that the Pru has been widely acknowledged for its role in boosting Boston's development prospects, the years have done little to soften the critical rejection of it as a piece of architecture. Robert Campbell of the *Globe* recently opined that "the tower's aluminum-curtain wall . . . still looks like mesh you'd pull down over the front of your pawnshop to defy burglars."[17] For many years Campbell bestowed an annual "Pru Award" — in honor of "the ghastly Prudential Center" — on what he considered the most objectionable building to grace the city's skyline that year.[18] Architect and critic Donlyn Lyndon has called the tower "an energetically ugly, square shaft that offends the Boston skyline more than any other structure."[19] It is possible that if the Prudential facade had been better received, the project as a whole might have also been considered more of an aesthetic success. (In 1987, Prudential hired the firm of Hugh Stubbins — the architect who had criticized the tower so vociferously — and Hellmuth, Obata, and Kassabaum to consider options to retrofit the tower's facade and roof profile, but nothing came of the study.)[20] But the most pointed criticism of the Prudential Center's original structures was that they did not fit into their urban context. "It ignored the old city around it," Campbell wrote in 1990, "the city of humanly scaled streets and squares and buildings. Instead, the Pru introduced what was then foolishly believed to be the model for a city of the future: a place of bold towers and vast open spaces."[21] "Alas," Campbell wrote, "the original Pru complex was an ugly alien." It looked like a "vast tourist capsule from Mars."[22]

In the last analysis, a balanced appraisal of the Prudential Center must include consideration of the project on the terms of its own sponsors and designers. In fact, Luckman's Prudential Center achieved to a great extent the company's desire to place its own stamp on Boston by anchoring a major expansion of the city's downtown. In a report to Prudential president Donald MacNaughton in 1969, Allsopp described positive results for the Prudential Center. The rental of all of the center's existing buildings was completed in 1969. The tower building was fully occupied and had attracted top-flight tenants, such as Gillette and Boston Edison. The three apartment towers, comprising 781 units, were fully rented and had a waiting list. The Lord and Taylor department store showed strong and increasing sales. The Sheraton-Boston Hotel had the highest occupancy rate in the city at eighty-six percent. Moreover, the Prudential Center garages were generating revenue, a gross income of $1.6 million in 1969. The second office tower, then in construction, was already seventy-seven percent rented, and the Saks Fifth Avenue department store was about to begin construction.[23]

Nonetheless, Allsopp reported that, on the whole, Prudential's return on investment was disappointing. Prudential was entitled to a six percent return and had not reached that mark. One of the main reasons was that the center was not succeeding as a retail destination. Prudential had promoted the civic qualities of the center by pointing to the large percentage of unbuilt plaza space. This was the keystone to Luckman's vision of "humanation." But sheer expanse did not contribute to a lively shopping atmosphere. Luckman's virtue — "freedom of space" — had become a liability.

Part of the problem came from a failure of the planners to anticipate how strong the winds would be in the retail areas. Heavy winds in the central plaza section and the pedestrian promenades at the base of the tower were a serious problem, recognized as early as 1965, soon after the plaza had opened. The associate general manager of Prudential's Northeastern Home Office, housed in the Prudential tower, fired off a note to his superior in Newark, the executive general manager of home office buildings and plant department, that the wind issue in the plaza had reached a crisis phase: "Yesterday afternoon and evening there were very high winds gusting more than 50 miles per hour which again highlighted the serious condition we have on the plaza level. It was virtually impossible for women to open the doors of the drug store. Furthermore, one of our men stayed out by the drug store for 15 or 20 minutes and observed that the doors facing the east would not close for at least ten minutes because of the wind pressure." If that wasn't enough, the associate general manager reported that a few people had almost been blown into the moat.[24]

An engineer from New York University was hired to study the wind issue with a scale-model wind tunnel, and produced a rudimentary proposal for wind barriers. As time went by, however, it became clear that wind barriers would not be enough to fix the retail situation. The larger problem was that the retail scheme simply did not work. "People don't know we're here," complained the manager of a Magnavox radio and television store.[25] The stores were not easily accessible from the surrounding streets. Indeed, they were practically invisible to anyone who was not already at work in the center. CLA had placed escalators at the ring road level that ascended to the covered porches of each commercial pavilion, intended as a functional complement to the more ceremonial staircases. But the escalators could not correct for the broader issue of the Prudential Center's remove from the streets around it. CLA's "moat" theme — the designers had set off each commercial block with a rectangular pool that potential shoppers could cross at only two points — accentuated this divide. Though they faced each other across a plaza, the retail arcades seemed to be "single-sided," explained urban designer Gary Hack, and they "lacked the intensity to seem more than an adjunct to the offices above."[26]

Part of the problem with the retail arcades may have been that the insurance executives at Prudential never took the retail aspect of their center seriously enough. In early meetings with the Boston Center Architects, Prudential's senior managers had dismissed the idea that a regional shopping center would be a key component of the overall plan. They were more interested in the office and convention center pieces of the ensemble. It turned out that the company underestimated the important role that shopping would play in revitalizing Boston. This point came home in a big way at the end of the 1970s, when the conversion of Faneuil Hall and Quincy Market from a forsaken wholesale location to a cleaned-up shopping mall and food court was heralded as the new answer to the problems of the city: not to offer bold, futuristic visions, but to carefully curate the city as a historical showpiece and to combine shopping and eating with a "sense of place." What sense of place could the Prudential Center offer to consumers, built as it had been over a long-erased rail yard?

The unmet challenges of the Prudential Center were underscored when a competing development got under way in the 1980s that was very much its progeny, a hotel, office, residential, and retail complex called Copley Place. Copley Place was an extension of the infrastructural investments of the Pike and Pru, built over the air rights of the Mass Pike ramps on the east side of Huntington Avenue and facing Copley Square. Although the site presented considerable difficulties, the trouble was worth it. Its developers, the Urban Investment and Development Corporation (UIDC), recognized an unmet demand for office and retail space as well as hotel rooms in the area. Largely capitalized by the Aetna Insurance Company, UIDC insisted that the development was impossible without public subsidy and applied to carry out the work under state urban redevelopment law, Chapter 121A. Ultimately, the project received its public subsidy through an Urban Development Action Grant, administered by the U.S. Department of Housing and Urban Development, which helped pay for site preparation costs. UIDC signed a ninety-nine-year lease with the Mass Pike, which supported air-rights projects such as Copley Place as another revenue stream. The Architects Collaborative — the same firm that was part of the team spurned by Prudential in the 1950s — was assigned the task of solving the complicated site planning and design challenges: the highway ramps had to be rerouted and the entire complex was coordinated with a new Back Bay transit station and the addition of a new transit route, the Orange Line.[27]

To assuage neighborhood apprehension raised by such a large development, a Citizens' Review Commission, made up of neighborhood associations and government agencies, was organized to identify local concerns and develop project guidelines. The building program consisted of a retail center anchored by a Neiman-Marcus department store, office space in four low-rise towers, two hotel towers, one hundred units of housing, and a parking structure for nearly fifteen hundred cars. Perhaps ironically, however, Copley Place, despite its name, had no more "sense of place" than its competitor did. It was essentially an enclosed suburban mall constructed on an urban site. Writing for the *Times*, Paul Goldberger echoed criticism of the Prudential Center when he said that Copley Place was "dropped like a flying saucer in the middle of the city."[28]

In two respects, however, Copley Place had learned from the Pru. Its shopping spaces were protected from the elements and it was better connected to mass transit.

It also tried to capitalize on the Pru's proximity by constructing an elevated skywalk between the two developments. Copley Place had only one department store anchor and hoped to benefit from the Lord and Taylor and Saks Fifth Avenue located at the Prudential Center. Unfortunately, however, pedestrians crossing to the Prudential side were deposited on a windswept plaza without a clear sense of how to proceed.[29]

Motivated primarily by commercial reality, in the 1980s Prudential began to look at how it might revamp its own complex to improve the retail environment and build out the site with a series of new office and residential structures.[30] As noted above, one of the problems with Luckman's scheme for the Prudential Center was that the plazas were too wide to create a cohesive, shopping mall environment. The new retail plan — designed by a partnership between Carr, Lynch, Hack, and Sandell of Cambridge, Sikes, Jennings, Kelly, and Brewer of Houston, and Communication Arts Incorporated of Boulder, Colorado — envisioned the Prudential Center as a sequence of enclosed streets (fig. 48).

The renovated retail component was ready in 1993. New shop fronts placed in the interior, skylit "street arcades" had bowed display windows and projecting signs. Planners encouraged individuality in storefront design. New public spaces were placed at the intersections of the arcade paths, including a ninety-foot-square Center Court, the "central city square of Prudential Center." An enclosed food court was placed in the North Plaza.[31] The plan included better links to a refurbished subway station, part of a renewed interest in providing convenient transit connections. On Boylston Street, architects designed an eye-catching, glass-enclosed escalator to draw shoppers from the street (fig. 49).

In the 1980s and early '90s, the standards of "good urbanism" had turned from open plazas to "busy streets."[32] In revamping the Prudential Center, planners invoked the language of traditional urban fabric and small-scale place-making as correctives to the old Pru, which seemed both out of scale and out of context. The new plan endeav-

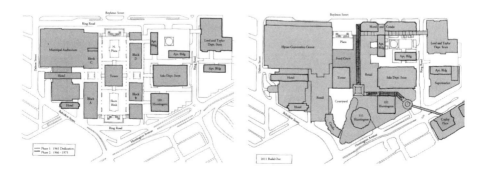

Figure 48 Diagrams of the Prudential Center in its several phases (Drawing by Amy DeDonato with James Andrachuk)

Figure 49 The Prudential Center in 2011: the new main entrance to the Pru from Boylston Street, with the new office tower, 111 Huntington, visible to the left of the original tower. At right, inside the new "street" of the Prudential Center. (Photo by Terah Maher)

ored to turn what had been viewed as an island separating the Back Bay from the South End into a bridge connecting them. The goal, according to one architect with Carr, Lynch, Hack, and Sandell, was "to knit the Prudential Center into its context."[33]

A key part of that reknitting was eliminating the ring road that divorced the Prudential Center from surrounding streets and placing new buildings there. The integrity of the ring road had begun to deteriorate when renovations and additions expanded the War Memorial Auditorium (later renamed the John B. Hynes Veterans Auditorium) toward Boylston Street in 1989. Urban designers from Carr, Lynch, Hack, and Sandell seized on this first move: "By displacing a portion of the ring road along Boylston, the Hynes expansion rendered the remainder of the roadway redundant, thus freeing up the Boylston frontage for other uses."[34]

Those other uses included new office, residential, and hotel facilities housed in a mix of mid-rise blocks and towers built up to the edges of the surrounding streets. On the south side of the site, an eleven-story condominium structure was designed to curve around the Huntington Avenue edge of the center. The Boston firm of Childs Bertman Tseckares Architects (CBT) designed the Pru's new signature skyscraper, 111 Huntington Street, a thirty-six-story tower — clad with reflective glass and crowned with an open-framed ornamental dome — that rests on a five-story base with office and retail functions as well as connections to a refurbished Metropolitan Boston Transit Authority station. It opened in 2002. These two structures framed a wedge-shaped south courtyard imagined as a green space, an antidote to the Pru's concrete plazas.

On Boylston Street, a mid-rise condominium and hotel structure (a branch of the Mandarin Oriental chain), also designed by CBT, has risen on the former site of the ring road. A "neighborhood supermarket" was placed at the eastern edge of the site. In 2007, the Hynes Convention Center was updated again to allow for retail space on Boylston Avenue. At the time of this writing, there are plans for rounding out the building program with two final towers. One of these, 888 Boylston Street, another CBT design, would stand on what was the north plaza of the Prudential Center, completing the reconstruction of a unified street wall on Boylston Street and wrapping the central tower in a cocoon of surrounding structures. There will also be a residential tower at the rear of the Lord and Taylor building on Exeter Street, designed by the Elkus Manfredi firm.[35]

In advance of these renovations, Prudential moved to terminate its Chapter 121A agreement with the Boston Redevelopment Authority. The Prudential Center would be split into two parts: the office, hotel, and commercial portion would be released from the 121A agreement, and the residential portion would retain 121A status. Prudential claimed that it would be impossible to seek outside investors to support its renovation under the financial strictures of 121A, and city planners agreed. The arguments to release the Pru from 121A echoed the arguments made less than thirty years before to put it in place. Coming as it did during the economic downturn of the early 1990s, the project should be encouraged, a BRA planner claimed, because it represented "a vote of confidence in the city's long-term economic health."[36]

In its application to terminate the Chapter 121A agreement, Prudential claimed that the center was already considered "outdated and obsolescent." In the first go-round, public benefits had accrued to the sheer scale and scope of the project. The definition of public benefits was different in 1989, including the goal to "redress the existing isolation and separation of the Prudential Center from the surrounding neighborhoods by producing continuous, active, and well-scaled urban arcades through the Prudential Center."[37] Prudential's request was granted.

At first, Prudential simply announced its ambitious plan to expand the building program at the Prudential Center. But times had changed: it quickly faced opposition from neighborhood groups in the adjacent communities. Kevin White, Boston's mayor from 1968 to 1984, and his successor, Raymond Flynn, had insisted on a new approach along a "participatory model" — likely inspired by the Citizens' Review organized for Copley Place — and they created the Prudential Property Advisory Committee, a consortium of twenty-two neighborhood, civic, and business groups to oversee, along with the Boston Redevelopment Authority, the development of a new plan. PruPAC, as the group was called, was given authority to establish planning guidelines, evaluate design concepts, and assess environmental impacts. What had previously been mediated largely through an internal bureaucratic decision-making process between corporations was now worked through more public channels.[38]

Perhaps surprisingly, in the midst of its renovation program and not long after the initial retail component opened, Prudential sold the center to Boston Properties, a real estate investment trust, which inherited the plans for its redevelopment. The reason given was that in the 1990s Prudential began planning for demutualization: the company was moving from the customer-owned model and becoming a joint stock company. In preparation, Prudential decided to sell off many of its most significant real estate assets to raise money to make the company more appealing as a stock offering. Selling the Prudential Center was part of this shift. In 1998, Boston Properties bought the Prudential Center for about $700 million.[39] The residential portion was eventually sold to Avalon Properties. Prudential carried out its demutualization in 2001.

DENOUEMENT: DIMINISHING LOCAL COMMITMENTS

Prudential's demutualization was an unmistakable sign that the insurance company was moving away from the characteristics that had defined it over the course of the twentieth century. During the 1980s and '90s, Prudential had expanded to become a diversified financial planning and services firm and not just a seller of life insurance policies.[40] One result of this corporate strategy is that the company streamlined its life insurance operations and hedged on its regional home office system. In fact, Prudential had formally closed its Northeastern Home Office as early as 1983. Though it maintained offices in the tower, the Prudential Center had become just one more real estate asset managed by the Prudential Realty Group, one of many subdivisions in an emerging vision of the insurance company as a multifaceted financial services and investment firm. By the mid-1990s, the rest of the regional home offices as they were envisioned in 1945 had been shuttered.[41]

For so long, Prudential's decentralization had been, in effect, an urban policy. In the final stages of the regional home office program, however, the company shifted away from this principle and began to leave the city. The Central Atlantic Home Office, announced in 1969, was built as an unabashedly suburban campus in Dublin Township, just off the Pennsylvania Turnpike some twenty miles north of Philadelphia. Designed by Philadelphia architect Vincent Kling, the CAHO building was a low-slung, four-story structure featuring a repeating pattern of rhomboid forms (fig. 50). Occupying only five percent of its eighty-two-acre site, the building was carefully placed in a richly landscaped campus with an artificial pond and surrounded by surface parking for more than two thousand cars. For the first time, Prudential abstained from labeling the building with its name or an emblem of the Rock of Gibraltar. Though visible — and easily accessible — from the Pennsylvania Turnpike, the CAHO building maintained a low profile. When it opened in 1972, the office stood alone in the landscape. Today it is surrounded by big-box retail stores and residential subdivisions organized around cul-de-sacs. The RHO program had finally gone suburban, and it seemed that Prudential's commitment to the center city was waning.[42]

The Central Atlantic Home Office pointed to a broader suburban strategy for Prudential's office location. In the late 1960s, Prudential executives considered what to do in Los Angeles, where the Western Home Office was at capacity. Prudential made studies for erecting a tall building on Wilshire and also considered a parcel in the Bunker Hill redevelopment area. Ultimately, Prudential eschewed both options and announced in 1976 that it was moving the WHO to a large site in Westlake Village in the San Fernando Valley. Ground was broken in 1979 on a three-level complex for twelve hundred employees on a nearly fifty-acre site. That same year Prudential sold the Wilshire Boulevard building.[43]

In 1977, twenty-five years after the Southwestern Home Office opened on Holcomb Boulevard and Old Main Street in Houston, Prudential moved to a low-slung office building just off the Interstate 610 loop highway that featured a freestanding garage nearly as large as the office building itself.[44] Prudential sold the Kenneth Franzheim–designed building in 1974 to the M. D. Anderson Cancer Center, and it was subsumed in the growing Texas Medical Center complex. After a rehabilitation study, M. D. Anderson announced its intentions to demolish the building in 2002, claiming that the foundation was cracking as it settled. Preservationists were unable to make the case that Franzheim's restrained moderne style warranted the landmark status that would have saved it from the wrecking ball. The building was not forward-thinking enough to stand as an early example of International Style modernism, nor was it seductive enough as a late example of the art deco style. Although designed to provide modern office space for Prudential, by the end of the twentieth century it was not modern enough to function efficiently for the hospital that had bought it. Caught in the middle in more ways than one, the SWHO is to be destroyed despite the protestations of a few local connoisseurs of regional modernist architecture.[45]

Administrative decentralization had begun as an urban policy; but its logical conclusion took Prudential to the suburbs. Between 1971 and 1974, Prudential sent

Figure 50 Two visions of the regional home office: Prudential's Central Atlantic Home Office, designed by Vincent G. Kling and Associates, in Dublin Township, Pennsylvania, ca. 1968. *right* The Prudential Center, Boston, not long after its dedication in 1965. (Courtesy of Prudential Financial, Inc.)

thousands of employees from Newark to satellite suburban offices.[46] Despite all of these changes, however, and to its credit, Prudential has maintained its corporate offices in downtown Newark, where the company's top executives continue to work. Still, in retrospect, the commitment Prudential made to locate its offices in cities in the 1950s and '60s now looks like the high-tide mark for corporate identification with civic interests.

CORPORATIONS AND COMMUNITIES

The Prudential Center represented one company's genuine, if naive, view that corporate interests could stand for the interests of a broader public. This belief suited the particular nature of the insurance enterprise. Executives believed that insurance company interests converged with the interests of people at large: not only by providing so many of them with life insurance and the foundations of fiscal security but also by reshaping the cities in which they lived.

In fact, the Prudential Center could hardly speak for all the people of Boston. In Boston, as in other cities, large-scale "urban renewal" projects in the center city stood at a considerable remove from neighborhood groups and less advantaged citizens who began stirring in the late 1960s to protest poverty, unemployment, poor housing, and bad schools. The Prudential Center, along with the Charlesgate Apartments built at the West End renewal site, had constructed residential towers to lure the middle classes back to the city. In the literal and allegorical shadow of the Prudential Center, South End community groups protested the city's recent renewal plan, which had demolished neighborhood housing and replaced it, among others things, with a parking lot. For several weeks, protesters established a "tent city" on the site, arguing against further demolition and asserting their right to affordable housing in their neighborhood.[47] The unified image of a prosperous Boston region, projected in large part by Prudential, was rupturing and showing signs of a split personality, in spite of glittering projects that stood like fortified enclaves.

Right after the Pru was opened, these tensions manifested themselves in another way. One of the first conventions held at the new municipal auditorium was a meeting of the National School Board Association. That morning, a thousand people gathered outside in protest, spilling onto the ring road adjacent to Boylston Street, in an effort to embarrass the Boston School Committee by accusing it of fostering racial imbalance in the school system. This had not been the sort of public gathering that Prudential officials had envisioned.[48]

On its own, the Prudential Center does not carry the same burden of collective trauma as urban redevelopment in the West End, New York Streets, or countless other places across American cities. Prudential bought the land independently — both the rail yard from the New York Central as well as the Mechanics Hall — without the benefit of eminent domain. However, the Boston Extension of the Mass Pike is not equally immune from those critiques that urban redevelopment came at the expense of marginal communities. The construction of the Pike extension was responsible for displacing many families and helped cultivate a resolve to oppose additional highways in the Boston area.

The Turnpike Extension, for all its promise, also created as many problems as it solved. Just as John Volpe and other advocates of an Inner Belt had feared, the Central Artery was choked with traffic soon after it was completed. The congestion was made worse by the fact that the extension fed directly into the Central Artery. The Inner Belt was viewed as necessary for proper traffic engineering, but the tide was turning away from big road projects. Early in the 1970s, urban planners were already looking at the possibility of depressing the Central Artery below ground to remove what was widely perceived as an obstruction and an eyesore and to enable reconstruction of the street surface — the project that ultimately came to pass as the "Big Dig."

One final legacy of the Prudential Center must be considered: the rise of the South End. Spared the fate of the West End and New York Streets, the South End retained much of its nineteenth-century architecture. After the Prudential Center eliminated the rail yard and suggested, if awkwardly, a connection between the South End and the Back Bay, this once grubby neighborhood was poised for a resurgence as an upscale residential district. In the late 1970s, journalists began writing about the "gentrification" of the South End, as affluent whites — "liberal, urban pioneers" — began moving back into center-city neighborhoods.[49]

The broader issue that the Prudential Center raised, however — that private development could in some way represent the legitimate will of the people — has had a mixed legacy. Are public-private partnerships in urban development desirable or even genuinely possible? The case of the Prudential Center can be used to support more than one set of answers to these questions. Several types of criticism can be leveled at the Pru. One of the richest companies in the world took advantage of urban redevelopment laws originally designed to help the poor. By its maneuvering for tax breaks, Prudential may have served its own goals of financial risk management but, at the same time, avoided paying its fair share of the freight. Yet its insistence on predictable tax rates came on the heels of an urban political regime that had consistently taken advantage of downtown property owners and dampened investment: it is important to remember that, outside of a few exceptions, the Prudential was the first major real estate project in Boston since the 1920s.

The Pru may also be sharply criticized — and indeed has been, rather unremittingly — for eschewing a design that might have more fully embraced the surrounding city and for building an undistinguished tower that marked (some would say "marred") the Boston skyline. From an architectural point of view, the design could certainly have been better: more interesting buildings were being built in comparable circumstances at that time. But nobody in the 1950s was producing urban ensembles that fit in with the surrounding neighborhood, because integration was not the ideal. In fact, most of these developments were designed not to blend in with the existing community but to replace it. Even the supposedly distinguished design for the Back Bay Center would have been a city within a city. Now such urban designs have fallen out of fashion, but they were very much in vogue when the Prudential Center was conceived.

Our contemporary criticisms for urban buildings designed around automobile transport are similarly anachronistic. Today, confronted with global warming, escalating gas prices, and social alienation, our romance with the car is waning, and an interest in public transportation, bicycling, and walking is on the rise. But when the Prudential Center plans were hatched, the train and its facilities were regarded by many — including the leading planners of the day — as a noisome scourge, whereas the car was seen as a progressive force.

Finally, critics have rightly attacked urban renewal for its unfair displacement of poor and politically marginalized communities. As early as the 1960s there were criticisms of urban renewal on fiscal, spatial, and social terms. Many claimed that urban renewal could not deliver on its promises — adding new tax revenue, rebuilding the business district, attracting the white middle classes back from the suburbs. By the 1980s, however, a few American cities had been able to capitalize on the desire of professional classes to return, and they are now thriving. It is the luxury of a successful city like Boston to regret particular development failures, especially in an era when many American cities are failing as a whole.

Of course, all of Boston's success cannot be laid at the feet of Prudential, but cities undeniably require a certain amount of financial investment before they can come back to the point where we mourn the old neighborhoods that have been lost. So when we cast a jaundiced eye at the Pru — while commuting to work on the Pike, or strolling on the esplanade by the Charles River, or cheering from the stands at Fenway Park — we should remember that at a time when American cities were struggling Prudential took a gamble and made a decisive investment in its new home. And perhaps the fact that we're all still here, criticizing it some fifty years later, is a sign that the gamble paid off.

Notes

ABBREVIATIONS

I have adopted the following shorthand to cite archival materials.

PA: Prudential Insurance Company of America archives, Newark, N.J. (followed by box number and folder name when possible)

BRA: Official documents and publications of the Boston Redevelopment Authority, held in Government Documents at the Boston Public Library (followed by document number when possible)

CLP: The Papers of Charles Luckman (followed by folder name when possible)

MTAA: The Massachusetts Turnpike Authority Archives, Weston, Mass. (followed by box number)

INTRODUCTION

1 See Robert Fogelson, *Downtown: Its Rise and Fall, 1880-1950* (New Haven: Yale University Press, 2001); Raymond Vernon, "The Changing Economic Function of the Center City," in *Urban Renewal: The Record and the Controversy,* ed. James Q. Wilson (Cambridge, Mass.: MIT Press, 1966).

2 "Is Boston 'Beginning to Boil'?" *Fortune* (June 1957), 288. The initial investment turned out to be closer to $200 million.

3 Interest in Robert Moses and New York City has been significant. See Joel Schwartz, *The New York Approach: Robert Moses, Urban Liberals, and the Redevelopment of the Inner City* (Columbus: Ohio State University Press, 1993); Robert A. Caro, *Power Broker: Robert Moses and the Fall of New York* (New York: Knopf, 1974); Hilary Ballon, "Robert Moses and Urban Renewal," in *Robert Moses and the Modern City: The Transformation of New York,* ed. Hilary Ballon and Kenneth T. Jackson (New York: W. W. Norton, 2007); Samuel Zipp, *Manhattan Projects: The Rise and Fall of Urban Renewal in Cold War New York* (New York: Oxford University Press, 2010). On federal policy, see Mark I. Gelfand, *A Nation of Cities: The Federal Government and Urban America, 1933-1965* (New York: Oxford University Press, 1975). For a study of corporate architecture, see Meredith L. Clausen, *The Pan Am Building and the Shattering of the Modernist Dream* (Cambridge, Mass.: MIT Press, 2005).

4 Chester Hartmann, *City for Sale: The Transformation of San Francisco* (Berkeley: University of California Press, 2002), 393. See John R. Logan and Harvey L. Molotch, *Urban Fortunes: The Political Economy of Place* (Berkeley: University of California Press, 1987); the essays in Susan Fainstein et al., *Restructuring the City: The Political Economy of Urban Redevelopment* (New York: Longman, 1986); John Mollenkopf, *The Contested City* (Princeton, N.J.: Princeton University Press, 1983); Jon Teaford, *The Rough Road to Renaissance* (Baltimore: Johns Hopkins University Press, 1990); David Schuyler, *A City Transformed* (University Park, Pa.: Pennsylvania State University Press, 2002); Martin Anderson, *The Federal Bulldozer: A Critical Analysis of Urban Renewal, 1949-1962* (New York: McGraw-Hill, 1967); Marc V. Levine, "The Politics of Partnership: Urban Redevelopment Since 1945," in *Unequal Partnerships: The Political Economy of Urban Redevelopment in Postwar America,* ed. Gregory D. Squares (New Brunswick: Rutgers University Press, 1989); James Q. Wilson, ed. *Urban Renewal: The Record and the Controversy* (Cambridge, Mass.: MIT Press, 1966).

5 Herbert Gans, *The Urban Villagers: Group and Class in the Life of Italian-Americans* (New York: Free Press, 1962); Marc A. Weiss, "The Origins and Legacy of Urban Renewal," in *Urban and Regional Planning in an Age of Austerity,* ed. Pierre Clavel, John Forester, and William M. Goldsmith (New York: Pergamon, 1980), 53-80. The 1954 amendment to the 1949 Housing Act, which formally inaugurated the Urban Renewal Administration, breathed new life into downtown redevelopment, giving local politicians, business elites, and real estate developers — who frequently had little interest in low-income housing — more flexibility in putting together commercial projects.

6 Lewis Weinstein, "Urban Renewal in Massachusetts," *Massachusetts Law Quarterly* 47 (1962).

7 Frank Norris, *The Octopus: A Story of California* (New York: Doubleday, Page, 1901).

8 Robert Sheehan, "That Mighty Pump, Prudential," *Fortune* (January 1964). The largest company in the world was AT&T (American Telephone and Telegraph).

9 See Alfred DuPont Chandler, Jr., *The Visible Hand:*

The Managerial Revolution in American Business (Cambridge: The Belknap Press of Harvard University Press, 1993); and Alfred DuPont Chandler, Jr., *Scale and Scope: The Dynamics of Industrial Capitalism* (Cambridge: The Belknap Press of Harvard University Press, 1994).

10 Walter Muir Whitehill and Lawrence Kennedy, *Boston: A Topographical History,* 3rd ed. (Cambridge: Harvard University Press, 2000), 102.

11 Wilfred Owen, *The Metropolitan Transportation Problem* (Washington, D.C.: Brookings Institution, 1966).

12 Transportation expert Wilfred Owen observed, "Relocation of [railroad] facilities is providing substantial real estate capable of conversion to more appropriate uses and has at the same time removed one of the principal causes of downtown decay." Ibid.

13 "Nation's Cities Fight Decay; Face-Lifting Now a 'Must,'" The Prudential Public Relations Department, Northeastern Home Office, PA 10-42.

14 Jeanne R. Lowe, *Cities in a Race with Time: Progress and Poverty in America's Renewing Cities* (New York: Vintage, 1968), 111. See also Gregory J. Crowley, *The Politics of Place: Contentious Urban Redevelopment in Pittsburgh* (Pittsburgh: University of Pittsburgh Press, 2005); Roy Lubove, *Twentieth-Century Pittsburgh,* volume 1: *Government, Business, and Environmental Change* (Pittsburgh: University of Pittsburgh Press, 1995 [originally published in 1969]); Robert C. Alberts, *The Shaping of the Point: Pittsburgh's Renaissance Park* (Pittsburgh: University of Pittsburgh Press, 1980).

15 Anderson, *The Federal Bulldozer,* 136–37.

16 Lowe, *Cities in a Race with Time,* 141. The original plan called for as many as seven cruciform-shaped office towers. Ultimately, three were built.

17 Ibid., 142.

18 "Architecture: Stepchild or Fashioner of Cities?" *Architectural Forum* (December 1953): 117. The editors at *Forum,* proponents of modernist design, deemed the design for Gateway Center not sufficiently progressive. The layout of buildings was "a little too near-symmetrical," implying Beaux-Arts and not modernist planning principles, and the architecture itself was merely "modernique," resembling "up-ended diners."

19 "Pittsburgh Renascent," *Architectural Forum* (November 1949): 68.

20 Lowe, *Cities in a Race with Time,* 318.

21 "Chances for Starting on Penn Center Seen by Spring; N.Y. Planner Shows Revised Model, Says Financing Is Certain," *Philadelphia Bulletin,* March 6, 1953, quoted in Guian McKee, "Blue Sky Boys, Professional Citizens, and Knights-in-Shining-Money: Philadelphia's Penn Center Project and the Constraints of Private Development," *Journal of Planning History* 6, no. 1 (February 2007): 60.

22 C. L. Baker, "Penn Center Plus 15," *Prudential Mortgage Loan Mirror* (January–February 1967): 23–26, Prudential Archives. The articles in the *Mirror* were written by appraisers from Prudential's vast network of mortgage loan offices.

23 S. Westcott Toole, "The Outlook for the Central City," October 13, 1955, PA 04-123, 9. In 1955, the year Toole delivered his speech, only a few high-profile firms had abandoned center-city locations for suburban campuses, including General Foods, which moved from Manhattan to Westchester in 1954. See Louise Mozingo, "Campus, Estate, and Park: Lawn Culture Comes to the Corporation," in *Everyday America: Cultural Landscapes Studies After J. B. Jackson,* ed. Chris Wilson and Paul Groth (Berkeley: University of California Press, 2003).

24 Kenneth Turney Gibbs, *Business Architectural Imagery in America, 1870-1930* (Ann Arbor: UMI Research Press, 1984), 119. The term "conspicuous consumption" was introduced by sociologist Thorstein Veblen in his 1899 book, *The Theory of the Leisure Class,* in which he explained how businesses, like individuals, used "the specialized consumption of goods as an evidence of pecuniary strength."

25 On the Woolworth tower, see Gail Fenske, *The Skyscraper and the City: The Woolworth Building and the Making of Modern New York* (Chicago: University of Chicago Press, 2008).

26 Viviana A. Zelizer, "Human Values and the Market: The Case of Life Insurance and Death in Nineteenth-Century America," *American Journal of Sociology* 84 (November 1978): 594.

27 Morton Keller, *The Life Insurance Enterprise, 1885-1910: A Study in the Limits of Corporate Power* (Cambridge: The Belknap Press of Harvard University Press, 1963), 27.

28 Sarah Bradford Landau and Carl W. Condit, *Rise of the New York Skyscraper, 1865-1913* (New Haven: Yale University Press, 1996).

29 Marquis James, *The Metropolitan: A Study in Business Growth* (New York: Viking, 1947), 174. On the Met Life tower, see Roberta Moudry, "Architecture as Cultural Design: The Architecture and Urbanism of the Metropolitan Life Insurance Company," Ph.D. diss., Cornell University, 1995; Roland Marchand, *Creating the Corporate Soul: The Rise of Public Relations and Corporate Imagery in American Big Business* (Berkeley: University of California Press, 1998).

30 See Keith D. Revell, "Regulating the Landscape: Real Estate Values, City Planning, and the 1916 Zoning Ordinance," and Gail Fenske and Deryck Holdsworth, "Corporate Identity and the New York Office

Building: 1895–1915," in *The Landscape of Modernity: New York City, 1900–1940,* ed. David Ward and Olivier Zunz (Baltimore: Johns Hopkins University Press, 1997).

31 "Aetna Life Insurance Company Building at Hartford, Conn.," *American Architect* 114, no. 2227 (August 28, 1918): 67–71. One interpretation of neocolonial style stresses the nationalistic discourse, a reaction to the industrial metropolis with its immigrant populations, by looking back to an imagined simplicity of early American cities.

32 "Rural Insurance Plant," *Architectural Forum* 101 (September 1954): 104–7; "Insurance Company Headquarters," *Architectural Design* 28 (July 1958): 174–81. See also Alexandra Lange, "Tower Typewriter and Trademark: Architects, Designers, and the Corporate Utopia, 1956–1964," Ph.D. dissertation, Institute of Fine Arts, New York University, May 2005; Louise A. Mozingo, "The Corporate Estate in the USA, 1954–1964: 'Thoroughly Modern in Concept, but . . . Down to Earth and Rugged,'" *Studies in the History of Gardens and Designed Landscapes* 20 (January–March 2000): 25. On Connecticut General's earlier buildings, see Jeffrey Karl Ochsner, *H. H. Richardson: Complete Architectural Works* (Cambridge, Mass.: MIT Press, 1982), 108; "Connecticut General Life Insurance Co.'s Building, Hartford, Conn.," *Architecture and Building* (November 1927): 354.

33 "Symposium in Symbolic Setting: Fine New Building Meets Challenge of City Crisis," *Life* (October 21, 1957), 49.

34 Fenske, *The Skyscraper and the City.* See also Robert Bruegmann, *The Architects and the City* (Chicago: University of Chicago Press, 1997).

35 Fitch and Waite, *Grand Central Terminal and Rockefeller Center;* Clausen, *The Pan Am Building.*

36 Sally A. Kitt Chappell, *Architecture and Planning of Graham, Anderson, Probst and White, 1912–1936: Transforming Tradition* (Chicago: University of Chicago Press, 1992); Walter C. Leedy, Jr., "Cleveland's Terminal Tower: The Van Sweringens' Afterthought," *The Gamut* 8 (Winter 1983): 39–62.

37 See Carol Herselle Krinsky, *Rockefeller Center* (New York: Oxford University Press, 1978), and James Marston Fitch and Diana S. Waite, *Grand Central Terminal and Rockefeller Center: A Historic-Critical Estimate of Their Significance* (New York: New York State Parks and Recreation, 1974).

38 Krinsky, *Rockefeller Center,* 56. Metropolitan Life ultimately furnished the crucial financing for Rockefeller Center when it agreed in 1931 to purchase up to $65 million in bonds. Krinsky reports that John R. Todd, who coordinated much of the Rockefeller Center project, also met with the president of Prudential,

Edward Duffield, to solicit his company's investment.

39 "The Pru Decentralizes: A Building Program for an Office Staff of 6,200," *Architectural Forum* 102 (1955): 143; Sheehan, "That Mighty Pump, Prudential," 102.

40 S. Westcott Toole, untitled article, *Boston Sunday Herald,* December 20, 1964.

41 See Robert A. Beauregard, *Voices of Decline: The Postwar Fate of U.S. Cities* (Cambridge, Mass.: Blackwell, 1993); Fogelson, *Downtown,* 250.

42 Vernon, "Changing Economic Function," 9.

43 Owen, *The Metropolitan Transportation Problem.*

44 Mildred F. Schmertz, "Planning the Downtown Center," *Architectural Record* (March 1964): 177; Wilfred Owen, *Cities in the Motor Age* (New York: Viking, 1959), 67. Government and insurance companies were the major patrons of the new urban form. Along with the Prudential Center, Schmertz mentioned Constitution Plaza in Hartford, financed by Travelers Insurance Company, as another example of the "downtown center," along with the Port Authority of New York's World Trade Center and Government Center in Boston.

45 "Insuring the Growth of Hartford," *Architectural Record* (March 1964): 178; Schmertz, "Planning the Downtown Center"; Charles F. J. Morse, "Organizes Corporation for Project," *Hartford Courant,* January 30, 1960; "Travelers Makes Offer to Finance Plaza; Phoenix Mutual Picks Site for New Home," *Hartford Courant,* January 30, 1960. The Phoenix Mutual developed its own independent project, connected to Constitution Plaza by a footbridge, featuring a distinctive fourteen-story, prow-shaped office tower designed by Harrison and Abramovitz.

46 Schmertz, "Planning the Downtown Center," 177.

47 This phrase is borrowed from Paul L. Knox, ed., *The Restless Urban Landscape* (Englewood Cliffs, N.J.: Prentice Hall, 1993).

CHAPTER 1 Extra Dividends

1 Robert Sheehan, "That Mighty Pump, Prudential," *Fortune* (January 1964), 98. Though Met Life held more assets than Prudential in 1964, the Pru had been outselling its rival in insurance policies since 1957. In 1966, *Fortune* reported that Prudential had overtaken Met Life in total assets, becoming the second largest company on the planet.

2 Ibid.

3 Earl Chapin May and Will Oursler, *The Prudential: A Story of Human Security* (Garden City, N.J.: Doubleday, 1950), 13. On the early development of life insurance as a business model, see Sharon Ann Murphy, *Investing in Life: Insurance in Antebellum America* (Baltimore: Johns Hopkins University Press, 2010). One of the myths surrounding Prudential's founder, John Dryden, was that his father had died when the boy was

only thirteen and his family suffered due to the sudden loss of its breadwinner. Dryden resolved to help other families protect themselves against similar privations. See William H. A. Carr, *From Three Cents a Week: The Story of the Prudential Insurance Company of America* (Englewood Cliffs, N.J.: Prentice-Hall, 1975), 10. In 1902, John Dryden was elected by the New Jersey state legislature to a seat in the United States Senate, where he lobbied for federal — and not state — regulation of the insurance industry.

4 Industrial insurance was in part viewed as "burial insurance," providing families with funeral expenses for the departed breadwinner. On the early days of Prudential, see Carr, *From Three Cents a Week*; Thomas Scanlon, "Our Great Life Insurance Companies — the Prudential," *Moody's Magazine* 13 (March 1912): 203-9; Frederick L. Hoffman, *History of the Prudential Insurance Company of America, 1875-1900* (Newark: Prudential Press, 1900). On mutual aid societies and voluntary associations, see Viviana A. Rotman Zelizer, *Morals and Markets: The Development of Life Insurance in the United States* (New York: Columbia University Press, 1979). The Knights of Columbus, founded in New Haven in 1882, is a good example of the origins of the religion-based fraternal organization that also collected and invested money from its members. See Christopher J. Kauffman, *Faith and Fraternalism: The History of the Knights of Columbus, 1882-1982* (New York: Harper and Row, 1982).

5 Dryden to W. H. Wells, September 1884, quoted in Morton Keller, *The Life Insurance Enterprise, 1885-1910* (Cambridge: The Belknap Press of Harvard University Press, 1963), 128.

6 Keller, *The Life Insurance Enterprise*, 128.

7 Government, the railroads, and insurance companies make up the key triumvirate of power in our story. Insurance companies underwrote the functions of government by funneling money to municipal, state, and federal bonds. In the 1880s, insurance companies, which were regulated by states and not the federal government, were allowed to purchase railroad securities. Later, Prudential invested in bonds offered by quasi-public authorities and was an early supporter of the Port Authority of New York and state turnpike authorities, a factor that also proved crucial in Boston.

8 Keller, *The Life Insurance Enterprise*, 253, 271. Metropolitan Life also mutualized in 1915. Some critics have held that in practice, mutualization insulated company directors from interference from stockholders as well as policyholders, who remained largely uninvolved in the corporate operations. See Robert E. Wright and George David Smith, *Mutually Beneficial: The Guardian and Life Insurance in America* (New York: New York University Press, 2004), 10.

9 May and Oursler, *The Prudential*, 203.

10 Harold Wayne Snider, *Life Insurance Investment in Commercial Real Estate* (Philadelphia: S. S. Heubner Foundation for Insurance Education, 1956), 2; Roberta Moudry, "Architecture as Cultural Design: The Architecture and Urbanism of the Metropolitan Life Insurance Company" (Ph.D. diss., Cornell University, 1995). As Olivier Zunz has argued, promoting reform movements such as modern housing and public health was ultimately "self-serving, for it was in the insurance companies' interest to help lengthen life." Olivier Zunz, *Making America Corporate, 1870-1920* (Chicago: University of Chicago Press, 1990), 96. On Prudential's Chellis Austin housing project in Newark, see Robert E. Schultz, *Life Insurance Housing Projects* (Philadelphia: S. S. Huebner Foundation for Insurance Education, 1956), and Roberta Moudry, "Prudential Insurance Housing Projects," *Encyclopedia of American Urban History* (Thousand Oaks, Calif.: Sage, 2007), 613-15.

11 On Stuyvesant Town and Peter Cooper Village, see Marc A. Weiss, "The Origins and Legacy of Urban Renewal," in *Urban and Regional Planning in an Age of Austerity*, ed. Pierre Clavel, John Forester, and William M. Goldsmith (New York: Pergamon, 1980), and Samuel Zipp, *Manhattan Projects: The Rise and Fall of Urban Renewal in Cold War New York* (New York: Oxford University Press, 2010).

12 Thomas Hanchett, "Financing Suburbia: Prudential Insurance and the Post-World War II Transformation of the American City," *Journal of Urban History* 26, no. 3 (2000): 315. See also Moudry, "Prudential Insurance Housing Projects."

13 The subcommittee was formally named the "Special Subcommittee on the Study of Monopoly Power of the Committee of the Judiciary of the United States House of Representatives," and was known as the Celler Committee, after Brooklyn's Emanuel Celler, who chaired the subcommittee.

14 Carrol M. Shanks, president of Prudential, to House Judiciary Committee, November 3, 1949, PA 01-07, 13. Progressive deregulation expanded the range of investment opportunities open to insurance companies. Though stocks were still rare, it was more and more common to offer direct loans to American industries through the 1950s and 1960s.

15 Ibid., 12.

16 Ibid., 9.

17 Carrol M. Shanks, "Address by Carrol M. Shanks, President of The Prudential Insurance Company of America, at the Sixty-Sixth Annual Banquet of the Chicago Real Estate Board in the Grand Ballroom of the Stevens Hotel, Chicago, Ill. at 6:30 p.m., Wednesday, May 4, 1949," PA 01-07.

18 Carrol M. Shanks, "Responsibilities of Business-men," a speech given by President Shanks of the Prudential Insurance Company of America before the Denver Rotary Club, October 7, 1948, PA 01-07.

19 May and Oursler, *The Prudential*, 176.

20 Carr, *From Three Cents a Week*, 43.

21 For reflections on corporate imagery, see Roland Marchand, *Creating the Corporate Soul: The Rise of Public Relations and Corporate Imagery in American Big Business* (Berkeley: University of California Press, 1998). In the 1970s and 1980s, Prudential advertised its products as the opportunity to own a "Piece of the Rock."

22 May and Oursler, *The Prudential*, 170.

23 Ibid., 175.

24 Carr, *From Three Cents a Week*, 123.

25 Ibid., 119.

26 "Memorandum for Mr. C. W. Shanks, Executive Vice President," PA 10-20, Correspondence/Memorandum 1945-1959, 1. What Green called "Branch Home Offices" were eventually renamed Regional Home Offices.

27 Ibid.

28 S. Westcott Toole, speech to Mortgage Loan Conference, Skytop, Pennsylvania, November 14, 1957, PA 04-123, 2.

29 Ibid.

30 Ibid., 3; S. Westcott Toole, "Some Decentralization Dividends," Biloxi, Miss., June 15, 1954, PA 04-123, 5.

31 S. Westcott Toole, "The Outlook for the Central City," October 13, 1955, PA 04-123, 9.

32 "Prudential Insurance to Spend $20 Million on Home Office Area," *Wall Street Journal*, November 14, 1955. Prudential's resolve to maintain its home office in Newark was likely influenced by the decision of a local rival, Mutual Benefit, to keep its corporate offices in the city. Prudential's new Corporate Home Office, called the Plaza Building, was ready for occupancy in 1961.

33 As we shall see, in the early stages of planning the Prudential Center, company executives did not expect a highway, just an outlying location along avenues and transit lines.

34 Prudential chose Jacksonville, Florida, as the home of its South Central Home Office in part because the city was already functioning as the "insurance capital of the south." Jacksonville also lured Prudential by dangling a tax abatement, a factor that proved decisive in Boston as well. The Jacksonville site was a wedge formed by a nexus of railroad lines, another foreshadowing of the Prudential Center. "South Central Home Office," PA 10-31.

35 One exception was in Toronto. At first Prudential rented space in the Bank of Nova Scotia building before building its own office tower in the central business district to house the Canadian Home Office.

36 Sheehan, "That Mighty Pump, Prudential."

37 "The Pru Decentralizes: A Building Program for an Office Staff of 6,200," *Architectural Forum* 102 (1955): 144.

38 *Architectural Forum* thought that the best-designed regional home office building was also the first, in Los Angeles.

39 See Richard Longstreth, *City Center to Regional Mall: Architecture, the Automobile, and Retailing in Los Angeles, 1920–1950* (Cambridge, Mass.: MIT Press, 1997); Larry R. Ford, "Midtowns, Megastructures, and World Cities," *Geographical Review* 88, no. 4 (1998).

40 The western office was responsible for California, Oregon, Washington, Montana, Utah, Idaho, Wyoming, Nevada, Arizona, New Mexico, Colorado, and what was then the Territory of Hawaii.

41 Carrol M. Shanks, "Outline of Address Before Board of Directors of Los Angeles Chamber of Commerce," May 2, 1947, PA 01-07.

42 Carrol M. Shanks, "The Shift from Center of Concentration," a speech to the Seattle Chamber of Commerce, September 24, 1948, PA 01-07.

43 Carr, *From Three Cents a Week*, 132.

44 May and Oursler, *The Prudential*, 321.

45 Carr, *From Three Cents a Week*, 131.

46 "Two Office Buildings in Los Angeles," *Architectural Forum* (May 1949).

47 Ibid.

48 "Prudential Co. Leases Space," *Los Angeles Times*, October 3, 1958; "Ohrbach's Opens West Coast Store," *New York Times*, December 3, 1948. Ohrbach's flagship store was on Union Square in New York City but the company maintained its administrative offices in Newark, New Jersey.

49 "Prudential's New Western Office Opens," *Los Angeles Times*, November 16, 1948; "Prudential Opens New Office Today," *Los Angeles Times*, November 15, 1948; "Prudential Will Erect $7,000,000 Western States Headquarters Here," *Los Angeles Times*, March 20, 1947.

50 Charles Fleetwood, "To Whom It May Concern in the Year 2000," 1952 Time Capsule, Event Files, 1952, PA 10-26, 1.

51 W. P. Hobby to Carrol M. Shanks, 1952 Time Capsule, PA 10-26, Event Files, 1952.

52 Ibid., 2, 3.

53 Fleetwood, "To Whom It May Concern."

54 Homer Hoyt Associates, "Survey of Regional Office Location in Houston, Texas, for the Prudential Insurance Company," February 27, 1950, PA 10-25. The nine states included Colorado, New Mexico, Kansas,

Oklahoma, Texas, Missouri, Arkansas, Louisiana, and Mississippi. On Hoyt, see Robert Beauregard, "More than Sector Theory: Homer Hoyt's Contributions to Planning Knowledge," *Journal of Planning History* 6, no. 3 (August 2007): 248-71.

55 Ibid., 5.

56 Ibid., 6.

57 Ibid., 7.

58 Ibid., 10. Hoyt's 1950 study was in advance of planning for Houston's express highway system, built in earnest in the 1960s based on a 1955 master plan. See Erik Slotboom, *Houston Freeways: A Historical and Visual Journey* (Houston: O. F. Slotboom, 2003).

59 I am using "modernistic" to describe a transitional style between art deco and the "International Style" that began to flourish in American corporate architecture in the mid-1950s. Welton Becket's design for the WHO in Los Angeles, though also "modernistic," carried out a horizontal emphasis. On Kenneth Franzheim, see Stephen Fox, "Franzheim, Kenneth," *Handbook of Texas Online* (http://www.tshaonline.org/handbook/online/articles/ffr26), accessed April 7, 2011, published by the Texas State Historical Association.

60 The mural by Peter Hurd, from New Mexico, picked up the realist tradition of the 1930s that focused on regional life. The Prudential mural borrowed its title from the insurance company's tag line, "The Future Belongs to Those Who Prepare for It."

61 "Building System Information," PA 10-26, Reports 1953-1954.

62 "District Home Office," *PPG Products* (January–February 1953): 4-8, repr., PA 10-25.

63 "At Home in the Great Southwest," brochure 1952, PA 10-25.

64 Ibid. In many ways these programs and facilities recalled the "welfare work" provisions of Progressive Era factories. See Andrea Tone, *The Business of Benevolence: Industrial Paternalism in Progressive America* (Ithaca: Cornell University Press, 1997).

65 "Conducted Tour for the Public," PA 10-26.

66 "Life Goes to Houston's Paradise for Office Girls, Prudential Life Insurance Company," *Life,* September 15, 1952, 150-55. The inclusion of employee amenities in an office building was not new, but those provided at Prudential's Houston building had few precedents. There was a tradition of extensive facilities in company towns and other large industrial estates to provide healthy and moral activities for workers. See William Littman, "The Architecture and Landscape of Welfare Capitalism," *International Labor and Working Class History,* no. 53 (Spring 1998): 88-114.

67 "The Story of the Prudential Building," *The Quadrennial Book of Valuations of the Central Business District of Chicago, 1951-1954,* repr., PA 10-37.

68 "Remarks of James J. Brennan," undated and untitled, but apparently made to a group of Chicago-based real estate brokers in a luncheon setting, PA 10-37.

69 Carl Condit, *Chicago, 1930-1970: Building, Planning, and Urban Technology* (Chicago: University of Chicago Press, 1974), 4. On the Field Building, see Sally A. Kitt Chappel, *Architecture and Planning of Graham, Anderson, Probst, and White, 1912-1936: Transforming Tradition* (Chicago: University of Chicago Press, 1992), 215.

70 "Remarks of James J. Brennan."

71 "Chicago's Prudential Building," *Architectural Forum* 97 (August 1952): 96.

72 The Illinois Central went on to develop the rest of its air rights parcels, announcing plans for the Illinois Center in 1961; "Center Is Slated by Chicago Group," *New York Times,* January 26, 1961. In 1990, Prudential constructed Two Prudential Plaza, on a site directly east of the original Prudential building, which was renamed One Prudential Plaza. In 1973, the Standard Oil Company of Indiana constructed an eighty-three-story skyscraper next to the Prudential building. (It is currently the headquarters of the Aon Corporation.)

73 "Remarks of James J. Brennan," 15.

74 Ibid., 17.

75 "The Story of the Prudential Building."

76 Martin H. Kennelly, "Address at the Ground-Breaking Ceremonies for The Prudential Building," August 12, 1952, PA 10-38, Event Files 1952.

77 "Remarks of Mayor Martin H. Kennelly," November 16, 1954, PA 10-39.

78 "Chicago's Prudential Building."

79 "The Pru Decentralizes," 141. In Jacksonville, Prudential initially planned to occupy the first eight floors of the tower, which was the tallest in Florida. "South Central Home Office," PA 10-31.

80 "Chicago's Prudential Building."

81 Ibid.

82 Ibid.; "Building and Office Highlights," PA 10-37.

83 Ibid.

84 "The Story of the Prudential Building."

85 "Remarks of J. M. Trissal, Assistant Chief Engineer, Illinois Central, Prudential Ground-Breaking Ceremony," August 12, 1952, Event Files 1952, PA 10-38.

86 Ibid.

87 "Remarks of Mayor Martin H. Kennelly."

88 Ibid.

CHAPTER 2 "I Hate Boston"

Epigraph I do not have an original source for this quotation, but it is quoted in both David McCord, *About Boston: Sight, Sound, Flavor, and Inflection* (Boston:

Little, Brown, 1948), and Patricia Harris and David Lyon, eds., *1001 Greatest Things Ever Said About Massachusetts* (Boston: Lyons Press, 2007), 56.

1 McCord, *About Boston,* 12.

2 On the rapid development of New York, see David Scobey, *Empire City: The Making and Meaning of the New York City Landscape* (Philadelphia: Temple University Press, 2002).

3 See Federal Writers Project of the Works Progress Administration for the State of Massachusetts, *Massachusetts: A Guide to Its Places and People* (Boston: Houghton Mifflin, 1937); Barry Bluestone and Mary Huff Stevenson, *The Boston Renaissance: Race, Space, and Economic Change in an American Metropolis* (New York: Russell Sage Foundation, 2000); Walter F. Carroll, *Brockton: From Rural Parish to Urban Center* (Northridge, Calif.: Windsor, 1989). On immigration and unions, see Oscar Handlin, *Boston's Immigrants: A Study in Acculturation* (Cambridge: The Belknap Press of Harvard University Press, 1959); Tom Juravich, William F. Hartford, and James R. Green, *Commonwealth of Toil: Chapters in the History of Massachusetts' Workers and Their Unions* (Amherst: University of Massachusetts Press, 1996).

4 See Russell B. Adams, Jr., *King C. Gillette: The Man and His Wonderful Shaving Device* (Boston: Little, Brown, 1978), and W. H. Bunting, *Portrait of a Port: Boston, 1852–1914* (Cambridge: The Belknap Press of Harvard University Press, 1994).

5 Gerald T. White, *A History of the Massachusetts Hospital Life Insurance Company* (Cambridge: Harvard University Press, 1955); King's *Handbook of Boston* (Cambridge, Mass.: Moses King, 1878), 238; Emil Schwab, *"The John Hancock": An Historical Sketch* (Boston: John Hancock, 1912).

6 On land-making and urban growth in Boston, see Walter Muir Whitehill and Lawrence Kennedy, *Boston: A Topographical History,* 3rd ed. (Cambridge: The Belknap Press of Harvard University Press, 2000); William A. Newman and Wilfred E. Holton, *Boston's Back Bay: The Story of America's Greatest Nineteenth-Century Landfill Project* (Boston: Northeastern University Press, 2006); Nancy S. Seasholes, *Gaining Ground: A History of Landmaking in Boston* (Cambridge, Mass.: MIT Press, 2003); Michael Rawson, *Eden on the Charles: The Making of Boston* (Cambridge: Harvard University Press, 2010); Sam Bass Warner, *Streetcar Suburbs: The Process of Growth in Boston, 1870–1900* (Cambridge: Harvard University Press, 1960); and Charles Cheape, *Moving the Masses: Urban Public Transit in New York, Boston, and Philadelphia, 1880–1912* (Cambridge: Harvard University Press, 1980).

7 See Henry Binford, *The First Suburbs: Residential Communities on the Boston Periphery, 1815–1860* (Chicago: University of Chicago Press, 1988), and Kenneth T. Jackson, *Crabgrass Frontier: The Suburbanization of the United States* (New York: Oxford University Press, 1985).

8 See Warner, *Streetcar Suburbs.*

9 "All houses had driveways and frequently garages to provide off-street parking, and one-family homes became the rule rather than duplexes and triplexes; still the suburbanization occurred only where there was good access to Boston by public transit." Matthew Edel, Elliott D. Sclar, and Daniel Luria, *Shaky Palaces: Homeownership and Social Mobility in Boston's Suburbanization* (New York: Columbia University Press, 1984), 59. See also Gerald Gamm, *Urban Exodus: Why the Jews Left Boston and the Catholics Stayed* (Cambridge: Harvard University Press, 2001).

10 On the MDC highways, including Storrow Drive, which was constructed along the Charles River in the early 1950s, see Karl Haglund, *Inventing the Charles River* (Cambridge, Mass.: MIT Press, 2003).

11 Bluestone and Stevenson, *The Boston Renaissance;* Anna Lee Saxenian, *Regional Advantage: Culture and Competition in Silicon Valley and Route 128* (Cambridge, Mass.: MIT Press, 1994); Otto J. Scott, *The Creative Ordeal: The Story of Raytheon* (New York: Atheneum, 1974); Alan R. Earls, *Route 128 and the Birth of the Age of High Tech* (Charleston, S.C.: Arcadia, 2002).

12 Robert S. Allen, *Our Fair City* (New York: Vanguard, 1947), 3, 15, 4. Allen was a veteran of World War I and served on General George Patton's staff in World War II.

13 Allen, *Our Fair City,* 6, 7.

14 Louis M. Lyons, "Boston: Study in Inertia," in Allen, *Our Fair City,* 16. Lyons goes on to say that "the descendants of those who pioneered the public school system in Boston now live in the suburbs, partly to have good schools for their children," 25.

15 Ibid., 18, 29.

16 Lawrence Kennedy, *Planning the City Upon a Hill: Boston Since 1630* (Amherst: University of Massachusetts Press, 1994), 142.

17 James Michael Curley, *I'd Do It Again: A Record of All My Uproarious Years* (Englewood Cliffs, N.J.: Prentice-Hall, 1957), 220–21.

18 Paul E. Peterson, *City Limits* (Chicago: University of Chicago Press, 1981), 24.

19 See Jack Beatty, *The Rascal King: The Life and Times of James Michael Curley, 1874–1958* (New York: Addison-Wesley, 1992), and Thomas H. O'Connor, *Building a New Boston: Politics and Urban Renewal, 1950 to 1970* (Boston: Northeastern University Press, 1993), 11.

20 Beatty, *The Rascal King,* 231.

21 Ibid., 231–32; see Cynthia Horan, "Organizing the 'New Boston': Growth Policy, Governing Coalitions, and Tax Reform," *Polity* 22, no. 3 (1990): 489–510.

22 Curley, *I'd Do It Again,* 220.

23 Phoebe Cutler, *The Public Landscape of the New Deal* (New Haven: Yale University Press, 1986), 10.

24 One notable exception was the Huntington Avenue subway, which was extended through the Back Bay district of Boston with Works Progress Administration (WPA) funds. See Kennedy, *Planning the City Upon a Hill,* 146–47.

25 See Gail Radford, *Modern Housing for America: Policy Struggles in the New Deal Era* (Chicago: University of Chicago Press, 1996); Jackson, *Crabgrass Frontier.*

26 The BHA used Public Works Administration (PWA) funds to construct Old Harbor Village in South Boston, a heavily Irish neighborhood. It was one of the PWA's first housing projects in the United States, and the first in Boston. Predictably, a crony of Curley's was chosen as the contractor, a coincidence that raised cackles from the City Planning Board. In 1937, the United States Housing Authority (USHA) was created under the Wagner-Steagall Act, and the USHA took over PWA projects. See Kennedy, *Planning the City on a Hill,* 148; Mark I. Gelfand, *A Nation of Cities: The Federal Government and Urban America, 1933–1965* (New York: Oxford University Press, 1975); and Lawrence Vale, *From Puritans to the Projects: Public Housing and Public Neighbors* (Cambridge, Mass.: MIT Press, 2000).

27 Horan, "Organizing the 'New Boston,'" 495.

28 The concept of urban political "managerialism" is drawn from David Harvey's essay "From Managerialism to Entrepreneurialism: The Transformation of Urban Governance in Late Capitalism," in *Spaces of Capital: Towards a Critical Geography* (New York: Routledge, 2001).

29 O'Connor, *Building a New Boston,* 22.

30 See Timothy Rose, "Civic War: People, Politics, and the Battle of New Boston, 1945–1967" (Ph.D. diss., University of California, Berkeley, 2006).

31 Elizabeth Hardwick, "Boston: The Lost Ideal," *Harper's Magazine* (December 1959), 64.

32 Russell B. Adams, Jr., *The Boston Money Tree: How the Proper Men of Boston Made, Invested, and Preserved Their Wealth from Colonial Days to the Space Age* (New York: Thomas Y. Crowell, 1977), 305–6.

33 *The Boston Contest of 1944* (Boston: Boston University Press, 1944), 10.

34 The "Boston Contest" was a postwar reincarnation of the "Boston-1915" movement, which advocated City Beautiful–era municipal reform, infrastructural modernization, and aesthetic embellishment of the city. "Boston — 1915" was the brainchild of Louis Filene, the city's leading Jewish businessman and owner of its most prestigious department store. Downtown department stores and insurance companies were also the essential backers of the Boston Contest of 1944. See Mel Scott, *American City Planning Since 1890* (Berkeley: University of California Press, 1972).

35 José Luis Sert, *Can Our Cities Survive?: An ABC of Urban Problems, Their Analysis, Their Solutions* (Cambridge: Harvard University Press, 1942). On CIAM, see Eric Mumford, *The CIAM Discourse on Modern Urbanism, 1928–1960* (Cambridge, Mass.: MIT Press, 2000). There were many other examples of modernists taking on the question of the city and congestion, starting perhaps most notably with Eliel Saarinen, *The City: Its Growth, Its Decay, Its Future* (New York: Reinhold, 1943). In 1964, more than twenty years later, the architect Victor Gruen published *The Heart of Our Cities: The Urban Crisis, Diagnosis, and Cure* (New York: Simon and Schuster, 1964).

36 Robert T. Norman, "The Harvard Plan for Metropolitan Boston," *Western Political Quarterly* 16, no. 3 (September 1963): 710; O'Connor, *Building a New Boston,* 3. See also Charles H. Trout, *Boston, the Great Depression, and the New Deal* (New York: Oxford University Press, 1977); William H. Bunting, *Portrait of a Port: Boston, 1852–1914* (Cambridge: Harvard University Press, 1971).

37 Lincoln Steffens, *The Shame of the Cities* (New York: McClure Philips, 1904); see Herbert Shapiro, *The Muckrakers and American Society* (New York: D. C. Heath, 1968).

38 See Roy Lubove, *Twentieth-Century Pittsburgh: Government, Business, and Environmental Change* (New York: John Wiley and Sons, 1969); Jon Teaford, *Rough Road to Renaissance* (Baltimore: Johns Hopkins University Press, 1990); Jeanne Lowe, *Cities in a Race with Time: Progress and Poverty in America's Renewing Cities* (New York: Vintage, 1967).

39 See Fred Powledge, *Model City: A Test of American Liberalism: One Town's Efforts to Rebuild Itself* (New York: Simon and Schuster, 1970); Allan R. Talbot, *The Mayor's Game: Richard Lee of New Haven and the Politics of Change* (New York: Harper and Row, 1968); Douglas Rae, *City: Urbanism and Its End* (New Haven: Yale University Press, 2003).

40 See Bennett Harrison, "Regional Restructuring and 'Good Business Climates': The Economic Transformation of New England Since World War II," in *Sunbelt/Frostbelt: Urban Development and Regional Restructuring,* ed. William K. Tabb (New York: Oxford University Press, 1984).

41 Quoted in O'Connor, *Building a New Boston,* 44.

42 Ibid., 112; see John H. Mollenkopf, *The Contested City* (Princeton, N.J.: Princeton University Press, 1983).

43 Gelfand, *A Nation of Cities*, 107.

44 O'Connor, *Building a New Boston*; Mel King, *Chains of Change: Struggles for Black Community Development* (Boston: South End, 1981); Herbert Gans, *The Urban Villagers: Group and Class in the Life of Italian-Americans* (New York: Free Press, 1962); David Kruh, *Always Something Doing: Boston's Infamous Scollay Square* (Boston: Northeastern University Press, 1999).

45 King, *Chains of Change*, 21. On the New York Streets, see also Whitehill and Kennedy, *Boston: A Topographical History*.

46 Robert Killam, "N.Y. Streets Area Sold for $400,000," *Boston Herald*, December 27, 1956; "Herald-Traveler Buys in South End," *Christian Science Monitor*, June 14, 1957.

47 Kennedy, *Planning the City Upon a Hill*, 162.

48 Gans, *The Urban Villagers*; Marc Fried, "Grieving for a Lost Home," in *The Urban Condition*, ed. Leonard J. Duhl (New York: Basic, 1963); Chester Hartmann, "The Housing of Relocated Families," in *Urban Renewal: People, Politics, and Planning*, ed. Jewel Bellush and Murray Hausknecht (New York: Clarion, 1967). For examples of how photographers sometimes manipulated images of housing interiors to accentuate "blighted" conditions, see Paul Groth, *Living Downtown: The History of Residential Hotels in the United States* (Berkeley: University of California Press, 1994), and Gabrielle Brainard, "Party Walls: Understanding Urban Change Through a Block of New Haven Row Houses, 1870–1979," *Journal of the New Haven Colony Historical Society* 48, no. 1 (2001).

49 Gans, *The Urban Villagers*, 285.

50 Ibid., 291.

51 For more on Boston's renewal-era public housing projects, see Lawrence Vale, *Reclaiming Public Housing: A Half Century of Struggle in Three Public Neighborhoods* (Cambridge, Mass.: MIT Press, 2002), and Lawrence Vale, *From Puritans to the Projects*; see also Langley Carleton Keyes, *The Rehabilitation Planning Game: A Study in the Diversity of a Neighborhood* (Cambridge, Mass.: MIT Press, 1971); Stephan Thernstrom, *Poverty, Planning, and Politics in the New Boston: The Origins of ABCD* (New York: Basic, 1969).

52 See O'Connor, *Building a New Boston*; Kennedy, *Planning a City on the Hill*; Harold D. Hodgkinson, "Miracle in Boston," *Proceedings of the Massachusetts Historical Society* 84 (1972); Edward Logue, "Boston, 1960–1970: Seven Years of Plenty," *Proceedings of the Massachusetts Historical Society* 84 (1972); and Rose, "Civic Wars." At first, GSA officials wanted to build a new federal building in the Back Bay and had already purchased land there. Federal GSA bureaucrats did not at first apprehend the fact that the entire district would be razed to make way for the new Government Center and that they would not have to locate in the middle of a notorious "vice district."

53 The architectural ensemble at Government Center included a federal office building, ultimately named after John F. Kennedy, Jr., designed by Walter Gropius and his firm The Architects Collaborative. Paul Rudolph designed the state Government Services Building, and the firm Kallmann, McKinnell and Knowles won the competition to design the City Hall and its surrounding plaza.

54 Logue, "Boston, Seven Years of Plenty."

55 Elmer Davis, "Boston: Notes on a Barbarian Invasion," *Harper's Magazine* (1928). Davis points out the irony of Boston's strict censorship statute: "The most obscene book I have ever read was an argument by an Irish judge against birth control; but I do not imagine that my protest would induce the Boston police to suppress it," 143.

56 Mencken was tried and acquitted. Later, he sued Reverend Frank Chase and won, when a federal judge ruled that a private organization had no right to govern the censorship of literature. See Neil Miller, *Banned in Boston: The Watch and Ward Society's Crusade Against Books, Burlesque, and the Social Evil* (Boston: Beacon, 2010), and Paul S. Boyer, *Purity in Print: Book Censorship in America from the Gilded Age to the Computer Age* (Madison: University of Wisconsin Press, 2002).

57 Hardwick, "Boston: The Lost Ideal," 62. See also John P. Marquand, *The Late George Apley* (Boston: Back Bay, 1936).

58 Mona Domosh, *Invented Cities: The Creation of Landscape in Nineteenth-Century New York and Boston* (New Haven: Yale University Press, 1996); Michael Holleran and Robert Fogelson, "'The Sacred Skyline': Boston's Opposition to the Skyscraper" (Working Paper 9, Center for Real Estate Development, Massachusetts Institute of Technology, 1987). This is not to say that there was not architectural diversity in the Back Bay. See Bainbridge Bunting, *Houses of Boston's Back Bay: An Architectural History, 1840–1917* (Cambridge: Harvard University Press, 1967).

59 O'Connor, *Building a New Boston*, 105.

60 The story of the John Hancock building's property assessment is reported in a few places, including Walter McQuade, "Urban Renewal in Boston," *Fortune* (June 1964).

61 Robert M. Fogelson, *Downtown: Its Rise and Fall, 1880–1950* (New Haven: Yale University Press, 2001), 117.

62 See Christine Meisner Rosen, *The Limits of Power: Great Fires and the Process of City Growth in America* (Cambridge, UK: Cambridge University Press,

1986). Arthur Gilman would also work in New York as one of the key designers of the Equitable Life Assurance Company building (1868–70) along with Edward Kendall and George Post, also done in the Second Empire style. On the Second Empire style in general and the Equitable Building in New York in particular, see Sarah Bradford Landau and Carl W. Condit, *Rise of the New York Skyscraper, 1865–1913* (New Haven: Yale University Press, 1996), 62–75.

63 The Second Empire style made its debut in Boston in the residential architecture of the Back Bay in the 1850s. Arthur Gilman is also credited with designing the street layout of the Back Bay district and a number of its houses. See Bunting, *Houses of Boston's Back Bay*; Douglass Shand-Tucci, *Built in Boston: City and Suburb, 1800–2000* (Amherst: University of Massachusetts Press, 1999), 35.

64 See David Ward, "The Industrial Revolution and the Emergence of Boston's Central Business District," *Economic Geography* 42, no. 2 (April 1966).

65 Owners of the Fiske Building mutilated the structure in 1964 when they covered the granite edifice with metal panels and destroyed the mansard roof. These "renovations" were so unsuccessful that the entire building was taken down in 1989.

66 See Holleran and Fogelson, "The Sacred Skyline," 17–18; Carl W. Condit, *The Chicago School of Architecture: A History of Commercial and Public Buildings in the Chicago Area, 1875–1925* (Chicago: University of Chicago Press, 1998); Kenneth Turney Gibbs, *Business Architectural Imagery in America, 1870–1930* (Ann Arbor: UMI Research Press, 1984).

67 Holleran and Fogelson, "The Sacred Skyline," 17, which cites the *Boston Real Estate Record,* October 15, 1892. At the time, real estate entrepreneurs were not adept at calculating the value of the "extra dividends" of architecture as advertisement. But Prudential later explicitly evoked this secondary source of value with respect to the buildings created during its regional home office building program.

68 Allen, *Our Fair City,* 29.

69 William Minot, letter to the *Boston Herald,* February 8, 1898, quoted in Holleran and Fogelson, "The Sacred Skyline," 17.

70 Holleran and Fogelson, "The Sacred Skyline." Height limits were not uncommon in American cities; by 1913 they existed in Chicago, Washington, D.C., Los Angeles, Baltimore, and Cleveland, among others.

71 Ibid., 28.

72 The Equitable Building (1915), a massive, forty-two-story edifice that filled its site on Broadway in downtown New York, spurred the movement toward zoning. See Keith D. Revell, "Regulating the Landscape: Real Estate Values, City Planning, and the 1916 Zoning Ordinance," in *The Landscape of Modernity: New York City, 1900–1940,* ed. David Ward and Olivier Zunz (Baltimore: Johns Hopkins University Press, 1997).

73 The new buildings produced under this regulatory framework were frequently designed with an art deco aesthetic that emphasized verticality and expressed streamlined modernity; see Hugh Ferriss, *The Metropolis of Tomorrow* (Princeton, N.J.: Princeton Architectural Press, 1986 (originally published in 1929)).

74 Holleran and Fogelson, "The Sacred Skyline," 34, quoting the *Boston Herald,* March 8, 1923.

75 Donlyn Lyndon, *Boston: The City Observed* (New York: Vintage, 1982), 265; Ethan Anthony, *The Architecture of Ralph Adams Cram and His Office* (New York: W. W. Norton, 2007).

76 Ibid., 192.

77 McCord, *About Boston.*

78 Lyndon, *Boston,* 147.

79 Other key examples of these sprawling colonial revival insurance buildings outside the central business district include the Massachusetts Mutual Insurance Company, 1928, based in Springfield and designed by Kirkham and Parlett, and the Connecticut Mutual Insurance Company, Hartford, from 1927 and designed by Benjamin Wistar Morris. In 1961, Hoyle, Doran, and Berry, successor to Cram and Ferguson, designed an addition to the New England Mutual building that filled in the space between the two wings with a solid office block that clipped the pediment of the temple front, though the clock tower and cupola were not compromised. A much more ambitious proposal, which would have replaced the existing building entirely with a modern skyscraper, was rejected.

80 The other notable "retardataire deco" building produced in this period was the New England Telephone and Telegraph Building on Post Office Square, also in 1947 and designed by Cram and Ferguson. Ralph Adams Cram died in 1942; the work of his office was continued by Cram and Ferguson and, later, Hoyle, Doran, and Berry. For an in-depth study of Ralph Adams Cram and his office, see Douglass Shand-Tucci, *Ralph Adams Cram: An Architect's Four Quests: Medieval, Modernist, American, Ecumenical* (Amherst: University of Massachusetts Press, 2005).

81 McCord, *About Boston,* 92.

82 Annie Haven Thwing, *The Crooked and Narrow Streets of Boston* (Boston: Marshall Jones, 1920).

83 Elisabeth M. Herlihy, "The History of Boston's Street System," in *Report on a Thoroughfare Plan for Boston* (Boston: City Planning Board, 1930), 156.

84 Whitehill and Kennedy, *Boston: A Topographical History,* 9. The basic form of the "Bulfinch Triangle" is still perceivable today, though obscured by the inter-

vention of rail lines, the North Station terminal, and the Central Artery (now covered over by the Big Dig and reconstructed as a surface boulevard).

85 Based on plans from 1856 by Arthur Gilman, using the Mill Dam as a guide to the northern edge of the grid. The railroads filled land between the crossing tracks of the Boston and Albany and the Boston and Providence lines in the 1870s and '80s. There was included a promenade along the Charles River Embankment (later the location of Storrow Drive and a redesigned esplanade). Before filling, the Back Bay was framed as a public health hazard. Much of the land was owned by the Commonwealth and the project was developed under the auspices of the Back Bay Commissions. A special railway was built to carry gravel from Needham. Issuing from South Station, the B&A and the B&P rails met at Back Bay Station, the Park Square terminal closed since 1899.

86 See Newman and Holton, *Boston's Back Bay;* Whitehill and Kennedy, *Boston: A Topographical History; Back Bay Boston: The City as a Work of Art,* with essays by Lewis Mumford and Walter Muir Whitehill (Boston: Museum of Fine Arts, 1969); Bunting, *Houses of Boston's Back Bay.*

87 Asha Elizabeth Weinstein, "The Congestion Evil: Perceptions of Traffic Congestion in Boston in the 1890s and 1920s" (Ph.D. diss., University of California, Berkeley, 2002); Asha Weinstein, "Curing Congestion: Competing Plans for a Loop Highway and Parking Regulations in Boston in the 1920s," *Journal of Planning History* 3, no. 4 (November 2004): 292–311.

88 Fogelson, *Downtown,* 59; see also Cheape, *Moving the Masses.* The Tremont Street subway became a key link in the West End Street Railway's broader network of electric streetcars. Ultimately, elevated streetcar lines were also built. The Boston Elevated Railway Company, chartered in 1894, took control of the West End in 1896, thus consolidating transit in Boston. The Atlantic Avenue elevated opened in 1901, articulating the future route of the Central Artery.

89 Arthur Shurtleff, "A Street Plan for Metropolitan District of Boston," *Landscape Architecture* 1 (January 1911): 71–83. Shurtleff's scheme followed a nineteenth-century tradition of metropolitanism first suggested by Frederick Law Olmsted, who designed an "Emerald Necklace" for Boston in the 1880s as a ring of parks and parkways — the Boston Common, Public Garden, and Commonwealth Avenue were its urban fountainhead — that also functioned as an urban drainage system for the Back Bay. In 1893, Charles Eliot, a landscape architect, and Sylvester Baxter, an urban reformer and journalist, proposed a more ambitious regional system of parks, open spaces, and parkways, as well as a new institutional body, the Metropolitan

District Commission, to procure and administer these new spaces.

90 See Weinstein, "The Congestion Evil."

91 "For Traffic Relief in Boston — New Two-Mile Thoroughfare Proposed," *American City* (February 1924): 215.

92 Elizabeth M. Herlihy, "Traffic Count Helps Boston Planning," *American City* (December 1926), 849. Throughout the 1920s, the pages of *American City* were littered with advertisements for inventions designed to regulate and improve traffic flow. These included the "Lehman Traffic Guide," which promised to "put an end to all traffic troubles." It was a small, heavy dome with reflective lenses that sat in the middle of streets to divide traffic. Or the Automatic Signal Corporation's "Electro-Matic vehicle-actuated traffic dispatching system," which could be installed at complicated intersections to control traffic and allow "non-interfering flows to move independently." The Electro-Matic was essentially a dressed-up version of traffic lights, designed to manage the flow of multimodal traffic through congested intersections and prevent collisions.

93 *Report on a Thoroughfare Plan for Boston,* 6.

94 "Speed and Safety for Boston's Traffic," *American City* (December 1930): 148.

95 Master Highway Plan for the Boston Metropolitan Area (1948), 12.

96 The remainder of the money was allocated to the Metropolitan District Commission (the successor of the Metropolitan Parks Commission) to construct a riverside drive — Storrow Drive — in conjunction with a landscaped esplanade along the Charles River in Boston. See Haglund, *Inventing the Charles River.*

97 See Yanni Tsipis and David Kruh, *Building Route 128* (Portsmouth, N.H.: Arcadia, 2003).

98 The planner Robert Whitten discouraged the use of Atlantic Avenue for the route of the Central Artery. The road was a major commercial thoroughfare that gave access to the wharves, but it already hosted an elevated train, and Whitten bemoaned losing transit access to the waterfront. See *Thoroughfare Plan for Metropolitan Boston,* p. 86.

99 Anthony David Green, "Planning the Central Artery: Constraints on Planners and the Limits of Planning, 1909–1979," A.B. Honors Thesis, Harvard University, 1979.

100 Governor Herter refused to save the meat processing structures, and blamed the recently created Massachusetts Market Authority for failing to locate new quarters. "State Refuses to Halt Work on Hub Artery," *Christian Science Monitor,* February 6, 1953; Everett M. Smith, "Leather District Fights Artery," *Christian Science Monitor,* November 6, 1953; Joseph

A. Keblinsky, "Artery Threatens Leather District and Chinatown," *Boston Globe*, March 25, 1953; John Volpe, then Public Works commissioner, insisted that the route was chosen to minimize impacts on the shoe and leather trades. The alternative route would have clung more closely to the northern edge of the Fort Point Channel, claiming land owned by the New York and New Haven Railroad, though it was ultimately dismissed; "Hynes Opposes State Route for Artery," *Christian Science Monitor*, March 25, 1953. Mayor Hynes supported many of these protests, expressing his concern that the highway sacrificed an inordinate amount of taxable property. "City and Chinatown Oppose Artery Route," *Boston Globe*, October 20, 1953. In the North End, merchants complained that the Central Artery ramps would disrupt the neighborhood. "No. Enders Protest Hanover St. Ramps for Central Artery," *Boston Globe*, January 27, 1953.

101 On the Interstate Highway Act, see Mark H. Rose, *Interstate: Express Highway Politics, 1939-1989* (Knoxville: University of Tennessee Press, 1979, revised edition 1990).

102 In the *1930 Thoroughfare Plan for Metropolitan Boston*, Robert Whitten had also proposed a direct connection to the Central Artery via a "B&A Highway" along the same rail corridor targeted by Callahan.

103 McCord, *About Boston*, 12.

104 Robert C. Bergenheim, "Realtors Expect New Skyscraper to Break Hub's 'Antique Barrier,'" *Christian Science Monitor*, February 1, 1957.

105 See Timothy Rohan, "Challenging the Curtain Wall: Paul Rudolph's Blue Cross and Blue Shield Building," *Journal of the Society of Architectural Historians* 66, no. 1 (March 2007); "Era of Commercial Building Looms, Says Real Estate Expert," *Boston Globe*, September 20, 1957; "Demolition of Famous Back Bay Landmark Begins," *Boston Globe*, February 3, 1957.

106 Frederick D. McCarthy, "Travelers' Building Good Sign for Boston Business," *Boston Globe*, October 20, 1957. Travelers had established a Boston branch office in 1909 and sold a diverse array of financial products, including accident, health, fire, automotive, and life insurance policies.

107 "Release After 9 p.m., Sept. 17, 1959," The Travelers Insurance Companies, Public Information Department.

108 McCarthy, "Travelers' Building Good Sign for Boston Business."

109 The lead designer was Elsa Gidoni. See Mary King, "There's a Quiet Woman's Quiet Touch in the Traveler's Insurance Building," *Boston Globe*, April 3, 1960. See also Jewel Stern and John A. Stuart, *Ely Jacques Kahn, Architect: Beaux-Arts to Modernism in New York* (New York: W. W. Norton, 2006).

110 "Remarks by Mr. J. Doyle DeWitt, President of the Travelers Insurance Companies, at Dedication Dinner at the Algonquin Club, Boston, Mass., Thursday evening, September 17, 1959, at 6:30 P.M," The Travelers Insurance Companies, Public Information Department.

111 At around the same time, William Zeckendorf of Webb and Knapp, the New York developer, was flirting with the idea of redeveloping a huge swath of land near South Station, including the terminal and the adjacent fan of tracks leading into it. Nothing would come of the Zeckendorf proposal, but news of the real estate magnate's interest in Boston formed part of the buzz that the city was "beginning to boil." "Is Boston 'Beginning to Boil'?" *Fortune* (June 1957), 286-90.

CHAPTER 3 "We Believe in Boston"

1 Richard Connolly, "Scope of Prudential Plans Astounds Business Leaders," *Boston Herald*, February 1, 1957.

2 Carrol M. Shanks, "We Believe in New England," address at a Luncheon of the Greater Boston Chamber of Commerce, January 31, 1957, PA 10-42, Press Kits 1960.

3 Ibid.

4 Ibid.

5 Ibid.

6 Arthur Stratton, "Huge Center to Make 12,000 New Jobs," *Boston Herald*, February 1, 1957.

7 Connolly, "Scope of Prudential Plans."

8 A. S. Plotkin, "Hail Prudential Center as City Reviver," *Boston Globe*, February 1, 1957.

9 Stratton, "Huge Center to Make 12,000 New Jobs."

10 "Hynes Stresses Development 'An Actuality, Not a Dream,'" *Boston Herald*, February 1, 1957.

11 Connolly, "Scope of Prudential Plans."

12 Ibid.

13 "Hynes Says Center Means New Life for City," *Boston Herald*, February 1, 1957.

14 Arthur Stratton, "Hynes Plans 6000-Seat Auditorium: Project Seen Key to 'Floodgates' for New Capital," *Boston Herald*, January 23, 1957.

15 Ibid.

16 "Statement of John B. Hynes, Mayor of Boston, on the Prudential Center," PA 10-43, Press Releases 1956-57.

17 Shanks, "We Believe in New England."

18 John B. Hynes, "How Hynes Steered the Pru to Boston," *Boston Sunday Globe*, January 11, 1970.

19 Robert C. Bergenheim, "Experts Say Years Needed to Develop Railroad Yard," *Christian Science Monitor*, December 17, 1951; W. Clifford Harvey, "Radio City for Boston?" *Christian Science Monitor*, April 15,

1949; Albert D. Hughes, "Metropolitan Freight-Passenger Heliport Projected," *Christian Science Monitor*, July 20, 1951; W. Clifford Harvey, "B&A Yards Plan Pivots on Convention Hall," *Christian Science Monitor*, December 31, 1951.

20 "Rockefeller Use of B&A Yard Eyed," *Christian Science Monitor*, September 14, 1951.

21 W. Clifford Harvey, "Rail Yard Study Keyed to $50 Million Price Tag," *Christian Science Monitor*, August 2, 1951; "28-Acre B&A Back Bay Yards, Valued at $8 Million, to Be Sold," *Boston Globe*, May 21, 1951.

22 Hynes, "How Hynes Steered the Pru to Boston."

23 Ibid.

24 "Proposed Back Bay Center Development," *Progressive Architecture* 35 (January 1954): 73–84. Walter Bogner was also part of Carl Friedrich's winning team in the Boston Contest of 1944, establishing himself as a key thinker on the topic of urban redevelopment.

25 The *Globe* reported in 1957 that Roger Stevens would work as a consultant to Prudential on the Boston project. Plotkin, "Hail Prudential Center as City Reviver."

26 Walter Bogner notes, October 26, 1955, Walter Bogner Collection, Frances Loeb Library, Harvard Graduate School of Design.

27 Hynes, "How Hynes Steered the Pru to Boston."

28 Stratton, "Hynes Plans 6000-Seat Auditorium."

29 Victor O. Jones, "The Man Who Believed in Boston," *Boston Globe*, July 15, 1966.

30 "Discussion of the Taxing Procedure of Prudential Center," PA 10-43, Event Files 1950s.

31 Ibid.

32 "Memorandum of Conference Held March 18, 1958, at the Sheraton-Plaza Hotel in Boston," MTAA, 01220, 2.

33 Hynes, "How Hynes Steered the Pru to Boston."

34 Ibid.

35 Ibid.

36 *Opinion of the Justices*, Massachusetts General Court, 332 Mass. 769, 770 (1955).

37 Cynthia Horan, "Organizing the 'New Boston': Growth Policy, Governing Coalitions and Tax Reform," *Polity* 22, no. 3 (1990): 501. One group of prominent Boston business leaders, organized as the greater Boston Economic Study Committee — which included the chairman of John Hancock, the president of the Federal Reserve Bank of Boston, and other leading financiers and industrialists — believed that the city needed comprehensive tax reform and not a continuation of the fickle system of individual dispensations. Cynthia Horan, "The Origins of 121A," unpublished manuscript, June 19, 1980.

38 *Opinion of the Justices*, 332 Mass. 769, 779.

39 Ibid., 783.

40 Thomas H. O'Connor, *Building a New Boston: Politics and Urban Renewal, 1950 to 1970* (Boston: Northeastern University Press, 1993), 101.

41 S. Westcott Toole, "Decentralization Dividends," address before the Savings Banks Association of Massachusetts, June 11, 1957, PA 04-123.

42 Ibid., 9.

43 Ibid.

44 Plotkin, "Merger of Toll Road–Prudential Center Planned in $300 Million Package Deal," *Boston Globe*, April 29, 1960.

45 "Memorandum, April 9, 1960, to Mr. Callahan, from N. T. Byrnes, Re: Prudential Center," MTAA 01220.

46 Michael Liuzzi, "Furcolo Carries Prudential Ball," *Christian Science Monitor*, May 2, 1960.

47 Plotkin, "Merger of Toll Road–Prudential Center."

48 Foster Furcolo to Senate and House of Representatives, May 2, 1960, MTAA 01220.

49 Copy of unnumbered Act, MTAA 01220.

50 Furcolo to Senate and House of Representatives.

51 *Opinion of the Justices*, 341 Mass. 738, 739.

52 Ibid., 759.

53 Ibid., 763.

54 The Urban Land Institute (ULI), among other development interests, lobbied state legislatures to create local enabling laws to facilitate large investments from insurance companies and other big financial institutions. Marc Weiss has argued that the ULI did not favor the Massachusetts type of redevelopment legislation because it focused too explicitly on housing. Marc A. Weiss, "The Origins and Legacy of Urban Renewal," in *Urban and Regional Planning in an Age of Austerity*, ed. Pierre Clavel, John Forester, and William M. Goldsmith (New York: Pergamon, 1980). See also Lewis H. Weinstein, "Urban Renewal in Massachusetts," *Massachusetts Law Quarterly* 47 (1962), and Mark I. Gelfand, *A Nation of Cities: The Federal Government and Urban America, 1933–1965* (New York: Oxford University Press, 1975).

55 Acts, 1960, Massachusetts General Court, Chap. 652, 558.

56 In 1975, the forty-year exemption was changed to fifteen years with the possibility of a further extension, and the six percent allowable return was enlarged to eight percent.

57 Acts, 1960, Massachusetts General Court, Chap. 652, 557.

58 Ibid.

59 Ibid.

60 Acts, 1960, Massachusetts General Court, Chap. 121A, 558.

61 Michael Liuzzi, "Prudential Center: Full Steam

Builds," *Christian Science Monitor,* June 16, 1960.

62 Michael Liuzzi, "Prudential Bill: Sides Deploy," *Christian Science Monitor,* June 27, 1960.

63 "Prudential Judged a Public Purpose," *Christian Science Monitor,* August 10, 1960.

64 *Opinion of the Justices,* 341 Mass. 760 (August 9, 1960).

65 Michael Liuzzi, "Boston Fuse Lit for Building Boom," *Christian Science Monitor,* August 24, 1960.

66 Ibid.

67 Edgar M. Mills, "Center Bill Near End of Gantlet," *Christian Science Monitor,* August 30, 1960.

68 "Light Is Green for Hub Centers," *Christian Science Monitor,* September 2, 1960; "Collins Blueprint for Rebuilding Boston," *Christian Science Monitor,* September 23, 1960.

69 Michael Liuzzi, "'Prudential Lake' Ripples in Back Bay," *Christian Science Monitor,* August 25, 1960.

70 Joseph W. Lund, chairman of the Boston Redevelopment Authority, to Louis R. Menagh, Jr., executive vice president of the Prudential Insurance Company of America, September 8, 1960, Papers of John Collins, box 397, folder "Prudential 1960," Boston Public Library.

71 I am quoting here from a June 1961 amended version of "Prudential's Application for Approval of Project under Chapter 121A of the General Laws and Chapter 652 of the Acts of 1960," Boston Redevelopment Authority Archives (hereafter cited as BRA) no. 621, pg. 18.

72 *Architectural Forum* quipped in 1964: "Boston is not only the most Irish city in the nation but the most Irish Catholic. Where else would the chairman of the redevelopment board be a priest? . . . As chairman of the BRA, Monsignor Lally is among other things a valuable buffer. When he presents a redevelopment plan to a hostile audience — whether it is the City Council or a neighborhood gathering — they are likely to listen to him more respectfully than to Ed Logue." See "Boston," *Architectural Forum* 120 (1964): 86.

73 Public Hearing, March 22, 1961, BRA no. 579, 12, 5, 16.

74 Ibid., 24.

75 Ibid., 45, 49–50.

76 Ibid., 67.

77 Ibid., 98.

78 Ibid., 124.

79 Ibid., 147, 148, 151.

80 Ibid., 152, 153, 154.

81 Ibid., 156.

82 Ibid., 158.

83 Ibid., 160.

84 Ibid., 178.

85 Ibid., 171, 162.

86 Ibid., 162–63.

87 Ibid., 173, 174.

88 "Court Weighs Pleas on Prudential Center," *Christian Science Monitor,* November 8, 1961.

89 Michael Liuzzi, "Court Says 'Yes' to Prudential in Boston," *Christian Science Monitor,* December 20, 1961.

CHAPTER 4 A Closed Loop

1 Albert D. Hughes, "Autos Stream Over New Pike; Extension into Boston Pushed," *Christian Science Monitor,* May 16, 1957.

2 See Wilfred Owen and Charles L. Dearing, *Toll Roads and the Problem of Highway Modernization* (Washington, D.C.: Brookings Institution, 1951).

3 Jameson Doig, "Joining New York City to the Greater Metropolis: The Port Authority as Visionary, Target of Opportunity, and Opportunist," in *The Landscape of Modernity: New York City, 1900–1940,* ed. David Ward and Olivier Zunz (Baltimore: Johns Hopkins University Press, 1997), and Jameson Doig, *Empire on the Hudson: Entrepreneurial Vision and Political Power at the Port of New York Authority* (New York: Columbia University Press, 2002); Robert A. Caro, *The Power Broker: Robert Moses and the Fall of New York* (New York: Vintage, 1975); Louise Nelson Dyble, *Paying the Toll: Local Power, Regional Politics, and the Golden Gate Bridge* (Philadelphia: University of Pennsylvania Press, 2009).

4 Charles Dearing, "Turnpike Authorities in the United States," *Law and Contemporary Problems* 26, no. 4 (Autumn 1961): 741.

5 "Excerpt from an Address by Hon. Paul L. Troast, Chairman of the New Jersey Turnpike Authority," included with a letter from Wm. R. McConochie of DeLeuw, Cather, and Company to William F. Callahan, February 13, 1952, MTAA 02333.

6 Ibid.

7 Dearing, "Turnpike Authorities in the United States," 751.

8 Ibid., 2.

9 Ibid.

10 Acts, 1955, Massachusetts General Court, Chap. 47, emphasis added.

11 Doig, *Empire on the Hudson.* See also Jean Riesman, "The Maharajah of the Macadam: William F. Callahan and His Fight for the Road to Boston" (Massachusetts Institute of Technology, 1991).

12 Volpe represented Italian-American political power that sought refuge in the Republic Party when elbowed from the Irish-dominated Democratic Party.

13 Anthony Lewis, "Boston Strong Man: William Francis Callahan," *New York Times,* June 20, 1961.

14 Ibid.

15 Harold K. Banks, "Mr. Callahan of Massachusetts: A Series on William F. Callahan," *Boston Sunday Advertiser and Record American,* September 9–22, 1962, quoted in Riesman, "The Maharajah of the Macadam."

16 Ibid., 6.

17 Lewis, "Boston Strong Man."

18 Tony Hill, "The Man Who Drove Hard to Build Roads," *Boston Globe,* August 25, 2002.

19 "New England Highway Upsets Old Way of Life," *Business Week,* May 14, 1955, 188.

20 "Renewing Our Cities," *Architectural Forum* 102 (1956): 13.

21 Edgar M. Mills, "Bay State's Toll Road to Boom Industrial Growth," *Christian Science Monitor,* November 26, 1954. On the parkways of the 1920s and '30s, see Thomas J. Campanella, "American Curves," *Harvard Design Magazine* (Summer 1997), 40–43; and Matthew Gandy, *Concrete and Clay: Reworking Nature in New York City* (Cambridge, Mass.: MIT Press, 2002), 115–52.

22 Ibid.

23 Hughes, "Autos Stream Over New Pike," 10.

24 William F. Callahan, "For Future Press Release," undated, MTAA 01321, Community Relations, Press Releases 1961–71.

25 Ibid. The parenthetical statement is Callahan's, not my own. He seemed intent on demonstrating his awareness of colonial history.

26 DeLeuw, Cather, and Company, "Estimated Traffic and Revenues, Proposed Massachusetts Turnpike," July 1953, MTAA 02333.

27 Ibid., 4.

28 Ibid., 9.

29 Ibid., 13.

30 Ibid., 6.

31 On the "billboard war" and highway beautification, see Catherine Gudis, *Buyways: Billboards, Automobiles, and the American Landscape* (New York: Routledge, 2004).

32 "Last-Minute Objections Snag Toll Road Extension," *Boston Herald,* July 19, 1956.

33 Robert C. Bergenheim, "Toll Road Entry to Hub Seen Via B&A Line," *Christian Science Monitor,* July 17, 1956.

34 Ibid.

35 Ibid.

36 Robert C. Bergenheim, "Prudential Unaffected: Toll Road to Follow B&A?" *Christian Science Monitor,* August 1, 1956.

37 Arthur Stratton, "Hynes Plans 6000-Seat Auditorium: Project Seen Key to 'Floodgates' for New Capital," *Boston Herald,* January 23, 1957.

38 "First Report of Mayor's Citizens' Committee on the Toll Road," October 23, 1956, Newton Historical Society Archives at the Jackson Homestead (hereafter cited as NHSA), Massachusetts Turnpike.

39 Bergenheim, "Toll Road Via B&A and Building Too?"

40 Albert D. Hughes, "Toll Road Bloc Gains Edge," *Christian Science Monitor,* February 13, 1957.

41 Undated, untitled memorandum, MTAA 01563, Federal Aid.

42 A. S. Plotkin, "Where Toll Road May Pinch Four Newton Villages," *Boston Globe,* November 22, 1956.

43 Undated press release, Newton Citizens' Committee Studying Toll Road Extension, NHSA, Werner Gumperts Papers.

44 Paul Heffernan, "Toll 'Pike Issues Losing in Favor," *New York Times,* January 6, 1957.

45 "The Toll Road Era Is Fading," *Christian Science Monitor,* December 5, 1956.

46 Press Release from Massachusetts Division AAA, "AAA Bill Proposes Suburban Freeway Along Charles River from Route 128 into Boston," NHSA, Werner Gumperts Papers.

47 "A Shot in the Dark," *Boston Herald,* March 20, 1957.

48 "Hanging a Toll Road on Us," *Boston Herald,* December 6, 1956.

49 "Our Western Gateway Squeeze," *Boston Herald,* July 17, 1956.

50 "Unscrambling the Highway Egg," *Boston Herald,* March 20, 1957.

51 Albert D. Hughes, "Inner Belt Roadway Held Boston 'Must,'" *Christian Science Monitor,* February 16, 1957.

52 "Notes for Future Press Release," undated, MTAA 01563, Federal Aid.

53 Hughes, "Toll Road Bloc Gains Edge."

54 Albert D. Hughes, "Cloud Seen on Hub Pike Link," *Christian Science Monitor,* October 29, 1958.

55 Albert D. Hughes, "DPW Urged to Speed Expressway to West," *Christian Science Monitor,* December 14, 1959. Though he was the commissioner of the DPW, Anthony DiNatale was an ally of Callahan's and later joined the Turnpike Authority as a member of the board.

56 A. S. Plotkin, "Merger of Toll Road–Prudential Center Planned in $300 Million Package Deal," *Boston Globe,* April 29, 1960.

57 Plotkin, "Merger of Toll Road–Prudential Center Planned."

58 S. J. Micciche, "Volpe to Speed Freeway Link, Race Callahan," *Boston Globe,* January 11, 1961.

59 A. S. Plotkin, "Pros, Cons of Volpe-Callahan Hassle on Highways," *Boston Globe,* January 13, 1961.

60 "Notes for Future Press Release," MTAA.

61 Frederick H. Guidry, "Volpe to Head U.S. Road

Program," *Christian Science Monitor*, October 12, 1956.

62 Undated press release, MTAA 01321, Community Relations and Press Releases.

63 Plotkin, "Pros, Cons of Volpe-Callahan Hassle."

64 Ibid.

65 Micciche, "Volpe to Speed Freeway Link."

66 S. J. Micciche, "Come Toll Link or Freeway, Prudential Going Up," *Boston Globe*, January 12, 1961.

67 Micciche, "Volpe to Speed Freeway Link."

68 S. J. Micciche, "Won't Bring Freeway Downtown: Volpe Plans Road from Prudential to Inner Belt," *Boston Globe*, January 13, 1961.

69 "Collision of Titans," *Boston Globe*, January 11, 1961.

70 Michael Liuzzi, "'Prudential Lake' Ripples in Back Bay," *Christian Science Monitor*, August 25, 1960.

71 Arthur Stratton, "Road Collapse Puts Prudential in Peril," *Boston Herald*, April 12, 1961.

72 Michael Liuzzi, "Ice Broken on Boston Boom," *Christian Science Monitor*, March 1, 1961.

73 Plotkin, "Pros, Cons of Volpe-Callahan Hassle."

74 Juan Cameron, "Toll-Road Backers Spy Green Light," *Christian Science Monitor*, December 5, 1960.

75 Ibid.

76 Stratton, "Road Collapse."

77 Unsigned memorandum to Monsignor Francis J. Lally, chairman, Boston Redevelopment Authority, May 2, 1961, PA 10–42, emphasis added.

78 Stratton, "Road Collapse."

79 "A Critical Review of the Boston Extension Project of the Massachusetts Turnpike Authority," BRA no. 3658.

80 Ibid., 7.

81 "Professors Explain Warning to Bankers on Pike Bonds," *Boston Herald*, April 12, 1961.

82 Ibid.

83 John H. Fenton, "Highway Delayed in Massachusetts," *New York Times*, May 20, 1961.

84 "Turnpike Bond Plan Fails in Bay State," *New York Times*, June 21, 1961.

85 Michael Liuzzi, "Massachusetts: Toll Bonds Fail," *Christian Science Monitor*, November 30, 1961.

86 A. S. Plotkin, "Hub Toll Road Assured; Work to Begin at Once," *Boston Globe*, January 23, 1962.

87 Peter B. Greenough, "New Deal and Faces Assure 'Pike Bond Underwriting," *Boston Globe*, January 23, 1962.

88 Robert B. Hanron, "Ask Speed on Toll Extension," *Boston Globe*, January 23, 1962.

89 A. S. Plotkin, "Road Marks High Point in Callahan's Career," *Boston Globe*, January 23, 1962.

90 John H. Fenton, "Massachusetts Turnpike Body

Places $180,000,000 of Bonds," *New York Times*, January 23, 1962.

91 Hanron, "Ask Speed on Toll Extension."

92 Plotkin, "Road Marks High Point."

93 "Callahan's Blast Opens Toll Road: A Wry Wish and a Whoosh!" *Boston Herald*, March 6, 1962, quoted in Riesman, "The Maharajah of the Macadam."

94 Gordon McClean, "Mass. Turnpike Work Gathers Speed," *New England Construction*, April 1, 1963, 60.

95 Press Release, January 22, 1962, MTAA 01321, Community Relations/Press Releases '61–'71.

96 Caro, *The Power Broker*, 218. On the impact of the Boston Extension in Newton, see Stacey A. Bancroft Neustadt, "The Impact of the Massachusetts Turnpike Extension on the Citizens of the City of Newton," master's thesis, Harvard University, November 1994, and Toby Berkman, "Six Lanes, Five Miles, a Decade of Controversy: The Construction of the Massachusetts Turnpike Extension Through the City of Newton," *The Concord Review*, 1998.

97 Alan Lupo, Frank Colcord, and Edmund P. Fowler, *Rites of Way: The Politics of Transportation in Boston and the U.S. City* (Boston: Little, Brown, 1971).

CHAPTER 5 Designing the Center

1 Charles Luckman, *Twice in a Lifetime: From Soap to Skyscrapers* (New York: W. W. Norton, 1988), 327.

2 "A Cavity in Boston — To Be Filled with Six Ideas," *Architectural Forum* 99 (1953): 103.

3 Kenneth Welch, who was based in Grand Rapids, Michigan, worked as a consultant on one of the earliest regional shopping centers, Shoppers World, which opened in the Boston suburb of Framingham, Massachusetts, in 1951. The Back Bay Center was intended to compete directly with suburban shopping centers like this, so it is no surprise that Roger Stevens wanted to engage a planner with direct experience working on such projects. See "'Shoppers' World' at Framingham Applies New Ideas," *Architectural Record* 110 (November 1951), 12–13; Geoffrey Harold Baker and Bruno Funaro, *Shopping Centers: Design and Operation* (New York: Reinhold, 1951), 198–99. See also Richard Longstreth, *City Center to Regional Mall: Architecture, the Automobile, and Retailing in Los Angeles, 1920–1950* (Cambridge, Mass.: MIT Press, 1997).

4 Ibid., 104, 107. Walter Bogner had been interested in renewing the urban core, and the language of illness and decay, at least since 1944, when he was a member of the winning "Harvard Team" in the Boston Contest for urban planning ideas.

5 Wilbur Smith and Associates, "Report on Traffic — Transportation — Parking for Back Bay Center Development, Boston, Massachusetts," December 1953, BRA no. 655.

6 Ibid.

7 Ibid., 112.

8 "A Cavity in Boston," 104. The architect Samuel Glaser collaborated on the design of the saucer-shaped convention center.

9 Ibid., 114.

10 "First Design Award," *Progressive Architecture* (January 1954), 73-78.

11 José Luis Sert, "Centres of Community Life," in *The Heart of the City: Towards the Humanisation of Urban Life*, ed. Jaqueline Tyrwhitt, José Luis Sert, and Ernesto N. Rogers (New York: Pellegrini and Cudahy, 1952), 11.

12 See Peter Blake, *The Master Builders: Le Corbusier, Mies van der Rohe, Frank Lloyd Wright* (New York: W. W. Norton, 1996 [originally published in 1960]); Siegfried Giedion, *Architecture You and Me: The Diary of a Development* (Cambridge: Harvard University Press, 1958).

13 "A Cavity in Boston."

14 Walter Bogner notes, October 26, 1955, Walter Bogner Collection, Frances Loeb Library, Harvard Graduate School of Design.

15 Luckman, *Twice in a Lifetime*, 327-28.

16 The son of Jewish immigrants, Luckman was involved with Jewish charities in Los Angeles.

17 "The Case of Charles Luckman," *Fortune* 41 (1950).

18 Luckman, *Twice in a Lifetime*, 241. Luckman aired his claim to the Lever House concept at length in a letter to the *American Institute of Architects Journal* in 1980: "Lever House — the Client's View," *AIA Journal* (August 1980): 8, 66-69. Lever House has been attacked by some critics, most notably the architectural historian Vincent Scully, for destroying the integrity of Park Avenue's street frontage by cutting a hole in its fabric. See Vincent Scully, *Architecture: The Natural and the Manmade* (New York: St. Martin's, 1991), 2-3.

19 There was also some evidence that Lever Brothers' profit margin was declining, and that it looked increasingly unlikely that the company's relatively new synthetic soap products would catch up with those already on the market from Procter and Gamble or Colgate. "Why Luckman Left," *Newsweek*, January 30, 1951, 52.

20 Luckman, *Twice in a Lifetime*, 277.

21 Ibid., 279.

22 "CBS TV City Starts," *Architectural Forum* (May 1952): 101-10.

23 "Southland Firm Will Plan Air Base Projects," *Los Angeles Times*, October 14, 1954; "L.A. Firms to Plan U.S. Bases in Spain," *Los Angeles Times*, October 10, 1953.

24 Luckman, *Twice in a Lifetime*, 332. Pereira's insistence on a more "artistic" practice has recently been rewarded with an emerging reputation for inventive modernist architecture. See James Steele, ed., *William Pereira* (Los Angeles: Architectural Guild, 2002).

25 "L.A.'s Tallest Building Set," *Los Angeles Times*, April 22, 1962; "New Giant of Wilshire Boulevard's Miracle Mile," *Los Angeles Times*, January 3, 1965.

26 Ada Louise Huxtable, "In Portland, Ore., Urban Decay Is Masked by Natural Splendor," *New York Times*, June 19, 1970. The First National Bank of Oregon building is now the Wells Fargo Center.

27 "100 Largest Firms in the U.S.," *Architectural Forum* (February 1964): 14-16. *Forum* noted that Skidmore, Owings, and Merrill did not make the list of America's largest architectural firms only because of insufficient data.

28 "He Sells Architecture the Way He Sold Soap," *Business Week*, October 28, 1967, 78.

29 Garry Stevens, *The Favored Circle: The Social Foundations of Architectural Distinction* (Cambridge, Mass.: MIT Press, 1998).

30 Ada Louise Huxtable, "Architecture: Felt Forum, New House Is Sensible and Quietly Attractive," *New York Times*, November 27, 1967. CLA designed other large arenas and sports facilities, including the Los Angeles Forum (1967) and the Oahu Bowl (1975) near Honolulu.

31 "Corporations: The Second Time Around," *Time*, March 20, 1962, 81.

32 "Repeat Performance," *New Yorker*, August 28, 1954, 16.

33 Ada Louise Huxtable, "A Fair U.S. Pavilion," *New York Times*, January 26, 1963; "U.S. Pavilion at N.Y. Fair Will 'Float' on 4 Columns," *New York Times*, January 22, 1963; "Preview: New York World's Fair 1964-1965," *Architectural Record* (February 1964): 137-39. See also Ron Robin, *Enclaves of America: The Rhetoric of American Political Architecture Abroad, 1900-1965* (Princeton, N.J.: Princeton University Press, 1992).

34 See "The Architects from 'Skid's Row,'" *Fortune* (January 1958), 137-40, 210-15; William Dudley Hunt, *Total Design: Architecture of Welton Becket and Associates* (New York: McGraw-Hill, 1972).

35 "Work to Start Soon on Broadway Plaza," *Los Angeles Times*, February 1, 1971; Lou Desser, "Plaza Welcomes New Broadway Store," *Los Angeles Times*, November 11, 1973. Prudential Insurance Company invested $65 million in finance capital for the Broadway Plaza. See Russ Leadabrand, "The Broadway Plaza, A Block Big . . . Vast, Complex, Bold," *Los Angeles Times*, November 18, 1973.

36 "Luckman Tells All About Ogden," *AIA Journal*

(June 1970): 52. Luckman's concept for Broadway Plaza bears resemblance to many of John Portman's projects from the same period, which created rich interior landscapes at the expense of engaging the surrounding streets. Both men emphasized the role of the architect-developer. See John Portman and Jonathan Barnett, *The Architect as Developer* (New York: McGraw-Hill, 1976).

37 "Luckman Firm Is Purchased by Ogden Corporation," *Architectural Record* (March 1968): 81–82; Robert A. Wright, "Ogden Corp. to Acquire Luckman Concern," *New York Times,* January 19, 1968. As an advocate of the architect as developer, Luckman was likened in the press to John Portman, the Atlanta-based architect who also took a stake in his large-scale urban development projects. See Gurney Breckenfeld, "The Architects Want a Voice in Redesigning America," *Fortune* (November 1971), 144–47, 198–206; Portman and Barnett, *Architect as Developer.*

38 Jan C. Rowan, untitled editorial, *Progressive Architecture* (March 1968), 97.

39 It turned out that Luckman's incorporation with Ogden was short-lived. As costs at Broadway Plaza ballooned, so did tensions between Luckman and Ogden chairman Ralph E. Ablom. In 1973, Luckman bought back his architectural firm, then under the leadership of his son James M. Luckman, from Ogden. "Luckman Goes Back to the Drawing Board," *Business Week,* November 24, 1973, 26. This is also the moment when Luckman ran out of steam in his autobiography: "The expansion years of the 1960s were gone; everybody was tightening their belts in the early 1970s"; Luckman, *Twice in a Lifetime,* 388. In 1977, CLA reorganized as the Luckman Partnership, moving from a corporate structure to a much smaller employee-owned partnership and consolidating its office in Los Angeles. James Luckman announced that the firm was "back practicing architecture, not business"; Ruth Ryon, "Luckmans Say Revamping Has Paid Off," *Los Angeles Times,* March 18, 1979.

40 Charles Luckman, "The Architect as Designer," February 23, 1961, CLP.

41 Luckman, "Planning for People," 3.

42 Charles Luckman, "Humanation of Cities," March 1960, CLP. Planning for Bunker Hill began in 1954, with Pereira and Luckman teaming up with Welton Becket to generate the first master plans. The 136-acre project required clearing countless individual homes and displacing thousands of people. The land was grouped in superblocks with plans for complete separation of pedestrian and vehicular traffic. "Bunker Hill Development Plans Told," *Los Angeles Times,* November 15, 1955.

43 Giedion, *Architecture You and Me,* 128, 172.

44 Luckman, "Humanation of Cities," 4.

45 Luckman, "Architecture IS a Business," 22.

46 Luckman, "Planning for People," 6, 7.

47 Luckman, *Twice in a Lifetime,* 328.

48 "Glass and Steel Will Predominate," *Christian Science Monitor,* February 1, 1957. It is difficult to be certain which office — Pereira and Luckman or HDB — produced the renderings that were circulated in 1957. My instinct is that HDB, which is listed at the top of the tag as the architect, was responsible for the renderings and for many of the initial architectural ideas, while Pereira and Luckman executed the broader site plan. The saucer-shaped building was a popular image at that time. It was used in the Back Bay Center, and the Shoppers World mall in Framingham also featured a saucer-shaped structure to punctuate the axis.

49 "A New View of the Prudential Center," *Christian Science Monitor,* May 6, 1957.

50 David Harvey, "Prudential Says 'This Is It,'" *Christian Science Monitor,* July 24, 1958.

51 By 1958, CLA, Luckman's new firm, had assumed responsibility for the project following the demise of Pereira and Luckman.

52 Earl W. Foell, "Hynes Unveils Plan for Auditorium," *Christian Science Monitor,* August 7, 1958.

53 "Prudential Awards Center's Hotel Pact," *Christian Science Monitor,* December 9, 1958.

54 Luckman, *Twice in a Lifetime,* 329.

55 "Officialdom Hails Prudential 'Start,'" *Christian Science Monitor,* January 9, 1959.

56 Frederick H. Guidry, "Fortresslike Mechanics Building Due to Crumble Before Back Bay Center," *Christian Science Monitor,* January 31, 1957.

57 "Begin Prudential Work in 2 Weeks," *Boston Sunday Globe,* March 29, 1959.

58 Earl W. Foell, "Prudential Center Started," *Christian Science Monitor,* April 3, 1959.

59 "C. W. Stanton Memorandum to Record," April 1, 1960, CLP, Pru — Plaza & Underground no. 860, 1960.

60 Public Hearing, March 22, 1961, BRA no. 579, 46, 56. Charles Stanton came to Luckman's firm after working for Victor Gruen in New York.

61 Ibid., 56, 27, 24.

62 Michael Liuzzi, "Prudential Faces a Winter Start," *Christian Science Monitor,* August 21, 1961.

63 "Court Weighs Pleas on Prudential Center," *Christian Science Monitor,* November 8, 1961; Michael Liuzzi, "Court Says 'Yes' to Prudential in Boston," *Christian Science Monitor,* December 20, 1961.

64 David Harvey, "Old Boston Pries Chains of Tradition as New Buildings Jab Skyline," *Christian Science Monitor,* November 24, 1961.

65 "Prudential Insurance Contract Let to Erect Boston

Office Center," *Wall Street Journal,* March 22, 1962.

66 A. S. Plotkin, "Here's 1962 Preview of Prudential Center as It Will Look in '64," *Boston Sunday Globe,* January 7, 1962. CLA's reference to "lacy" grillwork on the Prudential tower evoked the architecture of Edward Durrell Stone, who believed that modernist architecture had become too cold and would benefit from the warmth of additional visual interest.

67 "Charles Luckman Memorandum to Charles Stanton," November 9, 1962, CLP.

68 Leland Roth, *A Concise History of American Architecture* (New York: Harper and Row, 1979). On the Seagram Building, see also Alice T. Friedman, *American Glamour and the Evolution of Modern Architecture* (New Haven: Yale University Press, 2010), and Benjamin Flowers, *Skyscraper: The Politics and Power of Building New York City in the Twentieth Century* (Philadelphia: University of Pennsylvania Press, 2009). Pereira and Luckman had lost out to both of these firms in the past. Samuel Bronfman initially asked Pereira and Luckman to design the Seagram Building, but his daughter, Phyllis Lambert, objected to the design and it was rejected.

69 Meredith L. Clausen, *The Pan Am Building and the Shattering of the Modernist Dream* (Cambridge, Mass.: MIT Press, 2005), 272–76.

70 Albert D. Hughes, "Architects Seek to 'Humanate' Center," *Christian Science Monitor,* March 21, 1962.

71 W. Clifford Harvey, "Medieval Moat to Encircle Prudential 'Castle' in Boston," *Christian Science Monitor,* April 13, 1962.

72 Luckman made this recommendation after examining the rendering shown in figure 42. "Charles Luckman Memorandum to Charles Stanton," November 9, 1962, CLP, Pru 860.08 — Office Building.

73 "C. W. Stanton to Record," January 18, 1963, Pru-Miscellaneous-9–61.

74 "C. W. Stanton to Charles Luckman," October 28, 1965, Prudential Center 1965.

75 "C. W. Stanton to S. W. Toole," September 9, 1963, CLP, Pru — Miscellaneous 6/63.

76 George B. Merry, "Prudential Center to Expand," *Christian Science Monitor,* August 17, 1963.

77 "Westcott Toole to Charles Luckman," January 14, 1963, CLA, PRU-Miscellaneous-9.61. United Fruit had deep roots in Boston, having been formed from the Boston Fruit Company in 1899.

78 "Boston's New TV Station Goes on the Air Today," *Boston Globe,* October 12, 1964. The television channel was operated by the Catholic Archdiocese of Boston.

79 "Garber Travel to Open Office in Prudential Center," *Boston Globe,* December 6, 1964.

80 The Luckman Papers are now housed in the Department of Archives and Special Collections at Loyola Marymount University in Los Angeles.

81 Later, the New England Merchants National Bank decided to rent space for a small branch bank in a second commercial block "C" to gain exposure to the north side of the Prudential Center. C. W. Stanton to R. W. Jones, March 27, 1964, New England Merchants Bank, Pru Center.

82 Charles Luckman to N. Preston Breed, vice president, State Street Bank and Trust Company, August 1, 1962, CLP, New England Merchants Bank, Pru Center.

83 "R. W. Jones Memorandum to C. W. Stanton," December 18, 1962, CLP, New England Merchants Bank, Pru Center.

84 Charles Luckman to Charles Stanton, March 6, 1963, CLP, New England Merchants Bank, Pru Center.

85 Charles Luckman to Richard Chapman, April 19, 1963, CLP, New England Merchants Bank, Pru Center. As a gesture to his new client, Luckman shifted his firm's Boston bank account from the State Street Bank and Trust Company to the New England Merchants. Charles Luckman to N. Preston Breed, vice president, State Street Bank & Trust Company, August 1, 1962, CLP, New England Merchants Bank, Pru Center.

86 "Ron Getty Memorandum," December 23, 1960, CLP, Pru — HCA Hotel — July 1960. CLA said it would take a six percent fee (1.2 percent more than the firm charged for Prudential's tower, commercial pavilions, and other aspects.)

87 "3-in-1 Hotel Due at Prudential Site," *Christian Science Monitor,* September 13, 1960.

88 John T. Stofko to James S. Craig, vice president, Staff Services and New Projects Planning, Hotel Corporation of America, July 22, 1960, CLP, Pru — HCA Hotel — July 1960.

89 "John King Memorandum," December 5, 1960, CLP, Pru — HCA Hotel — July 1960.

90 "C. W. Stanton Memorandum," October 27, 1960, CLP, Pru — HCA Hotel — July 1960.

91 There was a small flurry of memoranda between CLA architects and Don Perry, CLA's director of publicity. Perry suggested that CLA architects let HCA executives know that a mention in future interviews would be appreciated. Pru — HCA Hotel — July 1960.

92 Donal White, "Sheraton Corp. Takes Over Hotel at Prudential Center," *Boston Globe,* May 29, 1964.

93 Anthony J. Yudis, "Hub's Behavior Key to Convention Success," *Boston Globe,* November 1, 1964.

94 Anthony Yudis, "BRA Permits Addition to Sheraton-Boston," *Boston Globe,* June 16, 1972.

95 Merry, "Prudential Center to Expand," 2.

96 W. Clifford Harvey, "Suburbanites Rap on Boston's Door," *Christian Science Monitor,* October 28, 1960; Wilfrid C. Rodgers, "West End for Disillusioned Sub-

urbanites," *Boston Globe*, February 7, 1960. In January 1960, the John Hancock Mutual Life Insurance Company announced that it would put up $55 million to finance the West End Redevelopment project, known as Charles River Park. Robert B. Hanron, "John Hancock Co. Financing $55 Million West End Project," *Boston Globe*, January 22, 1960.

97 W. Clifford Harvey, "Building Boom Shapes Up for Boston," *Christian Science Monitor*, April 13, 1962.

98 Anthony J. Yudis, "How Twin Apartment Towers Will Rise at Prudential Center," *Boston Globe*, June 18, 1964.

99 "Charles Stanton Memorandum," April 27, 1964, CLP, Pru Center Tenants.

100 George B. Merry, "Office Tower; Store Planned," *Christian Science Monitor*, July 28, 1967.

101 Ibid.

102 "Pru Complex Expanding — 28-Story Office, Garage," *Boston Globe*, July 27, 1967.

103 Alfred C. Linkletter to Charles Stanton, October 14, 1966, CLP, Pru — Center Apartments, 1964. The second office tower at 101 Huntington Avenue ultimately rose twenty-five stories above the plaza level.

104 "Minutes of Meeting on January 5, 1967," C. W. Stanton to Record, CLP, Prudential Center 1966.

105 "S. W. Toole and A. C. Linkletter Memorandum to CLA," December 3, 1962, CLP, Pru — Miscellaneous — 9.61.

106 Giedion, *Architecture You and Me*: the quotation is from Giedion's caption under the Back Bay Center opposite page 129. Giedion dismissed the Prudential Center as an "apartment house project," which understated the programmatic diversity of the complex. He may have associated the Pru with more single-use insurance company projects such as Stuyvesant Town in New York.

107 Anthony J. Yudis, "Says Hub Can Lead as 'City Beautiful,'" *Boston Globe*, December 12, 1962.

108 "Architectural Commentary on Boston Today and Tomorrow," address by Wolf Von Eckardt to the Urban Design Conference, Harvard Graduate School of Design, May 1, 1964.

109 Ada Louise Huxtable, "Renewal in Boston: Good and Bad," *New York Times*, April 19, 1964; Anthony J. Yudis, "Bouquet for Govt. Center — But Not for Prudential," *Boston Globe*, May 2, 1964.

110 John F. Collins, "The Prudential and Boston — A Dynamic Alliance," *Boston Sunday Herald*, December 20, 1964.

111 Gail Perrin, "Luckman Proud of Pru Design," *Boston Globe*, April 25, 1965; Anthony Yudis, "Prudential Center Designed with 'People in Mind,'" *Boston Globe*, February 7, 1965.

112 Robert Campbell and Peter Vanderwarker, "Prudential Center: Cityscapes," *Boston Globe*, August 2, 1998.

113 Mildred F. Schmertz, "Planning the Downtown Center," *Architectural Record* (March 1964): 177.

114 Clausen, *The Pan Am Building*.

115 June Bibb, "There's New Spark in Old Boston," *Christian Science Monitor*, April 17, 1965.

CHAPTER 6 The Legacy of the Prudential Center

1 John F. Collins, "The Prudential and Boston — A Dynamic Alliance," *Boston Sunday Herald*, December 20, 1964.

2 "Summary of Broadcast Coverage of Prudential Center's Dedication," PA 10-43, Event Files 1965.

3 "Dedication Event Schedule for Prudential and Sheraton Executives," PA 10-43, Event Files 1965.

4 Cronkite was a natural choice: Prudential was the chief sponsor of the newsman's weekly television program, *The Twentieth Century*. The symposium was broadcast live and included a pre-taped segment that summarized the dedication activities with commentary on the Prudential Center's role in the "New Boston."

5 The finish line for the marathon remained at the Prudential Center for the next twenty years. In 1965 the marathon was won by Japanese runner Morio Shigematsu in a time of 2:16:33. Women were not officially allowed to enter the marathon until 1971.

6 Thomas Allsopp, "Boston and the Prudential Center," *Journal of Contemporary Business* (Spring 1974), PA 10-43, 94. A key example came in 1976 when the Pru covered the south plaza with a tent and hosted an exhibit called "Where's Boston?" to celebrate the nation's bicentennial.

7 Ibid., 95.

8 "Press Conference Statement, Orville E. Beal, President, The Prudential Insurance Company," April 19, 1965, PA 10-42, "Press Releases, 1965."

9 Collins, "The Prudential and Boston."

10 Boston Redevelopment Authority, "Centripetal and Centrifugal Effects of the Prudential Center on the S.M.S.A. of Boston with Respect to the Location of Business Functions," 1969, Government Documents, Boston Public Library, BRA 577.

11 The State Street Bank building was also known as the "British Building" in recognition of the British lenders that financed it. Max Philippson, "State Street Building Project Stimulated Hub Construction," *Boston Globe*, June 5, 1966.

12 "Mother Church Announces 31-Acre Building Project," *Christian Science Monitor*, July 1, 1965.

13 Thomas Allsopp, "Boston and the Prudential Center," *Journal of Contemporary Business*, Spring 1974, PA 10-43, 96.

14 "The New John Hancock Building: An Example of Public and Private Decision-Making," Proceedings, Boston Architectural Conference, May 4, 1968, comments of Donald Graham, 11.

15 George B. Merry, "Booming Boston Reaches Skyward," *Christian Science Monitor,* June 5, 1965. A majority of 121A developments in the 1960s and '70s were multifamily housing projects financed with Federal Housing Administration insured loans. The small number of commercial projects that filed as a 121A corporation, however, made up a vast majority of the total dollars spent. In 1979, a city Finance Commission found that Boston had been too lenient in awarding Chapter 121A status to projects that did not merit tax concessions. Steve Trinward, "Fin Com Finds 121A Full of Holes," *Boston Ledger,* July 20–26, 1979, 5; Finance Commission of the City of Boston, "The Administration of Massachusetts General Law Chapter 121A by the City of Boston and the Boston Redevelopment Authority," July 18, 1979. See also Cynthia Horan, "Organizing the 'New Boston': Growth Policy, Governing Coalitions, and Tax Reform," *Polity* 22, no. 3 (Spring 1990): 489–510.

16 Scientists have analyzed the social nature of confidence and its effects on investment. A central tenet of *Animal Spirits,* by the economists George A. Akerlof and Robert J. Shiller, is that "when people make significant investment decisions, they must depend on confidence." The effect of confidence is not an entirely rational process, as standard economic theory would suggest, but in large part an emotional decision of individual actors that depends on "perceptions of other people's confidence, and of other people's perceptions of other people's confidence. . . . Just as diseases spread through contagion, so does confidence, or lack of confidence." George A. Akerlof and Robert J. Shiller, *Animal Spirits: How Human Psychology Drives the Economy, and Why It Matters for Global Capitalism* (Princeton, N.J.: Princeton University Press, 2009), 13, 55. Similarly, the organizational researcher Rosabeth Moss Kanter defines confidence as "positive expectations for favorable outcomes" and explains that it can be shaped by leaders who inspire initiative and innovation. She concludes: "Confidence influences the willingness to invest — to commit money, time, reputation, emotional energy, or other resources — or to withhold or hedge investment." Rosabeth Moss Kanter, *Confidence: How Winning Streaks and Losing Streaks Begin and End* (New York: Crown Business, 2004).

17 Robert Campbell and Peter Vanderwarker, "Self-Centered," *Boston Globe,* March 13, 2005.

18 Robert Campbell, "The Case for Better Buildings," *Boston Globe,* February 3, 2008.

19 Donlyn Lyndon, *Boston: The City Observed* (New York: Vintage, 1982), 196.

20 "Pru Tower Studies," TSA/HOK Architects, January 31, 1987.

21 Robert Campbell, "Rebuilding the Pru Disaster," *Boston Globe,* January 28, 1990.

22 Robert Campbell and Peter Vanderwarker, "Prudential Center; Cityscapes," *Boston Globe,* August 2, 1998.

23 "Northeastern Home Office," 1969, PA 04-103, Home Office Operations.

24 Donald Manchee to Art Linkletter, September 2, 1965, CLP, Pru Center 1965. Whitehill called the Prudential Center a "windy world of its own." Walter Muir Whitehill and Lawrence Kennedy, *Boston: A Topographical History,* 3rd ed. (Cambridge: Harvard University Press, 2000), 225. Eventually the open arcade that fronted the commercial pavilions was enclosed.

25 Carol Liston, "'Doesn't Anybody Know We're Here?'" *Boston Globe,* July 16, 1966.

26 Gary Hack, "Updating Prudential Center," *Urban Land* (October 1993): 88.

27 "Copley Place Project Information," Urban Investment and Development Company, July 17, 1980; Rachelle L. Levitt, ed., *Cities Reborn* (Washington, D.C.: Urban Land Institute, 1987), 37–40. The total cost of the project was $530 million, including a $19.7 million Urban Development Action Grant.

28 Paul Goldberger, "Urban Building Trends Lend Boston an Odd Mix," *New York Times,* June 16, 1985.

29 Ibid.; Hack, "Updating Prudential Center," 88.

30 Jonathan Wells, "Big Plans at the Pru," *Boston Tab,* February 5, 1985; Jane Holtz Kay, "Prudential Makeover," *Progressive Architecture* 67, no. 3 (March 1986): 21–23.

31 Hack, "Updating Prudential Center," 88.

32 Campbell, "Rebuilding the Pru Disaster"; "A New, Neighborly Pru," *Boston Globe,* May 1, 1989.

33 Mark Pickering, "The Pru Tries to Get It Right the Second Time," *Boston Business Journal,* August 24, 1992.

34 "Prudential Center Redevelopment, Draft Project and Environmental Impact Report, Volume I: Summary," I-6.

35 Casey Ross, "2 Towers Will Finish Prudential Center," *Boston Globe,* December 5, 2008.

36 Susan Diesenhouse, "Urban Mall Is Refocused in Boston," *New York Times,* October 2, 1991.

37 "Prudential Center Chapter 121A Separation and Termination," Boston Redevelopment Authority, December 14, 1989, 16.

38 "Prudential Center Redevelopment, Draft Project

and Environmental Impact Report, Volume I: Summary," I-6.

39 "Boston Properties to Buy Prudential Center," *New York Times,* January 12, 1998.

40 In 1981, Prudential acquired Bache Group, Inc., the Wall Street stock brokerage — it became known as Prudential-Bache Securities — an alliance that would ultimately damage Prudential's reputation when Prudential-Bache was accused of securities fraud in the 1980s. See Kurt Eichenwald, *Serpent on the Rock* (New York: Broadway, 1995).

41 Leon Lindsay, "A Fresh Face on the Growing Back Bay," *Christian Science Monitor,* June 3, 1985; Sandra Salmans, "Prudential Is Cutting 1,700 Jobs," *New York Times,* July 13, 1983; Joseph B. Treaster, "Patching the Cracks in the Rock," *New York Times,* February 23, 1997.

42 "Central Atlantic Home Office" and "For Release After 4 P.M., Tuesday, June 5," PA 10–44. The CAHO was a spinoff of the Eastern Home Office, established in 1966 to handle mid-Atlantic and metro New York business but located within the corporate headquarters complex in Newark. In the 1970s, the Eastern Home Office was itself suburbanized to three different locations in New Jersey.

43 "Proposed Western Home Office Building," February 8, 1969, PA 10–21; "Memorandum for All Western Home Office Employees," November 12, 1976, PA 10–21; "Ground Broken for Prudential Offices," *Los Angeles Times,* August 19, 1979; Nancy Yoshihara, "Pair Acquire Prudential Building, Adjacent Site," *Los Angeles Times,* February 9, 1979. Prudential already owned the land in Westlake Village. It was near a back-office complex also erected in the 1970s.

44 An American Institute of Architects jury called the 1977 Prudential office the "best freeway building" in Houston. It is now called the SBC Building. Greater Houston Preservation Alliance (www.ghpa.org/awards/ 2006/prudential.html), accessed April 10, 2011.

45 Nancy Sarnoff, "Preservationists Oppose Plan to Demolish Historic Building," *Houston Business Journal* 32, no. 46 (March 29, 2002): 8; Ralph Bivins, "Big Heads and Busted-Up Buildings: Prudential Goes Astrodome," *CultureMap Houston,* April 5, 2010 (http://houston.culturemap.com/newsdetail/04-05-10-big-heads-and-busted-buildings-prudential-goes-astrodome), accessed September 6, 2011. Arrangements have been made to preserve Peter Hurd's curved sixteen-by-forty-six-foot lobby mural, which will be featured in a new building for the library of Artesia, New Mexico, Hurd's home state. Allan Turner, "Medical Center Mural Saved," *Houston Chronicle,* November 1, 2010.

46 "Prudential Lessens Newark Base," *New York Times,* August 17, 1980.

47 Anthony J. Yudis, "U.S. 'Crisis Cities' Develop Split Personalities," *Boston Globe,* October 30, 1966; F. B. Taylor, Jr., "Renewal Foes Camp in So. End Parking Lot," *Boston Globe,* April 28, 1968.

48 Robert L. Levey, "Pickets Walk as School Boards Eye Their Task," *Boston Globe,* April 5, 1965. For a rich examination of race relations in Boston and the controversy over forced busing to desegregate the public schools, see J. Anthony Lukas, *Common Ground: A Turbulent Decade in the Lives of Three American Families* (New York: Vintage, 1986).

49 Robert A. Jordan, "A New Housing Threat to Blacks Living in the Inner City," *Boston Globe,* February 23, 1979; Ken Hartnett, "Tracking the Return of the Gentry: The Bad Side of Central-City Chic," *Boston Globe,* May 28, 1977; "Bringing It All Back Home," *Christian Science Monitor,* November 18, 1977; Victoria Everett, "Can Boston Be Saved?" *Black Enterprise* (February 1984), 99–105. See also Lukas, *Common Ground,* 168. Lukas pointed to the Prudential Center as a catalyst to new investment in the South End and wrote persuasively about one family's decision to come back to Boston from the suburbs and fix up a South End townhouse.

Index